THUNDER CAPE, ENTRANCE TO THUNDER BAY

OCEAN TO OCEAN

BUREAU OF ILLUSTRATION BUFFAL N. Y.

SHOOTING THE RAPIDS

OCEAN TO OCEAN

SANDFORD FLEMING'S EXPEDITION

THROUGH

CANADA IN 1872

BY

THE REV. GEORGE M. GRANT,
OF HALIFAX, N. S.

ENLARGED AND REVISED EDITION

ILLUSTRATED

CHARLES E. TUTTLE CO.: PUBLISHERS
Rutland, Vermont

Representatives
Continental Europe: BOXERBOOKS, INC., *Zurich*
British Isles: PRENTICE-HALL INTERNATIONAL, INC., *London*
Australasia: PAUL FLESCH & CO., PTY. LTD., *Melbourne*
Canada: m.g. hurtig ltd., *Edmonton*

Published by the Charles E. Tuttle Company, Inc.
of Rutland, Vermont & Tokyo, Japan
with editorial offices at Suido 1-chome, 2-6
Bunkyo-ku, Tokyo, Japan

Copyright in Japan, 1967 by m.g. hurtig ltd.

Library of Congress Catalog Card No. 67-19594

PRINTED IN JAPAN

INTRODUCTION

Ocean to Ocean, first published in 1873, is at once a superb
travel narrative, a declaration of faith in the future of
Canada and the Canadian West, and a record of a memora-
ble event in the careers of two famous Canadians, Sandford
Fleming (1827–1915) and George Munro Grant (1835–1902).
The journey described in this book was intimately associated
with one of the prominent objectives of the Fathers of
Confederation—the unlocking of the vast wilderness between the Great Lakes and the Pacific to settlement and
development. When Fleming and Grant left Toronto for the
West on July 16, 1872, only two years had elapsed since the
Hudson's Bay Company's domain, and the adjacent British
territory down to the Arctic coast had been transferred to
Canada, and it was but one year, less a few days, since
British Columbia had entered the union on the condition
that a transcontinental railway be constructed within a
decade. This commitment was a formidable challenge for a
young nation of little more than three and a half million
people, unsure of their capacities and possessing a still-
precarious sense of unity.

Even before a company was organized to build the railway, Prime Minister Sir John A. Macdonald's government,
as evidence of its determination, had appointed Fleming,
the Scottish-born civil engineer and surveyor who was
superintending the construction of the Intercolonial Railway, to direct the surveys for the new project. It was to
assess the reports of his field staff that Fleming, referred to
as "the Chief" in *Ocean to Ocean*, undertook the trans-Canada

journey which began on the shores of the Atlantic at Halifax, and ended at Victoria on the Pacific. Grant, secretary
to the expedition, was the minister of St. Matthew's Presbyterian Church in Halifax. Born in Pictou County, Nova
Scotia, and educated at Glasgow University, he had rejected
the prospects of a distinguished career in the Church of
Scotland to return to a life of service in his native land.
An eloquent preacher who believed that the Christian
should participate in public affairs, Grant was known as an
ardent supporter of Confederation in a province where this
policy was a highly contentious issue. Fleming's son Frank
and a Halifax physician, Dr. Arthur Moren, were also of the
party. From Toronto to Fort Garry they were accompanied
by Colonel Patrick Robertson-Ross, Adjutant-General of
the Canadian Militia, and his son Hugh. During the steamboat passage through Lakes Huron and Superior, John
Macoun, a botanist on the staff of Albert College, Belle-
ville, was invited to accompany the party and prepare a
report on the flora and agricultural potential of the country.
At Fort Garry, a member of Fleming's field staff, Charles
Horetzky, formerly with the Hudson's Bay Company and
one of the pioneer photographers in the Canadian West,
joined the expedition. On reaching Edmonton, Fleming
directed Horetzky and Macoun to explore an alternative
route to the ocean via the Peace River and northern British
Columbia, while the rest of the party proceeded due west
towards the Yellowhead Pass.

On the controversial questions of the best pass through
the mountains, and the best coastal terminus for Canada's
first transcontinental railway, Fleming was to opt for the
Yellowhead Pass, the North Thompson and Thompson
valleys, the Fraser valley, and Burrard Inlet—the route
traversed by his expedition of 1872 and never better described than by the author of *Ocean to Ocean*. Although the

Canadian Pacific Railway, when it was finally completed in 1885, followed only the westernmost part of this route, from Kamloops to the sea, the labors of Fleming and his staff were not without result, for much of the present-day Canadian National Railway main line coincides with Fleming's first choice. And today too, the motorist may follow closely the trails of Grant and Fleming as one traverses the highway from Winnipeg through Yorkton, and on to Saskatoon, Edmonton, Jasper, Tête Jaune Cache, Kamloops, and Vancouver.

Grant's philosophy of life emerges with increasing clarity as he conducts us over the waterways and trails of the vast land beyond the lakes and introduces us to the men and women who were the new Canadians of his day—Indians, Métis, pioneer settlers, prospectors, missionaries, surveyors, fur traders, Chinese laborers, businessmen and government officials. Although highly critical of what he conceived to be the ignorance and lack of vision of British statesmen in dealing with Canadian interests, he was a great admirer of British institutions. Few Canadians of today regret that his hopes of Imperial consolidation were not realized, more can approve his faith in classical conservative values, and all can share his pride in the physical grandeur of the Canadian land, and his confidence in the capacity of men and women of diverse races, skills, and faiths to achieve the goals decreed by ever-changing national needs and responsibilities.

University of Alberta   LEWIS H. THOMAS
Edmonton, Canada

CONTENTS

CHAPTER I.

CHAPTER II.

FROM HALIFAX, NOVA SCOTIA, TO THUNDER BAY, LAKE SUPERIOR.

CHAPTER III.

FROM THUNDER BAY TO FORT GARRY.

CHAPTER IV.

PROVINCE OF MANITOBA.

CHAPTER V.

FROM MANITOBA TO FORT CARLTON ON THE NORTH SASKATCHEWAN.

CHAPTER VI.

ALONG THE NORTH SASKATCHEWAN TO EDMONTON.

CHAPTER VII.

FROM FORT EDMONTON TO THE RIVER ATHABASKA.

CHAPTER VIII.

THE ROCKY MOUNTAINS.

CHAPTER IX.

YELLOW HEAD PASS TO THE NORTH THOMPSON RIVER.

CHAPTER X.

ALONG THE NORTH THOMPSON RIVER TO KAMLOOPS.

CHAPTER XI.

FROM KAMLOOPS TO THE SEA.

CHAPTER XII.

THE COAST, AND VANCOUVER'S ISLAND.

CHAPTER XIII.

CONCLUSION.

APPENDIX.

ILLUSTRATIONS

OCEAN TO OCEAN

THROUGH CANADA IN 1872.

CHAPTER I.

Introductory.

TRAVEL a thousand miles up the St. Lawrence; another thousand on great lakes and a wilderness of lakelets and streams; a thousand miles across prairies and up the valley of the Saskatchewan; and nearly a thousand through woods and over great ranges of mountains, and you have travelled from Ocean to Ocean through Canada. All this country is a single Colony of the British Empire; and this Colony is dreaming magnificent dreams of a future when it shall be the Greater Britain, and the highway across which the fabrics and products of Asia shall be carried, to the Eastern as well as to the Western sides of the Atlantic. Mountains were once thought to be effectual barrriers against railways, but that day has gone by; and, now that trains run between San Francisco and New York, over summits of eight thousand two hundred feet, why may they not run between Victoria and Halifax, over a height of three thousand seven hundred feet? At any rate, a Canadian Pacific Railway has been undertaken by the Dominion; and, as this book consists of notes made in connection with the survey, an introductory chapter may be given to a brief history of the project.

For more than a quarter of a century before the Atlantic was connected by rail with the Pacific public attention had been frequently called, especially in the great cities of the United

States, to the commercial advantage and the political necessity of such connection; but it was not till 1853 that the Secretary of War was authorized by the President to employ topographical engineers and others "to make explorations and surveys, and to ascertain the most practicable and economical route for a railroad from the Mississippi River to the Pacific Ocean." From that time the United States Government sent a succession of well-equipped parties to explore the western half of the Continent. The reports and surveys of these expeditions fill thirteen large quarto volumes, richly embellished, stored with valuable information concerning the country, and honestly pointing out that, west of the Mississippi Valley, there were vast extents of desert or semi-desert, and other difficulties so formidable as to render the construction of a railroad well nigh impracticable. Her Majesty's Government aware of this result, and aware, also, that there was a fertile belt of undefined size, in the same longitude as the Great American Desert, but north of the forty-ninth degree of latitude, organized an expedition, under Captain Palliser, in 1857, to explore the country between the west of Lake Superior and the Rocky Mountains; and also " to ascertain whether any practicable pass or passes, available for horses, existed across the Rocky Mountains within British Territory, and south of that known to exist between Mount Brown and Mount Hooker," known as the " Boat Encampment Pass." It was unfortunate that the limitation expressed in this last clause, was imposed on Captain Palliser, for it prevented him from exploring to the north of Boat Encampment, and reporting upon the Yellow Head Pass, which has since been found so favourable for the Railway and may soon be used as the gateway through the mountains to British Columbia and the Pacific. The difficulties presented by passes further south, and by the Selkirk Mountains, led Palliser to express an opinion upon the passage across the Mountains as hasty and inaccurate as his opinion about the possibility of con-

SAULT STE. MARIE (*from the South Side.*)

necting Ontario or Quebec with the Red River and Saskatchewan Country is now found to be. After stating that his expedition had made connection between the Saskatchewan Plains
and British Columbia, without passing through United States
Territory, he added :—" Still the knowledge of the country, on
the whole, would never lead me to advise a line of communication from Canada, across the continent to the Pacific, exclusive-
ly through British Territory. The time has forever gone by
for effecting such an object ; and the unfortunate choice of an
astronomical boundary line has completely isolated the Central
American possessions of Great Britain from Canada in the east,
and also almost debarred them from any eligible access from
the Pacific Coast on the west." The best answer to this sweeping opinion, is the Progress Report on the Canadian Pacific
Railway exploratory survey, presented to the House of Commons, in Ottawa, in the Session 1872, in which the advantages
of the Yellow Head Pass over every other approach to the
Pacific are shown ; and as complete an answer to the second
part is to be found in subsequent reports. The journals of
Captain Palliser's explorations, extending over a period of four
years, from 1857 to 1860, were printed *in extenso* by Her
Majesty's Government in a large Blue Book, which shared the
fate of all similar literature. There are, probably, not more
than half a dozen copies in the Dominion. A copy in the
Legislative Library at Ottawa is the only one known to the
writer. They deserved a better fate, for his own notes and the
reports of his associates, Lieutenant Blakiston, Dr. Hector, M.
Bourgeau and Mr. Sullivan, are replete with useful and interesting facts about the soil, the flora, the fauna, and the climate
of the plains and the mountains. M. Bourgeau was the botanist of the expedition. On Mr. Sullivan, an accomplished
mathematician and astronomical observer and surveyor, devolved the principal labours of computation. Dr. Hector, to
whose exertions the success of the expedition was chiefly owing,

had the charge of making the maps, both geographical and geological; and, whenever a side journey promised any result, no matter how arduous or dangerous it might be, Dr. Hector was always ready. His name is still revered in our Northwest, on account of his medical skill and his kindness to the Indians, and most astonishing tales are still told of his travelling feats in mid-winter among the mountains.

After printing Captain Palliser's journal, Her Majesty's Government took no step to connect the East of British America with the Centre and the West, or to open up the Northwest to emigration, although it had been clearly established that we had a country there, extending over many degrees of latitude and longitude, with a climate and soil equal to that of Ontario. In the meantime, the people of the United States, with characteristic energy, took up the work that was too formidable for their government. Public-spirited men, in Sacramento and other parts of California, embarked their all in a project which would make their own rich State the link between the old farthest East and the Western World on both sides of the Atlantic. The work was commenced on the east and west of the Rocky Mountains. Congress granted extraordinary liberal subsidies in lands and money, though in a half sceptical spirit, and as much under the influence of Rings as of patriotism. When the member for California was urging the scheme with a zeal that showed that he honestly believed in it, Mr. Lovejoy, of Illinois, could not help interjecting, "Does the honourable member really mean to tell me he believes that that road will ever be built?" "Pass the Bill, and it will be constructed in ten years," was the answer. In much less than the time asked for it was constructed, and it is at this day as remarkable a monument to the energy of our neighbours as the triumphant conclusion of their civil war, or the re-building of Chicago. Three great ranges of mountains had to be crossed, at altitudes of eight thousand two hundred and forty, seven

thousand one hundred and fifty, and seven thousand feet ; snow
sheds and fences to be built along exposed parts, for miles, at
enormous expense ; the work, for more than a thousand miles,
to be carried on in a desert, which yielded neither wood, water
nor food of any kind. No wonder that the scheme was
denounced as impracticable and a swindle. But its success has
vindicated the wisdom of its projectors ; and now no fewer than
four different lines are organized to connect the Atlantic States
with the Pacific, and to divide with the Union and Central
Pacific Railways, the enormous and increasing traffic they are
carrying.

While man was thus triumphing over all the obstacles of nature in the Territory of the United States, how was it that
nothing was attempted farther North in British America,
where a fertile belt stretches west to the base of the Rocky
Mountains, and where river-passes seem to offer natural highways through the mountains to the Ocean ? The North American Colonies were isolated from each other ; the North-west
was kept under lock and key by the Hudson Bay Company ;
and though some ambitious speeches were made, some spirited
pamphlets written, and Bulwer Lytton, in introducing the Bill
for the formation of British Columbia as a Province, saw, in
vision, a line of loyal Provinces, from the Atlantic to the
Pacific, the time had not come for a consummation so devoutly
to be wished. Had the old political state of things continued
in British America, nothing would have been done to this day.
But, in 1867, the separate Colonies of Canada, New Brunswick
and Nova Scotia, became the Dominion of Canada ; in 1869
the Hudson Bay Company's rights to the North-west were
bought up ; and, in 1871, British Columbia united itself to the
new Dominion ; and thus the whole mainland of British America became one political State under the ægis of the Empire.
One of the terms on which British Columbia joined the Dominion was, that a railway should be constructed within ten years

from the Pacific to a point of junction with the existing railway systems in the Provinces of Ontario and Quebec, and surveys with this object in view were at once instituted.

What did this preparatory survey-work in our case mean? It meant that we must do, in one or two years, what had been done in the United States in fifty. To us the ground was all new. Few of our public men had ever looked much beyond the confines of their particular Provinces ; our North-west, in some parts of it, was less an unknown land to the people of the States along the boundary line than to the people of the Dominion ; and, in other parts, it was unknown to the whole world. No white man is known to have crossed from the Upper Ottawa to Lake Superior or Lake Winnipeg.. There were maps of the country, dotted with lakes and lacustrine rivers here and there; but these had been made up largely from sketches, on bits of birch-bark or paper, and the verbal descriptions of Indians, and the Indian has little or no conception of scale or bearings. In drawing the picture of a lake, for instance, when his sheet of paper was too narrow, he would without warning, continue the lake up or down the side, and naturally an erroneous idea of the surface of the country was given. A lake was set down right in the path of what otherwise was an eligible line, and, after great expense had been incurred, it was found that there was no lake within thirty miles of the point. In a word, the country between Old Canada and Red River was utterly unknown, except along the canoe routes travelled by the Hudson Bay men north-west of Lake Superior. Not many years since, a lecturer had to inform a Toronto audience that he had discovered a great lake, called Nepigon, a few miles to the north of Lake Superior. When so little was known, the task was no light one. Engineers were sent out into trackless, inhospitable regions, obliged to carry their provisions on their backs over swamps, rocks, and barriers, of all kinds, when the Indians failed them ; with instructions simply to do their best to find out all they could, in as short a time as possible.

Far different was it with our neighbours. They could afford to spend, and they did spend, half a century on the preparatory work. Their special surveys were aided and supplemented by reports and maps extending back over a long course of years, drawn up, as part of their duty, by the highly educated officers of their regular army stationed at different posts in their Territories. These reports, as well as the unofficial narratives of missionaries, hunters, and traders, were studied, both before and after being pigeon-holed in Washington. The whole country had thus been gradually examined from every possible point of view ; and, among other things, this thorough knowledge explains the success of the United States' Government in all its treaty-making with Great Britain, *when territory was concerned.* The history of every such treaty between the two Powers is the history of a contest between knowledge and ignorance. The one Power always knew what it wanted. It therefore presented, from the first step in the negotiation to the last, a firm and apparently consistent front. The other had only a dim notion that right was on its side, and a notion, equally dim, that the object in dispute was not worth contending for.

Was it wise, then, for the Dominion to undertake so gigantic a public work at so early a stage in its history ? It was wise, because it was necessary. By uniting together, the British Provinces had declared that their destiny was—not to ripen and drop, one by one, into the arms of the Republic—but to work out their own future as an integral and important part of the grandest Empire in the world. They had reason for making such an election. They believed that it was better for themselves and for their neighbours ; better for the cause of human liberty and true progress, that it should be so. But it is not necessary to discuss the reasons. No outside power has a right to pronounce upon them. The fact is enough, that, on this central point, the mind of British America, from the Atlantic to the Pacific, is fixed. But, to be united politically and disunited physically, as the different parts of Prussia were for many a long year, is an anomaly only to be endured so long as it can not be helped ; and when, as in our case, the remedy is in our own hands, it is wise to secure the material union as soon as possible.

On the twentieth of July, 1871, British Columbia entered the Dominion. On the same day surveying parties left Victoria for various points of the Rocky Mountains, and from the Upper Ottawa westward, and all along the line surveys were commenced. Their reports were laid before the Canadian House of Commons in April, 1872. In the summer of the same year, Sandford Fleming, the Engineer in Chief, considered it necessary to travel overland, to see the main features of the country with his own eyes, and the writer of these pages accompanied him, as Secretary. The expedition started from Toronto on July 16th, and on October 14th, it left Victoria, Vancouver's Island, on the home stretch. During those three months a diary was kept of the chief things we saw or heard, and of the impressions which we formed respecting the country, as we journeyed from day to day and conversed with each other on the subject. Our notes are presented to the public, and are given almost as they were written so that others might see, as far as possible, a photograph of what we saw and thought from day to day. A more readable book could have been made by omitting some things, colouring others, and grouping the whole ; but the object was not to make a book. The expedition had special services to perform in connection with one of the most gigantic public works ever undertaken in any country by any people ; it was organized and conducted in a business-like way, in order to get through without disaster or serious difficulty ; it did not turn aside in search of adventures or of sport ; and therefore an exciting narrative of hair-breadth escapes and thrilling descriptions of " men whose heads do grow beneath their shoulders " need scarcely be expected.

CHAPTER II.

From Halifax, Nova Scotia, to Thunder Bay, Lake Superior.

1st July, 1872.—To-day, three friends met in Halifax, and
agreed to travel together through the Dominion from the Atlantic to the Pacific. All three had personal and business matters
to arrange, requiring them to leave on different days, and reach
the Upper Provinces by different routes. In these circumstances it was decided that Toronto should be the point of rendezvous for the main journey to the Far West, and that the
day of meeting should be the 15th of July. One proposed to
take the steamer from Halifax to Portland, and go thence by
the Grand Trunk Railway *via* Montreal ; another, to sail up
the Gulf of St. Lawrence from Pictou to Quebec ; and it was
the duty of the third—the chief of the party—to travel along
the line of the Intercolonial Railway. This narrative follows
the footsteps of the Chief, when more than one path is taken.
But, though it was his duty to make a professional examination
of all the engineering works in progress on the Intercolonial,—
the Eastern link of that great arterial highway which is to connect, entirely through Canadian Territory, a Canadian Atlantic
port with a Canadian Pacific port,—the reader would scarcely
be interested in an account of the culverts and bridges, built and
building, the comparative merits of wooden and iron work, the
pile driving, the dredging, the excavating, the banking and

blasting by over 10,000 workmen, scattered along 500 miles of road. The Intercolonial links, with rails of steel, the Provinces of Nova Scotia and New Brunswick with the Province of Quebec ; the Grand Trunk unites Quebec and Ontario ; and the Canadian Pacific Railway is to connect the latter with Manitoba and British Columbia, as well as with the various unborn Provinces which, in the rapid progress of events, shall spring up in the intervening region. But the work of actual railway construction is an old story ; and, if told at all, must be served up at some other time in some other way. It has now been told by Sandford Fleming, the Engineer-in-chief, in an interesting and well written volume, " The Intercolonial ; a Historical Sketch of the Inception, Location, Construction, and Completion of the Line of Railway uniting the Inland and Atlantic Provinces of the Dominion." The object of the present narrative is to give an account of what was observed and experienced in out-of-the-way places, over a vast extent of Canada little known even to Canadians. It will be sufficient for our purpose, therefore, to begin at Toronto, passing over all that may at any time be seen on the line from Halifax to Truro, and northerly across the Cobequid Mountains to Moncton. From Moncton, westward, there is much along the line worthy of description ;—the deep forests of New Brunswick, the noble Miramichi river with its Railway bridging on a somewhat gigantic scale, the magnificent highland scenery of the Baie des Chaleurs, the Restigouche, and the wild mountain gorges of the Matapedia. But, without delaying even to catch a forty or fifty pound salmon in the Restigouche, we hasten on with the Chief up the shores of the great St. Lawrence. Passing the cliffs of historic Quebec, we cross the broad St. Lawrence by that magnificent monument of early Canadian enterprise and triumph of engineering skill, the Victoria Bridge. Two days are necessarily spent at Ottawa in making final arrangements, and Toronto is reached at the time appointed for the rendezvous.

July 15th.—To-day, the various members of the overland expedition met at the Queen's Hotel, the Chief, the Adjutant General, the boys Frank and Hugh, the Doctor and the Secretary, and arranged to leave by the first train to-morrow morning. On the Chief devolved all the labour of preparation. The rest of us had little to do except to get ourselves photographed in travelling costume.

July 16th.—Took train for Collingwood, which is about a hundred miles due north from Toronto. The first half of the journey, or as far as Lake Simcoe, is through a fair and fertile land ; too flat to be picturesque, but sufficiently rolling for farming purposes. Clumps of stately elms, with noble stems, shooting high before their fan shape commences, relieve the monotony of the scene. Here and there a field, dotted with huge pine stumps, shows the character of the old crop. The forty or fifty miles nearest Georgian Bay have been settled more recently, but give as good promise to the settlers. Collingwood is an instance of what a railway terminus does for a place. Before the Northern Railway was built, an unbroken forest occupied its site, and the red dear came down through the woods to drink at the shore. Now, there is a thriving town of two or three thousand people, with steam saw-mills, and huge rafts from the North that almost fill up its little harbour, with a grain elevator which lifts out of steam barges the corn from Chicago, weighs it, and pours it into railway freight-waggons to be hurried down to Toronto, and there turned into bread or whiskey, without a hand touching it in all its transportations or transformations. Around the town the country is being opened up, and the forest is giving way to pasture and corn-fields. West of the town is a range of hills, about one thousand feet high, originally thickly wooded to their summits, but now seamed with roads and interspersed with clearings. Probably none of us would have noticed them, though their beauty is enough to attract passing attention, had they not been pointed out as the highest mountains in the great Province of Ontario !

THUNDER CAPE, ENTRANCE TO THUNDER BAY.

We reached Collingwood at midday, and were informed that the steamer *Frances Smith* would start for Fort William, at two P.M. Great was the bustle, accordingly, in getting the baggage on board. In the hurry, the gangway was shoved out of its place, and when one of the porters rushed on it with a box, down it tilted, pitching him head first into the water between the pier and the steamer. We heard the splash, and ran, with half a dozen others, just in time to see his boots kicking frantically as they disappeared. "Oh it's that fool S——," laughed a bystander, "this is the second time he's tumbled in." "He can't swim," yelled two or three, clutching at ropes that were tied, trunks and other impossible life-preservers. In the meantime S—— rose, but, in rising, struck his head against a heavy float that almost filled the narrow space, and at once sank again, like a stone. He would have been drowned within six feet of the wharf, but for a tall, strong fellow, who rushed through the crowd, jumped, in, and caught him as he rose a second time. S——, like the fool he was said to be, returned the kindness by half throttling his would-be deliverer; but other bystanders, springing on the float, got the two out. The rescuer swung lightly on to the wharf, shook himself as if he had been a Newfoundland dog, and walked off; nobody seemed to notice him or to think that he deserved a word of praise. On inquiring, we learned that he was a fisherman by name Alick Clark, on his way to the Upper Lakes, who, last summer also had jumped from the steamer's deck into Lake Superior, to save a child that had fallen overboard. Knowing that Canada had no Humane Society's medal to bestow, one of our party ran to thank him and quietly to offer a slight gratuity; but the plucky fellow refused to take anything, on the plea that he was a good swimmer and that his clothes hadn't been hurt.

At two o'clock, it being officially announced that the steamer would not start until six, we strolled up to the town to buy suits of duck, which were said to be the only sure defence against mosquitoes of portentous size and power beyond Fort William.   Meeting the Rector or Rural Dean, our Chief, learning that he was to be a fellow-passenger, introduced the Doctor to him. The Doctor has not usually a positively funereal aspect, but the Rector assumed that he was the clergyman of the party and a D.D., and cottoned to him at once.   When we returned to the steamer, and gathered round the tea table the Rector nodded significantly in his direction : he, in dumb show, declined the honor ; the Rector pantomimed again, and with more decision of manner ; the Doctor blushed furiously, and looked so very much as if an " aith would relieve him," that the Chief, in compassion, passed round the cold beef without a grace.   We were very angry with him, as the whole party doubtless suffered in the Rector's estimation through his lack of resources. The Doctor, however, was sensitive on the subject and threatened the secretary with a deprivation of sundry medical comforts, if he did not in future attend to his own work.

At six o'clock it was officially announced that the steamer would not start till midnight.

July 17th.—The *Frances Smith* left Collingwood at 5.30 A.M. " We're all right now," exclaimed Hugh, and so the passengers thought, but they counted without their host.   We steamed slowly round the Peninsula to Owen Sound, reaching it about eleven o'clock.

Leith, a port six miles from Owen Sound, was reached at 6.30, and we walked round the beach and had a swim, while two or three men set to work leisurely to carry on board a few sticks of wood from eight or ten cords piled on the wharf.   Half a dozen of the passengers volunteered help, and the Royal Mail steamer got off two hours after midnight.

An inauspicious beginning to our journey.   Aided all the way by steam, we were not much more than one hundred miles in a direct line from Toronto, forty-four hours after starting. At this rate, when would we reach the Rocky Mountains ? To make matters worse, the subordinates seemed also to have learned the trick of how not to do it. Seemingly the *Frances Smith* wanted a head, and, as the Scotch old maid lamented, " its an unco' thing to gang through the warld withcot a heid."

June 18th.—To-day, our course was northerly through the Georgian Bay towards the Great Manitoulin Island. This island and some smaller ones stretching in an almost continuous line westward, in the direction of Lake Superior, form in connection with the Saugeen Peninsula, the barrier of land that separates the Georgian Bay from the mighty Lake Huron. These two great inland waters were one, long ago, when the earth was younger, but the waters subsided, or Peninsula and Islands rose, and the one sea became two. Successive terraces on both sides of Owen Sound and on the different islands showed the old lake beaches, each now fringed with a firmer, darker escarpment than the stony or sandy flats beneath, and marked the different levels to which the waters had gradually subsided.

The day passed pleasantly, for, as progress was being made in the right direction, all the passengers willingly enjoyed themselves, while on the two previous days they had only enjoyed the Briton's privilege of grumbling. Crossing the calm breadth of the bay, past Lonely Island, we soon entered the Strait that extends for fifty miles between the North shore and Manitoulin. The contrast between the soft, rounded outlines of the lower Silurian of Manitoulin, and rugged Laurentian hills with their contorted sides and scarred foreheads on the mainland opposite, was striking enough to justify the declaration of a romantic fellow-passenger, " Why, there's quite a scenery here !" The entrance to the Strait has been called Killarney, according to our custom of discarding musical expressive Indian names for ridiculously inappropriate European ones. Killarney is a little Indian settlement, with one or two Irish families to whom the place appears to owe very little more than its name. On the wharf is an unshingled shanty or the store, the entrepôt for dry goods, hardware, groceries, Indian work and everything else that the heart of man in Killarney can desire.

The Indians possessed, until lately, the whole of the Island of Manitoulin as well as the adjoining Peninsula; but, at a grand *pow wow* held with their chiefs by Sir Edmund Head while he was Governor of Old Canada, it was agreed that they should, for certain annuities and other considerations, surrender all except tracts specially reserved for their permanent use. Some two thousand are settled around those shores. They are of the great Ojibbeway or Chippewa nation,—the nation that extends from the St. Lawrence to the Red River, where sections of them are called Salteaux and other names. West from the Red River to the Rocky Mountains, extend the next great nation of the Algonquin family,—the Crees. The languages of these two nations are so much alike, that Indians of the one nation can understand much of the speech of the other. The structure is simple, there being about a hundred and fifty monosyllabic radical roots, the greater number of which are common to Ojibbeway and Cree, and on these roots the language has grown up. Most of the Ojibbeways on Manitoulin are Christianized. At one point on the Island, where the steamer called, we met Mr. Hurlburt, a Methodist Missionary— a thoughtful, scholarly man—who has prepared, with infinite pains, a grammar of the language, and who gave us much interesting information. He honestly confessed that there was little if any difference in morals between the Christianized Indians around him and the two or three hundred who remain pagan; that, in fact, the pagans considered themselves superior, and made the immorality of their Christian countrymen their great plea against changing from the old religion.

July 19th.—This morning we entered a beautiful island-studded bay, on the north shore of which is the settlement round the Bruce and Wellington Copper Mines. The mines have been very productive, and give employment now to three or four hundred men and boys, whose habitations are, as is usually the case at mines, mere shanties. One, a little larger than the others, in which the Gaffer lives, is dignified with the title of "Apsley House." From the Bruce Mines we sailed westerly through a channel almost as beautiful as where the St. Lawrence runs through the thousand islands. A silver streak of sea, glittering in the warm sun, filled with rounded islets of old Huronian rock, that sloped gently into the water at one point, or more abruptly at another, and offered every variety and convenience that the heart of bather could desire; low, rugged, pine clad shores; soft bays, here and there, with sandy beeches; all that is required to make the scene one of perfect beauty is a back-ground of high hills. Everywhere through Ontario we miss the mountain forms, without which all scenery is tame in the eyes of those who have once learned to see the perpetual beauty that clothes the everlasting hills.

St. Joseph, Sugar, and Neebish Islands, now take the place of Manitoulin; then we come to the Ste. Marie River, which leads up to Lake Superior, and forms the boundary line between the Dominion and the United States. At the Sault, or rapids of the river, there is a village on each side; but as the canal is on the United States side, the steamer crosses to go through it to the great Lake. The canal has two locks, each three hundred and fifty feet long, seventy feet wide, twelve deep, and with a lift of nine feet. It is well and solidly built. The Federal Government has commenced the excavations for the channel of another. Though the necessity for two canals on the same side is not very apparent, still the United States Government, with its usual forethought, sees that the time will soon come when they shall be needed. The commerce on Lake Superior is increasing every year; and it is desirable to have a canal large enough for men-of-war and the largest steamers. We walked along the bank and found, among the men engaged on the work, two or three Indians handling pick and shovel as if to the manner born, and probably earning the ordinary wages of $2.25 per day. The rock is a loose and friable calciferous sandstone, reddish colored, easily excavated. Hence the reason why the Sault Ste. Marie, instead of being a leap, flows down its eighteen feet of descent in a continuous rapid, wonderfully little broken except over loose boulders. The water is wearing away the rock every year. As it would be much easier to make a canal on the British side of the river, one ought to be commenced withou delay. The most ordinary self-respect forbids that the entrance to our North-west should be wholly in the hands of another Power, a Power that, during the Riel disturbances at Red River, shut the entrance against even our merchant ships. In travelling from Ocean to Ocean through the Dominion, four thousand miles were all our own. Across this one mile, half-way on the great journey, every Canadian must pass on sufferance. The cost of a canal on our side is estimated by the Canal Commissioners, in a blue-book, dated February 2nd, 1871, at only $550,000. Such a canal, and a Railway from Nipigon, or Thunder Bay to Fort Garry, would give immediate and direct steam communication to our North West within our own territory.

At the western terminus of the canal, the Ste. Marie River is again entered. Keeping to the north, or British side, we come to the Point aux Pins, covered with the scrub pine (*Pinus Banksiana*) which extends away to the north from this latitude. Rounding the Point aux Pins, the river is two or three miles wide; and, a few miles further west, Capes Gros and Iroquois tower up on each side. These bold warders, called by Agassiz "the portals of Lake Superior," are over a thousand feet high; and rugged, primeval Laurentian ranges stretch away from them as far back as the eye can reach. The sun is setting when we enter the portals, and the scene is well worthy the approach to the grandest lake on the globe. Overhead the sky is clear and blue, but the sun has just emerged from huge clouds which are emptying their buckets in the west. Immediately around is a placid sea, with half a dozen steamers and three-masted schooners at different points. And now the clouds massed together rush to meet us, as if in response to our rapid movement towards them, and envelope us in a squall and fierce driving rain, through which we see the sun setting, and lighting up now with deep yellow and then with crimson glory the fragments of clouds left behind by the heavy columns. In ten minutes the storm passes over us to the east, our sky clears as if by magic, and wind and rain are at an end. The sun sets, as if sinking into an ocean; at the same moment the full moon rises behind us, and under her mellow light Lake Superior is entered.

Those who have never seen Superior get an inadequate, even inaccurate idea, by hearing it spoken of as a 'lake,' and to those who have sailed over its vast extent the word sounds ludicrous. Though its water are fresh and crystal, Superior is a sea. It breeds storms and rain and fogs, like the sea. It is cold in mid-summer as the Atlantic. It is wild, masterful, and dreaded as the Black Sea.

July 20th.—Sailed all night along the N. E. coast of the great Lake, and in the morning, entered the land-locked harbour of Gargantua.

Two or three days previously the Chief had noticed, among the passengers, a gentleman out for his holidays on a botanical excursion to Thunder Bay, and, won by his enthusiasm, had engaged him to accompany the expedition. At whatever point the steamer touched, the first man on shore was the Botanist, scrambling over the rocks or diving into the woods, vasculum in hand, stuffing it full of mosses, ferns, lichens, liverworts, sedges, grasses and flowers, till recalled by the whistle that the captain always obligingly sounded for him. Of course such an enthusiast became known to all on board, especially to the sailors, who designated him as 'the man that gathers grass' or, more briefly, 'the hay picker' or 'haymaker.' They regarded him, because of his scientific failing, with the respectful tolerance with which fools in the East are regarded, and would wait an extra minute for him or help him on board, if the steamer were cast loose from the pier before he could scramble up the side.

This morning the first object that met our eyes, on looking out of the window of the state-room, was our Botanist, on the highest peak of the rugged hills that enclose the harbour of Gargantua. Here was proof that we too had time to go ashore, and most of us hurried off for a ramble along the beach, or for a swim, or to climb one of the wooded rocky heights. Every day since leaving Toronto we had enjoyed our dip.

Half a dozen fishermen, Alick Clark among them, had come from Collingwood to fish in Superior for white-fish and salmon-trout, and having fixed on Gargantua for summer head-quarters, they were now getting out their luggage, nets, salt, barrels, boats, &c. We went ashore in one of their boats, and could not help congratulating them heartily on the beauty of the site they had chosen. The harbour is a perfect oblong, land-locked by hills three or four hundred feet high on every side except the entrance and the upper end, where a beautiful beach slopes gradually back into a level of considerable extent. The beach was covered with the maritime vetch or wild pea in flower, and beach grasses of various kinds. Our Botanist was in raptures over sundry rare mosses, and beautiful specimens of Aspidium fragrans, Woodsia hyperborea, Cystopteris montana, and other rare ferns, that he had gathered. The view from the summit away to the north, he described as a sea of rugged Laurentian hills covered with thick woods.

From Gargantua we steered direct for Michipicoten Island. In the cozy harbour of this Island, the S. S. Manitoba lay beached, having run aground two or three days before, and a little tug was doing its best to haul her off the rock or out of

the mud.   For three hours the *Frances Smith* added her efforts
to those of the tug, but without success, and had to give it up,
and leave her consort stranded.   In the meantime some of the
passengers went off with the Botanist to collect ferns and
mosses.   He led them a rare chase over rocks and through
woods, being always on the look-out for the places that promised
the rarest kinds, quite indifferent to the toil or danger.
Scrambling, puffing, rubbing their shins against the rocks, and
half breaking their necks, they toiled painfully after him, only
to find him on his knees before something of beauty that seemed to them little different from what they had passed by with
indifference thousands of times.   But if they could not honestly
admire the moss, or believe that it was worth going though so
much to get so little, they admired the enthusiasm, and it
proved so infectuous that, before many days, almost every one
of the passengers was bitten with ' the grass mania,' or ' hay-
fever,' and had begun to form collections.

   July 21st.—Sunday morning dawned calm and clear.   The
Rural Dean read a short service and preached.   After dinner
we entered Nepigon Bay, probably the largest and safest, and
certainly the most beautiful, harbour on Lake Superior.   It is
shut off from the Lake by half a dozen islands, of which the
largest is St. Ignace,—that seem to have been set on purpose to
act as break-waters against the mighty waves of the Lake, and
form a safe harbour ; while, inside, other islands are here and
there, as if for defence or to break the force of the waves of the
Bay itself; for it is a stretch of more than thirty miles from
the entrance to the point where Nepigon River discharges into
the Bay, in a fast flowing current, the waters of Nepigon Lake
which lies forty miles to the north.   The country between the
Bay and the Lake having been found extremely unfavourable
for railway construction, it will probably be necessary to carry
the Canadian Pacific Railway farther inland, but there must be
a branch line to Nepigon Bay, which will then be the summer

terminus for the traffic from the West, (unless Thunder Bay gets the start of it) just as Duluth is the terminus of the Northern Pacific.

The scenery of Nepigon Bay is of the grandest description. There is nothing like it elsewhere in Ontario. Entering from the east we pass up a broad strait, and can soon take our choice of deep and capacious channels, formed by the bold ridges of the islands that stud the Bay. Bluffs, from three hundred to one thousand feet high, rise up from the waters, some of them bare from lake to summit, others clad with graceful balsams. On the mainland, sloping and broken hills stretch far away, and the deep shadows that rest on them bring out the most distant in clear and full relief. The time will come when the wealthy men of our great North-west will have their summer residences on these hills and shores ; nor could the heart of man desire more lovely sites. At the river is an old Hudson Bay station, and the head-quarters of several surveying parties for the Canadian Pacific Railway. The Chief therefore has business here, and the Doctor also finds some ready to his hand, for one of the engineers in charge is seriously ill ; but the captain can spare only an hour, as he wishes to be out of the Bay by the western channel, which is much narrower than the eastern, before dark. We leave at 5.30, and are in Lake Superior again at 8.30. The passengers being anxious for an evening service, the captain and the Rural Dean requested our secretary to conduct it. He consented, and used, on the occasion, a form compiled last year specially for surveying parties. The scene was unusul and, perhaps, therefore all the more impressive. Our Secretary, dressed in grey homespun, read a service compiled by clergymen of the Churches of Rome, England, and Scotland ; no one could tell which part of it was Roman, which Anglican, or which Scottish, and yet it was all Christian. The responses were led by the Dean and the Doctor, and joined in heartily by Romanists, Episcopalians, Baptists, Methodists and Presbyterians. The hymns were, "Rock of Ages" and "Sun of my Soul;" these, with the "*Gloria Patri*," were accompanied on a piano by a young lady who had acted for years as the leader of a choir in an Episcopal Chapel, and she was supported right and left by a Presbyterian and a Baptist. The sermon was short, but, according to the Doctor, would "have been better, if it had been shorter;" but all listened attentively. The effect of the whole was excellent; when the service was over, many remained in the saloon to sing, converse, or join in sacred music, and the evening passed delightfully away. The ice was broken; ladies and gentlemen, who had kept aloof all the week, addressed each other freely, without waiting to be introduced, and all began now to express sorrow that they were to part so soon. It was near the "wee sma' hour" before the pleasant groups in the saloon separated for the night.

At one A. M., we arrived at Silver Island,—a little bit of rock in a Bay studded with islets. The most wonderful vein of silver in the world has been struck here. Last year, thirty men took out from it $1,200,000; and competent judges say that the mine is worth perhaps hundreds of milions. The original $50 shares sell for $25,000. The company that works it is chiefly a New York one, though it was held originally by Montreal men, and was offered for sale in London for a trifle. Such a marvellous find as this has stimulated search in every other direction around Lake Superior. Other veins have been discovered, some of them paying well, and, of course, the probability is that there are many more undiscovered; for not one hundredth part of the mineral region of Lake Superior has been examined yet, and it would be strange indeed if all the minerals had been stumbled on at the outset. Those rocky shores may turn out to be the richest part of the whole Dominion.

The steamer arrived at Thunder Bay early in the morning, and so ended the first half of our journey from Toronto to Fort

Garry ; by rail ninety-four miles, by steamboat five hundred and thirty miles. The second half was to be by waggons and canoes ;—waggons at the beginning and end ; and, in the middle, canoes paddled by Indians or tugged by steam launches over a chain of lakes, extending like a net work in all directions along the watershed that separates the basin of the great Lakes and St. Lawrence from the vast Northern basin of Hudson's Bay. The unnecessary delays of the *Frances Smith* on this first part of our journey had been provoking ; but the real *amari aliquid* was the Sault Ste. Marie Canal. The United States own the southern shores of Superior, and have therefore only done their duty in constructing a canal on their side of the Ste. Marie River. The Dominion not only owns the northern shores, but the easier access to its great North-west is by this route ; a canal on its side is thus doubly necessary. The eastern key to two-thirds of the Dominion is meanwhile in the hands of another power ; and yet, if there ought to be only one gateway into Lake Superior, nature has declared that it should be on our side. So long ago as the end of the last century, a rude canal, capable of floating large loaded canoes without breaking bulk, existed on our side of the river.* The report of a N. W. Navigation Company in 1858 gives the length of a ship canal around the Ste. Marie rapids on the Canadian side as only 838 yards, while on the opposite side the length is a mile and one-seventh. In the interests of peace and commerce, because it would be a convenience to trade now, and may be ere long an absolute national necessity, let us have our own roadway across that short half mile. Canada can already boast of the finest ship canal system in the world ; this trifling addition would be the crowning work, and complete her inland water communication from the Ocean, westerly, across thirty degrees of longitude to the far end of Lake Superior.

(*) May 30th (1800), Friday, Sault Ste. Marie. Here the North-West Company have another establishment on the North side of the Rapid.   *   *   *   Here tne North-West Company have built locks, in order to take up loaded canoes, that they may not be under the necessity of carrying them by land, to the head of the Rapid, for the current s too strong to be stemmed by any craft.—*Hamorn's Journal.*

CHAPTER III.

From Thunder Bay to Fort Garry.

July 22nd.—At 5 A.M., arrived at Prince Arthur's Landing,
Thunder Bay, a fine open harbour, about four miles from the
mouth of the Kaministiquia river, with dark cliffs of basaltic
rock and island scenery second only to Nepigon. Population
is flowing rapidly to these shores of Lake Superior. Already
more than a hundred stores, shanties, or houses are scattered
about 'the Landing.' The chief business is silver mining, and
prospecting for silver, copper, galena, and other valuable minerals known to exist in the neighbourhood.

The engineer of the surveying parties between Ottawa and
Red River, and the assistant superintendent of the Dawson
Road to Fort Garry met us at the Landing and invited us to
breakfast in their shanty. After breakfast, our baggage was
packed on a heavy waggon, and instructions were given to the
driver to keep moving till he reached Shebandowan Lake, the
first of the chain to be traversed in canoes.

Shebandowan is forty-five miles from Lake Superior, about
800 feet higher, and near the summit or watershed of the district. At 10.30 A.M., we started for that point, the Chief and
the Doctor in a buggy, the others in a light waggon. Drove in

three hours to " fifteen-mile shanty " through a rolling country with a steady upward incline, lightly wooded for the first half and more heavily for the latter half of the distance. The flora is much the same as in our Eastern Provinces ; the soil light, with a surface-covering of peaty or sandy loam, and a subsoil of clay, fairly fertile and capable of being easily cleared. The vegetation is varied, wild fruit being especially abundant,— raspberries, currants, gooseberries, and tomatoes ; flowers like the convolvulus, roses, a great profusion of asters, wild kallas, water-lilies on the ponds, wild chives on the rocks in the streams, and generally a rich vegetation. It is a good country for emigrants of the farmer class. The road, too, is first-rate, a great point for the settler ; and a market is near. Whatever a settler raises he can easily transport to the ready market that there always is near mines. Miners are not particular about their lodging, but good food and plenty of it they must have.

At the fifteen-mile shanty, we stopped for an hour and a half to feed the horses and to dine. Bread, light and sweet as Paris rolls, was baked in Dutch ovens, buried in the hot embers of a huge fire outside, near the door. The Scotch boss of the shanty accepted the shower of compliments on its quality with the canny admission that there were " waur bakers in the warld than himsel.' "

We walked on for the next three or four miles till the waggon overtook us. The soil became richer, the timber heavier, and the whole vegetation more luxuriant. Six miles from the fifteen mile shanty we crossed the Kaministiquia—a broad and rapid river, which, at this point, is, by its own course forty-five miles distant from where it falls into Lake Superior. The valley of the river is acknowledged to be a splendid farming country. A squatter, who had pitched camp at the bridge end last year, on his way to Red River, and had remained instead of going on because everything was so favourable, came up to have a talk with us, and to grumble, like a true Briton, that the Government wasn't doing more for him. Timothy was growing to the height of four and five feet, on every vacant spot, from chance seeds. A bushel and a-half of barley, which seemed to be all that he had sown, was looking as if it could take the prize at an Ontario Exhibition.

The soil, for the next five miles, was covered luxuriantly with the vetch, or wild pea. The road led to the Matawan,— a stream that runs out of Lake Shebandowan into the Kaministiquia. Both rivers are crossed by capital bridges. The station at the Matawan was in charge of a Mr. Aitken and his family, from Glengarry. He had arrived exactly two months ago, on the 22nd of May, and he had now oats and barley up, potatoes in blossom, turnips, lettuce, parsnips, cucumbers, etc., all looking healthy, and all growing on land that, sixty days before, had been in part covered with undergrowth, stumps, and tall trees, through which fires had run the year previous. Mr. Aitken was in love with the country, and, what was of more consequence, so was Mrs. Aitken, though she confessed to a longing for some neighbours. They intended to make it their future home, and said that they had never seen land so well suited for farming. Everything was prospering with them. The very hens seemed to do better here than elsewhere. One was pointed out with a brood of twenty strong healthy chickens around her ; Guinea hens and turkeys looked thriving.

Everything about this part of the country, so far, has astonished us. Our former ideas concerning it had been that it was a barren desert ; that there was only a horse trail, and not always that, to travel by ; that the mosquitoes were as big as grasshoppers, and bit through everything. Whereas, it is a fair and fertile land, undulating from the intervals of the river up to hills and rocks eight hundred feet high. The road through it is good enough for a king's highway, and the mosquitoes are not more vicious than in the woods, and by the streams of the Lower Provinces ; yet, not half a dozen settlers are on the road for the first twenty-six miles; and for the next twenty, not half that number. How many cottars, small farmers, and plough boys in Britain, would rejoice to know that they could get a hundred acres of such land for one dollar an acre, money down; or at twenty cents per acre after five years' settlement on it! They could settle along the high road, take their produce to a good market, and be independent landholders in five years. This was the information about the price of land that the settlers gave us. Why free grants are not offered, as in other parts of Ontario or in Manitoba, it is impossible to say.

From the Matawan to Shebandowan lake was the next stage, twenty miles long. We passed over most of it in the dark, but could see, from the poor timber and other indications, that the latter half was not at all as good as the first. The road was heavy, varying between corduroy, deep sand, and rutty and rooty stretches, over which the waggon jolted frightfully.

So passed the first day of our expedition, for we counted that the journey only began at Thunder Bay.

July 23rd.—Rose at sunrise, and found that the baggage waggon had not arrived. An hour after it came in, and, along with it, two young gentlemen, M . . . . and L . . . with a canoe and Indians on their way to Red River. They were travelling for pleasure, and as they had been on the road all night, and were tired, seedy and mosquito-bitten, they represented very fairly, in their own persons, the Anglo-Saxon idea of pleasure.

At 8 A. M., the baggage having been stowed in the canoes, the Indians paddled out, and hooked on to a little steam tug, kept on the lake for towing purposes; a line was formed, and after a few preliminary puffings, the start was made and we proceeded along the lake. The mode of locomotion was, to us, altogether new, and as charming as it was picturesque: The tug led the way at the rate of seven knots, towing first a large barge with immigrants, second a five fathom canoe with three of our party and seven Indians, third a four fathom canoe with two of us and six Indians, fourth same as number three, fifth M . . . and L . . . .'s canoe. We glided along with a delightful motion, sitting on our baggage in the bottoms of the canoes. The morning was dull and grey, and the shores of the lake looked sterile and fire-swept, with abundant indications of mineral wealth. Gold and silver have been found at Shebandowan and prospecting parties are now searching all accessible spots.

Our Indians were Iroquois from Caughnawaga near Montreal, and a few native Ojibbeways. Their leader was Ignace Mentour, who had been Sir George Simpson's guide for fifteen years ; and the steersman of his canoe was Louis, who had been cook to Sir George on his expeditions, and looked every inch the butler of a respectable English family ; we fell in love with him and Ignace from the first. Another of the Iroquois had been one of the party which sought for Franklin by going down the McKenzie River to the Arctic Sea. Two old pupils of Ignace, named respectively Baptiste and Toma, were the captains of the two smaller canoes. All were sinewy, active, good looking men. Ignace's hair was gray, but he was still as strong as any of the young men ; he paddled in the bow of the big canoe, leading the way, and quietly chewing tobacco the whole time. In his young days he had been a famous runner, and had won foot races in every town on both sides of the St. Lawrence. These Iroquois, and most of the Ojibbeways we have met, are men above the medium size, broad shouldered, with straight features, intelligent faces, and graceful, because natural, bearing.

At the west end of the lake we came to a camp of seventy or eighty Ojibbeways—two-thirds of them children. They had been there for three weeks, of course doing nothing, and the camp was very dirty. More were expected, and when all assembled, a grand pow-wow would be held, and a Treaty made between them and the Indian Commissioner of the

Dominion. So at least they hoped and they declared themselves willing to cede, for a consideration, all their rights to the land, that would hinder settlers from coming in. Poor creatures ! not much use have they ever made of the land ; but yet, in admitting the settler, they sign their own death warrants. Who, but they, have a right to the country ; and if a man may do what he likes with his own, would they not be justified in refusing to admit one of us to their lakes and woods, and fighting us to the death on that issue ?

Three hours' steaming brought our flotilla to the west end of the lake. A portage of three quarters of a mile intervenes between it and Lake Kashaboiwe. The Indians emptied the canoes in a trice ; two shouldered a canoe, weighing probably three hundred pounds, and made off at a rapid trot across the portage. The others loaded the waggon of the station with the luggage, and carried on their backs, by a strap passed over their foreheads, what the waggon could not take. This portage strap is three or four inches broad in the middle, where it is adjusted to the forehead ; its great advantage to the voyageur is that it leaves him the free use of his arms in going through the woods. A tug has been placed on Kashaboiwe, but as the machinery was out of gear the Indians paddled over the lake, doing the ten miles of its length in two hours. The wood on this lake is heavier than on Shebandowan : poplars, white birch, red, white and scrub pine, all show well. The second portage is between Kashaboiwe and Lac des Mille Lacs, and is the Height of Land where the water begins to run north and west instead of east and south. The lakes, after this, empty at their west ends. At the east end of Lac des Mille Lacs, a little stream three yards wide, that flows in a tortuous channel with gentle current into the lake, eventually finds its way to Hudson's Bay. The Height of Land is about a thousand feet above Lake Superior.

We now entered Lac des Mille Lacs—a lovely lake twenty-two miles long ; its name explains its characteristic. As the steam launch, stationed on it, happened unfortunately to be at the west end, the Indians again paddled for about four miles, when we met the lauch coming back ; it at once turned about and took us in tow. After a smart shower the sky cleared, and the sun shone on innumerable bays, creeks, channels, headlands, and islets, which are simply larger or smaller rocks of granite covered with moss and wooded to the water's brink. Through these labyrinths we threaded our way, often wondering that the wrong passage was never taken, where there were so many exactly alike. An Indian on his own ground or water is never mistaken, and we went on as surely as if on a king's highway. Fortunately, the fire-demon has not devastated the shores. The timber, in some places, is heavy : pine, aspen, and birch being the prevailing varieties. Every islet in the lake is wooded down to the water's edge. Our Botanist exulted in his holiday and looked forward with eager hope to the flora of the plains. As we drew near our third portage for the day, his face clouded. " Look at the ground burnt again." One asked if it was the great waste of wood he referred to. " It's not that, but, they have burned the very spot for botanizing over." What is a site for shanty and clearing, compared to botany.

At the end of Lac des Mille Lacs is Baril Portage, less than a quarter of a mile long. No steamer has been put on Baril lake; but the Indians paddled over its eight miles of length in an hour and forty minutes. The bluffs around Baril are bolder than those rising from the previous lakes, and the vegetation very similar. We hurried over the next portage, and, at the other end met the station-keeper, who had a comfortable tent pitched for the emigrants, strewn with fragrant pine and spruce branches.

It was impossible to avoid admiring the activity and cheerfulness with which our Indians worked. They would carry as heavy a load as a Constantinople porter, at a rapid trot across the portage, run back for another load without a minute's halt, and so on till all the luggage was portaged, and everything in readiness for starting on the next lake. The canoes were always their first care. As a jockey cherishes his horse, and a shepherd his collie, so do they care for and actually love their canoe,

A fire was quickly kindled, and search made for the eatables. blankets, and everything needed for the night, when the discovery was made that, though the colonel had his blankets and the botanist his pair, a big package with the main supply had been left behind, very probably as far back as the "Height of Land." The frizzling of the ham in the frying pan, and the delicious fragrance of the tea, made us forget the loss for the time. We all sat around the fire, gipsy-like, enjoying our first gipsy meal, and very soon after threw ourselves down on the water-proof, that covered the sweet-smelling floor of the tent, and slept the sleep of the just.

July 20th.—The Chief awoke us in the grey misty dawn. It took more than a little shaking to awaken the boys; but the botanist had gone off, no one knew when, in search of new species. As we emerged from our tent, Louis and Baptiste appeared from theirs, and kindled the fire. They next took from a wallet scented soap, brush and comb; went down to the stream, washed and made their toilettes, and then set to work to prepare for breakfast. It never seemed to occur to our Ojibbeways to wash, crop, or dress their hair. They let it grow, at its own sweet will, all around their faces and down their necks, lank and stiff, helping the growth with fish oil. Every one of the Iroquois had good head of hair, thick, well cropped, and, though always black, quite like the hair of a civilized man instead of a savage. Our Ojibbeways had silver rings on their fingers, broad gaudy sashes and bedraggled feathers bound round their felt hats. The Iroquois dressed as simply and neatly as blue jackets.

It had been chilly through the night, and the cold mist clung heavily to the ground in the morning. The air is colder than the water from evening till morning. Hence the evening and morning mists, which disappear an hour or two after sunrise, rise and form into clouds, which sooner or later empty themselves back again on the land or lakes.

After breakfast we embarked on the mist-covered river that runs into Lake Windegoostigwan. The sun soon cleared away the mists and we glided on pleasantly, down long reaches of lake, and through narrow winding reedy passages, past curved shores hidden by rank vegetation, and naked bluffs and islets covered with clumps of pines. Not a word fell from the Indians' lips, as they paddled with all the ease and regularity of machinery. The air was delightful, and all felt as if out on a holiday. In three hours the fifteen miles of Windegoostigwan were crossed, and we came to a portage nearly two miles long. This detained us three hours, as the waggon had to make two trips from lake to lake, over a new road, with our luggage.

A man from Glengarry was in charge of the portage; he had lived here all winter, and said that he preferred the winter weather to that of the Eastern Provinces. Great as is the summer rainfall, it is quite different in winter; then the days are clear and cloudless, and so sunny and pleasant that he was accustomed to go about in his summer clothing, except in the mornings and evenings. Three feet of snow fell in the woods after Christmas, and continued dry and powdery till April, when it commenced to melt, and soon after the middle of May it was all gone, and vegetation began to show itself at once.

At the west end of the portage is a small encampment of Ojibbeways, around the wigwam of Blackstone, said to be their most eloquent chief, and accordingly set down as a great rascal by those who cannot conceive of Indians as having rights, or tribal or patriotic feelings. He was absent, but we saw one of his three wives sitting on a log, with two or three papooses hanging round her neck, and his oldest son, a stout young fellow, who could not speak a word of English or French, but who managed to let us know that he was ill. The Doctor was called, and he made out that the lad had a pain in his back, but, not being able to diagnose more particularly, was at a loss what to do for him. Our Chief suggested a bit of tobacco, but the Doctor took no notice of the profane proposal; luckily enough, or the whole tribe would have been ill when the next Medicine-man passed their way. Blackstone's wife was not more comely than any of the other Indian women; that is she was dirty, joyless-looking and prematurely old. All the hard work falls to the lot of the women; the husband hunts, fishes, paddles, or does any other work that a gentleman feels he can do without degradation; his wife is something better than his dog, and faithfully will he share with her his last morsel; but it's only a dog's life that she has.

Our next lake was Kaogassikok, sixteen miles long. The shores of this, too, were lined with good-sized pine, white, red, and scrub. To-day more larch and cedar shewed among the birch and pine than yesterday. When the country is opened up, all this timber will be very valuable, as sleepers and ties for the Pacific Railway, and lumber, for building purposes, can be obtained here in abundance, if nowhere nearer the plains. Numbers of fine trees are now growing in the water; for, by damming up the outflow of the lakes to make the landing places, the water level has been raised and the shore trees have thus been submerged several feet. They will rot, in consequence, and fall into the lakes sooner or later, and perhaps obstruct the narrow channels. The timber gets heavier as we go on; at the west of Kaogassikok are scrub pines, three feet in diameter; but, unfortunately, about one-third of them are punky or hollow. Here are two portages, Pine and Deux Rivières, separated by only two miles of water; consequently much detention owing to our magnificent quantities of baggage. Two Indians suffering from dysentery, applied for relief at Pine Portage, and received it at the hands of the Doctor : he has already had about a dozen cases, either of white or red men, since we left Owen Sound. Our party have, thus far, received little at the Doctor's hands, sundry medical comforts always excepted.

After paddling over four miles of the next lake the Indians advised camping, though the sun was more than an hour high. As we had experienced the discomforts of camping in the dark the night before, and as the men were evidently tired, we landed and pitched the tents on a rocky promontory at the foot of a wooded hill. Scarcely were our fires lighted, when M————'s canoe came up, and then another with a stray Indian, his wife, papooses, dog—that looked half wolf, and all their traps. After a good swim, we sat down to our evening meal, which Louis had spread on a clean table-cloth on the sward. In front of us was the smooth lake ; on the other side of it, two miles off, the sun was going down in the woods. The country ahead broke into knolls, looking in many parts like cultivated parks; around us the white tents and the ruddy fires, with Indians flitting between, or busy about the canoes, gave animation to the scene and made up a picture that will long live in the memory of many of us.

The Indians never halt without at once turning their canoes upside down, and examining them. The seams and crevices in the birch bark yield at any extra strain, and scratches are made by submerged brushwood in some of the channels or the shallow parts of the lakes. These crevices they carefully daub over with resin, which is obtained from the red pine, till the bottom of an old canoe becomes almost covered with a black resinous coat. Of course, the more uniform the blackness, the harder the service the canoe has seen.

The stray Indian pitched camp a hundred yards off from us ; and, with true Indian dignity, did not come near to ask for anything, though quite equal to take anything that was offered or left behind.

July 25th.—Up before four A.M., and, after a cup of hot tea, that always has a wondrous fragrance in the wilderness, started in excellent spirits. Our three canoes had tried a race the night before, over the last four miles of the day's journey, and they renewed it this morning. The best crew was in the five-fathom boat, of which Ignace was captain, and Louis steersman. The captains of the other two, Baptiste and Toma, pushed their old master hard to-day; as one or the other stole ahead, not a glance did Ignace give to either. Doggedly, and with averted head, he dug his paddle deeper in the water, and pegged away with his sure, steady stroke, and though the others, by spurting, forced themselves half a canoe length ahead at times, they had not the stay of the older men, and every race ended with Ignace leading. Then he would look up, and with sunshine on his broad handsome face, throw a good humoured joke back, which the others would catch up with great glee. These races often broke the monotony of the day. "Up, up," or "hi, hi," would break suddenly from one of the canoes that had fallen behind. Everyone answered with quickened stroke that sent it abreast of the others. Then came the tug of war. The graceful, gondola shaped canoes cut through the water as though impelled by steam. The *Buffalo* or Ignace's canoe— so called from the figure of an Indian with a gun standing before a buffalo that he had painted on the bow—always led at the first; but often the *Sun*, Baptiste's lighter craft, would shoot ahead, and sometimes Toma's, the *Beaver*, under the frantic efforts of her crew, seconded by one or two of us snatching up a paddle, would lead for a few minutes. The chivalry of our Indians in the heat of the contest contrasted favourably with that of professionals. No "foul" ever took place, though the course often lay through narrow winding reedy channels. Once, when Baptiste at such a place might have forced ahead by a spurt, he slacked speed gracefully, let Ignace take the curve and win. Another time, when neck and neck, he saw a heavy

line dragging at the stern and called Louis' attention to it. No
one ever charged the other with being unfair, and no angry
word was ever heard; in fact, the Indians grow on us day by day.
It is easy to understand how an Englishman, travelling for weeks
together with an Indian guide, so often contracts a strong
friendship for him; for Indian patience, endurance, dignity, and
self-control, are the very qualities to evoke friendship.

The sun rose bright but was soon clouded. Ten good miles
were made and then the halt called for breakfast. at a beautiful
headland, just as it commenced to rain. Now we got some
idea of what a rainy day in these regions means. After breakfast we put on our water-proofs, covered up our baggage and
moved ahead, under a deluge of rain that knew no intermission
for four hours. Most of the water-proofs proved to be delus-
ions ; they had not been made for these latitudes. The canoes
would have filled, had we not kept bailing, but, without a word
of complaint, the Indians stuck to their paddles.

From the lake we passed into the Maligne river, and there
the current aided us. In this short, but broad and rapid
stream, are six or seven rapids, which must be shot or portaged
round ; we preferred the shooting, wherever it was practicable
for such large and deeply-laden canoes as ours.

To shoot rapids in a canoe is a pleasure that comparatively
few Englishmen have ever enjoyed, and no picture can give an
idea of what it is. There is a fascination in the motion, as of
poetry or music, which must be experienced to be understood.
The excitement is greater than when on board a steamer, because you are so much nearer the seething water, and the canoe
seems such a fragile thing to contend with the mad forces, into
the very thick of which it has to be steered. Where the stream
begins to descend, the water is an inclined plane, smooth and
shining as glare ice. Beyond that it breaks into curling, gleaming rolls which end off in white, boiling caldrons, where the
water has broken on the rocks underneath. On the brink of

the inclined plane the motion is so quiet that you think the
canoe pauses for an instant. The captain is at the bow,—a
broader, stronger paddle than usual in his hand—his eye kindl-
ing with enthusiasm, and every nerve and fibre in his body at
its utmost tension. The steersman is at his post, and every
man is ready. They know that a false stroke, or too weak a
turn of the captain's wrist, at the critical moment, means death.
A push with the paddles, and, straight and swift as an arrow,
the canoe shoots right down into the mad vortex ; now into a
cross current that would twist her broadside round, but that
every man fights against it ; then she steers right for a rock, to
which she is being resistlessly sucked, and on which it seems as
if she would be dashed to pieces ; but a rapid turn of the captain's paddle at the right moment, and she rushes past the black
mass, riding gallantly as a race horse. The waves boil up at the
side, threatening to engulf her, but except a dash of spray or
the cap of a wave, nothing gets in, and as she speeds into the
calm reach beyond, all draw long breaths and hope that another
rapid is near.

At eleven o'clock we reached Island Portage, having paddled
thirty-two miles—the best forenoon's work since taking to the
canoes—in spite of the weather. Here a steam launch is
stationed ; and, though the engineer thought it a frightful day
to travel in, he got ready at our request, but said that he could
not go four miles an hour as the rain would keep the boiler wet
the whole time. We dined with M——'s party, under the
shelter of their upturned canoe, on tea and the fattest of fat
pork, which all ate with delight unspeakable, for every one had
in himself the right kind of sauce. The day, and our soaked
condition, suggested a little brandy as a specific ; but their bottle was exhausted, and, an hour before, they had passed round
the cork for each to have a smell at. Such a case of potatoes
and point moved our pity, and the chief did what he could for
them. The Indians excited our admiration ;—soaked through,

and over-worked as they had been, the only word that we heard, indicating that they were conscious of anything unusual, was an exclamation from Baptiste, as he gave himself a shake,— " Boys, wish I was in a tavern now, I'd get drunk in less than tree hours, I guess."

At two o'clock, the steam launch was ready. It towed us the twenty-four miles of Lake Nequaquon in three and a quarter hours.

Next came Loon portage ; then paddling for five miles ; then Mud portage, worthy of its name ; another short paddle ; and then American portage, at which we camped for the night— the sun having at last come out and this being the best place for pitching tents and the freest from mosquitoes. Tired enough all hands were, and ready for sleep, for these portages are kill- ing work. After taking a swim, we rigged lines before huge fires, and hung up our wet things to dry, so that it was eleven o'clock before anyone could lie down. The Doctor and Secretary had stowed their luggage in water-proof bags, kindly lent them by the Colonel ; but the bags proved a fallacious as our water- proofs ! Part of the Botanist's valise was reduced to pulp, but he was too eager in search of specimens to think of such a trifle, and, while all the rest of us were busy washing and hanging out to dry, he hunted through woods and marshes, and, though he got little for his pains, was happy as a king.

Our camping ground had been selected by the Indians with their usual good taste. A rocky eminence, round two sides of which a river poured in a roaring linn ; on the hill sombre pines, underneath which the tents were pitched ; and lower down a forest of white birch. More than one of the party dreamed he was in Scotland, as he was lulled to sleep by the thunder of the waterfall.

July 26th.—Up again about three, A.M., and off within an hour, down a sedgy river, with low swampy shores, into Lake Nameukan. The sun rose bright, and continued to shine all

day ; but a pleasant breeze tempered its rays.   At mid-day, the
thermometer stood at 80° in the shade, the hottest since leaving
Owen Sound.   One day on Lake Superior it was down to 48°,
and the average at mid-day since we landed at Thunder Bay was
from 55° to 60°.

After twelve miles paddling, halted at a pretty spot on an
islet for breakfast.   Frank caught a large pickerel and M——
shot a few pigeons, giving us a variety of courses at dinner.
M——'s Indians tried a race with us to-day, and after a hard
struggle got ahead of Toma and Baptiste, but Ignace proudly
held his own and would not be beaten.   However, among the
many turns of the river, Toma, followed by Baptiste, circum-
vented their old master, by dashing through a passage overgrown with weeds and reeds instead of taking the usual channel.
When Ignace turned the corner he saw the two young fellows
coolly waiting for him a hundred and fifty yards ahead.   They
gave a sly laugh as he came up, but Ignace was too dignified to
take the slightest notice.   Baptiste was so pleased that he sang
us two Iroquois canoe songs.

Eighteen miles, broken by two short portages (for we took a
short-cut instead of the public route), brought us about mid-day
to Rainy Lake.

The engineer of the steam launch here promised to be ready
in two hours, and to land us at Fort Francis, at the west end of
Rainy Lake, forty-five miles on, by sundown.   But in half an
hour the prospect did not look so bright, as, across the portage,
by the public route, came a band of eighteen emigrants, men,
women and children, who had left Thunder Bay five days before
us, and whom we had passed this forenoon, when we took our
short cut.   They had a great deal of baggage, and were terribly
tired.   One old woman, eighty-five years of age, complained of
being ill, and the doctor attended to her.   As we had soup for
dinner, he sent some over to her, and the prescription had a
good effect.   While waiting here we took our half dried clothes

out of the bags, and, by hanging them on lines under the warm sun, got them pretty well dried before starting.

At three P.M., at the cry of " All aboard," our flotilla formed at once,—the steam launch towing two large barges with the emigrants and their luggage, and the four canoes. The afternoon was warm and sunny, and there was a pleasant breeze on the Lake. In half an hour every Indian was asleep in the bottom of his canoe.

The shores of Rainy Lake are low, especially on the northern side, and the timber is small ; the shores rocky, with here and there sandy beaches that have formed round little bays ; scenery tame and monotonous, though the islets, in some parts, are beautiful.

By nine o'clock, we had made only thirty miles. Our steamer was small, the flotilla stretched out far and the wind was ahead. We therefore determined to camp ; and, by the advice of the engineer, steered for the north shore to what is called the Fifteen Mile House from Fort Francis, said house being two deserted log huts. Our botanist, learning that we would leave before day-break, lighted an old pine branch and roamed about with his torch to investigate the flora of the place. The others visited the emigrants to whom the log-huts had been assigned, or sat round rousing fires, smoking, or gathered bracken and fragrant artemisia for the beds.

July 27th.—Had our breakfast before four A.M., and in less than half an hour after, were *en route* for Fort Francis. Two miles above the Fort the Lake ends and pours itself into Rainy River, over a rapid which the emigrants' barges had not oars to shoot. They were cast off, and we went on to the Fort and sent men up to bring them down. The Fort is simply a Hudson's Bay Company's trading post ;—the shop and the cottages of the agent and employés in the form of a square, surrounded by stockades about ten feet high. From the Fort is a beautiful view of the Chaudière Falls which have to be portaged round.

These are formed by the river, here nearly two hundred yards wide, pouring over a granite ridge in magnificent roaring cascades. A sandy plain of several acres, covered with rich grass extends around the Fort, and wheat, barley, and potatoes are raised; but beyond this plain is marsh and then rock. A few fine cattle, in splendid condition, were grazing upon the level. On the potato leaves we found the Colorado Bug, that frightful pest which seems to be moving further east every year.

Half a dozen wigwams were tenanted in the vicinity of the Fort, and there were scores of roofless poles, where, a fortnight ago, had been high feasting for a few days. A thousand or twelve hundred Ojibbeways had assembled to confer with Mr. Simpson, the Dominion Indian Commissioner, as to the terms on which they would allow free passage through, and settlement in the country. No agreement had been come to, as their terms were considered extravagant.

Justice, both to the Indians and to the emigrants who are invited to make their home in this newly opened country, demands that a settlement of the difficulty be made as soon as possible. It may be true that they are vain, lazy, dirty, and improvident. The few about Fort Francis did not impress us favourably. They contrasted strikingly with our noble Iroquois. The men were lounging about, lolling in their wigwams, playing cards in the shade, or lying on their faces in the sun; and, though not one of them was doing a hand's turn, it was a matter of some difficulty to get four or five to go with us to the North-west Angle, to replace those who had come from Shebandowan and whose engagement ended here. There were some attempts at tawdry finery about them all. The men wore their hair plaited into two or more long queues, which, when rolled up on the head, looked well enough, but which usually hung down the sides of the face, giving them an effeminate look, all the more so because bits of silver or brass were twisted in or ringed round with the plaits. One young fellow that consented to paddle, had long streamers of bright ribbon flying from his felt hat.   Another poor looking creature had his face streaked over with red ochre—to show how great a brave he was. Some wore blankets, folded loosely and gracefully about them, instead of coats and trousers.   Indeed, every one had some good clothes ; the construction of the road being the cause of this, for all who wish can get employment in one way or another in connection with it.   At Fort Francis the hulls of two steamers, to be over a hundred feet in length, for use on Rainy river and Lake of the Woods, are now being built; and Indians who cannot work at bringing in timber or at ship carpentering, can be employed as voyageurs, or to improve the portages, or to fish or hunt, or in many other ways.   But whatever the benefits that have been conferred on them, or whatever their natural defects, they have rights to this country, though they have never divided it up into separate personal holdings.   They did not do so, simply because their idea was that the land was free to all. Each tribe had its own ground, which extended over hundreds of miles, and every man had a full right to all of that as far as he could occupy it.   Wherever he could walk, ride, or canoe, there the land and the water were his.   If he went to the land of another tribe, the same rule held good.   There he might be scalped as an enemy, but he ran no risk of being punished as a trespasser.

And now a foreign race is swarming over the country, to mark out lines, to erect fences, and to say " this is mine and not yours," till not an inch shall be left the original owner.   All this may be inevitable.   But in the name of justice, and of the sacred rights of property, is not the Indian entitled to liberal and, if possible, permanent compensation ? What makes it difficult to arrange a settlement with the Ojibbeways is, that they have no chiefs who are authorized to treat for them. This results from their scattered and dispersed state as a nation. The country they live in is poorly supplied with game, and pro_ duces but little of itself, and the Indian does not farm.   It is thus impossible for them to live in large bodies. They wander in groups and families from place to place, often suffering the extreme of hunger, and sometimes starved outright. Each group has generally one or more men of greater moral or physical power than the rest, and these are its chiefs, chiefs who have no hereditary rank, who have never been formally elected, and who are quietly deposed when greater men than they rise up. Their influence is indirect, undefined, wholly personal, and confined to the particular group they live with. They can scarcely speak for the group, and not at all for the nation. When anything has to be done for the nation as a whole, there is then no other way but for the nation to meet *en masse*. Even then they elect no representative men, unless specially requested. Those of greatest age, eloquence, or personal weight speak for the others; but decisions can be come to only by the crowd. Of course they could not have existed, thus loosely bound together, had they lived in large bodies, or being pressed by powerful enemies. But they are merely families and groups and their lands have no special attraction for other Indian tribes. Neither can they be formidable as enemies to settlers on this same account, should the worst come to the worst; but their feebleness makes it the more incumbent on the Government of a Christian people to treat them not only justly but generously.

After breakfast we paddled down the river, till overtaken by the steam launch with the emigrants. The day was very warm; when we landed, about twelve miles on, to dine, the thermometer stood at 87 ° in the shade.

Rainy River is broad and beautiful; flowing with an easy current through a low-lying and evidently fertile country. For the whole of its length—about eighty miles—it forms the boundary between Canada and the United States. For the first twenty-five miles, twenty or thirty feet above the present beach or intervale, rises in terrace form another, evidently the old shore of the river, which extends far back like a prairie. The richness of the soil is evident from the luxuriance and variety of the wild flowers. Much of the land could be cleared almost as easily as prairie ; other parts are covered with pines, elms, maples and aspens.

Thirty-five miles from Fort Francis we ran the Manitou rapids and, five miles further on, the Sault, neither of them formidable. A moderately powerful steamer could easily run up as well as shoot them. Beyond the Sault we landed to take in wood for the tug, and dinner for ourselves. The Botanist came up to us in a few minutes with wild pea and vetch vines eight feet high, which grew so thickly, not far off, that it was almost impossible to pass through them. The land is a heavy loam,—once the bed of the river, and the luxuriance of the vegetation shows that it is of the best quality. He made a list of the following plants while we halted, "and these," he truly remarks " are only an index to the vast profusion of nature's beauties in this region :—

Lilium Canadense,	Lathyrus venosus,
" Philadelphicum,	" ochroleucus,
Vicia Americana,	Monarda fistulosa,
Calystegia spithamea,	Viburnum pubescens,
" sepium,	Astragalus Canadensis,
Aralia hispida,	Erysimum chieranthoides,
Lobelia Kalmii,	Asarum Canadensis,
Similacina stellata,	Lopanthus anistatus."

Besides these there were grasses and sedges in abundance and many other species not worth mentioning. Enough was seen, however, to satisfy the writer that Rainy River will yet support a large population, mainly composed of agriculturists.

On we swept, down the broad pleasant river, with its long reaches, beautiful at night as they had been in the bright sunshine. At times a high wall of luxuriant wood rose on each side, and stretched far ahead in curves that looked in the gloam-

ing like cultivated parks. Occasionally an islet divided the
river; and, at such places, a small Indian camp was usually
pitched. Of the seventy-five miles of Rainy River, down which
we sailed to-day, every mile seemed well adapted for cultivation and the dwellings of men. At eleven o'clock the moon
rose; at half-past twelve we reached Hungry Hall, a post of
the H. B. Company and a village of wigwams, out of which all
the natives rushed, some of them clothed scantily and others
less than scantily, to greet the new comers, with " Ho! Ho!"
or " B'jou, B'jou." Baptiste urged us not to stop here, as the
Indians of the place were such thieves that they would " steal
the socks off us," and spoke of good camping ground a mile and
a half further on. We took his advice, after getting a supply
of flour, pork, and tea from the store.

July 28th.—This morning, for the first time since leaving
Lake Superior, we enjoyed the luxury of a long sleep, and the
still greater luxury of an hour's dozing, that condition between
sleeping and waking in which you are just enough awake to
know that you are not asleep.

At 8.30, A. M., a distinguished visitor appeared, an old stately
looking Indian, a chief, we were informed, and the father of
Blackstone. He came with only one attendant; but two or
three canoes made their appearance about the same time, with
other Indians, squaws, and papooses who squatted in groups on
the banks at respectful distances. The old Indian came up
with a " B'jou, B'jou," shook hands all round, and then drawing
himself up—knife in one hand, big pipe in the other, the em-
blems of war and peace—commenced a long harangue. We
didn't understand a word; but one of the men roughly interpreted, and the speaker's gestures were so expressive that the
drift of his meaning could be easily followed. Pointing, with
outstretched arms, north, south, east and west, he told us that
all the land had been his people's, and that he now, in their
name, asked for some return for our passage through it. The

bearing and speech were those of a born orator. He had good straight features, a large Roman nose, square chin, and, as he stood over six feet in his moccasins, his presence was most commanding. One great secret of impressive gesticulation—the free play of the arm from the shoulder, instead of the cramped motion from the elbow—he certainly knew. It was astonishing with what dignity and force, long, rolling, musical sentences poured from the lips of one who would be carelessly classed by most people as a savage, to whose views no regard should be paid. When ended, he took a seat on a hillock with the dignity natural to every real Indian, and began to smoke in perfect silence. He had said his say, and it was our turn now. Without answering his speech, which we could only have done in a style far inferior to his, the Chief proposed that he should have some breakfast. To show due respect to so great an O-ghe-mah, a newspaper was spread before him as a tablecloth, and a plate of fried pork placed on it, with a huge slapjack or thick pancake made of flour and fat, one-sixth of which was as much as any white man's stomach could digest. A large pannikin of tea, a beverage the Indians are immoderately fond of, was also brought, and, by signs, he was invited to fall to. For some moments he made no movement, either from offended pride or expectation that we would join him, or, more likely, only to show a gentleman-like indifference to the food. But the fat pork and the fragrant tea were irresistible. Many a great man's dignity has been overcome by less. After he had eaten about half, he summoned his attendant to sit beside him and eat, and to him too a pannikin of tea was brought. We then told the old man that we had heard his words ; that we were travellers carrying only enough food for ourselves, but that we would bring his views to the notice of the Government, and that his tribe would certainly receive justice, as it was the desire of our Great Mother the Queen, that all her children— red as well as white—should be well cared for. He at once

assented, though whether he would have done so with equal
blandness had we given him no breakfast is questionable. He
was entitled to the breakfast and perhaps to something more ;
for as no treaty had been made we were certainly trespassers on
his domains.

At ten o'clock the steamer came along.

A few miles through long reaches of wide expanding sedge
and marsh brought us to the Lake of the Woods. An unbroken
sheet of water, ten miles square, called The Traverse, is the
first part of this Lake that has to be crossed ; but, as a thunder
storm seemed brewing behind us, the captain steered to the
north, behind a group of islets that fringe the shore. In half
an hour an inky belt of cloud stretched over us from north to
south, and, when it burst, the torrent was as if the lake had
turned upside down. The storm moved with us, as in a circle,
flashes of lightning coming simultaneously from opposite quarters of the heavens. First we had the wind and rain on our
backs, then on the left, then in our faces, and then on the right.
The captain made for a little bay in an islet near at hand, and,
though the weather cleared, it looked threatening enough to
make him decide to put the steamer's fire out and wait. The
islet was merely a sand dune, covered with coarse grasses and
small willows, though in a storm these sand hills might be mistaken for formidable rocks. As there was not enough wood on
it for both parties, we gave it up to the crew and the emigrants,
and paddled to another a mile ahead. This islet was of gneissoid rock, and had a bold headland covered with good wood.
The botanist found the ash-leaved maple, the nettle tree, and
twenty-four kinds of wild flowers that he had not seen since
joining the expedition, and, of these, eight with which he was
unacquainted.

Scarcely were our canoes hauled up, when the Colonel came
along. His men had been so anxious to have all their party
together that they had paddled steadily at their hardest for

seven hours. Louis at once set to work to get dinner; and, it being Sunday, several delicacies were brought out in addition to the standing dishes of pork, biscuit and tea. From the Colonel's stores came Mullagatawny soup, Bologna sausage, French mustard, Marmalade, and, as every one carried with him an abundant supply of "black sauce," we had a great feast.

After dinner, all the party, except the pagan Ojibbeways, assembled for divine service. The form compiled for the surveying parties was read; the "*Veni Creator*" sung in Iroquois by the Indians; and a short sermon preached. Although the Iroquois understood but few words of English, they listened most devoutly, and we listened with as much attention to their singing. To hear those children of the forest, on a lonely isle in a lake that Indian tradition says is ever haunted by their old deities, chanting the hymn that for centuries has been sung at the great Councils and in the high Cathedrals of Christendom, moved us deeply.

After tea, candles were lit in the tents, as this evening we were not too tired to read. Our candlestick was a simple and effective Indian contrivance. A stick of any length you desired was slit at the top and then stuck in the ground. A bit of birch-bark or paper was doubled; in the fold the candle was placed, and the ends were then inserted in the slit. The stick thus held the ends tight, and the candle upright. We spent a quiet pleasant evening, and about ten o'clock turned in.

July 29th.—There was a heavy sea on The Traverse, and, as the little steamer was not very sea-worthy, it was doubtful if she would attempt the passage. But, while we were at breakfast, she was announced as making in our direction. Orders were at once given to take down the tents and embark the stores, but the Indians showed some reluctance to move. They said that it would be safer to trust to the paddles; that the waves in the middle of the *traverse* would be heavy, and that, if the canoes were forced through them, the bow or side would be broken in. We overruled their doubts, with a show of confidence, and started at 7.30 A.M.

Instead of the long single line of canoes that had been formed on previous days, they were now formed two abreast, and the connecting lines of the first two were shortened, and tied to the middle bench of the big barge which contained the emigrants' luggage. This worked admirably, as the barge broke the waves, and, in the comparatively smooth water immediately behind her, the two canoes rode easily, the five-fathom one to windward and a smaller one under her lee; close after these came the other two canoes. The passage was made safely, and the water for the rest of the day was only rippled slightly, as we took a circuitous route through innumerable islets, instead of the short and direct one over the unbroken part of the lake. The forenoon was cold and cloudy, but occasionally the sun shone cheerily out. All were thankful for the clouds and coolness, as they could note and enjoy the changing scenery, whereas the day before yesterday, in coming down Rainy River, they had suffered from the rays of the sun beating down fiercely, and reflected on every side from the water. To sit still in the canoes and suffer headache and drowsiness was a heavy price to pay for the pleasure of a glowing sun. The Indians who seemed able to do without sleep, if necessary, but willing to take any quantity when they could get it, slept soundly in the bottom of the canoes.

At mid-day we landed for dinner in a bay on a fire-swept islet. The Colonel and the boys made the circuit of the islet with their guns; but saw nothing worth shooting at except a solitary duck, which they did not get.

Lake of the Woods has been shorn of much of its beauty by fires. The fires have also revealed the nakedness, as far as soil is concerned, of its shores and islets which are low, hard, gneissoid rocks, covered with but poor timber even where it has been spared.

In the afternoon a favourable wind helped us on ; the barge hoisted a sail, and between wind and steam we made seven or eight miles an hour. The tug stopped twice for wood ; but such despatch was shown that though there was neither wharf nor platform, and the tug had to be held by boat hooks to the rocks, and at the same time kept from dashing against them, the whole thing was done at each place in ten minutes.

The last eight or nine miles of the Lake, which were to be the last of our journey by water, led up a long bay to what is called the North-west Angle, a point from which a road has been made to Fort Garry, so that travellers by this route now escape the terrible portages of the Winnipeg river and the roundabout way by Lake Winnipeg. The breeze chased us up finely, and we congratulated ourselves on having started in the morning, as the passage across The Traverse would have been an impossibility with the afternoon's wind. The land became lower as we sailed west. We were approaching the Eastern boundary of the great prairies, that extend to the west for the next thousand miles. A vast expanse of reeds lined both sides of the channel, and beyond these the wood looked poor and scrubby. The Indians, however, assured us that the land was good,—indeed that it was the only lake of all that we had seen that had any good land.

At sunset, the North-west Angle was reached. This point, though far North of the 49th degree—the boundary line be- tween the Dominion and the United States, is claimed by the Republic, and their claim is sustained by an evident verbal mistake in the Treaty that defines the boundary. " North- west " has been inserted instead of " South-west." This is only another instance in which the diplomatists of the Empire have been outwitted by the superior knowledge and unscrupulous- ness of our neighbours. A glance at the map reveals to any one the ugly jog in the boundary line here, and the absurdity of the claim which now cannot be gainsaid.

As we rounded out of the Bay into a little creek, the Angle appeared a place of importance in the eyes of travellers who had not seen anything like a crowd in their last four hundred miles of travel. Fifty or sixty people, chiefly Indians, crowded about the landing place, and the babble and bustle were to us like a return to the world ; but, after having satisfied themselves with a good look at us, and a joyous boisterous greeting to our Ojibbeways, whom they carried off to an Indian and half-breed ball in the neighbourhood, we were left alone in the dirtiest, most desolate-looking, mosquito-haunted of all our camping grounds. In such circumstances it was indispensable to be jolly ; so Louis was summoned and instructed to prepare for supper everything good that our stores contained. The result was a grand success, and the looks of the place improved materially.

The chief received two letters at this point ; one from Governor Archibald inviting us to come direct to Government House at Fort Garry ; another from the District Superintendent of the road, putting his half-breed cook at our disposal. As cook had taken advantage of his master's absence to treat and be treated up to the hilarious point, his services, much to his amazement, were quietly dispensed with. At 11 o'clock we turned in under our canvas, having arranged that waggons should be ready at 4 a. m.

July 30th.—Waked at 4.30, by the sound of heavy rain. Drank a cup of tea and were off in an hour on the hardest day's journey that we had yet had. It was two o'clock the following morning when we got out of the waggons for the night's rest, having travelled eighty miles in the twenty hours.

Those eighty miles, between the North-west Angle ank Oak Point, were through a country utterly uninteresting in appearance. The first twenty miles are across a flat country, most of it marshy, with a dense forest of scrub pine, spruce, tamarack, and, here and there, aspens and white birch. On both sides of

the road, and in the more open parts of the country, all kinds
of wild fruit grow luxuriantly ; strawberries, raspberries, black
and red currants, etc., and, as a consequence, flocks of wild
pigeons and prairie hens are numerous. The pigeons rest calmly
on the branches of dead trees by the roadside, as if no shot had
ever been fired in their hearing. Great difficulties must have
been overcome in making this part of the road, and advantage
has been skilfully taken of dry spots and ridges of gravel or
sand, running in the same general direction as the road. All
this part of road has been corduroyed and covered over with
clay and sand, or gravel. The land is loam with clay underneath, like prairie ; with the prairie so near, it is not likely to
be soon cultivated ; but the wood on it will be in immediate
demand.

The next section of the country is of a different character. It
is light and sandy, getting more and more so, every ten miles
further west. This change in the character of the soil afforded
a feast to our Botanist. In the course of the day he came on
two or three distinct floras ; and although not many of the species were new, and in general features the productions of the
heavy and the light soils were similar to those of like land farther east in Ontario and the Lower Provinces, yet the luxuriance
and variety were amazing. He counted over four hundred different species in this one day's ride. Great was the astonishment of our teamsters, when they saw him make a bound from
his seat on the waggon to the ground, and rush to plain, wood,
or marsh. At first, they all hauled up to see what was the matter.
It must be gold or silver he had found ; but when he came back
triumphantly waving a flower or bunch of grass, they exclaimed,
" Did you ever see the like of that ?" they looked angry or
amused, according as they were sober minded teamsters or the
reverse. The internal cachinnation of a Scotch lad, from the
kingdom of Fife, over the phenomenon, was so violent, that he
would have exploded had he not relieved himself by occasional

witticisms ; " Jock," he cried to the teamster ahead, " tell yon
man if he wants a load o' graiss, no' to fill the buggy noo, an'
a'll show him a fine place where we feed the horse." But when
one of us explained to the Scot that all this was done in the interests of science, and would end in something good for schools,
he ceased to jibe, though he could not altogether suppress a deep
hoarse rumbling far down in his throat—like that of a distant
volcano,—when the Professor would come back with an unusually large armful of spoil. The bonny Scot was an emigrant
who had been a farm servant in Fife five years ago. He had
come to the Angle this spring, and was getting thirty dollars a
month and his board, as a common teamster. He was saving
four-fifths of his wages, and intended in a few months to buy a
good farm on the Red River among his countrymen, and settle
down as a Laird for the rest of his life. How many ten
thousands of Scotch lads would follow his example if they only
knew how.

At our first station, White Birch river, thirty miles from the
Angle, the keeper of the Station was a very intelligent man, a
Scotchman, who had once been a soldier. He was studying
hard at the Cree and Ojibbeway languages, and gave us much
interesting information about the country and the Indians.
He attributed the failure of Mr. Simpson to make a treaty with
the Indians at Fort Francis, in great measure to the fact
that Indians from the United States had been instigated by
parties interested in the Northern Pacific Railway to come across
and inflame their countrymen on our side to make preposterous
demands. The story does not sound improbable to those who
know the extremes which Railway Kings and companies in New
York, and elsewhere in the Republic, have gone to in pushing their own line and doing everything *per fas atque nefas* to
crush opposition. It is a little remarkable that the Indians all
over the Dominion are anxious to make Treaties, and are easily
dealt with, except in the neighbourhood of the boundary line.

Mr. Simpson, in his Report dated November, 1871, states that he had no difficulty with the Indians in Manitoba Province, except near Pembina; and there he says, "I found that the Indians had misunderstood the advice given them by parties in the settlement, well disposed towards the Treaty, or, as I have some reason to believe, had become unsettled by the representations made by persons in the vicinity of Pembina whose interests lay elsewhere than in the Province of Manitoba; for, on my announcing my readiness to pay them, they demurred at receiving their money until some further concession had been made by me."

Seventeen miles further on—at White Mud river—we dined. Had we known what was before us, some would have voted for remaining all night.

The next stage was to Oak Point, thirty-three miles distant. The first half was over an abominable road, and, as we had to take on the same horses, they lagged sadly. The sun had set before we arrived at Broken Head creek, half-way to Oak Point. Hereabouts is the eastern boundary of Manitoba, and we are not likely to forget the rough greeting the new Province gave us. Clouds gathered, and, as the jaded horses toiled heavily on, the rain poured down furiously and made the roads worse. It was so dark that the teamsters couldn't see the horses; and, as neither of them had been over this part of the road before, they had to give the horses free rein to go where they pleased, and—as they were dead beat—at the rate they pleased. The black flies worried us, and we were all heavy with sleep. The hours dragged miserably on, and the night seemed endless; but, at length emerging from the wooded country into the prairie, we saw the light of the station two miles ahead. Arriving there wearied and soaked through, we came to what appeared to be the only building—a half-finished store of the Hudson Bay Company;—entering the open door, barricaded with paint pots, blocks of wood, tools, etc., we climbed up a shaky ladder to the second story, threw ourselves down on the floor, and slept heavily beside a crowd of teamsters whom no amount of kicking could awake. That night-drive to Oak Point we made a note of.

July 31st.—Awakened at 8 A. M., by hearing a voice exclaiming, " thirty-two new species already; it's a perfect floral garden." Of course it was our botanist, with his arms full of the treasures of the prairie. We looked out and beheld a sea of green sprinkled with yellow, red, lilac, and white, extending all round to the horizon. None of us had ever seen a prairie before, and, behold, the half had not been told us ! As you cannot know what the ocean is without seeing it, neither can you in imagination picture the prairie. The vast fertile beautiful expanse suggests inexhaustible national wealth. Our uppermost thought might be expressed in the words, " thank God, the great North-west is a reality."

Oak Point is thirty miles east from Fort Garry, and a straight furrow could be run the whole distance, or north all the way up to Lake Winnipeg. A little stream—the Seine—runs from Oak Point into the Red River. The land along it, in sections extending two miles into the prairie, is taken up by the French half-breeds ; all beyond is waiting for settlers.

After breakfast we started in our waggons for Fort Garry. Tall, bright yellow flowers, as golden rods ; red, pink, and white roses; asters, and an immense variety of compositæ, thickly bedded among the green grass, made up a bright and beautiful carpet. Further on, the flowers were fewer ; but everywhere the herbage was luxuriant, admirable for pasturage, and, in the hollows, tall enough for hay. Even where the marshes intervened, the grass was all the thicker, taller and coarser, so that an acre of marsh is counted as valuable to the settler as an acre of prairie.

The road strikes right across the prairie, and, though simply a trail made by the ordinary traffic, is an excellent carriage road. Whenever the ruts get deep, carts and waggons strike off a few feet, and make another trail alongside ; and the old one, if not used, is soon covered with new grasses. Immense numbers of fat plover and snipe are in the marshes, and prairie hens on the meadow land.

At 3 P. M., we reached the Red River, a broad, deep, muddy coloured stream, winding sluggishly and tortuously through a land fat and level as Holland, till it empties itself into the great lake Winnipeg. At a point below its junction with the Assiniboine we crossed in a scow ; drove across the tongue of land, formed by it and the Assiniboine coming from the west, into the village of Winnipeg, and from there to the Fort, where the Government House is at present.

Thus we finished our journey, from Lake Superior to Red River, by that Dawson road, of which all had previously heard much, in terms of praise or disparagement. The total distance is about five hundred and thirty miles ; forty-five at the beginning and a hundred and ten at the end by land ; and three hundred and eighty miles between, made up of a chain of some twenty lakes and lacustrine rivers, separated from each other by spits, ridges, or short traverses of land or granite rocks, that have to be portaged across. Over those three hundred and eighty miles the only land suitable for agriculture is along Rainy River, and, perhaps, around the Lake of the Woods. North and south the country is a wilderness of lakes, or tarns on a large scale, filling huge holes scooped out of primitive rock. The scenery is picturesque, though rather monotonous, owing to the absence of mountains ; the mode of travelling, whether the canoes are paddled or tugged, novel and delightful ; and, if a tourist can afford a crew of Indians and three or four weeks' time, he is certain to enjoy himself, the necessity of roughing it adding zest to the pleasure.

The road has been proved on two occasions to be a military necessity for the Dominion, until a railway is built farther back from the boundary line. If Canada is to open up her North-west to all the world for colonization, there must be a road for troops, from the first : there are sufficient elements of disorder to make preparedness a necessity. As long as we have a road of our own, the United States would perhaps raise no objection to Canadian volunteers passing through Minnesota ; were we absolutely dependent, it might be otherwise.

In speaking of this Dawson road it is only fair to give full credit for all that has been accomplished. Difficulties have been overcome, insomuch that, whereas it took Colonel Wolsley's force nearly three months to reach Fort Garry from Thunder Bay, a similar expedition could now do the journey in two or three weeks.

But, as a route for trade, for ordinary travel or for emigrants to go west, the Dawson road is far from satisfactory. Only by building a hundred and fifty-five miles or so of railway at the beginning and the end, and by overcoming the intervening portages in such a way that bulk would not have to be broken, could it be made to compete even with the present route by Duluth and the railway thence to Pembina. The question, then, is simply whether or not it is wise to do this, at an expenditure of some millions on a road the greater part of which runs along the boundary line, after the Dominion has already decided to build a direct line of railway to the North-west. The station-masters and other agents on the road, as a rule, do their utmost ; they have been well selected, and are spirited and intelligent men ; but the task given them to do is greater than the means given will permit. The road is composed of fifteen or twenty independent pieces ; is it any wonder if these often do not fit, especially as there cannot be unity of understanding and of plan, for there is no telegraph along the route and it would be extremely difficult to construct one.

CHAPTER IV.

Province of Manitoba.

August 1st.— Fort Garry.—The Province of Manitoba, in
which we now are, is the smallest Province in the Dominion,
being only three degrees of longitude, or one hundred and
thirty-five miles long, by one and a half degrees of latitude, or
a hundred and five miles broad ; but, as it is watered by two
magnificent rivers, and includes the southern ends of the two
great lakes, Winnipeg and Manitoba, which open up an immense extent of inland navigation, and as almost every acre of
its soil is prairie, before many years it may equal some of the
larger Provinces in population. At present the population
numbers about fifteen thousand, of whom not more than two
thousand are pure whites. One-fifth of the number are Indians,
either living in houses or wanderers, one-third English or
Scotch half-breeds, and rather more than a third French half-
breeds. Order reigns in Manitoba, though wise ruling is still
required to keep the conflicting elements in their proper places.
By the legislation that made Manitoba a Province, nearly one-
sixth of the land was reserved for the half-breeds ; owing to
some delay in carrying out this stipulation, the Metis, last year,
got suspicious and restless, and the Fenians counted on this
when they invaded the Province from Pembina and plundered

the Hudson's Bay Company's post near the line. As the half-breeds live along the Red River from Pembina north, the situation was full of danger; had they joined the Fenians, the frontier would have been at once moved up to Fort Garry. Everyone can understand the serious consequences that would have followed the slightest success on their part. Happily the danger was averted by prompt action on the part of the Governor. The whole population rallied around him, and the Fenians, not being able to advance into the country, were dispersed by a company of United States regulars, after being compelled to disgorge their plunder. A battalion of Canadian militia, stationed at different points along Red River, now keeps the peace and guarantees its permanence. The land difficulty has been settled by faith being kept with the half-breeds; a treaty has been made with the Indians that extinguishes their claims to the land; and, as the whole of the Province has been surveyed, divided off into townships, sections and sub-sections, emigrants as they come in can either get accurate information in the Winnipeg Land-office as to where it would be best for them to settle, or they can visit and then describe the piece of land they wish to occupy. There is room and to spare for all, after doing the fullest justice to the old settlers. Even the one-sixth reserved for them cannot, in the nature of things, be permanently held by those among whom it may now be divided. There is no Jewish law preserving to each family its inheritance forever. The French half-breeds do not like farming, and they therefore make but poor farmers; and, as enterprising settlers with a little capital come in, much of the land is sure to change hands. The fact that land can be bought from others, as well as from the Government, will quicken instead of retarding its sale.

After breakfast this morning, we had an opportunity of conversing with several gentlemen who called at Government House: the United States Consul, the Land Commissioner,

Officers of the Battalion, Dr. Schultz, and others. All spoke in the highest terms of the climate, the land, and the prospects of the Province and of the North-west. Nothing shows more conclusively the wonderful progress of Manitoba and the settled condition into which it has emerged from the chaos of two or three years ago, than the fact that the Hudson's Bay Company sold at auction, the other day, in building lots, thirteen acres of the five hundred of their Reserve around Fort Garry, at the rate of $7,000 per acre. At half the rate, for the rest, the Hudson's Bay Company will receive for this small reserve more than the money payment of £300,000 stg., which Canada gave for the whole territory; and, if a few acres favourably situated bring so much, what must be the value of the many millions of acres transferred to the Dominion? The policy of the Company now is exactly the opposite of what it used to be; formerly all their efforts were directed to keep the country a close preserve; now they are doing all in their power to open it up. The times have changed and they have changed with them. And, regarding them merely as a Company whose sole object has been and is to look after their own interests and pay good dividends to the shareholders, their present policy is as sagacious for to-day as the former was for yesterday. While a fur trading Company with sovereign rights, they did not look beyond their own proper work; they attended to that, and, as a duty merely incidental to it, governed half a continent in a paternal or semi-patriarchal way, admirably suited to the tribes that roamed over its vast expanses. But, as they can no longer be supreme, it is their interest that the country should be opened up; and they are taking their place among new competitors, and preparing to reap a large share of the fruits of the development. For many a year to come they must be a great power in our North-west.

To-day was spent in seeing men and things, the land and the rivers, in and around Fort Garry. The Chief drove twenty

miles down the Red River, to the Stone Fort, the Governor
and the rest of the party accompanying him five miles to Kil-
donan, where they called on the Rev. Mr. Black.   The farms
have a frontage of eight chains on the river, and run two miles
back, with the privilege of cutting hay on two miles more in
the rear.   The people are Highlanders from Sutherland-shire,
and, they knew but little about scientific farming when they
settled: the excellence of the land and their own thrifty habits
have stood them in good stead.   They have all saved money,
though there was no market for produce, except what the
Hudson's Bay Company required, till within the last two or
three years.   Mr. Black has been their minister for twenty
years.   All the original emigrants were Presbyterians, but as
no minister was sent to them from the Church of Scotland, the
missionaries of the Church of England attracted great numbers
to their communion, by wisely adapting their service to Scottish tastes.   Till recently, the Scottish version of the psalms
was sung in the Cathedral, and the afternoon service was altogether on the Presbyterian model.   The missionaries, arch-
deacons, and bishops have been earnest evangelical men, several of them Scotchmen too.   It is, therefore, no wonder if even
Scottish dislike of prelacy gave way before such a combination.
There are now Methodist and Presbyterian clergymen in the
Province, as well as Roman Catholic and Episcopal.   They all
have missions to the Indians, and report that, while the great
majority of the Crees and other tribes to the north-west are
Christianized, the majority of the Ojibbeways around Fort
Garry and to the east are still pagans.   The Ojibbeway seems
to have more of the gipsy in him than any of the other tribes,
and to cling more tenaciously to the customs, traditions, and
habits of life of his ancestors.   It may be that the rivalry of the
Churches that he sees at Red River, and the vices of the white
men that he finds it easy to pick up—drunkenness especially—
have something to do with the obstinacy of his paganism.   The

drunkenness of Winnipeg is notorious; the clergy do all in their power, by precept and example, to check it, but they accomplish little. The Roman Catholic bishop and his priests, all the Presbyterian and Methodist ministers, the Episcopal archdeacon and several of his clergy are teetotalers; but the saloons of Winnipeg are stronger than the Churches.

In conversation with the archdeacon and Mr. Black, we learned that the various denominations were building or preparing to build colleges. A common school system of unsectarian education has been established by the Local Government, one-twentieth of the land reserved as a school endowment, and power given to the townships to assess themselves; but strange to say, nothing has been done to establish a common centre of higher education. The little Province with its fifteen thousand inhabitants will therefore soon rejoice in three or four denominational Colleges.

We called on the Wesleyan minister and Archbishop Tache; but as both were from home, we went to the camp and saw the battalion reviewed. After the review the Adjutant-General complimented the men deservedly on the order and cleanliness of the camp, the excellence of the galley, and their good conduct in their relations with the citizens. The men were smart, stout, clean-looking soldiers, and went through various movements with steadiness and activity. Many of them settle in the country, as their term of service expires, free grants of land being given to all who have served for a year.

August 2nd.—Archbishop Taché called this morning, and delighted us with his polished manners and knowledge of the country, He does not think very highly of the Saskatchewan valley as a future grain-producing country, differing in this respect from every other authority; but he speaks in glowing terms of the Red-deer Lake and River which runs into the Athabaska, sometimes called Lac la Biche, a better name, because there are innumerable "Red-deer" lakes. In that far

away country, extending to the north of the North Saskatchewan, the wheat crops of the mission have never suffered from
summer frosts but once. It certainly is one of the anomalies
of the North-west, that the way to avoid frosts is to go farther
north. To hear on the same day the U. S. Consul and the
Archbishop speak about the fertile belt is almost like hearing
counsel for and against it. The Consul believes that the world
without the Saskatchewan would be but a poor affair; the
Archbishop that the fertile belt must have been so called because it is *not* fertile. But how explain the Archbishop's
opinions? The evidence he adduced in support of them suggests
the explanation; he confined himself to facts that had been
brought before him; but his induction of facts was too limited.
It doubtless is true that at Lac la Biche wheat is raised easily,
and that at the R. C. Missions, near the Saskatchewan, it suf-
fers from summer frosts; but the only two R. C. settlements
that we heard of in the Saskatchewan country, viz. : those at St.
Albert's and Lake St. Ann's, we visited, and could easily understand why they suffered. They are on the extreme north-west
of the fertile belt, at an altitude above sea-level of from 2000
to 2500 feet, and were selected by the half-breeds not with a
view to farming, for the French half-breed is no farmer, but
because of the abundance of white-fish in the lake, and sturgeon
in the river, and because they were convenient for buffalo hunting and trapping, as well as for other reasons. The substance
of the disputed matter seems to be this: every one else believes
in the fertile belt of the Saskatchewan; the Archbishop believes
that there is a belt farther north much more fertile.

At Fort Garry farewell greetings had to be exchanged with
the Colonel and his son. Military duties required his presence
in the Province for ten days, and we could not wait. Horetski,
who had been sent on ahead to make the necessary arrangements
for the journey westward, joined us; so that our party from
this date numbered six. A French half-breed, named Emilien,

had been engaged to conduct us across the plains as far as Fort
Carleton, after the approved style of prairie travel.   Emilien's
cavalcade for this purpose was, in our ignorant eyes, unnecessarily large and imposing ; but before many days we found that
everything was needed.   The caravan is not more needed in
the East, across the deserts, than it is in the West, across the
fertile but uninhabited prairies.   Provisions for the whole
party and for the return journey of the men must be carried—
unless you make frequent delays to hunt.   Your tents and
theirs, in other words, house and furniture ; kitchen, larder and
pantry ;   tool-chest and spare axle-trees ;   clothes, blankets,
water-proofs, arms and ammunition, medicine-chest, books,
paper boxes for specimens to be collected on the way, and things
you never think of till you miss them, all are or may be
required.

Our caravan consisted of six Red River wooden carts, in
which were stowed the tents, baggage and provisions ; a horse
to each cart, and three drivers, one of them the cook for the
party, two buckboards, or light four-wheeled waggonettes, for
any of us to use when tired of the saddle ; saddle horses, and
two young fellows with Emilien to drive along a pack of
eighteen horses, as a change of horses is required once or twice
a day when it is intended to travel steadily at the rate of two
hundred and fifty miles a week.   The native horses are small,
except those that have been crossed with Yankee or Ontarian
breeds ; but, though small and often mean-looking, it is doubtful if the best stall-fed horses could keep up with them on a
long journey.

Emilien started from the Fort with his carts and bands of
horses at 10 A.M.   We followed at mid-day, the Governor
accompanying us to Silver Heights, six miles up the Assiniboine.   This had been his own country residence, but is now
owned by D. A. Smith, Esq., M. P., the head of the H. B.
Company in America.   We met here Mr. Christie, late chief

factor at Edmonton, Mr. Hamilton, of Norway House, Mr. McTavish and others from different parts of the great Northwest; and received from Mr. Smith assistance and highland hospitality, of the same kind that every traveller has experienced, in crossing the continent, wherever there is an H. B. post.

A few words about this Hudson's Bay Company may be allowed here, not only because of the interest attaching to it as the last of the great English monopolies, but because, to this day, it is all but impossible for a party to cross the country from Fort Garry to the Pacific without its co-operation. Its forts are the only stations on that long route where horses can be exchanged, provisions bought, and information or guides obtained. The Company received its charter in the year 1670. The objects declared in that charter were fur-trading and the Christianizing of the Indians. The two objects may be considered incongruous in these days; but history must testify that the Company as a rule sought to benefit the Indians as well as to look after its own interests. At first, and for more than a century, it displayed but little activity, though its profits were enormous. Its operations were chiefly confined to the shores of Hudson's Bay; but in 1783, a rival Company called the Northwest,—consisting chiefly of Canadians—disputed their claims, entered the field, and pushed operations so vigorously that the old Company was stirred into life and activity. A golden age for the red man followed. Rival traders sought him out by lake and river side; planted posts to suit every tribe; coaxed and bribed him to have nothing to do with the opposition shop; assured him that Thomas Codlin and not Short had always been the friend of the Indian; gave him his own price for furs, and—what he liked much better—paid the price in rum. Over a great part of North America the conflict raged hotly for years, for the Territory over which the Hudson's Bay Company claimed jurisdiction was the whole of British America,—outside of the settled Eastern Provinces of Upper and Lower Canada, New Brunswick, and Nova Scotia,—a territory twenty-six hundred miles long and fourteen hundred broad. The rival Companies armed their agents' servants, and half-breed voyageurs, and many a time the quarrel was fought out in the old-fashioned way, in remote wildernesses, where there were no Courts to interfere and no laws to appeal to.

In 1821 the two Companies, tired of this expensive contest, agreed to coalesce, and the present Hudson's Bay Company was incorporated. Some details as to its constitution may be gleaned from a work published in 1849, entitled "Twenty-five years in the Hudson's Bay Territory," by John McLean. The shareholders elected a Governor and Committee to sit in London and represent them. This body sent out a Governor to the Territory, whose authority was absolute. He held a Council at York Factory in Hudson's Bay, of such chief factors and chief traders as could be present; but these gentlemen had the right only to advise, they could not veto any measure of the Governor. The vast territory of the Company was divided into four departments, and those departments into districts. At the head of each department and district a chief factor or chief trader generally presided, to whom all officials within its bounds were amenable. The discipline and etiquette maintained were of the strictest kind, and an *esprit de corps* existed between the 3,000 officers—commissioned and non-commissioned, voyageurs and servants, such as is only to be found in the army or in connection with an ancient and honourable service. The Company wisely identified the interests of its agents with its own, by paying them not in fixed salaries, but with a certain share of the profits; and the agents served it with a devotion and pride honourable to all parties. The stock of the Company was divided into an hundred shares, sixty of these belonging to the capitalists, and forty being divided among the chief factors and chief traders.

The first territory lost by the Company was two-thirds of

that lying between the Rocky Mountains and the Pacific. Oregon was lost to them when yielded in 1846 to the United States, after the ten years' joint occupancy; and Vancouver's Island and British Columbia, when they were formed into Provinces. The fertile plains along the Red River, the Assiniboine, and the two Saskatchewans ought to have been opened up by the Empire and formed into Colonies long ago : but their real value was not known. It was not the business of the Company to call attention to them as fitted for any other purpose than to feed buffalo : for those plains were their hunting grounds, and their posts on them were kept up chiefly for the purpose of supplying their far northern posts with pemmican or preserved buffalo-meat. The Company did what every other corporation would have done, attended simply to its own business. The more sagacious of its leading men knew that the end was coming, as the country could not be kept under lock and key much longer. They could not enforce their monopoly ; for they had no authority to enlist soldiers, they were not sure of their legal rights, and the tide of emigration was advancing nearer every day. Eight or nine years ago, when Governor Dallas was shown some gold washed from the sand-bars of the Saskatchewan, his remark was, " the beginning of the end has come." Gold would bring miners, merchants, farmers, and free-trade, so that fur-bearing animals and monopolies would need to fall back to the frozen north ; still, the end would have been longer delayed had the British Provinces not united. But, in 1869, the Company's rights to all its remaining territories were bought up, under Imperial authority, by the Dominion of Canada, and, as a monopoly and semi-sovereign power, the Company ceased to exist.

To return to our diary. A walk in the garden at Silver Heights was sufficient to prove to us the wonderful richness of the soil of the Assiniboine valley. The wealth of vegetation and the size of the root crops astonished us, especially when informed that no manure had been used. The soil all along the Assiniboine is either a dark or light-coloured loam, the vegetable or sandy loam that our gardeners are anxious to fill their pots with ; a soil capable of raising anything. After dinner we said good-bye to the Governor, a statesman of whom even opponents will hereafter record that he deserved well of the country, because on all great occasions he preferred country to self or party, and of whose work in Manitoba we ought to say and would say much more, were it not for the fact that we had partaken of his hospitality. Driving rapidly on for five or six miles, we overtook our cavalcade, which had made but indifferent progress on account of sundry leave-takings by the way. The country along the road is partly settled, but, with few exceptions, the farmers do not farm. Till lately they had not much inducement, for there was no market : but they have neither the knowledge nor the inclination to farm systematically ; and, in a few years, most of the present occupants will be bought out and go west.

As specimens of what may be done here, the farm of one Morgan was pointed out. He had bought it some years ago, for £50 ; and this year, he had already been offered £450 for the potatoes growing on it. A Wesleyan missionary told us that, last year, he had taken the average of ten good farmers near Portage la Prairie, and found that their returns of wheat were seventeen bushels to one,—and that on land which had been yielding wheat for ten years back, and which would continue to yield it, on the same terms, for the next thirty or forty.

We drove on in the quiet, sunny afternoon, at a pleasant rate, over a fine farming but unfarmed country, to the White Horse Plains, and rested at " Lane's Post," about twenty-five miles from Fort Garry. Lane is a North of Ireland man, a good farmer, and, like all such, enthusiastic in praise of the country. " What about wood and water ?" we asked. " Plenty of both everywhere," was his answer. Wherever wells had been dug on the prairie near to his place, water had been found. On the Assiniboine and the creeks running into it, or north into Lake Manitoba, there was abundance of good timber ; and, where none existed, if aspens were planted, they grew in five years big enough for fence poles.

Our first evening on the prairie was like many another which followed it. The sky was a clear soft unflecked blue, save all around the horizon, where pure white clouds of many shapes and masses bordered it, like a great shield of which only the rim is embossed. The air was singularly exhilarating, yet sweet and warm, as in more southern latitudes. The road was only the trail made by the ordinary traffic, but it formed nevertheless an excellent carriage road. Far away stretched the level prairie, dotted with islets of aspens ; and the sun, in his going down, dipped beneath it as he does beneath the sea. Soon after sunset, we reached our camping place for the night, an open spot on the banks of the river, thirty-three miles from Fort Garry, on the east side of Long Lake, with plenty of dry wood for our fires, and good feed for the horses near at hand. Scarcely were our fires lighted when another traveller drove up, the Rev. Mr. McDougal, Wesleyan missionary at Fort Victoria near Edmonton. We cordially welcomed him to our camp, and asked him to join our party. He was well known to us by reputation as a faithful minister, and an intelligent observer of Indian character. He had been nine times over the plains, and evidently knew the country better than our guides. On this occasion, he was accompanied only by his Cree servant Souzie, which being interpreted is Joseph.

August 3rd.—We found this morning that it was not so easy to make an early start with a pack of horses as with canoes. Two or three of the pack were sure to give trouble, and the young fellows in charge had at least half an hour's galloping about,—which they didn't seem to regret much,—before all were brought together. Watering, harnessing, saddling, and

such like, all took time.   To-day the Chief and Secretary drove
on ahead twenty-seven miles to Portage la Prairie.   The rest
followed more slowly, and the whole party did not reunite for
the second start of the day till four P.M.

The road and the country were much the same as yesterday.
We were crossing the comparatively narrow strip of land between the Assiniboine and Lake Manitoba.   Long Lake, or a
creek that is part of it, is near the road for the greater part of
the distance.   It is difficult to get at the water of the lake,
because of the deep mire around the shores; and so we took
the word of one of the settlers for it, that it is good though
warm.   Water from a well by the roadside was good, and cold
as ice.   All the land along this part of the Assiniboine, north
to what is called the " Ridge," for eight miles back has been
taken up, but a great part is in the hands of men who do not
understand the treasures they could take out of it ; and there
is abundance of the same kind of land farther back, for new
settlers.   As we drove on in the early morning, prairie hens
and chickens rose out of the deep grass and ran across the road,
within a few feet of us ; while, on mounds of hay in a field
lately mown, sat hawks looking heavy and sated as if they had
eaten too many chickens for breakfast. On the branches of oaks
and aspens sat scores of pigeons, so unmoved at our approach that
they evidently had not been much shot at.   We asked a farmer
who had recently settled, and was making his fortune at ten
times the rate he had done in Ontario, if he ever shot any of
the birds.   " No," he contemptuously answered ; " he was too
busy ; the half-breeds did that sort of thing, and did little else."
Day after day, he would have for dinner fried pork or bacon,
and tea, when he could easily have had the most delicious and
wholesome varieties of food.   He told us that, in the spring,
wild geese, wavies, and ducks could be shot in great numbers,
but he had eaten only goose in Manitoba.

Portage la Prairie is the centre of what will soon be a

thriving settlement.　On the way to the little village, we passed, in less than ten miles, three camps of Sioux—each with about twenty wigwams,—ranged in oval or circular form.　The three camps probably numbered three hundred souls.　The men were handsome fellows, and a few of the women were pretty. We did not see many of the women, however, as they kept to the camps doing all the dirty work, while the men marched about along the road, every one of them with a gun on his shoulder.　The Indian would carry his gun for a month, though there was not the slightest chance of getting a shot at anything. These Sioux fled here nine or ten years ago, after the terrible Minnesota massacre, and here they have lived ever since.　One amiable-looking old woman was pointed out as having roasted and eaten ten or twelve children.　No demand was made for their extradition, probably because they had been more sinned against than sinning.　Frightful stories are told of the treatment of Indian by miners ; and there are comparatively few tales of Indian atrocities to balance them.　When the Sioux entered British territory they had with them old George III medals, and they declared that their fathers had always considered themselves British subjects and that they would not submit to the rule of the " long knives."　They are and always have been intensely loyal to their great mother, and during Riel's rebellion, were ready and anxious to fight for the Queen.　We were told that the United States authorities had offered pardon if they would return to their own lands, for the Government at Washington is desirous now to do justice to the Indians, though its best efforts are defeated by the cupidity and knavery of its agents ; but the Sioux would not be charmed back.　The settlers all around the Portage speak favourably of the Sioux. They are honest and harmless, willing to do a day's work for a little food or powder, and giving little or no trouble to anybody.

The Doctor at the portage entertained us hospitably.　He spoke highly of the healthiness of the climate, showing himself as an example. There seems nothing lacking in this country but good industrious settlers.

At four P.M. we started for the next post, Rat Creek, ten miles off. The sky was threatening, but, as we always disregarded appearances, no one proposed a halt. On the open prairie, when just well away from the Hudson Bay Company's store, we saw that we were in for a storm. Every form of beauty was combined in the sky at this time. To the south it was such blue as Titian loved to paint : blue, that those who have seen only dull English skies say is nowhere to be seen but on canvas or in heaven ; and the blue was bordered to the west with vast billowy mountains of the fleeciest white. Next to these and right ahead of us and overhead, was a swollen black cloud, along the under surface of which greyer masses were eddying at a terrific rate. Extending from this, and all around the north and east, the expanse was a dun-coloured mass livid with lightning, and there, to the right, and behind us, torrents of rain were pouring, and nearing us every moment. The atmosphere was charged with electricity on all sides, lightning rushed towards the earth in straight and zigzag currents, and the thunder varied from the sharp rattle of musketry to the roar of artillery ; still there was no rain and but little wind. We pressed on for a house, not far away ; but there was to be no escape. With the suddenness of a tornado the wind struck us, at first without rain—but so fierce that the horses were forced again and again off the track. And now, with the wind came rain— thick and furious, and then hail—hail mixed with angular lumps of ice from half an inch to an inch across, a blow on the head from one of which was stunning. Our long line of horses and carts was broken. Some of the poor creatures clung to the road, fighting desperately ; others were driven into the prairie, and, turning their backs to the storm, stood still or moved sideways with cowering heads, their manes and long tails floating wildly like those of Highland shelties. It was a picture for Rosa Bonheur; the storm driving over the vast treeless prairie, and the men and horses yielding to or fighting against it. In half an hour we got under the shelter of the log house a mile distant; but the fury of the storm was past, and in less than an hour the sun burst forth again, scattering the the clouds, till not a blot was left in the sky, save fragments of mist to the south and east.

Three miles farther on was the camping place. The houses of several settlers were to be seen on different parts of the creek. One of them was pointed out as the big house of Grant, a Nova Scotian, and now the farthest west settler. We were on the confines of the " Great Lone Land."

August 4th.—Enjoyed a long sleep this morning. Had intended to rest all day, but Emilien refused. He had contracted to do the journey in so many days, and would do it in his own way; and his way was to travel on all days alike. He agreed, however, to make a short journey so that we might be able to overtake him, though not starting till late in the afternoon.

At 10 a. m., we went over to Grant's house to service. Mr. McDougall and a resident Wesleyan missionary officiated. About fifty people were present, and in the afternoon a Sunday School of thirty children was held in the same room. Some of us dined at Grant's, and the rest with one of his neighbours —McKenzie. Both these men seem to be model settlers. They had done well in Ontario, but the spirit of enterprise had brought them to the new Province. One had come three years ago, and the other only last year; and now one had a hundred and twenty acres under wheat, barley and potatoes, and the other fifty. In five years both will have probably three or four hundred acres under the plough. There is no limit to the amount they may break up except the limit imposed by the lack of capital or their own moderation. This prairie land is the place for steam ploughs, reaping, mowing and threshing machines. With such machinery one family can do the work of a dozen men. It is no wonder that these settlers speak enthusiastically of the country. The great difficulties a farmer encounters elsewhere are non-existent here. To begin with, he does not need to buy land, for a hundred and sixty acres are given away gratuitously by the Government to every *bona fide* settler ; and one-third of the quantity is a farm large enough for any one who would devote himself to a specialty, such as the raising of beets, potatoes, or wheat. He does not need to use manure, for, so worthless is it considered, that the Legislature has had to pass a law prohibiting people from throwing it into the rivers. He has not to buy guano, nor to make compost heaps. The land, if it has any fault, is naturally too rich. Hay is so abundant that when threshing the grain at one end of the yard, he burns the straw at the other end to get rid of it. He does not need to clear the land of trees, stumps or rocks. Very little fencing is required, for he can enclose all his arable land at once with one fence, and pasture is common and illimitable. There is a good market all over Manitoba for stock or produce of any kind, and if a settler is discontented he can sell his stock and implements for their full value to new comers.

And what of the Indians, the mosquitoes, and the locusts ? Neither Crees nor Sioux have given those settlers the slightest trouble. The Sioux ask only for protection, and even before Governor Archibald made the Treaty with the Salteaux and Crees by which they received a hundred and sixty acres of land per family of five, and three dollars per head every year for their rights to the country, they molested no one. Poor whites, were they about in equal numbers, would give ten times as much trouble as the poor Indians, though some of the braves still paint ferociously and all carry guns. And the mosquitoes, and the grasshoppers or locusts, no one ever spoke of, probably because the former are no greater nuisance in Manitoba than in Minnesota or Nova Scotia, and the latter have proved a plague only two or three times in half a century. Every country has its own drawbacks. The question must always be, do the advantages more than counterbalance the drawbacks? Thus, in returning home through California we found that the wheat crop, this year, amounted to twenty millions of bushels. The farmers told us that, for the two preceding years, it had been a failure owing to long continued drought, and that, on an average, they could only count on a good crop every second year, but, so enormous was the yield then, that it paid them well to sow wheat. Take, too, the case of the great wheat-raising State of what, as distinguished from the Pacific, may be called the Eastern States. The wheat crop of Minnesota this year amounts to twenty millions of bushels. But, up to 1857, enough wheat was not raised in the State to supply the wants of the few thousands of lumbermen who first settled Minnesota. Flour had to be sent up the Mississippi from St. Louis, and the imprsssion then was very general that one half of Minnssota consited of lakes, sandhills, sandy prairies and wilderness, and that the winters were so long and so cold in the other half that farming could never be carried on profitably. Severe remarks could be made with truth against Minnesota, but it is also the truth that twenty years ago its population was five thousand, and that now it is five hundred thousand. The soil of Minnesota is not equal in quality to the soil of Manitoba. Calcareous soils are usually fertile. And Manitoba has not only abundant limestone everywhere, but every other element required to make soil unusually productive. Whereas, when you sail up the Red River into Minnesota, the limestone disappears, and the valley contracts to a narrow trough, only two or three miles wide, beyond which the soil is often thin and poor. But, notwithstanding all difficulties, most of the emigrants to Minnesota are prospering. Hundreds of thousands of hardy Welshmen and Scandinavians poured into the new State, secured land under the Homestead Acts or bought it from Railway Companies, lived frugally—shiefly on a bred and milk fare—for the first few years, and they are now well-to-do farmers. Seeing that all the conditions for prosperous settlement are more favourable in Manitoba, is it not easy to foresee a similarly rapid development, if those entrusted with its destinies and with the destinies of our great North-west act with the energy and public spirit of which our neighbours show so shining an example?

It is not hard to trace the sources of those alarming rumours, that we heard so much of at a distance, concerning the soil and climate of Manitoba. Our friends on Rat Creek gave us an inkling of them. On their way from St. Paul's, with their teams and cattle, at every post they were repeatedly warned not to impoverish their families by going to a cold, locust-devoured, barren land, where there was no market and no freedom, but to settle in Minnesota. Agents offered them the best land in the world, and when, with British stupidity, they shut their ears to all temptations, obstacles were thrown in the way of their going on, and costs and charges so multiplied, that the threatened impoverishment would have become a fact before they reached Manitoba, had they not been resolute and trusted entirely to their own resources. Even when they arrived at Winnipeg the gauntlet had still to be run. In that saloon-crowded village were certain touters and indefatigable sympathizers with American institutions, men who had always calculated that our North-west would drop like a ripe pear into the lap of the Republic, who had been at the bottom of the half-breed insurrection, and who are now bitterly disappointed to see their old dream never likely to be more than a dream. These worthies told Grant's party confidentially that they had been years in the country, and had not once seen a good crop. Who could doubt such disinterested testimony?

But what of the terrible frost, the deep snow, and the long winters? These must be stern realities. The answer of every man and woman we spoke to, in town or country, was that the winter was pleasanter than in Ontario, Quebec, or the Maritime

Provinces. There is no severe weather till the beginning of December. The average depth of snow from that time is two feet, and there is no thaw till March. The severity of the intervening months is lessened by the bright sun, the cloudless skies, the stillness and dryness of the air. On account of the steady cold the snow is dry as meal, and the farmers' wives said that "it was such an advantage that the children could run about all winter, without getting their feet wet." They could not say as much in Nova Scotia. This dryness of the snow is also an important fact as regards railway construction. Let the rails be raised two or three feet above the level of the prairie, and they are sure to be always clear of snow. In fact there is much less risk of snow blockades in the winter on our western plains than in the older Provinces or in the North-eastern States. In March, and even in April, there are sometimes heavy snow-storms. But the snow soon melts away. It is what was intended for spring rain. Hay is needed in those months more than in the winter, when the horses and even the cattle can paw off the snow and eat the nutritive grasses underneath ; whereas, in March and April a crust is often formed, too hard for their hoofs to remove ; and the more hay that is cut in the autumn the less risk from prairie fires, as well as the better provision for the live stock.

This hopeful—even enthusiastic—language about Manitoba may be discounted by some readers, in view of the locust plagues that have retarded the prosperity of the Province since 1872. Our hopes were founded not only on what we saw, but on the descriptions of the settlers and on their brave and cheery tone. They ignored rather than anticipated difficulties. They had a pride in the new land they had made their own, and faith in its future. Everywhere, in conversation with them, we found combined with this confidence, the rising of that national sentiment, that pride in their country, which is both a result and a safe-guard of national dignity and independence, as distinguished from a petty provincialism.   This Great West will, in the future, probably manifest this spirit more than even the Eastern Provinces, and so be the very backbone of the Dominion ; just as the prairie States of the neighbouring republic are the most strongly imbued with patriotic sentiments.   The sight, the possession of these boundless sees of rich land stirs in one that feeling of—-shall we call it bumptiousness—that Western men have been accused of displaying.   It is easy to ridicule and caricature the self-sufficiency, but the fact is, a man out West feels like a young giant, who cannot help indulging a little tall talk, and in displays of his big limbs.

At 4 P.M., we prepared to follow our party, but at this moment, a body of sixty or eighty Sioux, noble looking fellows, came sweeping across the prairie in all the glory of paint, feathers, and Indian warlike magnificence.   They had come from Fort Ellice, had recently travelled the long road from Missouri, and were now on their way to Governor Archibald to ask permission to live under the British flag, and that small reserves or allotments of land should be allowed them, as they were determined to live no longer under the rule of "the long knives."   Some of them rode horses, others were in light baggage-carts or on foot.   All had guns and adornment of one kind or another.   A handsome brave came first, with a painted tin horse a foot long hanging from his neck down on his naked brawny breast, skunk fur round his ankles, hawk's feathers on his head, and a great bunch of sweet-smelling lilac bergamot flowers on one arm.   An Indian brave has the vanity of a child. We went forward to address him, when he pointed to another as O-ghe-ma (or chief) ; and, as the band halted, the O-ghe-ma then came up with the usual " Ho, Ho ; B'jou, B'jou," and shook hands all round with a dignity of manner that whites in the new world must despair of ever attaining.   His distinction was a necklace of bears' claws, and mocassins belted with broad stripes of porcupines' quills dyed a bright gold.   Next to him came the medicine man, six feet three inches in height, gaunt and wasted in appearance, with only a single blanket to cover his nakedness. They would have liked a long *pow wow*, but we had time only for hasty greetings and a few kindly words with them.

It was late before we reached the tents, for Emilien had gone on to "the three creeks," twenty-two miles from Rat Creek—or "crick," as the word is universally pronounced in the North-west. Every stream, two small to be dignified with the name of river, is a " crick."

In to-morrow morning's journey we are to pass out of the Province of Manitoba. This, then is probably the best place for a few additional words on it as a home for emigrants ; on the subject of emigration generally ; and on the settlement of the Indian difficulty in the Province.

How is it that the United States have risen so rapidly from the condition of a fringe of provinces along the At-lantic to that of a mighty nation spreading its arms across a continent ? The question is one that the New Dominion ought to ask, for the Dominion also aspires to greatness, and believes that it has within its borders all the resources required to make a nation materially great. A principal cause of the rapid development of the United States is that it has absored, especially within the last quarter of a century, so many millions of the population of the old world. It had a great West, boundless expanses of fertile land, and had the wis-dom to see that, while the soil is the great source of wealth, untilled soil is valueless ; and that therefore every inducement should be held out to the masses, overcrowded in Europe, to seek homes within its borders. Each emigrant who landed at Castle Garden represented the addition of hundreds of dollars to the wealth of the country. He represented the cultivation of some land and an increased value to more, addi-tional imports and exports, taxes, and national strength. With the same apparent generosity, but with as cool a calculation of profits as that which sent Stanley to discover Livingstone, free grants of land were therefore offered to the whole world. Homestead laws provided that those farms should not be liable to be seized for debt. As it was necessary that the emigrant should be able to get easily to his farm and to send to market what he raised, companies were chartered to build railways in every direction, the State subsidising them with exemptions, money bonuses, and enormous land grants. The ancient maxim had been, "settle up the country and the people will build railways if they want them." The new and better maxim is, "build railways and the country will soon be settled." These railway corporations became the emigration agents of the United States, and well have they done the public work, while directly serving their own interests. With the one aim of securing settlers, whose labour on parts of their land would make the other parts valuable, they organized, advertised, and worked emigration schemes with a business-like thoroughness that has attracted far less attention than it deserves. What a proud position the United States, as a country, was thus made to occupy in the eyes of the whole world ! "Ho, every one that wants a farm, come and take one," it cried aloud, and in every language. Poor men toiling for a small daily wage in the old world, afraid of hard times, sickness and old age. heard the cry, and loved the land that loved them so well, and offered so fair. They came in thousands and found, too, that it kept its word ; and then they came in tens and hundreds of thousands, till now less liberal offers have to be made, because most of the public domain that is worth anything has been absorbed. Those hardworking masses prospered, and they made the country great. Some of them who had been rudely expatriated, who had left their mother land with bitterness in their hearts, vowed vengeance and bequeathed the vow to their children. Others attributing their success to the new institutions, began to hate

the forms of government that they identified with their days of
penury and misery. Others were wiser, but their interests
were bound up with their adopted country, and, when it came
to the question, they took sides against the old and with the
new. Had the State held aloof, maintaining that any inter-
ference or expenditure on its part in connection with emigration
was inconsistent with political economy, that the tide of population must be left to flow at its own sweet will, and railways
be built only where there was a demand for them, the great west
of the United States would not have been filled up for many
a year to come. And had the Imperial authorities thought
less about imaginary laws of political economy and more about
pressing practical necessities, millions, who are now in a strange
land bitter enemies of the British crown, would have been its
loyal subjects in loyal colonies.

The past is gone ; but it is not yet too late to do much. We
now stand on a more favourable vantage ground than before,
not only positively but comparatively, for our vast virgin
prairies are thrown open, while there is but little good land
left in the United States available for settlement under the
homestead laws. The great lines of communication from the
sea-board are beginning to touch our North-west territory ; and,
if we act with the vigour and wisdom of which our neighbours
have set the example, the ever-increasing current of emigration
from the old world must flow into Manitoba, and up the Assiniboine and Saskatchewan rivers.

We must act, to bring about such a result. It will not come
of itself. While we stand looking at the river, it flows past.
Labour is required to divert it into new channels, or it will flow
over the courses that have been made for it, or simply overflow
them. We are now able to offer better land, and on easier terms,
to immigrants than the United States or any of its railway companies offer, but they will continue to attract them if we fold
our arms while they work. They have many influences on their

side ; the gravitating force of numbers ; past success on a grand
scale ; grooves worn smooth by the millions tramping westward ;
a vast army of agents paid in proportion to their succes ; every
principal railway station in Furope, and even in the Dominion,
papered with their glowing advertisements ; floods of pamphlets in every language; arrangements perfected to the minutest
details for forwarding the ignorant and helpless stranger from
New York and Chicago to any point he desires ; and perhaps a
comfortable log shanty ready for him when he gets there. They
offer great inducements to men to organise colonies ; advise
neighbours to club their resources and emigrate together, so that
one may help the other ; lay off village plats and draw beautiful
sketches of future cities ; and cheer the drooping spirit of the
foreigner, when he is discouraged with difficulties that had not
been advertised, with brilliant prophecies and an infusion of the
indomitable Yankee spirit.   They make the doubter believe
that it is better to pay their company from $5 to $15 an acre
for " the best land in the world," " rich in minerals," " no long
winters," accompanied with free passes over the railway, and
long credits, " one-tenth down, and the rest when it suits you,"
than to take up free grants elsewhere.

In all this business, for it is purely a business transaction,
though gilded with soft hues of buncombe, references to down-
trodden millions, American generosity, free institutions, and such
like, they have hitherto had no competitor; for, until our North-
west was opened up and proved to contain farms for the million,
we could not well compete.   What the mass of emigrants wanted
was prairie soil ; land that they could plough at once without
the tedious and exhausting labour of years required in wood-
land farming, chopping, rolling, burning, grubbing, stumping,
and levelling.   Such land the Dominion can now offer, and it is
therefore the great and immediate duty of the Government to
see that it be opened up, and brought within reach of the ordinary class of settlers.

To what point in the Dominion should the emigrant turn his eyes? Each province presents special inducements, but no part of America now offers so many as Manitoba. The land farther west and to the north-west is equally good, but, until opened up by railway or steamboats, it is comparatively valueless to the settler; for there is little use in raising stock, wheat, or potatoes, if they cannot be conveyed to market. But Manitobe is now within reach of the emigrant, and there is a good market in Winnipeg. This little village is becoming a town; houses are springing up in all directions with a rapidity known only in the history of Western towns; and the demand for provisions, stock, farm implements, and everything on which labour is expended, is so much greater than the supply, that prices are enormously high. The intending settler, therefore, should bring in with him as much of what he may require as he possibly can.

Besides a rich soil, a healthy and—for the hardy populations of northern and central Europe—a pleasant climate, law and order, and all the advantages of British connection, Manitoba offers other inducements to the emigrant.

The Government of the Dominion has opened the country for settlement on the most liberal terms possible. Any person, the subject of Her Majesty by birth or naturalization, who is the head of a family or has attained the age of twenty-one years, is entitled to be entered for one hundred and sixty acres, for the purpose of securing a homestead right in respect thereof. To secure this land he has only to make affidavit to the above effect, and that he purposes to be an actual settler. On filing this affidavit with the land officer, and on payment to him of $10, he is permitted to enter the land specified in his application. Five years thereafter, on showing that he has resided on or cultivated the land, he receives a patent for it; or any time before the expiration of the five years he can obtain the patent by paying the pre-emption price of one dollar an acre. This farm,

no matter how valuable it may become, and his house and furniture, barns, stables, fences, tools, and farm implements are
declared free from seizure for debt ; and in addition to the exemption of all those, there are also exempted, " one cow, two
oxen, one horse, four sheep, two pigs, and the food for the same
for thirty days."

There are, and can be, no Indian wars or difficulties in Manitoba. This is a matter of the utmost importance to the intending settler. When we returned from our expedition, the Chief
was interviewed at Ottawa by a deputation of the Russian sect
of Mennonites, who are looking out for the best place in America
for their constituents to settle in, and one of their first questions
referred to this. He answered it by pulling a boy's knife out of
his pocket, small blade at one end cork-screw at the other, and
told them that that was the only weapon he had carried while
travelling from Ocean to Ocean ; adding that he had used only
one end of even so insignificant a weapon, and that end not so
often as he would have liked.

As the mode of settling with the Indians adopted in Manitoba is based on the system that has been long tested in the older
provinces, and that will probably be extended to the whole of
the North-west, a few words on the general question may not
be out of place. There are three ways of dealing with the less
than half-million of red men still to be found on the continent
of America, each of which has been tried on a smaller or larger
scale. The first cannot be put more clearly or badly than it
was in a letter dated San Francisco, Sept. 1859, which went the
round of the American press, and received very general appro-
val. The writer, in the same spirit in which Roebuck condemned the British Government's shilly-shally policy towards
the Maories, condemned the Federal Government for not having
ordered a large military force to California when they got possession of it, " with orders to hunt and shoot down all the Indians from the Colorado to the Klamath." Of course the wri

ter adds that such a method of dealing with the Indians would have been the cheapest, "and perhaps the most humane." With regard to this policy of no nonsense, thorough-going as selfishness itself, it is enough to say that no Christian nation would now tolerate it for an instant.

The second way is to insist that there is no Indian question. Assume that the Indian must submit to our ways of living and our laws because they are better than his ; and that, as he has made no improvement on the land, and has no legal title-deeds, he can have no right to it that a civilized being is bound to recognize. Let the emigrants, as they pour into the country, shove the old lords of the soil back ; hire them if they choose to work ; punish them if they break the laws, and treat them as poor whites have to be treated. Leave the struggle between the two races entirely to the principle of natural selection, and let the weaker go to the wall. This course has been practically followed in many parts of America. It has led to frightful atrocities on both sides, in which the superior vigour of the civilized man has outmatched the native ferocity of the savage. The Indian in such competition for existence, soon realizing his comparative weakness, had resource to the cunning that the inferior naturally opposes to the strength of the superior. This irritated even the well-disposed white, who got along honestly, and believed that honesty was the best policy. It was no wonder that, after a few exchanges of punishment and vengeance, the conviction became general that the presence of the Indian was inconsistent with public security ; that he was a nuisance to be abated ; and that it was not wise to scrutinize too closely, what was done by miners who had to look out for themselves, or by the troops who had been called in to protect settlers. The Indians had no newspapers to tell how miners tried their rifles on an unoffending Indian at a distance, for the pleasure of seeing the poor wretch jump when the bullet struck him ; or how, if a band had fine horses, a charge was trumped up against them, that the band might be broken up and the horses stolen ; or how the innocent were indiscriminately slaughtered with the guilty ; or how they were poisoned by traders with bad rum, and cheated till left without gun, horse, or blanket. This policy of giving to the simple children of the forest and prairie, the blessings of unlimited free-trade, and bidding them look after their own interests, has not been a success. The frightful cruelties connected with it and the expense it has entailed, have forced many to question whether the fire and sword plan would not have been " cheaper and, perhaps, more humane."

The third way, called sometimes the paternal, is to go down to the Indian level when dealing with them ; go at least halfway down ; explain that, whether they wish it or not, immigrants will come into the country, and that the Government is bound to seek the good of all the races under its sway, and do justly by the white as well as by the red man ; offer to make a treaty with them on the principles of allotting to them reserves of land that no one can invade, and that they themselves cannot alienate, giving them an annual sum per family in the shape of useful articles, establishing schools among them and encouraging missionary effort, and prohibiting the sale of intoxicating liquors to them. When thus approached, they are generally reasonable in their demands ; and it is the testimony of all competent authorities that, when a treaty is solemnly made with them, that is according to Indian ideas of solemnity, they keep it sacredly. They only break it when they believe that the other side has broken faith first.

Such has been the policy of the old Canadas and of the Dominion, and it is now universally adopted in America. True, the agents of the United States Government have often defeated its attempts to do justice and show mercy, by wholesale frauds ; and the Indians, believing themselves deceived, have risen with bursts of fury to take vengeance ; and, like all

children, if deceived once, they are very unwilling to believe
you the next time.   General Howard has therefore advised the
removal of many of the Indian agents, with the remark that
" when agents pay $15,000 for a position, the salary of which
is only $1500, there must be something wrong."   But this cor-
ruption of individual agents is a mere accident, an accident
that seems to be inseparable from the management of public
affairs in the Republic.   The great thing is that the United
States Government has taken its stand firmly on the ground
that the Indians are to be neither exterminated nor abandoned
to themselves, but protected and helped.   In a letter to George
H. Stewart, dated October 28th, 1872, President Grant writes
with his customary directness and plainness of speech : "If
the present policy towards the Indians can be improved in any
way, I will always be ready to receive suggestions on the subject ; but if any change is made, it must be made on the side of
the civilization and christianization of the Indians.   I do not
believe our Creator ever placed the different races of men on
this earth with the view of the stronger exerting all his energies in exterminating the weaker."

It may be said that, do what we like, the Indians as a race,
must eventually die out.   It is not unlikely.   Almost all the
Indians in the North-west are scrofulous.   But on the other
hand, in the United States and in Canada, they exist, in not a
few cases, as christianized self-supporting communities, and have
multiplied and prospered.   These are beginning to ask for full
freedom.   It was all right, they argue, to forbid us to sell our
lands, when we did not know their value, and to keep us as
wards when we could not take care of ourselves ; but it is
different now ; we are grown men ; and it is an injustice to
prevent us from making the most we can out of our own.

At all events, there are no Indian difficulties in our North-
west.   For generations the H. B. Company governed the tribes
in a semi-paternal way, the big children often being rude and

noisy, sometimes plundering a fort, or even maltreating a factor, but in the end always returning to their allegiance, as without the Company, they could not get tea or tobacco, guns or powder, blankets or trinkets.

Since the transfer of the country to the Dominion the Indians, except when operated on by foreign influences, have been anxious for treaties. In the year 1871, Governor Archibald made a treaty at the Stone Fort or Lower Fort Garry, with the Ojibbeways and Swampy Crees, the only two tribes in his Province, and a second treaty with the Indians further north, as far as Lake Winnipegosis and Beren's River, and to the west as far as Fort Ellice. This second treaty comprises a tract of country two or three times as large as Manitoba. About four thousand Indians assembled on those occasions, and, after a good deal of preliminary feasting, consulting, and *powwowing*, arrangements were made with them. The objects aimed at by the Governor and the Indian Commissioner were to extinguish the Indian title to the land, and, at the same time, do substantial justice and give satisfaction to the Indians.

The treaty-making process is interesting, as illustrative of several points in the Indian character. Though it took ten days to make the first, yet, in the light lately thrown on the difficulties of drawing up a treaty that shall express the same thing to both parties, the time cannot be considered unreasonably long.

The Indians first elected chiefs and spokesmen to represent them. On these being duly presented and invited to state their views, they said that there was a cloud before them which made things dark, and they did not wish to commence the proceedings till the cloud was dispersed. It was found that they referred to four Swampies who were in prison for breach of contract, and the tribe felt that it would be a violation of the brotherly covenant to enter upon a friendly treaty, unless an act of indemnity were passed in favour of the four. As they begged their discharge on the plea of grace and not of right, the Governor acceded to their petition ; and the Indians thereupon declared that henceforth they would never raise a voice against the law being enforced.

The real business then commenced. Being told to state their views on reserves and annuities, they did so very freely, and, substantially, to the effect that about two-thirds of the province should be reserved for them. But when it was explained that their great mother must do justly to all her children, " to those of the rising sun as well as to those of the setting sun," and that it would not be fair to give much more than a good farm for each family, they assented. Fortunately the Governor could point out to them a settlement of Christianized Ojibbeways numbering some four hundred, between the Stone Fort and the mouth of Red River, as a proof that Indians could live, prosper, and provide like the white man. This mission was established by Archdeacon Cochrane, and has now a full-blooded Indian for its clergyman. Many of them have well-built houses and well-tilled fields, with wheat, barley and potatoes growing, and giving promise of plenty for the coming winter.

The Indians of this district form a parish of their own, called St. Peter's, and return a member to the House of Assembly ; they have the honour of being represented by a gentleman who has successively held the offices of Minister of Agriculture, Provincial Secretary, and who is now Provincial Treasurer.

In the end, it was agreed that reserves should be allotted sufficient to give one hundred and sixty acres to each family of five ; that the Queen should maintain a school on each reserve when the Indians required it ; and that no intoxicating liquors be allowed to be introduced or sold within the bounds of the reserves ; also, that each family of five should receive an annuity of $15, in blankets, clothing, twine, or traps ; and, as a mark of Her Majesty's satisfaction with the good behaviour of Her Indians, and as a seal to the treaty, or Indian luck-penny, a present of $3 be given to each man, woman, and child. Every one being satisfied, the treaty was signed, the big orna-mented calumet of peace smoked all round, and the Governor then promised each chief a buggy, to his unbounded delight.

One important consequence of these Indians being pleased is that the Indians farther west, having heard the news, are all anxious for treaties, and have been on their good behaviour ever since.

CHAPTER V.

From Manitoba to Fort Carlton on the North Saskatchewan.

Fine fertile country.—The water question.—Duck shooting.—Salt Lakes.—Camping on
the plains.—Fort Ellice.—Qu'appelle Valley.—" Souzie "—The River Assiniboine.—
The Buffalo.—Cold nights.—Rich soil.—Lovely Country.—Little Touchwood Hills.—
Cause of prairie fires.—A day of rest.—Prairie uplands.—Indian family.—Red
River Carts.—Buffalo skulls.—Desolate track.—Quill Lake.—Salt water.—Broken
prairie.—Round hill.—Prairie fire.—Rich black soil.—Red River Brigades.—
Magnificent Panorama.—Break-neck speed.—The South Saskatchewan,—Sweet⁻
hearts and wives.—Fort Carlton.—Free traders.—The Indians.—Crop raising.

August 5th.—This morning it rained heavily, and delayed us
a little ; but by the time we had our morning pannikin of tea,
the carts packed, and everything in its place, the weather cleared
up. We got away at 5 A.M., and rode sixteen miles before
breakfast, reaching Pine Creek, a favourite camping ground ;
still following up the course of the Assiniboine, though never
coming near enough to get a sight of it, after leaving our first
camp from Fort Garry. The next stage was fourteen miles to
Bog Creek ; and after dinner, eleven miles more, making forty-
one for the day. Instead of the level prairie of the two preceding days and the black peaty loam, we had an undulating
and more wooded country, with soil of sandy loam of varying
degrees of richness. Here and there ridges of sand dunes,
covered with vegetation, sloped to the south, having originally
drifted from the north, probably from the Riding Mountains, of
which they may be considered the outlying spurs. From the
top of any one of these a magnificent view can be had. At
our feet a park-like country stretched far out, studded with
young oaks ; vast expanses beyond, extending on the north to
the Riding Mountains, and on the south to the Tortoise Mountain on the boundary line ; a beautiful country extending
hundreds of square miles without a settler, though there is less

bad land in the whole of it than there is in the peninsula of
Halifax, or within five or ten miles of any of our eastern
cities. This almost entire absence of unproductive land is to
us very wonderful. If we except the narrow range of sandhills, there is actually none ; for the soil, even at their base, is
a light sandy loam which would yield a good return to the
farmer. The soil about these hills is not equal to prairie. Its
flora is not that of the prairie. Both soil and flora are like
those of the Rice Lake plains, and the County of Simcoe in
Ontario, where excellent wheat crops are raised. The only
question, suggestive of a doubt, that came up was the old one
of " Is there plenty of water ? " The rivers are few ; the
creeks small. Along their banks there is no difficulty, but
what of the intervening ground ? We had heard of wells sunk
in different places, and good water found from four to fifty
feet down. But, yesterday, Grant informed us that a beautiful stretch of prairie, immediately to the west of his location,
which had been taken up by a friend of his, had been abandoned because no water could be got. They had sunk wells in
three places, one of them to the depth of seventy-five feet, but
pierced only hard white clay. Grant believed that this stratum of clay extended over a limited area, and that, under it,
water would be tapped if they went deep enough. But the
matter is of too great importance to be left to conjecture.
Test wells should be sunk by the Government in different
places ; and where there are saline or brackish lakes, or even
should the first water tapped prove saline, artesian wells might
be tried, so as to get to the fresh water beneath. Till it is
certain that good water can be easily had all over the prairie,
successful colonization on a large scale cannot be expected.
The general belief is that there is water enough everywhere.
There is an abundant rain fall, and the water does not form
little brooks and run off, but is absorbed by the rich, deep,
porous ground. Still the claims of our North-west on the at-

tention of emigrants would be rendered all the stronger, were
they assured that the water supply was unfailing everywhere.
Up to this time the question has not been started, because
much of the land on the river-banks has not yet been taken
up. But it would be well to be prepared with an answer.

Nothing could be more exhilarating than our rides across
the prairie, especially the morning ones. The weather, since
our arrival at Fort Garry, had been delightful, and we knew
that we had escaped the sultry heat of July, and were just at
the commencement of the two pleasantest months of the year.
The nights were so cool that the blanket was welcome, and in
the evenings and mornings we could enjoy the hot tea. The air
throughout the day was delicious, fresh, flower scented, health-
ful, and generally breezy, so that neither horse nor rider was
warm after a fifteen or twenty miles' ride. We ceased to wonder that we had not heard of a case of sickness in the settlers'
families. Each day was like a new pic-nic. Even the short
terrific thunder storm of the day before yesterday had been
enjoyed because of its grandeur. Grant told us that it was
the heaviest he had ever seen in the country, and that we had
felt its full force. Three miles away there had been no hail.

August 6th.—Up before four A. M., but were delayed some
time by the difficulty of lassoing the horses that were wanted.
The Doctor had, meanwhile, some shooting round the little
lake by which we had camped ; and getting some more on the
way, Terry the cook was enabled to serve up plover duck and
pigeons, with rice curry, for breakfast. Our morning's ride was
sixteen miles, and brought us to the Little Saskatchewan,—a
swift-flowing pebbly-bottomed stream, running south into the
Assiniboine. Its valley was about two miles wide and two
hundred and fifty feet deep. All the rivers of the North-west
have this peculiarity of wide valleys, and it constitutes a serious
difficulty in the way of railroad making ; they must be crossed,
but regular bridging on so gigantic a scale is out of the ques-

tion. The hill sides sloping down into the valley or intervale of the river are green and rounded, with clumps of trees, most of them fire scorched, in the depressions.

We hailed the sight of this flowing stream with peculiar delight ; for it was the first thing that looked, to our eyes, like a river in all the hundred and twenty miles since leaving the Assiniboine. The creeks crossed on the way were sluggish and had little water in them, and most of the swamps and lakelets were dried up, and their bottom covered with rank coarse grass, instead of the water that fills them in the spring. This morning, however, we passed several pretty-well-filled lakes,—plover and snipe about most of them,—on the height of land from which the ground slopes toward the little Saskatchewan.

Our second stage for the day was only eleven miles ; but the next was fourteen, and we drove or rode along the winding road at a rattling pace, reaching our camping ground, at Salt Lake, an hour before sunset. This lake is bitter or brackish, but, on the opposite side of the road, there is good water ; and, although the mosquitoes gave us a little trouble, we fared well —as at all our camps. This was the first salt lake we had seen, but farther on the way there are many such ; and grievous has been the disappointment of weary travellers, on drawing near to one of them and preparing to camp. The causes are probably local, for good water is found near, and, all around the grass is luxuriant. A white crust forms on the dried up part of the bottom and the shores are covered with saline plants, chiefly reddish-coloured, thick, succulent samphire and sea-blite growing together and extending over several acres of ground. The following are the principal plants:—*Scirpus maritimus, L.; Salicornia herbacea, L.; Glaux maritima, L.; Suada maritima, Dumot, var. prostrata; Pall. Glyceria distans.* These have a wide range over the whole interior wherever salt lakes are found."

A bathe in the little Saskatchewan before breakfast was our

first good wash for two or three days, and we enjoyed it pro-
portionately. Our horses did their forty-one miles to-day,
seemingly with greater ease than they had any previous day's
work. Most of them are of pure native breed; some of them—
the largest—have been crossed with Canadian, and the swiftest
with Yankee breeds. In all our pack there are only two or
three bad horses; none of them looked well at first, but,
though small and common looking, they are so patient, hardy
and companionable, that it is impossible for their riders to
avoid becoming attached to them. Hardly two of the saddles
provided for our party were alike. There was choice of English,
American, Mexican, and military,—the first being the favourite.

August 7th.—Made a good day's journey of forty-five miles,
from the Salt Lake to the junction of the Qu' Appelle and
Assiniboine rivers. The first stage was ten miles, to the Shoal
Lake—a large and beautiful sheet of water with pebbly or
sandy beach—a capital place for a halt or for camping. The
great requirements of such spots are wood, water, and feed for
the horses; the traveller has to make his stages square with
the absence or presence of those essentials. If he can get a
hilly spot where there are few mosquitoes, and a sheet of water
large enough to bathe in, and a resort of game, so much the
better. Arrived at the ground, the grassiest and most level
spots, gently sloping, if possible, that the head may be higher
than the feet, are selected. The tents are pitched over these,
one tent being allotted to two persons, when comfort is desirable, though sometimes a dozen crowd inside of one. A water-
proof is spread on the ground, and, over that, a blanket. Each
man has another blanket to pull over him, and he may be
scund asleep ten minutes after arriving at the ground, if he has
not to cook or wait for his supper. The horses need very little
attention; the harness is taken off and they are turned loose—
the leaders or most turbulent ones being hobbled, i. e., their
fore feet are fettered with intertwined folds of shagannappi or

raw buffalo hide, so that they can only move about by a succession of short jumps. Hobbling is the western substitute for tethering. They find out, or are driven to the water, and, immediately after drinking begin grazing around ; next morning they are ready for the road. A morning's swim and wash in Shoal Lake was a luxury, and the Doctor had some good shooting at loons, ducks, yellowlegs, and snipe.

Our second stage was twenty-one miles to Bird's Tail Creek, a pretty little running stream, with valley nearly as wide, and banks as high as the Little Saskatchewan. It is wonderful to see the immense breadth of valley that insignificant creeks, in land where they have not to cut their way through rocks, have eroded in the course of ages.

At this creek, we were only twelve miles distant from Fort Ellice. The true distance from Fort Garry, as measured by our odometer, is two hundred and fifteen miles. As our course lay to the north of Fort Ellice, the Chief and two of the party went on ahead to get provisions and a half dozen Government horses that had been left to winter there, and to attend to some business, while the rest followed the direct trail and struck the edge of the plateau overlooking the Assiniboine,—which was running south—just where the Qu'Appelle joined it from the west. The view from this point is magnificent ; between two and three hundred feet below, extending far to the south and then winding to the east, was the valley of the Assiniboine,— at least two miles wide.

Opposite us, the Qu'Appelle joined it, and both ran so slowly, that the united river meandered through the intervale as circuitously as the links of the Forth, cutting necks and promontories of land that were almost islands, some of them soft and grassy, and others covered with willows or timber. The broad open valley of the Qu'Appelle stretched along to the west, making a grand break in what would otherwise have been an unbroken plateau of prairie. Three miles to the south

of this valley, and therefore opposite us but farther down, two
or three small white buildings on the edge of the plateau were
pointed out as Fort Ellice. To the north of the Qu'Appelle,
the sun was dipping behind the woods far away on the edge of
the horizon, and throwing a mellow light on the vast expanse
which spread around in every direction.

We descended to the intervale by a much-winding path, and
moved on to the crossing, three miles above the Fort, and immediately above where the Qu'Appelle flows into the main
river. Scarcely had the tents been pitched and the fires lighted,
when the Chief appeared bringing supplies of flour, pemmican,
dried meat, salt, etc., from Fort Ellice. He reported that there
were several parties of Indians about the Fort, who had emi-
grated two or three years ago from the United States, anxious
to settle in British territory. One of them, from Ohio, spoke
good English, and from him he had gained the information
about them.

This portion of our journey from Fort Garry to Fort Ellice,
we had accomplished in less than six days. The last stage had
been over the worst road—a road winding between broad hill-
sides strewn with granite boulders, and lacking only brawling
streams and foaming fells to make it like Moffatdale, and many
another similar dale in the south of Scotland. But here there
never had been bold moss troopers, and no Tales of the Borders
had ever been written: Crees, Sioux, and Ojibbeways may have
gone on the war path against each other, and hunted the buffalo over the plains to the west, but there has been no Walter
Scott nor even Wilson to gather up and record their legends,
and hand down the fame of their braves. And there are no
sheep grazing on those rich hill-sides, and there was neither
wigwam, steading, nor shieling on the last hundred and sixty
miles of road. Silence reigned everywhere, broken only by the
harsh cry of wild fowl rising from lakelets, or the grouse-like
whirr of the prairie hen on its short flight. We had seen but a

small part, and that by no means the best of the land. The trail follows along the ridges, where there is a probability of its being dry for most of the year, as it was not part of its object to shew the fertility of the country or its suitableness for settlers. But we had seen enough to show that, even east of Fort Ellice, there is room for a large population. Those great breadths of unoccupied land are calling " come, plough, sow, and reap us." The rich grass is destroyed by the autumn fires, which a spark kindles, and which destroy the wood, which formerly was of larger size and much more abundant than now. This destruction of wood seriously affects the water supply. Lakes that once had water all the year round are now dry, except in the spring time. But, when settlers come in, all this shall be changed. The grass will be cut at the proper time, and stacked for the cattle, and then there shall not be the wide spreading dried fuel to feed the fires, and give them ever increasing force. Fields of ploughed land, interspersed here and there, shall set bounds to the flames, and tourists and travellers will be less likely to leave their camp-fires burning, when they know that there are settlers near, whose property would be endangered, and who would not tolerate criminal carelessness on the part of strangers.

8th August.—Being in the neighbourhood of a fort, and having to re-arrange luggage and look after the new horses, we did not get away till nine o'clock. An hour before, greatly to the surprise of Emilien, who had calculated on keeping in advance the twenty-two miles he had gained on Sunday, and greatly to our delight, Mr. McDougal drove up and rejoined us with his man Souzie. Souzie had never been east before, and the glories of Winnipeg had fairly dazzled him. He was going home heavy laden with wonderful stories of all he had seen ;— the crowd hearing Mr. Punshon preach and the collection taken up at the close, the review of the battalion of militia, the splendour of the village stores, the Red River Steamboat, the quantities of rum, were all amazing. When the plate came round at the church Souzie rejoiced, and was going to help himself, but, noticing his neighbours put money in, he was so puzzled that he let it pass. He chuckled for many a day at the simplicity of the Winnipeggers :—"Who ever before saw a plate handed round except to take something from it ?" The review excited his highest admiration :—"Wah, wah ! wonderful ! I have seen a hundred men turned into one !"

Our first work this morning was to cross the Assiniboine. The ford was only three feet deep, but the bottom was of shifting sand, so that it did not do to let the horses stand still while crossing. The bank on the west side is bold, and the sand so deep, that it is a heavy pull up to the top. After ascending, we moved west for the first few miles along the north bank of the Qu'Apelle. Our Botanist went down to the intervale and sand hills near the stream, to inspect the flora, and was rewarded by finding half-a-dozen new species. We soon turned in a more northerly direction, though, had there been a fortnight to spare, some of us would have gone a hundred miles up the Qu'Apelle, where we had been told yesterday by a Scotch half-breed called Mackay, the buffalo were in swarms. Mackay was on his way back to Fort Garry with the spoils of his hunt. He had left home with his wife and seven children and six carts, late in May, joined a party at Fort Ellice and gone up to the high plains at the source of the Qu'Appelle, near the elbow of the South Saskatchewan, to obtain his food for the year in the way most pleasing to a half-breed. All had lived sumptuously while near the buffalo, and when they had dried enough meat to fill their carts, at the rate of ten buffaloes to a cart, they parted company ; he and his wife and family, with the meat and skins of sixty buffaloes, turned homewards, to do little for the rest of the year, but enjoy themselves. This is all very well when the buffalo are plenty ; but as they get scarcer or move farther away, what is to be done? A man cannot be both a hunter and a farmer; and, therefore, as the buffalo go west, so must the half-breeds.

But, fascinating as a buffalo-hunt seemed to us, described in all the glowing language and gesticulations of a successful hunter, the time could not be spared, and so we jogged along our road, hoping that we might fall in with the lord of the prairies as far north as Carlton or Fort Pitt.

The first part of the day's ride, like the last part of the previous day's, was over the poorest ground we had seen—light and sandy—and yet the grass nowhere presented the dried up, crisp, brownish look that is so often seen in the eastern provinces at this time of the year. Still the land about Fort Ellice is not to be recommended.

Nine miles from the Assiniboine, we breakfasted beside a spring in the marsh where the water is good, but where a barrel or some such thing sunk in the ground would be desirable. This is every traveller's business, and therefore is not done. We are now in No-man's Land;—where the Governor of Manitoba has a nominal jurisdiction, but where there are no taxes and no laws; where every man does what is right in his own eyes, and prays the great Manitou to prosper him in his horse-stealing or scalping expeditions.

Our next stage was twenty-two miles to Broken Arm River —a pretty little stream with the usual deep and broad valley. The soil improved as we travelled west. The grass was richer, and much of the flora that had disappeared for the previous twenty miles began to show again. On the banks of the river there was time before tea to indulge in a great feast of raspberries, as we camped early this evening, after having travelled only thirty-one miles. The Botanist had found exactly that number of new species,—the largest number by far on any one day since leaving Fort Garry. The explanation is, that he had botanized over the valleys of two rivers and several varieties of soil.

August 9th.—Last night the thermometer fell to 34 °, and we all suffered from the cold, not being prepared for such a sudden change. There was heavy dew, as there always is on prairies, and at four o'clock, when we came out of the tents, shivering a little, the cold wet grass was comfortless enough ; but a warm cup of tea around the camp fire put all right. We were on horseback before sunrise, and a trot of thirteen miles, over a beautiful and somewhat broken country, fitted us for breakfast. Mr. McDougal told us that in the elevated part of the country in which we were, extending north-west from Fort Ellice, light frosts were not unusual in July or August. They are not so heavy as seriously to injure grain crops ; but still they are an unpleasant feature in this section of the country. The general destruction of the trees by fires makes a recurrence of these frosts only too likely. If there were forests, there would be a greater rainfall, less heavy dews, and probably no frosts. But it will be little use for the government to issue proclamations in reference to the extinguishing of camp fires, until there are settlers here and there, who will see to their observance for their own interest. Settlers will plant trees, or give a chance of growing to those that sow themselves, and prevent the spread of fires.

Our second stage for the day was sixteen miles over an excellent road and through an undulating country that evoked spontaneous bursts of admiration from every one. The prairie was broken into natural fields by rounded hillocks and ridges crowned with clumps of aspens—too often fire-scathed. In the hollows grew tall rich grass which would never be mowed ; everywhere else, even on the sandy ridges, was excellent pasture.

We met a half-breed travelling, with dried meat and buffalo skins, to Fort Garry, in his wooden cart covered with a cotton roof, and he informed us that men were hunting, two days' journey ahead, about the Touchwood Hills. This excited our men to the highest pitch, for the buffalo have not come on this route for many years, and eager hopes were exchanged that we might see and get a shot at them.   Wonderful stories were told of the buffalo-hunts in former days, and men hitherto taciturn, perhaps because they knew little English, began explaining volubly—eking out their meaning with expressive gesticulation—the nature of a buffalo hunt.   Fine fellows all our half-breeds were as far as riding, hunting, camping, dancing and such like were concerned ; though they would have made but poor farm-servants.   Two of them had belonged to Riel's body-guard in the days of his little rebellion.   The youngest was Willie, a boy of sixteen who rode and lassoed and raged and stormed and swore on the slightest provocation better than any of them.   He looked part of the horse when on his back, and never shirked the roughest work.   We were horrified at his ready profanity, and the Doctor rowed him up about it ; but, though they all liked the Doctor, for he had physicked two or three of them successfully, and had even bound up the sore leg of one of the horses better than they could, the jawing had no effect.   The Secretary then tried his hand.   Finding that Willie believed in his father, an adventurous daring Scot who had married a squaw, he accosted him one day when none of the others were near, with : "Willie, would you like to hear me yelling out your father's name, with shameful words among strangers?"   He looked up with a half-puzzled, half-defiant air, and shook his head.   "Well, how can I like to hear you shouting out bad language about my best friend?"   A few more words on that line, and Willie was converted.   We heard no more oaths from him except the mild ones : "By George," "by Jing" or "by Golly," and in sundry ingenious ways thereafter he showed a sneaking fondness for the Secretary.

We rested to-day for dinner on a hillock beside two deep pools of water, and the Doctor made us capital soup from preserved tomatoes and mutton.   Ten or eleven miles from our

dining table brought us to the end of this section of wooded
country, where we had intended to camp for the night, but the
ponds were empty and no halt could be made.   We therefore
pushed on across a vast treeless plain, twenty miles wide, with
the knowledge that if there was no water in a marsh beside a
solitary tree four miles ahead, we would have to go off the road
for five miles to get some, and, as the sun was setting, the
prospect for the first time looked gloomy.   Making rapidly for
the lonely tree, enough water for ourselves and horses was
found, and with hurrahs from the united party, the tents were
pitched.   Forty-two and a half miles the odometer shewed to
be our day's travel.

August 10th.—The night of the 8th having been so cold,
we divided out more blankets the following evening by dispen-
sing with one tent, and sleeping three, instead of two, in each.
The precaution turned out to be unnecessary, though we kept
it up afterwards, for the nights were always cool.   This feature
of cool nights after hot days is an agreeable surprise to those
who know how different it usually is in inland countries, or
wherever there is no sea breeze.   It is one of the causes of
the healthy appearance of the new settlers even in the summer
months.   In the hottest season of the year the nights are cool,
and the dews abundant, except when the sky is covered with
clouds.   No wonder that the grass keeps green.

Our morning's ride was across sixteen miles of the great plain,
four miles from the easterly edge of which we had camped.   The
Secretary walked the distance and got to the breakfast-place
ten minutes after the mounted party.   A morning's walk or
ride across such an open has a wonderfully exhilarating effect.
The air is so pure and bracing that little fatigue is felt, even
after unusual exertion ; seldom is a hair turned on horse or
man.

The plain was not an unbroken expanse but a succession of
very shallow basins, enclosed in one large basin, itself shallow,

from the rim of which you could look across the whole, whereas, at the bottom of one of the smaller basins, the horizon was exceedingly limited. No sound broke the stillness except the chirp of the gopher, or prairie squirrel, running to his hole in the gound. The character of the soil every few yards could be seen from the fresh earth, that the moles had scarcely finished throwing up. It varied from the richest of black peaty loam, crumbled as if it had been worked by a gardener's hand for his pots, to a very light sandy soil. The ridges of the basins were often gravelly. Everywhere the pasturage was excellent, though it was tall enough for hay only in the depressions or marshy spots.

Our two next stages carried us over twenty-five miles of a lovely country, known as the Little Touchwood Hills ; aspens were grouped on gentle slopes, or thrown in at the right points of valley and plain, so as to convey the idea of distance and every other effect that a landscape gardener could desire. Lakelets and pools, fringed with willows, glistened out at almost every turn of the road, though unfortunately most were saline. Only the manor houses and some gently-flowing streams were wanting, to make out a resemblance to the most beautiful parts of England. For generations, all this boundless extent of beauty and wealth had been here, owned by England ; and yet statesmen had been puzzling their heads over the " Condition of England, the Poor, the Irish Famine, the Land and Labour, and similar Questions," without once turning their eyes to a land that offered a practical solution to them all. And the beauty in former years had been still greater, for though the fires have somehow been kept off this district for a few years, it is not very long since both hardwood and evergreens as well as willows and aspens, grew all over it ; and then, at every season of the year, it must have been beautiful. Of late years fires have been frequent ; and they are so disastrous to the whole of our North-west that energetic action should be taken to prevent them. Formerly, when the Hudson's Bay Company was the only power in this Great Lone Land, it was alive to the necessity of this, and very successful in impressing its views on the Indians as well as on its own servants. Each of its travelling parties carried a spade with which the piece of ground on which the fire was to be made was dug up, and as the party moved off, earth thrown on the embers extinguished them. But since miners, traders, tourists and others have entered the country, there has been a very different state of affairs. Some of the spring traders set fire to the grass round their camps, that it may grow up the better and be fresh on their return in autumn. The destruction of forests, the drying up of pools, and the extermination of game by roasting the spring eggs, are all nothing compared to a little selfish advantage. And the Indians and the Hudson's Bay parties seeing this, have become nearly as reckless.

This afternoon we had some idea of the lovely aspect that this country would soon assume, if protected from the fire-demon. The trees grow up with great rapidity ; in five or six years the aspens are thick enough for fencing purposes. There was good sport near the lakes and clumps of trees, and Frank shot prairie-hen, partridge and teal, for dinner and next day's breakfast. As he was confined to the roadside, and had no dog, he had but indifferent chances for a good bag. We had to push on to do our forty-one miles, and could not wait for sportsmen. At sunset the camp was selected, by a pond in the middle of a plain, away from the bush so as to avoid mosquitoes ; and as Emilien was tired enough by this time, he agreed readily to the proposal to rest on the following day.

August 11th.—Breakfast at 9 a.m., having allowed ourselves the luxury of a long sleep on the Day of Rest. The water beside our camp was hard and brackish, scarcely drinkable, not good even to wash with. It gave an unpleasant taste to the tea, and even a dash of spirits did not neutralize its brackish-

BUFFALO-SKIN LODGE AND RED RIVER CARTS.

ness.   Here again the necessity of finding out the real state of
the water-supply of this country was forced on our attention.
Even if the pools do not dry up, the water in them at this time
of the year is only what is left of melted snow and the spring
and summer rains, tainted with decayed vegetable matter, and
filled with animalculæ.

This was a grand day for horses and men.   Most of the latter
rose early and had their breakfasts and then went to sleep again;
others did not rise from under the carts and shake themselves
out of their buffalo blankets, till after ten o'clock.   At 11:15
all assembled for service—Roman Catholics, Methodists, Episcopalians, and Presbyterians.   The Secretary sat on a box in
front of the tents, with Frank by his side holding an umbrella
over both heads, as the sun shone fiercely.   The congregation,
thirteen in number, sat in the doors, or shade of the tents.
Mr. McDougal led the responses, and all joined in devoutly.
After the service had been read and hymns sung, a short sermon was preached.

The advantages of resting on the Lord's Day, on such expeditions as this, and of uniting in some common form of worship,
are manifest.   The physical rest is needed by man and beast.
All through the week there has been a rush ; the camp begins
to be astir at three in the morning, and from that hour till nine
or ten at night, there is constant high pressure.   At the halting places, meals have to be cooked, baggage arranged and re-
arranged, horses looked to, harness mended, clothes washed or
dried, observations and notes taken, specimens collected, and
everything kept clean and trim ; rest is therefore impossible.
From four to six hours of sleep are all that can be snatched.
The excitement keeps a mere tourist up, so that on Saturday
night he feels able to go ahead ; and possibly grudges what
seems the unnecessary loss of a day ; but if he insists on pushing on, the strain soon becomes too much, and he loses all the
benefit to his health that he had gained : and as the men have

none of the excitement of novelty, they need the periodic rest all the more.

But the great advantages of the day, to such a party, are lost if each man is left the whole time to look after himself, as if there was no common bond of union, and no sacredness about the day. They then sleep or gamble, ramble or shoot, snare gophers or prairie dogs, read or write, eat and drink, are benefitted as their horses are, but nothing more, perhaps less. There is a more excellent way, for the Sabbath was made for the whole man. Let the head of the party ask them to meet for common prayer or some simple service, ever so short ; all will come if they believe that they are welcome. The question, what denomination are you of ? need not be asked. The singing of a hymn will bring them round the tent or hillock where the service is held. The kneeling together, the alternate reading, a few earnest kindly words, do more than anything else to awaken old blessed remembrances, to stir the better nature of all, to heal up the little bitternesses and squabbles of the week and gives each that sentiment of common brotherhood that cements into one the whole party. They have been brought into the presence of the Great Preserver and the rest of the day and of the week is hallowed by that hour. Cut off from the world of men, they are made to feel their dependence on Him and on each other ; and master and man are all the better for is.

The large body of Canadians that preceded Milton and Cheadle in their journey across these same plains ten years ago, would hardly have held together, had it not been for their observance of the Sunday rest. In an account of their arduous expedition by this route to the Cariboo gold mines, one of themselves gives this earnestly-worded testimony :—" The fatigues of the journey were now beginning to have an injurious effect upon our animals, as well as upon the tempers and dispositions of the men, and especially towards the end of the week were these effects more apparent, when frequent disagreements and petty disputes or quarrels of a more serious kind would take place, when each was ready to contradict the other, and, at the slightest occasion or without any occasion, to take offence. But to-morrow would be the Sabbath; and no wonder that its approach should be regarded with pleasurable anticipations, as furnishing an opportunity for restoring the exhausted energies of both man and beast, for smoothing down the asperities of our natures, and by allowing us time for reflection, for regaining a just opinion of our duties towards one another; and the vigour with which our journey would be prosecuted, and the cordiality and good feeling that characterized our intercourse after our accustomed rest on the first day of the week, are sufficient evidence to us that the law of the Sabbath is of physical as well as moral obligation, and that its precepts cannot be violated with impunity. We certainly have had much reason gratefully to adore that infinite wisdom and goodness that provided for us such rest."—All which is sound common sense. *Crede expertis !*

Our Sunday dinner was a good one. Terry had time and did his best. The Chief gave a little whiskey to the men, to take the bad taste from the water and kill the animalculæ ; and Emilien took as kindly to resting as if he had never travelled on Sundays in his life.

The afternoon was sultry and thundery. Heavy showers, we could see, were falling ahead and all around, but although the clouds threatened serious things, we got only a sprinkling, and the evening cleared up with a glorious sunset.

After tea Mr. McDougal led our family worship. We did not ask the men to come, but the sound of the hymn brought them round, and they joined in the short service with devoutness, Willie, who had done a good day's work in snaring fat gophers, being particularly attentive. They were all thankful for the rest of the day.

August 12th.—" The 12th " found us up early, as if near a highland moor, and away from camp a few minutes after sunrise. Another delightful day; sunny and breezy. First stage, thirteen miles; the second, sixteen; and the third, fourteen miles, or forty-three for the day; every mile across a country of unequalled beauty and fertility; of swelling uplands enclosing in their hollows lakelets, the homes of snipe plover and duck, fringed with tall reeds, and surrounded with a belt of soft woods; long reaches of rich lowlands with hillsides spreading gently away from them, on which we were always imagining the houses of the owners; avenues of whispering trees through which we rode on, without ever coming to lodge or gate.

Our first " spell "* was through the most beautiful country, simply because longest spared by fire. Many of the aspens were from one to two feet in diameter. Most of the water was fresh, but probably not very healthy, for the lakes or ponds were shallow, and the water tainted by the annual deposition of an enormous quantity of decomposed organic matter. In summer when the water is low, it is difficult to get at it, because of the depth of the mire. When the buffalo ranged through this country and came to ponds to drink, they often sank so deep in the mud that they were unable to extricate themselves, especially if the foremost were driven on by those behind, or the hunter was pressing them. The harder the poor beasts struggled, the deeper they sank; till, resigning themselves to the inevitable, they were trampled over by others of the herd. The old deeply indented trails of the herd, in the direction of the saline lakes, are still visible. They used to lick greedily the saline incrustations round the border, as they do still when near such lakes. Like domestic cattle, they instinctively understand the medicinal value of salt. From this

---

* The term " spell" is commonly used, all over the plains, to indicate the length of journey between meals or stopping-places; the latter are sometimes called spelling-places, by half-breeds and others.

point of view, it is doubtful if the saline lakes will prove a
serious disadvantage to the stock-raising farmer.   In British
Columbia and on the Pacific Coast generally, such lakes are
found, and the cattle that are accustomed to the water, receive
no injury from drinking it.

On our way to dinner, two large white cranes rose swan-like
from a wet marsh near the road.   Frank with his gun and
Willie with a stone made after them.   The larger of the two
flew high, but Willie's stone brought down the other.   As he
was seizing it, the big one, evidently the mother, attacked him,
but seeing the gun coming, flew up in time to save herself.
The young one was a beautiful bird, the extended wings measu-
ring over six feet from tip to tip.   As soon as Willie had killed
his game, he rode off in triumph with it slung across his shoulders.   In twenty minutes after his arrival at camp, he and his
mates had plucked, cooked and disposed of it, all uniting in
pronouncing the meat " first class."

After dinner a good chance of killing a brown bear was lost.
At a turn of the road he was surprised on a hillock, not twenty
yards distant from the buckboard that led our cavalcade.   Had
the horsemen and guns been in front as usual, he could have
been shot at once ; but before they came up he was off, at a
shambling but rapid gait among the thickets, and there was not
time to give chase.   This was a disappointment, for all of us
would have relished a bear-steak.

The low line of the Touchwood Hills had been visible in the
forenoon ; and, for the rest of the day's journey, we first skirted
them in a north westerly direction, and then turning directly
west, we gained the height by a road so winding and an ascent
so easy, that there was no point at which we could look back
and get an extended view of the ground travelled in the course
of the afternoon.   It is almost inaccurate to call this section of
country by the name of Hills, little or big.   It is simply a series of prairie uplands, from fifty to eighty miles wide, that

swell up in beautiful undulations from the level prairies on each side. They have no decided summits from which the ascent and the plain beyond can be seen; but everywhere are grassy or wooded rounded knolls, enclosing fields, with small ponds in the windings, and larger ones in the lowest hollows. The land everywhere is of the richest loam. Every acre that we saw might be ploughed. Though not as well suited for steam-ploughs as the open prairie, in many respects this section is better adapted for farming purposes, being well wooded, well watered, and with excellent natural drainage, not to speak of its wonderful beauty. All that it lacks is a murmuring brook or brawling burn; but there is not one, partly because the trail is along the watershed. On a parallel road farther north passing by Quill Lake, Mr. McDougal says that there are running streams, and that the country is, of course, all the more beautiful.

Our camp for the night was beside two lakelets near forks where the road divides, one going northerly from our course to the old Touchwood trading-post, fifteen miles distant.

So passed the 12th with us. If we had not sweet-scented heather and Scotch grouse, we had duck and plover and prairie hen; and, beside the cheery camp-fires under a cloudless star-lit-sky, we enjoyed our feast as heartily as any band of gypsies or sportsmen on the moors.

August 13th.—Heavy rain this morning which ceased at sunrise. Got off an hour after, and descended, in our first stage of fourteen and a half miles, the western side of the Touchwood Hills. This side is very much like the other; the descent to us was so imperceptible that nowhere could we see far ahead or feel certain that we were descending, until the most western upland was reached, and then, beneath and far before us, stretched a seemingly endless sea of level prairie, a mist on the horizon giving it still more the look of a sea. Early in the morning we came upon two buffalo-tents by the roadside. In these were the first Indians we had fallen in with since meeting the Sioux at Rat Creek, with the exception of two or three tents at the crossing of the Assiniboine. They were two families of Bungys (a section of the Salteaux or Ojibbeway tribe) who had been hunting buffalo on the prairie to the south-west. They had a good many skins on their carts, and the women were engaged at the door of a tent chopping up the fat and meat to make pemmican. Marchaud, our guide, at once struck a trade with them, a few handfuls of tea for several pieces of dried buffalo meat. The men seemed willing that he should take as much as he liked, but the oldest squaw haggled pertinaciously over each piece, and chuckled and grinned horribly when she succeeded in snatching away from him the last piece he was carrying off. She was the only ugly being in their camp. The men had straight delicate features, with little appearance of manly strength in their limbs ; hair nicely trimmed and plaited. Two or three young girls were decidedly pretty, and so were the pappooses. The whole party would have been taken for good looking gypsies in England.

The road on this stage was the worst we had travelled over ; so full of ruts and boulders that the axle of one of the carts snapped, and as there was not time to make another, the cart had to be abandoned by the road-side till Emilien's return from Carlton. It was a marvel how well those Red River carts stood out all the jolting they got. When any part broke before, a thong of shaganappi or buffalo raw-hide thong had united the pieces. Shaganappi in this part of the world does all that leather, cloth, rope, nails, glue, straps, cord, tape, and a number of other articles are used for elsewhere. Without it the Red River cart, which is simply a clumsy looking but really light box cart with wheels six or seven feet in diameter, and not a bit of iron about the whole concern, would be an impossibility. These small-bodied high-wheeled carts cross the miry creeks, borne up by the grass roots, and on the ordinary trail the horses jog along with them at a steady trot of four or five miles an hour. Ordinary carts would stick hopelessly in the mud at the crossings of the creeks and marshes, and travel slowly on a good trail. A cart without an ounce of iron was a curiosity to us at first, but we soon found that it was the right thing in the right place.

After breakfast we entered on a plain that stretched out on every side, but the one we had left, to the horizon. This had once been a favourite resort of the buffalo, and we passed in the course of the day more than a score of skulls that were bleaching on the prairie. All the other bones had been chopped and boiled by the Indian women for the oil in them. The Chief picked up two or three of the best skulls to send as specimens to Ottawa. Great was Souzie's amazement at such an act. He had been amused at the Botanist gathering flowers and grasses ; but the idea of a great O-ghe-ma coming hundreds of miles, to carry home bones without any marrow in them, was inexplicable. He went up to Frank and explained by gestures that they were quite useless, and urged him to throw them out of the buckboard, and when Frank shook his head he appealed to Mr. McDougal to argue with us. All his efforts failing, he gave it up ; but whenever his eyes caught sight of the skulls it was too much for even Indian gravity, and off he would go into fits of laughing at the folly of the white men.

Our second spell was nineteen, and the third, nine miles across this treeless desolate-looking prairie. Towards evening the country became slightly broken and wooded, but we had to camp on a spot where there was not enough wood to make the fires for the night. Knowing this, Marchaud passed the word to the men on horseback, two or three miles before arriving at the camp. They dashed into the thicket, pitched some small dead dry wood into the carts, and then each throwing an uprooted tree from fifteen to twenty-five feet long, and four to six inches in diameter across his shoulders or on the pommel of his saddle, cantered off with it, Sancho Panza like, as easily as if it was only a long whip.   They had done this several times before, Willie generally picking out the biggest tree to carry.   No matter how unwieldy the load, they rode their horses firmly and gracefully as ever.

The prairie crossed to-day extends north-easterly to Quill Lake, the largest of the salt lakes.   Just on that account, and because all the ponds on it are saline, clearly shown even where dried up by the reddish samphire or white incrustations about the edges, one or two test wells should be sunk here.

To-day we had two opportunities of sending to Red River letters or telegrams for home, and—lest one should fail—availed ourselves of both.   Tying our packets with red tape, to give them an official look and thus impress Posty with due care, and sealing the commission with a plug of tobacco, we trusted our venture with the comfortable feeling that we had re-established our communications with the outer world. *

All day our men had been on the outlook for buffalo but without result.   Marchaud rode in advance, gun slung across his shoulders, but although he scanned every corner of the horizon eagerly, and galloped ahead or on either side to any overhanging lip of the plateau, no herd or solitary bull came within his view.   They were not far off, for fresh tracks were seen. The tracks of former times are indented in the ground like old furrows and run in parallel lines to the salt lakes, as if in those days the prairie had been covered with wood, and the beasts had made their way through in long files of thousands.

August 14th.—The thermometer fell below freezing point last night, but the additional allowance of blankets kept us warm enough.   At sunrise there was a slight skiff of ice on some water in a bucket; and, in the course of the morning's ride, we noticed some of the leaves of the more tender plants

---

* It is only fair to mention that both messengers, one of them a French, and the other a Scotch half-breed and parishioner of Mr. McDougal's, proved trusty.   Every letter or telegram we sent from the plains reached home sooner than we had counted on.

withered, but whether from the frost or blight, or natural decay—they having reached maturity,—we could not determine.

The sun rose clear, and the day like its predecessors was
warm and bracing, the perfection of weather for travelling.
We had hitherto been on the height of land that divides the
streams running into the Assiniboine from those that run into
the Qu'Appelle, and this, in part, accounted for the absence of
creeks near our road. To-day we got to a still higher elevation, the watershed of the South Saskatchewan, and found, in
consequence, that the grass and flowers were in an advanced
stage as compared with those farther east. The grass was grey
and ripe, and flowers, that were in bloom not far away, were
seeding here. The general upward slope of the plains between
Red River and Lake Winnepeg, and the Rocky Mountains, is
towards the west. The elevation at Fort Garry is 700 feet, at
Fort Edmonton 2088 feet, and at the base of the Mountain
Chain 3000 feet above the sea. This rise of 2,300 feet is spread
over a thousand miles, but Captain Palliser marked three distinct steppes in this great plain. The first springs from the
southern shore of the Lake of the Woods, and, tending to the
south-west, crosses the Red River well south of the boundary
line ; thence it runs irregularly in a north-westerly direction,
by the Riding Mountains towards Swan River, and thence to
the Saskatchewan—where the north and south branches unite.
The average altitude of this easterly steppe is from 800 to 900
feet above the sea level. The second or middle steppe, on
which we now are, extends west to the elbow of the South Saskatchewan, and thence northwards to the Eagle Hills, west of
Fort Carlton. Its mean altitude is 1608 feet. The third prairie steppe extends to the mountains. Each of these steppes,
says Palliser, is marked by important changes in the composition
of the soil, and consequently in the character of the vegetation.*

* For an exceedingly clear description of the boundaries of these three steppes, and
of the Western, Eastern and transverse watersheds of the whole area, see "Report of
the Geology and Resources of the region in the vicinity of the 49th parallel, by George
Mercer Dawson," p. 2--10.

Our first spell to-day was fifteen, and our second, twenty miles, to the Round Hill, over rolling or slightly broken prairie; the loam was not so rich as usual and had a sandy subsoil. Ridges and hillocks of gravel intersected or broke the general level, so that, should the railway come in this direction, abundant material for ballasting can be promised.

The prairie to-day had an upward slope till about one o'clock, when it terminated in a range of grassy round hills. For the next hour's travelling the road wound through these; a succession of knolls enclosing cup-like basins, which in the heart of the range contained water, fresh and saline. Wood also began to re-appear; and, when we halted for dinner, at the height of the range, the beauty that wood, water, and bold hill-sides give were blended in one spot. We were three or four hundred feet above the prairie; the scenery round us was bolder than is to be found in any part of Ontario, and resembled that of the Pentlands near Edinburgh. The hill at the foot of which we camped rose abruptly from the rest, like the site of an ancient fortalice. Horetski described it as a New Zealand pah; one hill like a wall enclosing another in its centre, and a deep precipitous valley, that would have served admirably as a moat, filled with thick wood and underbrush, between the two. Climbing to the summit of the central hill, we found ourselves in the middle of a circle, thirty to forty miles in diameter, enclosing about a thousand square miles of beautiful country. North and east it was undulating, studded with aspen groves and shining with lakes. To the south and west was a level prairie, with a sky line of hills to the south-west. To the north-west—our direction—a prairie fire, kindled probably by embers that had been left carelessly behind at a camp, partly hid the view. Masses of fiery smoke rose from the burning grass and willows, and if there had been a strong wind, or the grass less green and damp, the beauty of much of the fair scene we were gazing on would soon have vanished, and a vast blackened surface alone been left.

It was nearly 4 P.M. before we left the Round Hill, and then we passed between the remaining hills of the range, and gradually descended to the more level prairie beyond, through a beautiful, boldly irregular country, with more open expanses than in the Touchwood Hills, and more beautiful pools, though the wood was not so artistically grouped.   Passing near the fire, which was blazing fiercely along a line of a quarter of a mile, we saw that it had commenced from a camping grouud near the roadside.   Heavy clouds were gathering that would soon extinguish the flames.   As there was the appearance of a terrific thunder storm, we hurried to a sheltered spot seven or eight miles from Round Hill, and camped before sunset, just as heavy drops commenced to fall.   The speed with which our arrangements for the night were made astonished ourselves. Every one did what he could ; and in five minutes the horses were unharnessed, the tents pitched, the saddles and all perishable articles covered with waterproofs ; but, while exchanging congratulations, the dense black clouds drove on to the south, and, though the sky was a-flame with lightning, the rain scarcely touched us.

August 15th.—Early in the morning rain pattered on our tents, but before day-light it had passed off, and we started comfortably at our usual hour, a little after sunrise.   Our aim was to reach the south branch of the Saskatchewan, forty-six miles away, before night ; the distance was divided into three spells of thirteen, seventeen and sixteen miles.

The scenery in the morning's ride was a continuation of that of last night ; through a lovely country, well wooded, abounding in lakelets, swelling into softly-rounded knolls, and occasionally opening out into a wide and fair landscape.   The soil was of rich loam and the vegetation correspondingly luxuriant ; the flora the same, and almost at the same stage as that we had first seen on the prairie, a fortnight before, near Red River ;— the roses just going out of bloom ; the yellow marigolds and

golden-rods, the lilac bergamot, the white tansey, blue bells and
hare-bells, and asters of many colours and sizes, in all their
splendour.   We were quite beyond the high and dry region ;
and again in a country that could easily be converted into an
earthly paradise.

We met or passed a great many teams and " brigades " to-
day ; traders going west, and half-breeds returning east with
carts well-laden with buffalo skins and dried meat.   A number
of Red River people club together in the spring, and go west
to hunt the buffalo.   Their united caravan is popularly called a
brigade, and very picturesque is its appearance on the road or
round the camp-fire.   The old men, the women and little children are engaged on the expedition, and all help.   The men
ride and the women drive the carts.   The children make the
fires and do chores for the women.   The men shoot buffalo; the
women dry the meat and make it into pemmican.

Hundreds of half-breeds often start together on these expeditions with horses and carts, oxen and dogs, and remain out in
the plains for two months at a time.   The discipline maintained
by the half-breeds on these occasions is enough to prove what
formidable enemies they could be if they were determined to prevent the settling of the country. They are all supplied with arms,
they shoot and ride well, and could find food and water where
regular troops would starve.   They elect their own captains and
policemen when out on the plains, set outposts, make camping
laws and laws for the hunt, and strictly enforce them by fines,
or the destruction of the clothes and gear of the offender, or by
expulsion from the band.   When near a great herd of buffalo,
the excitement becomes intense.   The approach is made cauti-
ously, but not till the captain gives the word is the charge
made.   Then like hounds slipped from the leash, in the hunters' dash, their horses quivering with the excitement of the
riders.   Each man selects his cow or bull, and unless his horse
trips in a mole or badger hole and throws him, he is taken

safely within a few yards of its flanks. Aim is seldom missed, and the hunter dashes off instantly after another, and so on till the herd is far away. The half-breed would not exchange the pleasure of one such " run " for a whole year's profitable farm work. After the hunt the work of the women and children begins. They have to prepare the dried meat and pemmican, and dress the hides. And when the carts are well filled, the band returns home.

Our breakfast place was a neck of land between two lakes, one of them sweet, the other bitter. The elevation of the two seemed to be the same, but, on a closer look, the fresh lake was seen to be the higher of the two, so that when full it would overflow into the other. This was invariably the case, as far as we saw, when two or more of such lakes were near each other. The salt lakes had no outlet, the natural drainage passing off only by absorption and evaporation.

The country between this first halt and the Saskatchewan consisted of three successive basins ; each bounded by a low ridge, less or more broken. Everywhere the ground was uneven, not so well suited as the level for steam agricultural imple-ments, but the very country for stock raising or dairy farms. The road was bad, and no wonder, according to the axiom that good soil makes bad roads. The ruts were deep in black loam, and rough with willow roots. Even when the wheels sank to the axles, they brought up not clay, but moist dripping black muck, that would gladden the eyes of a farmer.

Soon after dinner, we came to the last ridge, and before us spread out a magnificent panorama. Fifteen miles further west rolled the South Saskatchewan. We could not see the river, but the blue plateau that formed our sky line was on the other side of it. And those fifteen miles at our feet, stretching to an indefinite horizon on the south, and bounded five miles away to the north by Minitchenass or "the lumping hill of the woods," showed every variety of rolling plain, gentle upland, wooded

knoll, and gleaming lake.   Where hundreds of homesteads
shall yet be there is not one.   Perhaps it is not to be regretted
that there is so much good land in the world still unoccupied.
The intense saltness of many of the lakes was the only doubtful feature in the landscape.   One at our feet several miles long
had a shore of brightest red, sure sign of how it would taste.
All at the foot of the ridge with one exception are saline ; after
going on a few miles and mounting a slope, they are fresh.

The sun set when we were still five miles from the river.
Another axle had broken and heavy clouds threatened instant
rain.   Some advised halting ; but the desire to see the Saskatchewan was too strong to be resisted, and we pushed on at a
rattling rate over the rutty uneven road.   Never were buckboards tested more severely, and no carts but those of Red River
could have stood for ten minutes the bumps from hillock to
hillock, over boulders, roots and holes, as we dashed forward at
a break-neck rate.   The last mile was down hill.   The Doctor
and the Chief put their horses to the gallop, and only drew rein
when, right beneath, they saw the shining waters of the river.
The rest of us were scarcely a minute behind, and three rousing
cheers sent back the news to the carts.   In twelve working
days, we had travelled five hundred and six miles, doing on this
last forty-six ; and the horses looked as fresh as at the beginning
of the journey ; a fact that establishes the nutritious properties
of the grasses, their only food on the way, as well as the
strength and hardihood of the breed.

The first thing the Chief saw to, after pitching the tents, was
the preparation of a kettle of whiskey-toddy, of which all who
were not teetotallers received an equal share.   The allowance
was not excessive after nearly a fortnight's work ; about three
half-pints to thirteen men, six of them old voyageurs ; but they
had been so abstemious on the road that it was quite enough,
and great was the hilarity with which each one drank his mug-
full, pledging the Queen, sweethearts and wives, the Dominion

and the Chief.   It shakes a company together to share anything in common ; and by this time we felt a personal interest in every member of the party, and looked forward with regret to the farewells that would be exchanged to-morrow.

While at supper, rain began to fall, and it continued with intermissions all night, but we slept soundly in our tents,— caring nothing, for were we not faring on in good style ?   A month from Toronto and we were on the Saskatchewan.

August 16th.—A grey and chilly morning.   There was some delay in getting the scow, that is kept on the river by the Hudson's Bay Company, up from a point where it had been left, so that we did not move from camp till 8 o'clock.   This delay gave the Botanist an hour or two to hunt for new species, which he did with all diligence.   He had been slightly cast down of late by finding few new varieties.   The flora of the five hundred and thirty miles between the eastern verge of the prairie at Oak Point and the Saskatchewan is wonderfully uniform.   The characteristic flowers and grasses are everywhere the same.   We expect, however, to meet with many varieties after crossing the two Saskatchewans.

At this point of the river, where the scow is usually kept and where a regular ferry is to be established next year, crossing is an easy matter.   When there was no scow, every party that came along had to make a raft for their baggage, and a whole day was lost.   Our buckboard carts and Mr. McDougal's waggons made two scow-loads, and the horses swam across.   Some were reluctant to go into the water, but they were forced on by the men, who waded after them—shouting and throwing stones —to the very brink of the channel.   Once in there, they had to swim.   Some, ignorant of how to do it, struggled violently against the full force of the current or to get back, when they were stoned in again.   Others went quietly and cunningly with the current, and got across at the very point the scow made. The river for a few minutes looked alive with horses' heads, for that was all that was seen of them from the shore. As the water was lower and the force of the stream less than usual, all got across with comparative ease. The river at this point is from two hundred to two hundred and fifty yards wide. A hand-level showed the west bank to be about a hundred and seventy feet high, and the east somewhat higher. Groves of aspens, balsams, poplars, and small white birch are on both banks. The valley is about a mile wide, narrower therefore than the valley of the Assiniboine or the Qu'Appelle, though the Saskatchewan is larger than the two put together. The water now is of a milky grey colour, but very sweet to the taste, especially to those who had not drunk of living water for some days. A month hence Mr. McDougal says it will be clear as crystal. In the spring it is discoloured by the turbid torrents along its banks, composed of the melting snows and an admixture of soil and sand ; and this colour is continued through the summer, by the melted snow and ice and the debris borne along with them from the Rocky Mountains. In August it begins to get clear, and remains so till frozen, which usually happens about the end of November.

Near the ferry an extensive reserve of land has been secured for a French half-breed settlement. A number of families have already come up from Fort Garry. We did not see them, as the buffalo-magnet had drawn them away to the plains.

After crossing, most of us drove rapidly to Fort Carlton— eighteen miles distant on the North Saskatchewan,—being anxious to see a house and civilized ways and people again. Mr. Clark, the agent, received us with customary Hudson's Bay hospitality. The eighteen miles between the two rivers is a plateau, not more at its highest than three hundred feet above either stream. The soil looked rather light and sandy, but sufficiently rich for profitable farming. There is capital duck-shooting on lakes near the road. From the ancient bank of the river, above the Fort, is a good view of the course of the north

stream. It is a noble river, rather broader, with higher banks
and a wider valley, than the south branch. The usual square
of four or five wooden buildings, surrounded by a high plank
fence, constitutes "the Fort," and having been intended for
defence against Indians only, it is of little consequence that it
is built on the low ground, so immediately under the ancient
bank of the river that you can look down into the inclosure,
and almost throw a stone into it from a point on the bank.
Fifty miles down stream is the Prince Albert Presbyterian
Mission to the Crees, where there is also the nucleus of a thriving Scotch settlement.   Fifty miles farther down, in the same
north-easterly direction, the two Saskatchewans unite, and then
pursue their way with a magnificent volume of water—broken
only by one rapid of any consequence—to Lake Winnipeg.

We dined with Mr. Clark on pemmican, a strong but savoury
dish, not at all like " the dried chips and tallow" some Sybarites
have called it.   There is pemmican and pemmican however,
and we were warned that what is made for ordinary fare needs
all the sauce that hunger supplies to make it palatable.

A few hours before our arrival, Mr. Clark had received intelligence from Edmonton, that Yankee free-traders from Belly
River had entered the country, and were selling rum to the
Indians in exchange for their horses.   The worst consequences
were feared, as when the Indians have no horses th ey cannot
hunt.   When they cannot hunt they are not ashamed to steal
horses, and horse-stealing leads to wars.   The Crees and Blackfeet had been at peace for the last two or three years, but, if
the peace was once broken, the old thirst for scalps would revive
and the country be rendered insecure.   Mr. Clark spoke bitterly
of the helplessness of the authorities, in consequence of having
had no force from the outset to back up the proclamations that
had been issued.   Both traders and Indians, he said, were
learning the dangerous lesson that the Queen's orders could be
disregarded with impunity.   We comforted him with the assu-

rance that the Adjutant-General was coming up to repress all
disorders and see what was necessary to be done for the future
peace of the country.

Making allowances for the fears of those who see no protection for life or property within five hundred or a thousand
miles of them, and for the exaggerated size to which rumours
swell in a country of such magnificent distances, where there
are no newspapers and no means of communication except
expresses, it is clear that if the government wishes to avoid
worrying, expensive, murderous difficulties with the Indians,
" something must be done." There must be law and order all
over our Northwest from the first. Three or four companies
of fifty men each, like those now in Manitoba, would be sufficient for the purpose, if judiciously stationed. Ten times the
number may be required if there is long delay. The country
cannot afford repetitions of the Manitoba rebellion. The Crees
are anxious for a treaty. The Blackfeet should be dealt with
firmly and generously ; treaties made with both on the basis of
those agreed upon in the east ; a few simple laws for the protection of life and property explained to them, and their observance enforced ; small annuities allowed ; the spirit-traffic
prohibited, and schools and missionaries encouraged.

On asking Mr. Clark why there was no farm at Carlton, he
explained that the neighbourhood of a fort was the worst possible place for farm or garden ; that the Indians who come
about a fort from all quarters, to trade and to see what they
can get, would, without the slightest intention of stealing, use
the fences for firewood, dig up the potatoes and turnips, and
let their horses get into the grain-fields. He had therefore
established a farm at the Prince Albert Mission, fifty miles
down the river. With regard to crops, barley and potatoes
were always sure, wheat generally a success, though threatened
by frosts or early drought, and never a total failure. This year,
he expected two thousand bushels of wheat from a sowing of a

hundred.   The land at Carlton, and everywhere round, is the
same as at Prince Albert.   Its only fault is that it is rather
too rich.

After dinner, three or four hours were allowed for writing
letters home, and making arrangements for the journey farther
west.   We got some fresh horses and provisions from Mr.
Clark ; said good-bye to Emilien, Marchand, Willie, Frederick,
and Jerome ; and taking two of our old crew, Terry and
Maxime, along with two half-breeds and a hunch-backed Indian
from Carlton, crossed the North Saskatchewan before sunset.
In addition to Mr. McDougal, two Hudson's Bay officers joined
us—one of whom, Mr. Macaulay, had been long stationed at
Jasper House and Edmonton, and the other, Mr. King, far
north on the McKenzie River.   The scow took everything
across in two loads, and the horses swam the river ; but it was
after dark before the tents were pitched on the top of the hill,
and nearly midnight when we got to bed.

CHAPTER VI.

Along the North Saskatchewan to Edmonton.

August 17th.—The distance from Fort Garry to Edmonton is nine hundred miles, and is usually regarded as consisting of three portions ; two hundred and fifteen miles to Fort Ellice on the Assiniboine ; three hundred and nine more to Fort Carlton ; and about three hundred and eighty up the North Saskatchewan to Edmonton. On this third part of the journey we were now entering.

It rained this morning, but we rose early, as usual, and prepared to start. There was a good deal of confusion and delay, as Horetsky, who had employed the new men and made the arrangements, had remained over night at the fort. The new horses could not be found for some time ; and, with one thing and another, it was seven o'clock before we got off on this stage of our journey. The sky soon cleared and the day turned out as sunny and breezy as any of its predecessors.

The road follows the upward course of the Saskatchewan, but as the river soon makes an almost semi-circular sweep, first south and parallel to the South Saskatchewan, then northerly as far as Fort Pitt, the road strikes across the chord of the arc, over a broken and hilly country called the Thickwood Hills.

Lakes are always in sight,—one of them very large and very salt—and extensive views of fine pasture lands are had from every elevation. The soil and its productions, greatly to the disappointment of our Botanist, resembled what we had everywhere seen for the last fortnight. The soil in some places was equally rich and deep ; but generally not quite as good. Everything indicated a cool and moist climate. There were few of the prairie flowers, but a great variety of grasses, of wild peas, and beans, all green succulent herbage ; a country better adapted for stock raising than for wheat. The road was rough with roots, stones, and occasionally deep ruts, and so hilly that the jog-trot had often to be exchanged for a walk. Mr. Clark's horses, with the exception of a span attached to a large waggon of his own that he had lent us, turned out to be miserable beasts ; stiff-jointed or sore backed, and obstinately lifeless ; so that we would have fared badly, had it not been for the six government horses brought on from Fort Ellice. The two Carlton half-breeds, employed to drive the carts or horses, were old and stupid, incurable smokers and talkers. The one called Legrace was dried up as a mummy ; the other fat and greasy, popularly known among us as " Haroosh." He owed the name to Terry, who, hearing him drive his red horse with frequent howls of " Ho Rouge ! Ho Rouge !" took for granted that this was the " Haroosh" familiar to himself in early days, and the proper north-west cry to lazy horses. Terry, accordingly, never whacked his unfortunate white nag without yelling " Haroosh !" The only acquisition to the party from Carlton, was the young hunchbacked Indian called Keasis or the little bird.

Our breakfast-place was fifteen miles from camp, beside a marsh or pool on the road, twenty feet wide, and so deep that the water came into the buck-boards and up to the axles of the carts. It is well enough named the Slough of Despond. Often have carts stuck, and whole brigades come to grief in it. Why the H. B. Company has never bridged it is a puzzle, except on the principle that no private company cares to do any work that will be a public benefit, for it has lost enough by it to build ten bridges. Where there is any considerable traffic, nothing is so expensive as a slough, a hole, or any serious obstruction on the road.

We took dinner fifteen miles further on, beside a pretty little running stream, and camped before sunset, after making only eight miles more, beside The Bears Paddling Lake, a good place to stay over Sunday, as there is abundance of wood, water and pasture. The lake is very shallow but has a firm sandy bottom and the Indians have often seen bears about its shores, enjoying themselves in the water. Hence its name, a translation of which is sufficient for us.

Every one from the Saskatchewan that we previously met, had spoken so enthusiastically of this river and of the great country it waters, that we were somewhat disappointed with what we had seen to day. True, we had passed over only a speck, and that so elevated that much could not be looked for from it. The soil appeared good, and the grasses were so thick that they almost formed a sward ; but the larger wood had been burnt, and willow bushes, scattered all round, indicated an indifferent sub-soil. Besides, we had not got rid of the salt lakes. Mr. McDougal, however, ridiculed our doubts : we had only to go out of our road a little, to find a rich and beautiful country, extending north to the line of continuous forest, and to-morrow and every successive day, as we journeyed west, would show pretty much the same.

Faith in the future of the Saskatchewan and its fertile belt is strong in the mind of almost every man who has lived on it, and it is impossible to see even the little of the two great branches of the river that we saw, without being convinced that they are natural highways along which many steamers will soon be plying, carrying to market the rich produce of the plains that extend to the east, west, and north. When the tents were pitched Souzie went down to the lake and shot four or five ducks, as a contribution to our Sunday dinner. The night was cool, as we had expected at the elevation; but there was no frost.

August, 18th.—Took a much-needed long sleep, as usual on Sunday mornings; breakfasted at nine o'clock, and had service at eleven, Mr. McDougal assisting. We think ourselves fortunate in having fallen in with Mr. McDougal. He is thoroughly acquainted with the country, a man of ready resources and an obliging fellow traveller.

Widely different opinions have been expressed, about the value of missionary work among the Indians, by the half dozen persons we have hitherto met, who profess to be less or more acquainted with the subject. One gentleman's information was very decided :—" The Protestant missionaries had made no converts ; the Roman Catholic missionaries had made some, and they were the greatest scoundrels unhung." Another was equally emphatic on the other side. One witness was doubtful, thinking that something could be said on both sides, and he was therefore subjected to a little cross-examination :—" Many of the Indians are now professing Christians ; but, no doubt, some of them are great hypocrites." Asked if there was not a share of hypocrisy in all of us, and if such a charge was not made against Christians everywhere. Admitted that it was so. Pressed on the point, whether the old child-like frankness on the part of the Indian along with a vast fund of reserve on the part of the trader, made commercial transactions equally fair to both parties ; admitted that it did not, and that thus the charge of hypocrisy might be retorted in the wigwam on the trader, or explained in the store on the part of the Indian. Asked if he could name any positive improvement in morality, that had resulted from missionaries' labours. " Yes ; Christianized Crees would not steal your horses,—at least not openly— when you were passing through their country." Well, you

could not say more for Christianized Englishmen, or Yankees, if so much.   Could he mention any other improvement ?
" Yes ; they had all been polygamists to as great an extent
as they could afford (a new wife being bought for a horse
or a blanket) and they used to exchange wives to suit
each others' convenience ; but such practices among several
tribes had passed away, or were considered disreputable.''
Urged to remember what they were when he first went among
them, so as to say fairly if there was any other gain.   " Yes ;
away to the north the Dogribs and other tribes on the Mc-
Kenzie, had a practice of strangling or smothering all their
infant daughters after the first ; even the mother would stuff a
handful of grass into the mouth of the poor little thing and
choke it ; now the practice was unknown."   A decided gain for
the daughters. Any more.   " Yes ; some of them did keep the
Lord's Day after a fashion, treated their women rather better,
were more comfortable, a little cleaner, sent their children to
school for a while, and—well, there had been improvement,
but after all, if you only knew how superstitious they still are,
how dirty, vicious, miserable, you would not consider them
much better than pagans.

The style of argument seemed ungenerous. Here were men,
self-exiled, toiling all their lives without prospect of earthly
promotion or reward, from the Blackfeet on the Bow River to
the Loocieux on the Yucan, from Winnipeg to where the Mc-
Kenzie empties into the Arctic sea ; among the Indians of the
lakes and the plains, and the still more degraded Indians of the
woods ; living, many of them, in frozen wildernesses, where the
year is made up of a six weeks' summer of West India heat,
six or seven weeks more of warm days and cold nights, and
nine months of stern and dreary winter ; and when they see
some results of their labour, some small improvements struggling to show themselves in spite of all the dismal surround-
ings, they find that the necessarily slow process has made men

forget the raw material they had to begin upon; they are sneered at as making hypocrites, or are pointed only to what remains to be done, because their converts are not equal to the descendants of fifty generations of Christian forefathers. It is so easy to forget what once was, or to kick away the ladder by which we ourselves have risen. Changes take place so imperceptibly that even those living among them do not notice there has been change, and they assume that nothing has been done, when a great work is going on around them. Missionaries on the plains say, that now there has been peace for the last two or three years, they can call to mind only with an effort the once familiar scenes of bloodshed, and the universal craving for scalps.

The uniform policy of the Hudson's Bay Company was to encourage missionary effort among the Indians. Their charter bound them to this, and especially since 1820 they have done so to a considerable extent. Sir George Simpson always offered the protection of the Company to missionaries, on condition that they attended to their own business and did nothing prejudicial to the interests of the Company. When a missionary was stationed near a Hudson's Bay Fort, he had the position also of Chaplain to the Fort, free passage in and out of the country by the Company's boats, and £50 a year. For some time the Anglican and the Roman Catholic were the only Churches that entered on the work, perhaps because the Company was most ready to invite and assist these. During the last quarter of a century the Wesleyans also have worked in this field with their usual energy. They have now nine missionaries, and it is much to the credit of the two Protestant Churches, that they do not interfere with the stations of one another. The Presbyterians have only one mission, that at Prince Albert, and, though in a prosperous state, its work is in a great measure confined to a congregation of half-breed and white settlers.

A practical vindication both of the general dealings of the

Company with the Indians and of missionary work among them is the fact that the survey of the Canada Pacific Railway, from the Upper Ottawa to the Pacific coast, has in no case been interfered with. The engineers and others have been welcomed ; and very often, the Indians have proved extremely serviceable. The contrast with the state of things on the other side of the boundary line,—where surveys have been summarily stopped, engineers killed, and where every Indian scalp is estimated to have cost the country $100,000,—is marked indeed.

Of course the missionary work has another and altogether higher aspect, from which it is only fair to look at it also. We must judge it from its own as well as from the world's standpoint. Christian men and women give their means, their labours, and their lives to the heathen, not for social, political, or economical results, though they believe that such results follow their success, but for Christ's sake, because the heathen are their brethren, dear to them because dear to their Lord. It is not fair, thererefore, to leave the decision as to the value of their labours wholly to men of the world, who judge only from the lower point of view,—whose immediate interests may be injured, or on whose passions a bridle may be put by " the impertinent intermeddling " of missionaries, or who may be bitterly opposed to true Christianity—for it is not extravagant to suppose that there have been such men. To preach the Gospel of the wonderful love of God to a few degraded Indians, may seem a small thing in the eyes of tourist or trader, in comparison with the gospel of plenty of tobacco for peltries.

Far otherwise is it in the eyes of the missionary and his Master; far otherwise when weighed in the balances of eternity.

August 19th.—Rose at 3 A. M., thanks to the Sunday rest, and got away from camp before sunrise.

Our first spell was thirteen miles, over a rich undulating country, little wooded, but, judging from the strong green grasses and vetches, well suited either for stock-raising or cereals.   We breakfasted in a lovely hollow, watered by springs of delicious water the banks lined with balsam, poplars from one to two feet in diamater. The road here is about forty miles from the river on account of the bend, to the south, that the latter makes.   The Thickwood Hills are not more than two hundred feet high.

Terry gave us pemmican for breakfast, and, from this date, pemmican was the staple of each meal.   Though none of us cared for it raw at first, we all liked it hot.   Cooked for a few minutes in a frying pan with a little water and flour, and a dust of pepper and salt, onions added if you have any, it is called réchaud, and a capital dish it is, looking like Rodney, and tasting not very differently from well roasted beef.   Pemmican and sun-dried thin flitches of buffalo meat are the great food staples of the plains, so much so that when you hear people speak of provisions, you may be sure that they simply mean buffalo meat, either dried or as pemmican.

The second spell was twenty miles over round or sloping hills, enclosing lakes aud affording good pasturage, though the most of the land was sandy or gravelly and not up to the average.   The country resembled the Cheviots and the south of Scotland—two or three places reminding us of Drumlanrig. The road followed the high lands where the streamlets or creeks that flow into the Saskatchewan, take their rise.   We crossed one of these three times, and then halted beside it for dinner. In the afternoon we followed along its course, through a succession of very pretty lakes, that are almost covered with wild fowl, till it issued from the largest, Jack-fish Lake.   We should have crossed it there, but the water was too high, and we had to follow down its left bank to a ford three miles to the south.   When within quarter of a mile of the ford,—the big waggon and buck-boards going before, the carts following at some distance, and the horses driven behind them,—the humpbacked Indian galloped to the front, and pointed back.   There was Souzie crossing the river in his light waggon, and the carts and the horses following lead. They floundered across pretty well, except the cart of Haroosh, which stuck in the mud. Though angry at the check of the thing, it was thought best to follow, and Souzie being recalled and rowed up for his impudence, most of the articles that a wetting would damage, were transferred from the buckboards to his waggon and sent safely across. The big waggon, with the Chief and the Doctor mounted on the highest pinnacle, followed ; but when near the other side, its iron wheels sank in the black muddy bottom, and the horses, while struggling to extricate them, broke the whipple-tree and parts of the harness, leaving the waggon and contents in the middle of the stream. Maxime and Keasis rushed to the rescue and untackled the horses. The Chief and the Doctor, stripping from feet to waist jumped down into the water, and putting their shoulders to the wheels while the other two pulled, amid cheers from the rest of us on the other side, and countless bites from the mosquitoes, shoved the big thing to the bank. The buckboards followed, and then Greasy, who had been left all the time in the middle of the stream, cudgelling his horse, and yelling " Ho Rouge ! Ho Rouge !" supplicated help, as his arm and throat had quite given out. He was told to help himself, and to our great satisfaction, the old fellow had to jump down into the water and shove his cart out. All got safely across, nothing had been hurt, only Souzie looked woe-begone for the night, and Greasy continued sulky for two days. We camped at once on the bank, though the mosquitoes, that always haunt woods and streams, tormented our horses so much that the poor brutes could not eat, but crowded round the smoke of our fires, making the place look even more like a gipsy encampment than usual.

The Jackfish-lake River runs, through a beautiful park-like country from this point into the Saskatchewan, fifteen miles to the south. It would be a good location for a missionary or general settlement, for the lakes above are filled with jackfish or pike, and with white fish,—the finest fresh water fish, perhaps, in the world. There is also good water power, as the stream descends about a hundred and fifty feet in the course of the next fifteen miles, and the land is slightly rolling and of excellent quality. It is the favourite ground of a large mixed band of Crees and Salteaux, who were away hunting buffalo. On a little hill, near the stream, a great annual pow-wow is held in the spring, by the heathen Crees and Salteaux who come from long distances to have a high time. Their medicine men who have still much influence among them, take the lead and hold a revival meeting. All the old incantations and wild dances are practised, and as the excitement gets up, they abandon themselves to the foulest licentiousness.

We had driven forty-eight miles to-day, the longest journey yet made. Except the first and last part, the land was apparently not very good.

August 20th.—Instead of following up the right bank of the stream to the main road near Jack-fish Lake, we struck a new trail direct for Tortoise River, twenty-five miles distant. On the way we saw a fine buck and two or three antelopes, but they were too far off for a shot. In the spring, several varieties of deer are abundant hereabouts, but at this season, most of them are away with their young on the treeless prairies to the south. Halted on the road for breakfast ; but, to our disgust the water was salt. A breakfast of dry bread and dry pemmican was hurriedly made ; and we found that, on the plains, any meal without tea, is as poor an affair as bacon and beans without the bacon.

At Tortoise River had a most reviving swim, and a long halt. Beyond it is Horse Hill, so called from a fight between the Crees and Blackfeet, forty years ago. The Crees were encamped near a thicket at the foot of the hill, and a party of Blackfeet, that had made a successful raid far from their own borders, discovered them and charged. But the Crees were prepared, and, a still larger body of them on the slope of the hill, hidden by a ravine, swept round and drove their enemies into the ravine ; and though many of the Blackfeet escaped, all their spoil was retaken and forty horses were killed; an extraordinary number, for the aim is always to capture the horses, —horses and buffalo being the all-in-all to the Indians of the plains. In their wars the Blackfeet often suffered from similar haste and over-boldness. Not long ago, a party a hundred strong, out raiding in the winter time, discovered a Cree camp among the hills, and rushed on it ; but when they entered the pass, a second and a third camp appeared on each side. Their only hope was escape, and they dashed straight on, to find that they had rushed into a deep hollow, the opposite rim of which was topped high with snow-banks curling over in folds, so that there was no possibility of mounting it. The Crees closed with yells of triumph, and for once they had their will on their enemies It was not a fight but a massacre. Seventy were killed in a few minutes, and then the Crees, in a fit of generosity, or because they were glutted with blood, opened out and let the rest go.

Not that the Blackfeet disdain to exercise strategy. Cunning is natural to every Indian, in war and peace, in hunting and trading. We were told of a successful ambuscade of theirs at the Round Hill so like a New Zealand pah, on the other side of the Saskatchewan. A large body of Crees had camped by one of the lakes near the open. Towards evening they espied a buffalo grazing on the top of the inner hill. He fed so quietly, that they were a little suspicious at first, but soon others emerged from the coppice in the dip between the two hills. Hungry Crees could be suspicious no longer. They drew near quietly, and were all ready to run the buffalo, when every bush opened fire and a score of them dropped. The buffalo became Blackfeet and turning the tables ran the Crees to some purpose.

The characteristic of the Blackfeet braves, however, is daring. Many a stirring tale of headlong valour they tell round their camp fires, as, long ago in moated castles, bards sang the deeds of knights-errant, and fired the blood of the rising generation. Such a story we heard of a chief called the Swan, once the bravest of the brave, but now, tho' in the prime of life, dying of consumption. Dressing himself one day in all his bravery, he mounted his fleet horse and rode straight for the Cree camp. A hundred warriors were scattered about the tents, and in the centre of the encampment two noted braves sat gambling. Right up to them the Swan rode, scarcely challenged, as he was alone, clapped his musket to the head of one and blew his brains out. In an instant the camp was up ; dozens of strong arms caught at the reckless foe, dozens of shots were fired, while others rushed for their horses. But he knew his horse, and, dashing through the encampment like a bolt, made good his escape, though chased by every man that could mount.

Many a story of this kind we heard from poor old mummy Legrace, who boasted for himself in a dignified way that in his time he had killed two Blackfeet, but how much is truth and how much fiction, deponent saith not.

This afternoon we drove sixteen miles, from Tortoise River to English River, another stream running south into the Saskatchewan, so called from the fact that an Englishman had been drowned while crossing it in the spring time, when very insignificant creeks are dangerous. The soil all the way was sandy and mossy, except in patches or near either river, where it was excellent ; the country was undulating and suited for sheep grazing. At one point, the road ran within two or three miles of the Saskatchewan, and a prominent hill on the other side was recognized by Souzie. " Ah ! " said he to his master, "I know now where I am " ; and, on arriving at the camp, he went up to Frank and formally shook hands with him, to indicate that he welcomed him to his country. He had established confidential relations with Frank from the first, taught him Cree words, and told him long stories, explaining his meaning by gesticulations of fingers, hands, shoulders, mouth, and eyes, so expressive that Frank understood as well as if all had been broad Lowlands.

A clump of tall pointed white and branching poplar spruce, on the banks of English River, was the first variety from the universal aspen or occasional balsam poplar, that we had seen since leaving Fort Garry, with the exception of a few white birches on the banks of the Saskatchewan. The aspen is the characteristic tree, just as the buffalo is the characteristic animal of our North-west ; the other trees have in great measure been burnt out. Fortunately the aspen is good wood for carpenter work ; good also for fuel, being kindled easily and burning without sparks.

In the course of the afternoon, the Little Bird having gone in too extensively for pemmican became so ill that he gave out altogether. This generally happens with the new men that are picked up at the forts along the route. They are often half-starved, except when employed, and then it takes them a week to go through the surfeiting and sick stages before shaking down into proper condition. Legrace and Haroosh were far too old hands to suffer any evil consequences, no matter what the quantity they ate. One of us took the Little Bird's work, and made him get into a buckboard where he lay prone, head wrapped up in his blanket, till the camping ground was reached. Then he stretched himself beside the fire, the picture of utter wretchedness. The Doctor prescribed castor oil, and Terry put the dose to his mouth. As the Little Bird took the first taste, he looked up ; noticing the comical look about Terry's amorphous mouth, he thought that a practical joke was being played at his expense, and with a gleam of fire in his eyes spit it out on him. The Doctor had now to come up and with his most impressive Muskeekee ohnyou (chief medicine man) air, intimate that the dose must be taken. The Little Bird submitted, drank it as if it were hemlock, and rolled himself up in his blanket to die. But in the morning he was all right again, though weak ; and gratefully testified that castor oil was the most wonderful medicine in the world.

August 21st.—Our destination to-day was Fort Pitt on the Saskatchewan, but learning that a visit to it involved twelve or fifteen miles additional travelling, as the main road keeps well to the north of the river, it was decided that Horetzky, and Macaulay—one of the Hudson's Bay officers that joined our party at Carlton—should ride ahead to the Fort for supplies, and meet us if possible in the evening at the guard. Every station of the Hudson's Bay Company has a guard, or judiciously selected spot, well supplied with good water, wood, pasturage, and shelter, where the horses are kept. From this depôt we expected to be furnished with fresh horses and men in place of those brought from Carlton.

To-day's travel was through a hilly well-watered country. The first spell brouught us to the base of the Red Deer Hill, close to a spring of cold clear water beside a grove. The soil was a deep loam all the way. The grasses and flowers resembled those of Ontario and the Lower Provinces rather than the prairie flora. Such common wild fruits as currants, goose-berries, choke-cherries, &c., were in abundance. We seemed to have taken leave of the prairie and its characteristic flowers since crossing the North Saskatchewan. The road from Carlton to Fort Pitt runs among the sandy hills, that skirt the course of the river. The nearer the river the more sandy the soil, and the less adapted for cereals, because of droughts, and early frosts which are attributed to the heavy mists that cling about the river banks.

After breakfast, the road ran through a still more broken country and along a more elevated plateau. The windings of the Red Deer and its little tributaries have cut out, in the course of ages, great valleys and enormous "punch bowls," resembling the heaviest parts of the south of Scotland, on the rich grassy sides of which thousands of cattle or sheep ought to be grazing to make the resemblance complete. At a point where the plateau is about 400 feet above the level of the Saskatchewan, a round sugar-loaf hill rises abruptly from the road nearly 200 feet, called the Frenchman's Knoll, because long ago a Frenchman had been killed here. We cantered or walked to the top, and had a far extending view of level, undulating, and hilly country. Most of the wood was small because of recent fires, and it was all aspen, except a few clumps of pines far away. The sky line beyond the Saskatchewan was an elevated range with distinct summits, several of which must have been as high as the Mountain behind Montreal. The smallness and sameness of the wood gave monotony to the view, which was redeemed only by its vastness.

Near this, the trail to Fort Pitt branched off. Keeping the main road for a mile, we halted for dinner; then moved on, first descending the long winding slopes of a hill to the south, and afterwards going west, up a valley that must have been formerly the bed of a river, or cut out by an overflow of the Saskatchewan. In the course of the afternoon, we crossed three clear streamlets running over soft black bottoms; in spite of this abundance of good water the lakelets in the lowest hollows were saline. The soil everywhere was of the rich loam that had become so familiar to our eyes; uplands and valleys equally good. The grasses were thick and short, almost forming a sward; green and juicy, though they had been exposed to all the summer's heat. In the marshes the grass was from four to six feet high, and of excellent quality for hay.

After crossing the last creek, a handsome young Indian came galloping towards us, to say that Horetzky and Macauley were already at the guard ahead, with Mr. Sinclair, the Hudson's Bay agent at Fort Pitt. This was good news, for we had cal-

culated on having to wait several hours for our two outriders.
Getting to the guard before sunset, tents were at once pitched.
We had ridden more than 40 miles, and our avant-couriers
about 52, besides attending to all our commissions at the Fort.

This was the first guard we had seen. They are usually at
a distance from the Forts, and it so happened that this one, although ten miles from the Fort, was by the roadside. We could
not have seen a better specimen, for, on account of the grasses
being so good, more horses are kept at Fort Pitt than at any
other post on the Saskatchewan. There are 300 now, and they
increase rapidly, though the prairie wolves destroy many of
the foals. All were in prime condition and some of them
very handsome. Not one in ten of those horses had ever got
a feed from man. They cropped all their own food ; and sleek
and fat as they are now, they are equally so in midwinter :
pawing off the dry snow they find the grasses abundant and succulent beneath. Better witnesses to the suitableness of this
country for stock raising on an extensive scale, than those 300
horses, could not be desired. When weak or sickly, or returned from a trip, knocked up with hard driving and cudgelling, for the half-breed looks upon cudgeling as an essential
and inevitable part of driving, they may be taken into the
barn at the Fort for a time and fed on hay, but not otherwise.
At the guard only one Indian is in charge of the whole herd.
The horses keep together and do not stray, so gregarious are
they. The chief difficulty in obtaining some for a journey is
to detach them from the pack. There is a thick grove of aspens where they take shelter in the coldest weather, and near
it is the tent of the keeper. His chief work seems to be making little inclosures of green logs or sticks, and building fires
of green wood inside to smoke off the mosquitoes. Round
these fires the horses often stand in groups, enjoying the smoke
that keeps their active tormentors at a little distance. In considering this fact of horses feeding in the open all winter, it is

well to remember that Fort Pitt is between two and three hundred miles farther north than Fort Garry.

After inspecting the horses, we were taken into the keeper's tent to see how he was housed. It was a roomy lodge, called a fourteen skin, because constructed of so many buffalo hides stretched and sewed together ; the smallest lodges are made of five or six, and the largest of from twenty to twenty-five skins. The fire is in the centre, and the family sleep round the side, each member having his or her appointed corner, that nobody else ever dreams of encroaching upon. The smoke of the fire dries the skins thoroughly, keeps out the mosquitoes, and gives the inmates sore eyes. We all pronounced it very comfortable, but many people would probably prefer a house with more than one room.

Mr. Sinclair showed us the utmost kindness, giving us good advice, good horses, good men, and with no more show than if he had merely run down to the guard on his own business. The kindness we appreciated most at the time, it must be con-. fessed, was a huge shoulder of fresh buffalo meat, some tongues, and a bag of new potatoes. Terry was at once set to work on the fresh meat, with orders to cook enough for twenty, with a corresponding allowance of potatoes. None of us had ever tasted fresh buffalo before, nor fresh meat of any kind since leaving Red River ; and as we had resolved not to go out of our way to hunt, though Mr. Sinclair told us that buffalo were in vast numbers twenty miles to the south of Fort Pitt, it was only fair that our self-denial should be repaid by a good supper at the guard. And that supper was an event in our journey. Falling to with prairie appetites, each man disposed of his three portions with ease. The prairie wolves were yelping not far off, but nobody paid any attention to them. Tender buffalo steak, and new potatoes in delicious gravy, absorbed everyone's attention. The delights of the table when you are in the best of health and keen-set are wonderful, as a junior member of the party remarked, handing in his plate for a fourth or fifth helping, "man, what a lot more you can eat when the things are good"! Getting out of the tent after supper with an effort, a spectacle to gladden a philanthropist's heart was presented round Terry's fire. The men were cooking and eating, laughing and joking, old Haroosh presiding as king of the feast. He sat on a hillock, holding tit-bits to the fire on a little wooden spit, for Terry's frying pan could not keep up to him, and his greasy face shone in the ruddy light. So they continued till we went to bed. That they were at it all night cannot be positively affirmed, but in the morning the first sight that met our eyes was Haroosh in the same place and attitude, cooking and eating in a semi-comatose state.

August 22nd.—There was at least an hour's racing and chasing of the guard horses this morning, before our quota could be caught ; but, we got such good horses in exchange for our poorest that the delay was not grudged ; and three smart Indians, Louis, Cheeman (the little fellow), and Kisanis (the old man), instead of the Carlton three. We breakfasted at sunrise and said good-bye to Mr. Sinclair at 7 o'clock. On account of the lateness of the start, we divided the day's journey into two spells, one of nineteen, and the other of twenty-one miles.

The country round the guard is fertile, and beautiful in outline ; Mr. Sinclair said that it would yield anything. At the Fort and along the sandy banks of the river, their crops often suffered from Indians, droughts, and early frosts ; but it was impossible to have their farm ten miles away from where they lived.

Our first spelling-place to-day was Stony Lake ; after dinner we crossed Frog Creek, Middle Creek, and Moose Creek, and camped on the banks of the last named.

This was one of our best days. Everything contributed to make it supremely enjoyable. We had fresh spirited horses under us, a cloudless sky and bright sun above ; and an atmosphere exhilarating as some pure gentle stimulant. The country was of varied beauty ; rich in soil, grasses, flowers, wood, and water ; infinitely diversified in colour and outline. From elevated points, far and wide reaches could be seen. Here was no dreary monotonous prairie such as fancy had sometimes painted, but a land to live in and enjoy life. Last but not the least important item, Terry had in his cart new potatoes and buffalo steak, good as any porter-house or London rump steak ; man could want nothing more for animal enjoyment. In the forenoon, we rode up two or three hill-sides to get wider views. With all the beauty of former days, there was now what we had often craved for, variety of wood. Clumps and groves of tall white spruce in the gullies and valleys, and along lake sides, branching poplars with occasional white birch and tamarack, mingled with the still prevailing aspen. The sombre spruces were the greatest relief. They gave a deeper hue to landscape, and their tall pointed heads broke the distant sky line. Recent fires had desolated much of the country, but there was enough of the old beauty left to show what it had been and what it could soon be made. Sometimes our course lay across a wide open, or up or down a long bare slope ; sometimes through a forest where the trees were far enough apart for easy riding, while a little beyond the wood seemed impenetrably close. In the afternoon we crossed plateaux extending between the different streams that meander to the south ; and here the trail ran by what looked like well cultivated old clearings, hemmed in at varying distances by graceful trees, through the branches of which the waters of a lake, or the rough back of a hill gleamed, while high uplands beyond gave a definite horizon. The road was not very good in many places because of the steep little hills near the creeks, or boulders, deep ruts, mole and badger holes ; but ten dollars a mile would put it in good repair, and, as it was, our carts did their usual forty miles easily.

After dinner we came on our first camp of Crees—a small body, of five or six tents, that had not gone after the buffalo, but had remained quietly beside some lakes, living on berries and wild ducks.   Two broad-backed healthy young squaws met us first, coming up from a lake with half-a-dozen dogs.   One squaw had a bag, filled with ducks, on her neck, and the other had tied her game around the back of a dog.   Some of the men came up to shake hands all round and to receive the plug of tobacco they looked for.   Others, manly looking fellows, lounged round in dignified indifference, with blanket or buffalo robe folded gracefully about them,—evidently knowing or hoping that every attitude was noticed.   Not a man was doing a single hand's turn, and not a woman was idle.   The women wished to trade their ducks for tea or flour; but if we stopped the carts and opened the boxes there would be no getting away from them that night, so the word was passed to push ahead. We were not to be let off so easily.   Eight or ten miles further on, two elderly men on horseback—evidently Chiefs—overtook us, and riding up to our Chief with all the grace of gentlemen of the old regime, extended their hands.   Being welcomed and invited to ride on and camp with us, they bowed with an ease and self-possession that any of us might have envied, and joined our party.   At the camp, the Chief treated them with great civility, ordering pemmican, as they preferred it to fresh buffalo, and handing them the fragrant tea they love so well; not a muscle of their faces moved, though their souls were rejoicing ; a soft smile when they first came upon us, and a more melancholy smile in the morning when departing, were the only indications of feeling that either gave.   With the exception of the dull half-opened Mongolian cross-eyes, they had all the appearance of Italian gentlemen, and they were really handsome fellows, with well cut refined features—handsomer than any of us, or even than the young English trader, who " never allowed an Indian to enter his rooms ; if a Chief came along, he might sit in the kitchen awhile." So far below the salt have the sons of the soil to sit now. But "Rolling Mud" and the "Walker with out-turned feet," as our two guests were called, were entitled to move in the highest circles, as far as appearance and a perfect *nil admirari* manner were concerned. They could be guaranteed to look on, without opening their eyes at a modern ball.

After supper, one of our party lolling lazily on a hillock, happened to stretch out his long legs between the two and the big open fire. In an undertone, the Chief called his attention to the undesigned rudeness. "Oh" said he "they'll never mind." And certainly they smoked on and looked as tho' they saw not. "They will not say anything, but they will mind and not forget," quietly remarked Mr. McDougal. The long legs were withdrawn.

Our Chief always treated the poorest Indian with perfect courtesy. So as a rule do the H. B. officials, and much of their success in dealing with the Indians is due to this simple fact. We Anglo-Saxons are apt to sneer at French politeness. I verily believe that the chief reason why the French have often succeeded better than ourselves with the North American Indians was in virtue of that same politeness of theirs. The average Briton seems incapable of understanding that " a nigger " that is, any man whose skin is not white, has exactly the same rights as, and perhaps finer feelings than, he himself. But prick the redskin and he'll bleed just as if he were white and a Christian.

In the afternoon's drive, the big Carlton waggon, drawn by the span, broke down. The iron bolt, connecting the two fore wheels with the shaft, broke in two. Shaganappi had been sufficient for every mishap hitherto, but this seemed too serious a case for it; but, with the ready help of Mr. McDougal, shaganappi triumphed, and we were delayed only an hour. No one ever seems non-plussed on the plains; for every man is a Jack of all trades, and accustomed to make shifts. When an

axle broke, the men would haul out a piece of white birch, shape
it into something like the right thing, stick it in, tie it with
shaganappi, and be jogging on at the old rate, before a professional carriage builder could have made up his mind what was
best to be done.   Mr. McDougal in particular, was invaluable.
In every difficulty we called upon him and he never failed us.
He would come up with his uniform sober pleasant look, take
in the bearings of the whole case, and decide promptly what
was to be done.   He was our *deus ex machina*.   Dear old fellow-traveller ! how often you are in our thoughts ! Your
memory is green in the heart of every one who ever travelled
with you.

Both yesterday and to-day, the sasketoon berries, that are put
in the best of berry pemmican, were pointed out to us, and the
creeper which the Indians make into kinni-kinnick, when they
can't get the bark of the red willow to mix with their tobacco.
The sasketoon are simply what are known in Nova Scotia as
Indian pears, and the kinni-kinnick creeper is our squaw-berry
plant.

Just as the sun was setting behind the Moose Mountain, we
had ascended the high ridge that rises from Middle Creek, and
were crossing the narrow plateau that separates it from Moose
Creek.   Getting across the plateau to the edge of the descent
to Moose Creek, a glorious view opened out in the glowing
twilight.   To our immediate left, coming from the west, and
winding south and east, the Saskatchewan, not quite so broad
as at Carlton, but without any break or sand-bar, flowed like a
mass of molten lead, between far extending hills, covered with
young aspens ; like the Rhine with its vine-clad slopes near
Bingen.   Right beneath, was the deep rugged valley of Moose
Creek, broken into strange transverse sections by its own action
and by swirling overflows of its great neighbour, and running
round north and north-west into the heart of the mountain that
fed it, and that formed our horizon.   Crossing the creek we

camped on its bank. Our tents were pitched and fires burning brightly, long before the twilight had forsaken the west. Then a mighty supper of buffalo steak for us, and limitless pemmican for our Cree visitors, rounded off one of the pleasantest days of the expedition.

August 23rd.—Away from camp before sunrise. The sun usually rose and set in so cloudless a sky on the prairies that the Chief had all along roughly determined the longitude of our camps and the local time in a simple way that may as well be mentioned. His watch kept Montreal time, and he knew that the longitude of Montreal was 73 ° 33'. Sunset last night was at 0.34 p.m., and sunrise this morning at 7.26 a.m., by his watch. That gave fourteen hours and eight minutes of sunlight : the half of that added to the hour of sunrise made 2.30 p.m., on his watch, to be mid-day. We were thus two hours and a half behind Montreal time, and as four minutes are equal to a degree of longitude, we learned that we were 37 ° 30' west of Montreal, or in longitude 111 ° . At the same time we were in latitude 54 ° , 350 miles north of the boundary line, and 700 miles north of Toronto. Yet the vegetation was of the same general character as that of Ontario ; and Bishop Tache had told us that at Lac la Biche, 100 miles further north, they had their favourite wheat ground, where the wheat crop could always be depended on. But we can go still farther north. Mr. King, the second H. B. officer who had joined our party at Carlton, told us that he had never seen better wheat or root crops than are raised at Fort Liard on the Liard river—a tributary of the MacKenzie, in latitude 60 ° . This testimony is confirmed by Sir John Richardson who says " wheat is raised with profit at Fort Liard, latitude 60 ° 5' North, longitude 122 ° 31' West, and four or five hundred feet above the sea." And numerous authorities, from MacKenzie in 1787, whose name the great river of the Arctic regions bears, down to H. B. officers and miners of the present day, give similar testimony concerning immense tracts along the Athabaska and the Peace rivers.

There are several reasons why the isothermal lines should extend so far north in this longitude, and why there should be the same flora as farther south, though the summers are shorter.

The low altitude of the Rocky Mountains, as they run north, permits the warm moisture-laden air of the Pacific to get across ; meeting then the colder currents from the north, refreshing showers are emptied on the plains. These northern plains of ours have also a comparatively low elevation, while farther south in the United States, on the same longitude, the semi-desert rainless plateaux are from five to eight thousand fet high. Combined with these reasons, another may be suggested, that —the summer days being much longer as you go north—plants get more of the sun, that is, more light and warmth within the same period of growing weather. The summer days where we are now, for instance, must be two hours longer than at Toronto.

But these and such like general reasons by no means determine the fitness of every section of the country for cereals. Much land south of 54 ° is unsuited for wheat because of drought or early frosts. Probably this is so with much along the banks of the Saskatchewan. It has been proved at any rate that there is less or more risk, in places ; but those places are as a rule adapted for stock-raising, and, in such a country as this, cattle and sheep are as much needed as flour.

To-day we travelled 42 miles. The first spell, ten miles to the Little Lake, was over a cold and moist soil as shown by the more northern character of the vegetation. The ground was profusely covered with the low scrub birch, which is found everywhere in the extreme north. The second spell was fourteen miles, over ground that improved as we journeyed west, across Dog-rump Creek, up the opposite hill, and four miles farther on to two beautiful lakes well stocked with wild fowl. The creek gets its peculiar name from a bluff, projecting beyond a bold ridge that bounds the valley to the west. A lively fancy

sees in the bluff a resemblance to a dog's rump. Beavers had
built a dam a few days before across the creek below the road,
and in consequence the water was too deep for the buckboards.
Untackling the horse we ran the buckboards across a slight
bridge of willow rods that some good Samaritan had made for
foot passengers. The road then wound up to the top of the
ridge and gained the plateau beyond, through an extremely picturesque narrow steep pass.   From the summit we had a good
view of the creek meandering through valley and lake towards
the Saskatchewan.

At the second spelling-place we caught up to a large brigade
of Hudson's Bay carts, that had left Carlton for Edmonton a
week before us, heavily laden with stores.   They were driven
by several of Mr. McDougal's people, half-breeds and Crees from
Victoria, an united family of husband, wife and half-a-dozen
young children being at the head of the brigade.   The expense
of bringing anything into or sending anything out of the country by this old-fashioned way is enormous.   The prime cost of
the articles is a bagatelle.   Transport swallows up everything.
No wonder that the price of a pound of tea, sugar, or salt is exactly the same.   The weight is the same, and the cost for
carriage the same, and that determines the price.   One of the
Crees in this brigade, called Jack, was pointed out to us as
having in the last Indian war done a very plucky thing.   A
company of Crees and half-breeds from Victoria were hunting
buffalo on the plains.   One morning Jack and an old man were
left behind to bring up the kitchen and baggage carts, while the
main body started ahead for another camp.   Just as the main
body got over the first ridge, a war-party of Blackfeet swooped
down on them with their usual terrific yells.   They turned
campwards, from the mere instinct of flight, though knowing
that no relief could be there.   The Blackfeet had just got up
to them, shot and scalped the two hindmost, and would soon
have massacreed every one, when Jack, who had heard the

yells, appeared over the ridge, and firing his gun at the enemy, shouted to an imaginary force behind him, "hurrah! here they are boys; we've caught them at last." The old man at the same moment was seen hurrying up, and the Blackfeet imagining that they had fallen into a trap, turned tail and fled precipitately. With the best intention in the world, we voted Jack the Victoria Cross.

The third spell was eighteen miles, over fine meadow land, covered with rich pasturage that extended without break for fifty miles to the north. On the road the Doctor shot some ducks for the pot. Every lakelet had at least one flock among the reeds, or swimming about; but not having a dog to bring them out, it was unsatisfactory work shooting them, unless they were close to the shore. A little after sunset, we camped near the Riding or Snake Lake.

As we were now only 110 to 120 miles from Edmonton, it was proposed at supper that Horetzky should ride ahead with our letters of introduction to Mr. Hardisty; order pack-saddles, secure a guide, and make as many arrangements as possible, for our journey over the mountains. At Edmonton, or at any rate at Lake St. Ann's, fifty miles farther west, wheels must be discarded and everything carried on pack horses. A different outfit is required and as some of it has to be made to order, time would be gained for the whole party if one got to the Fort before the others. Macaulay who had been away on a visit to Scotland for the last twelve months, and whose wife and family were at Edmonton, offered to accompany Horetzky. So it was decided that after an early breakfast next morning, the two should ride on rapidly, each taking two horses, a blanket, and some pemmican.

August 24th.—Rose early, but as for the sake of Horetzky and Macaulay, breakfast was served before our first spell, it was 6 o'clock before we got away. Our two couriers preceded us by half an hour, but expected to be at Edmonton a day and a half before us. Passing the Riding or—as it is called on Palliser's Map —the Snake Lake, the smell of decaying fish-offal explained the object for which a number of log shanties had been erected at two points near its shores. The lake swarms with white-fish. Soon after, we crossed the creek that issues from the lake. The cellar of a deserted shanty by the roadside showed the character of the soil ; eighteen inches of black loam, and then successive layers of tenacious clay, through the uppermost of which the tissues of plants extended.

The country now became more hilly ; the hill-sides covered with heavy wood, and the hollows with marshes or lakelets. Vegetation everywhere was wonderfully luxuriant. Flowers re-appeared, but the general color was blue in place of the former yellow or lilac ; mint, blue bells, a beautiful tall larkspur, but principally light and dark blue asters. Our Botanist was disappointed to find that, amid such wealth of vegetation, there were few new species. The same plants have kept by us for a thousand miles. Mint and a saxifragaceous plant had accompanied us from Rainy Lake ; gentians, asters, castilia, anemones, and golden rods from the eastern verge of the prairie.

We divided the day into two spells,—sixteen miles of the richest soil and pasturage ; and twenty-four miles to Victoria over a great deal of inferior ground. One large section of this showed little but scrub birch. Another, ten miles broad, near Victoria, was a sandy ridge producing scrub pine, or as the people here call it cypress, very like the country between Bathurst and Miramichi, that was burnt over by the great Miramichi fire, and where in the Lower Provinces the scrub pine is chiefly found. The ground was literally covered with cranberries, bear-berries, the uva ursi, and other creepers.

In the forenoon the water was in the lakes ; in the afternoon in streams, all of which fortunately for us were bridged, rough-ly indeed, but the worst bridge was a great improvement on deep black quagmire. Pine, White Mud, and Smoking Lake

Creeks were the suggestive names of the chief streams, names that we had heard before and probably would hear again. America has been called the country of inventions,—but it cannot invent names. In the North-west, there are half-a-dozen " Red Deers," " White Muds," " Vermilions " ; next in popularity to these come the names of members of the Royal Family.

The first part of the day was bright and pleasant ; but at two o'clock heavy clouds gathered in the north-west. The wind drifted the thickest masses completely to our right, while all to the left the sky remained a clear bright blue. It thundered on the right ; and then we could see the rain falling in half-a-dozen different places while intervening districts escaped. At one point, not very far from us, the rain must have been terrific, and right thankful were we that our course had not taken us there, or we would have had Rat Creek over again. The central mass of cloud hung over this point, and all at once seemed to have the bottom knocked out of it, when a deluge either of rain or hail—probably of both—descended, like a continuous pillar, to the ground for a quarter of an hour, uniting the earth to the clouds as if by a solid band. The end of the tail of this cloud swept round over our heads, and gave us first a gust of wind, and then a smart shower of rain and hail for two or three minutes. The sky cleared completely at 3 o'clock ; but, two hours later, as we crossed Smoking Lake Creek, and entered again on good land, thundery clouds rose the second time from the western horizon, and soon covered the sun and sky before us. We were now in the bounds of Mr. McDougal's old mission settlement ; and at his word we " hustled up," or pushed our horses to their utmost speed to reach a good camping ground before the storm would burst. We got to the spot aimed at in time, our course for two miles being up a rich valley that is now behind the northern ridge or bank of the Saskatchewan, but that formerly, when the river was higher, must have been one of its beds, the

FORT EDMONTON.

intervening ridge being then an island. The settlement and
Hudson's Bay fort of Victoria is on the river slope of this
ridge, and thus travellers, passing along the main trail up the
valley, might be in entire ignorance that there was a settlement
near. When we rode up, however, two or three men were
making hay in the valley, and, hailing the sight as a sure sign
that civilized beings and dwellings must be not far off, we
camped at a spring beside them ; and, with a rapidity, that
astonished them and ourselves, had everything made tight before the rain commenced. After all the threatening the shower
did not amount to much. In half an hour the sky was clear
again and the Doctor and Mr. McDougal drove over to the fort, a
mile distant, for supplies, and to announce that there would be
service in the church next day. They returned after dark with
beef, bread, and milk. Mr. Tait, the Hudson's Bay agent, had
no fresh meat ; but, hearing of our arrival, he with oriental
hospitality had ordered a young ox to be killed and a quarter
sent over for our use.

August 25th.—Another day of rest, and a long sleep to begin
it with. At 10 A. M. walked over the ridge to service, at Victoria. The church is also used as a school-room, the Mission
House, and Fort are all at the west end of the settlement. The
log-houses of the English and Scotch half-breeds, intermingled
with the tents of the Crees, extend in a line from this west end
along the bank of the river, each man having a frontage on the
river, and his grain planted in a little hollow that runs behind
the houses, beneath the main rise of the ridge. Most of their
hay they cut in the valley, on the other side of the ridge, where
we had camped.

The farming is on a very limited scale, as the men prefer
hunting buffalo, fishing, or freighting for the Company to
steady agricultural labour, and neither farming nor gardening
can succeed well, when the seeds are merely thrown into the
ground in spring, and the ground is not looked at again till

autumn, when every thing is expected to be ripe and ready for ingathering. The settlement is seven years old, and consists now of between twenty and thirty families of half-breeds and from ten to a hundred tents of Crees, according to the time of the year, each tent housing on an average seven or eight souls. It ows its origin to Mr. McDougal who selected the place as a mission field because the Crees resorted to it ; and as a suitable locality for a half-breed settlement, on account of its advantages of soil, river, lakes abounding in fish and wild fowl, and near-ness to the plains where the buffalo are always found. Last year Mr. McDougal was removed to Edmonton, and the charge of Victoria given to Mr. Campbell who had been conducting a successful mission among the Stonies at Woodville to the south-west. Mr. Campbell was at present on his way home from Red River, where he had gone to attend the first Wesleyan conference of Manitoba, and consequently there had been no one attending to the mission for some weeks, except the school-master. This removal of missionaries from one tribe or even station, where they have gained the confidence of the Indians, to another locality, seems a mistake to outsiders. The personal influence of the missionary is the only thing that can be counted upon in work among heathen, or any rude and primitive people, and personal influence can be gained only after a long inter-course with them.

When we arrived at the church it was almost filled with about eighty whites, half-breeds, and Crees. The men sat on one side, the women on the other, and the children in a little gallery or loft with the schoolmaster and monitors. The ser-vice was in English, but some Cree hymns were sung, and Mr. McDougal announced that there would be service in Cree in the evening, through the medium of an interpreter. The conduct of all present from first to last was most devout, notwithstand-ing that many present understood English imperfectly. The children led the singing, and though there was lack of bass-

voices on account of the absence of the principal members of
the choir, it was singularly sweet and correct. Some of us were
moved more than we cared to show, when we heard the first
Cree hymn sung.

Service over, two of our party dined at the Mission House,
and the others at the Fort ; and, after a walk through the settlement along the bank of the river, we returned to the church
to see the Sunday School. Mr. McKenzie, the teacher, was
about to leave for another mission, and his successor Mr. Snyder was also present. There were sixty names, forty of them
half-breeds, and twenty Indians, on the roll ; but only thirty-
two were present, as whole families were absent, freighting or
hunting. We examined the three advanced classes, numbering
twenty-one, of the biggest boys and girls. All read the English
Bible more or less fluently and with understanding, for they
answered every question put to them. Their knowledge of
hymns was such as could be found only in a Methodist school ;
if any of us named a hymn in the collection, the tune was at
once raised and all joined in without books. The more ambitious tunes were of course the favourites with the children.
The Indians delight in hymn singing, and the missionaries take
advantage of this, making it one great means of reaching their
hearts. Heathen Crees who come to Victoria only for a few
weeks send their children to the school ; they pick up some
hymns at any rate, and sing them when far away on the plains.

Mr. Snyder had been schoolmaster for the last few years at
White-fish Lake, a settlement of Crees fifty miles to the north,
where good work has been done. He had eighty Cree children
at his school. When the Indians moved out to the plains to
hunt buffalo, the master would pack up his spelling books and
slates, and go off with them, setting up his establishment
wherever they halted. He spent from two to six months of the
year, teaching in this rotary style,—hunting half the day, teaching the other half. The Crees at White-fish Lake are all

Christianized and value the school highly.   They are beginning
to settle down to steady farming-work too, several families not
going to the plains now, but raising wheat, barley and potatoes
instead.   At Victoria wheat has been sowed for seven successive
years, and was a failure only once, the cause then being an extreme local drought.   At White-fish Lake it has never been a
total failure.   Victoria is on the most northerly bend of the
North Saskatchewan ; the plateau is very elevated ; and many
of the plants in the country round, have more of the sub-arctic
character than in any other part of the fertile belt ; so that we
were not surprised when told that there were generally light
frosts in July and August.   Indeed Mr. McDougal had been
warned in planting the settlement, that he was choosing one of
the worst spots on the river. The future may show that he was
wiser than his friends.

In the evening, we went to church again ; more Crees were
present than in the forenoon, but not so many of the half-breeds.
Mr. Tait acted as interpreter and also led the meeting, with
modesty and fervour, in prayer in Cree.   It must be a great
advantage to a missionary to have such a man in charge of the
Fort.

We had seen enough to-day to convince us, more than all
the arguments in the world, that missionary labour among the
Indians is a reality, and that the positive language on the
other side is the language of ignorance, self-interest, or down-
right opposition to the Gospel.   The aims of traders and missionaries with regard to the Indians are different ; the former
wish that they should continue hunters, the latter that they
should take to steady employment.   It is not wonderful then
that some traders should feel annoyed at what they regard as
a steady working against their interest.   But, as the Indian
has no chance of existence except by conforming to civilized
ways, the sooner that the Government or the Christian people
awake to the necessity of establishing schools among every

tribe the better. Little can be done with the old, and it may be two three or more generations before the old habits of a people are changed; but, by always taking hold of the young, the work can be done. A mission without schools is a mistake, almost a crime. And the Methodists deserve the praise of having seen and vigorously acted on this, and they can point to visible proofs of success in their Indian missions.

It is greatly to the credit of the Indians in British America, that they have never injured or stolen from any missionary. They have plundered posts, stripped traders naked, and murdered some who perhaps had given them cause; but even when at war, the missionary is allowed to enter and speak in their great councils and is everywhere treated with respect. Reverence is a strong trait in the Indian character. His own language supplies no words for profane swearing; if he wishes to blaspheme, he must borrow from the French or English. Is not his dignity of speech and manner connected with this veneration for Deity?

We invited Mr. Tait and the schoolmasters to walk over the ridge and have supper with us. Mrs. Campbell also did us the honour of coming, and, so for the first time, our camp was graced with the presence of a lady. Her presence lighted up everything, and had a very appreciable effect on our style of passing things round the table; every one was as anxious to help her to something as if she had been Her Majesty in person; Terry, naturally and nationally the soul of politeness, was especially attentive. Rather than let her put preserved peaches on the plate beefsteak had been on, he removed the plate and whipping out his pocket handkerchief, that had not been washed since he left Fort Garry, proceeded to clean it. Luckily the Doctor noticed him in time to snatch the plate away, or— but we must draw a veil over Terry as cook or table-maid; in no house is it wise to look too closely into how things are done in the kitchen.

Since the commencement of our journey, Sundays had invariably been our most pleasant and profitable days, and this was no exception. The kindness of every one at Victoria was something not soon to be forgotten. They welcomed us for our own sakes, and for the end the expedition had in view, as they had long prayed for the opening up of the country. It was in our favour also here as elsewhere that a Doctor was with us. He visited and prescribed for all the sick in the settlement, and finding in the Fort a medicine chest that had been sent out as a present by Dr. Ray but had never been used, he explained to Mr. Tait how and when to give the different medicines, and wrote out general directions that could be easily understood and acted upon.

August 26th.—Rose very early, the Doctor acting as campmaster and making every one fly around, so that we got off half an hour before sunrise. The thermometer then stood at thirty degrees, and heavy hoar-frost lay on the rich deep grass. A dense fog rose as the frost exhaled in dew, and, the sun's rays striking on this, formed a beautiful fog-bow that hung before us during more than an hour's travelling. Passing up the valley parallel to the river, we then skirted the edge of the plateau that bounded it on the north, going through tall heavy grass and a country which seemed to possess every qualification for stock-raising. The road showed the influence of recent rains that, the Victoria settlers told us, had been so heavy this August as to have completely stopped haying operations. Every marsh was a bog, every creek swollen, and as good soil makes bad roads, our progress was slow. Still by pegging away we made forty-four miles in our three spells. The first was to the Wassetenow, (or opening in the bank) so called from the cleft it has made, in the ridge, to get to the Saskatchewan. The cleft, instead of showing the usual broad rounded valley, is cut sharp and clean as if with a knife, partly by the force of the stream and partly by land slides. We next passed successively

Sucker, Vermilion and Deep Creeks, besides several smaller ones, and camped at the last named. The road descended twice to the Saskatchewan, which showed the same clayey look as at Carlton, and ran with almost as great a volume, though more than three hundred miles nearer its source. For thirty miles to-day the trail was through thick woods of aspen, poplars, birch, tamarack, spruce and pine. Much of the wood was good timber, from one to two feet in diameter with tall straight shafts, as thick fifty or sixty feet up as when five or six feet from the ground. There are occasionally alternate sections of aspen and spruce for half a mile or so; in one place the underbrush thick and green; in another the soil so bare and the trees so branchless, that movement in any direction is easy.

Camped before sunset within twenty-seven miles of Edmonton, and in honour of the event brought out our only bottle of claret. As we had no ice, Terry shouted to Souzie to bring some cold water, but no Souzie appearing he varied the call to "Pemmican!" This brought Souzie, but great was his indignation when a bucket was put into his hands, instead of the rich pemmican he was never tired of feasting on. Terry had a decidedly Irish contempt for Indians, half-breeds, or coloured gentlemen of any kind; and Souzie was especially obnoxious, because of his magnificent appetite, and because with Indian carelessness he often mislaid the belongings of the party, "as if," remarked Terry confidentially to the Secretary, "I carried tillygraph wires in my head."

August 27th.—Off this morning again before sunrise, and breakfast fourteen miles from camp at a little creek near Horse Hill, where the guard of Edmonton was formerly located. On the way crossed a strong rapid-running stream called Sturgeon Creek, from which twenty-five pound fish are often taken. We had left the thick woods last evening, and the country to-day was open and elevated. Thirty miles to our left the Beaver

Hills, on the other side of the Saskatchewan, formed a bold background of deep blue. Mr. McDougal pointed out a spot near our breakfast spelling place, where his predecessor had a remarkable escape when travelling. He had intended to camp on Horse Hill, but when within a mile of it, so furious a storm came on that he dismounted and crouched for protection under a bank with overhanging low willow bushes. When the storm passed over, he rode on to the hill and found on the very spot where he intended to have camped, a horse that had just been killed by the lightning.

At eleven o'clock, arrived at Edmonton and found that Horetsky had made arrangements to enable us to start next day. Mr. Hardisty, in the quiet business-like way, and with the kindness that many a traveller has experienced before, had done everything to forward our views. We pitched tents on the bank three quarters of a mile down the river from the Fort, near Mr. McDougal's house and the new church he is building, and had the whole party photographed; tents, carts, buckboards, with Terry, seated on his pots and pans, mending his pants and smoking the inevitable cutty, in the foreground.

The first great half of our journey from Fort Garry, the prairie as distinguished from the mountain part, was over. It had not been all prairie or anything like it, and the second part would not be all mountain. We would not discard our carts for another fifty miles, and the mountains were still two hundred miles distant. But, Edmonton may be considered the end of the journey across the plains and the beginning of the woods, and is the point at which to prepare for crossing the Rocky Mountains. It is the headquarters of the Company's posts on the Saskatchewan, and here we were to take our leave of the great river Up to this point it had been all plain sailing, but now we were told to expect toil and trouble.

At Edmonton we looked with great interest for the section of coal that crops out on the river bank. "Is it coal or not,' was the question, no matter whether it was called bituminous shale or lignite. A bushel or two was brought up from the river side at our request. Trying it in the smiddy, it burnt well and gave a good heat when the bellows was applied, but it would be very difficult to kindle without the bellows. It keeps burning a long time and leaves a great deal of dirt, dust and ash, " at the rate of two ton of ashes to one of coal." The section at Edmonton is three feet thick, and it crops out in several places, with a conglomerate beneath it that resembles ironstone in nodules ; at the Pembina river, seventy miles to the west, there is a seam ten feet thick ; and Mr. Hardisty informed us that at the Rocky Mountain House, one hundred and forty miles to the south-west, the seam is ten feet, the coal of a superior quality, and used regularly in the forge. Many other seams are found over a wide extent of country, and it is reasonable to infer that several of these will yield good fuel, for even in the richest coal countries there is no such abundant outcrop as here. What we tried was picked up from the river or from the outcrop, and was hard, shaly and inferior as fuel ; but had it not been very hard it would have crumbled away by exposure to the rain, snow and frost, and its face been covered up completely with earthy and vegetable matter, so that no traces of its presence would have been left. A little boring would settle the matter, for the beds are horizontal and not very deep.

The Company works a large farm at Edmonton, and with a success that is encouraging, especially when it is remembered that the methods are comparatively rude. They have raised wheat for thirty years, and it has failed only two or three times ; barley and potatoes and turnips are sure crops. The usual difficulties from the Indians camping near a fort have been experienced. A band of strange Indians come along, and, without the slightest idea that they are doing anything objectionable, use the fences for tent poles or fuel ; and their horses then getting into the fields destroy much of the crop. But in spite of these and other hindrances, a thousand bushels of wheat are usually stored from a sowing of a hundred ; and last year, two hundred and fifty kegs of potatoes (eight gallon kegs used instead of bushels) were planted, and about five thousand were dug. The same land has been used for the farm for thirty years, without any manure worth speaking of being put on it. Part is intervale and part upland.

The uplands do not yield such good crops because there is a slight infusion of alkali in the surface soil, which subsoil ploughing would probably do away with.

In the evening the Secretary held Divine service in the ball room of the Fort. About fifty men, most of them employed about the post, were present. There were also some miners who had recently arrived from Peace River, and whose reports of the Ominica gold-mines were not very encouraging. The men who wash the Saskatchewan sand bars for gold make on an average four dollars per day, but that does not satisfy them ; five dollars a day is called wages. This year there are only fifteen miners on the Saskatchewan.

Three or four intend starting to-morrow for the Red Deer, a tributary of the Bow River, in some canyons of which heavier grains of gold than usual have been found.

On the North Saskatchewan the gold miners or washers range up and down for about one hundred and thirty miles, Edmonton being the central point of this distance. It was for a long time supposed that all the gold in the Saskatchewan and the other rivers—in the same longitude—came from the Rocky Mountains, and these were diligently prospected near their sources. But not a trace of gold has been found there, and it is now thought probable that a stratum of gold-bearing quartz extends across the country, some distance on the west side of the mountains. Float silver is also found in some of the rivers, but not in sufficient quantities to encourage prospecting.

This seems the proper place, before going on with our diary, for some general observations on the country, between the North-West Angle of the Lake of the Woods and Edmonton ; particularly with a view to its capabilities as a great field for colonization. We can speak positively only of what we saw, and that includes a very narrow strip. All admit that the line of our route does not show the best land, however much they differ as to the quantity that is available for settlement. Some observers, long resident in the country, declare that the fertile belt practically means the whole distance between the North and South Saskatchewan, and other vast regions to the east, north, and west, especially a broad belt along the basis of the Rocky Mountains to the south of Edmonton, two hundred miles long by fifty broad, the home of the Blackfeet, and pronounced by many to be the garden of the North-west. Others maintain that, as far as the Saskatchewan country is concerned, only a narrow belt along such rivers as the Battle, Vermilion, and Red Deer can be cultivated with success. It is not necessary to decide between those views now. We know on the authority of Captain Palliser, who crossed and re-crossed the plains several times, that the central American desert does extend into British Territory forming a triangle, having for its base the forty-ninth parallel from longitude 100 ° to 114 ° W., with its apex reaching to the fifty-second parallel of latitude. But the first emigrants will select land along the courses of streams, especially the navigable rivers, and they will soon find out all about the intervening districts.

Speaking generally of Manitoba and our North-west, along the line we travelled, it is impossible to doubt that it is one of the finest pasture countries in the world, and that a great part of it is well adapted for cereals. The climatological conditions are favourable for both stock raising and grain producing. The spring is nearly as early as in Ontario ; the summer is more humid and therefore the grains, grasses, and root crops grow better ; the autumn bright and cloudless, the very weather for

harvesting ; and the winter has less snow and fewer snow-storms
and though, in many parts colder, it is healthy and pleasant
because of the still dry air, the cloudless sky, and bright sun.
The soil is almost everywhere a peaty or sandy loam resting on
clay. Its only fault is that it is too rich. Crop after crop is
raised without fallow or manure.

As regards the practical experience of farmers on the subject
there is little to appeal to, and that little is chiefly favourable.
The only large settlement is about Red River. The farms there
are most inconveniently shaped, being very narrow long strips ;
none of the people were skilled farmers to begin with, and, till
the last two or three years, they had no market except the H.
B. Company. But the Scotch farmers there are all making
money now, and their testimony is uniformly in favour of the
country for farming purposes.

The other settlements are few and far between, on the edges
of rivers or lakes, where wood and water are easily obtainable.
The population of these consists entirely of half-breeds, and
their method of farming is unique. They are farmers, hunters,
fishermen, voyageurs, all in one ; the soil is scratched, three
inches deep, early in May, some seed is thrown in, and then
the whole household go off to hunt the buffalo. They get back
about the first of August, spend the month haying and harvesting, and are off to the fall hunt early in September. Some are
now so devoted to farming that they only go to one hunt in the
year. It is astonishing that, though knowing so well how not
to do it, they raise some wheat and a good deal of barley, oats
and potatoes. There is a great difference, however, between
the Scotch and French half-breeds. The French who intermarried with the Indians, often became as the Indians ; just as
the Spaniards in Mexico and South America who intermarried
with the natives sank to their level. The squaw was treated
as his wife. Her people became his people, but his God her
God. The children have Indian characteristics, the habits,

weaknesses, and ill-regulated passions of nomads.   They excel the Indian in strength of body and endurance.   They beat him on his own field of hunting, running, riding, power of eating, or when necessary of abstinence ; with these are united much of French vivacity, love of amusement, hospitality, patience, courtesy of manner, and warmth of affection.   When a Scotch-man married a squaw, her position, on the contrary, was fre-quently not much higher than a servant's. He was the superior person of the house.   He continued Christian after his fashion, she continued pagan.   The granite of his nature resisted fusion in spite of family and tribal influences, the attrition of all sur-rounding circumstances, and the total absence of civilization ; and the wife was too completely separated from him to be able to raise herself to his level.   The children of such a couple take more after the father than the mother.   As a rule they are shrewd, steady, and industrious.   A Scotch half-breed has generally a field of wheat before or behind his house, stacks, barn, and provision for a year ahead, in his granary.   The Métis has a patch of potatoes or a little barley, and in a year of scarcity draws his belt tighter or starves.   It is interesting as one travels in the great North-west to note, how the two old allies of the middle ages have left their marks on the whole of this great country.   The name of almost every river, creek, mountain, or district is French or Scotch.

The climate and the soil are favourable !   What about water, fuel, and the summer frosts, the three points next in import-ance ?

A large population cannot be expected unless there is good water in the form of rivers, lakes, springs, or wells.   In many parts of the prairies of the U. S., dependence is placed mainly on rain water collected in cisterns ; but such a supply is un-wholesome, and to it may be attributed much of their prairie sickness.   In connection with this question of water, the exist-ence of the numerous saline lakes, that has been again and again

noted, forces itself on our attention ; the wonder is that former
observers have said so little about them.   Palliser marks them
on his map in two places, but they are really the characteristic
feature of the country for hundreds of miles.   In many parts
they so completely outnumber the fresh water lakes, that it is

> "Water, water, everywhere
> And not a drop to drink."

Some of them are from five two twenty miles long, others only
little pools.   Some are so impregnated with salt that crystals of
sulphate of soda are formed on the surface, and a thick white
incrustation is deposited round the shores.   Others are brackish
or with a salt taste that is scarcely discernible.   We noted
several facts about these lakes that may be stated.   (1) That
they have no outlet.   (2) That they are often side by side
with fresh water lakes, and that in these cases the latter occupy
the higher situation and their outflow consequently falls into
the former.   (3) That a few feet away from their immediate
shores, on which marine plants grow, the usual flora and grasses
of the country flourish.   (4) That the tracks of the buffalo
show that the water is drunk by them, and horses drink it when
they cannot get fresh water, though it acts medicinally on
them.

Whence have they originated ?   Several theories may be
suggested.   Here is one that explains all the facts so far as
known to us.   Suppose that formerly a superabundant quantity of alkaline matter was diffused through the soil generally,
over our Northwest, as we know it is over a wide extent of the
American desert and in sections on the Pacific coast.   We found
it so in some places where there are no lakes, and where it
could be carried off by rivers.   On the bank of the Assiniboine
near Fort Ellice, similarly on the Saskatchewan near Edmonton,
and at other points it was observed.   If it had once been generally diffused through the soil, what must have happened in the
course of centuries wherever there was an ordinary rainfall ?

The water, percolating through the soil, would carry off the alkaline matter into lakes and rivers, and it would be retained only in those lakes that had no outlet. This theory explains all the features of the case, and starts no new difficulties. It suggests too, that the one great reason why the American Desert must remain both desert and bitter is, that there is no rainfall on it, whereas farther north in the same longitude there is abundance of rain.

Apart from those saline lakes, is there a sufficient supply of water? In brief we must answer that, in many parts there is, in others we do not know yet. Test wells must be sunk and then we can speak positively.

The question of fuel is next in importance in a country where the winters are severe, for corn cannot be grown for fuel in our North-west as it has been on the prairies of Illinois. At present there is little wood except along the rivers and creeks, and on some of the hills, until we go back to the continuous forest on the north, or to within two hundred miles of the Rocky Mountains. This scarcity of wood is of little consequence, if the vast coal-measures, that extend from the Red Deer and Bow Rivers to the McKenzie, prove to contain good coal in large enough seams to be worked with profit. By river or rail, coal can be carried in all directions for every purpose ; and it is highly probable that we have the most extensive coal fields in the world. The importance of definitely ascertaining the quality of each prominent seam is very great. But even though wood may not be absolutely required for fuel, every encouragement for its growth should be given. Wood is needed for many purposes, and the plains would be warmer in winter if they were not treeless.

The remaining difficulty is the recurrence of summer frosts. In many localities these are dreaded more than anything else. At one place in June or July, at another in August, sharp frosts have nipped the grain, and sometimes even the potatoes.

At Edmonton, 2088 feet above the sea there is invariably a night or two of frost between the 10th and 20th of August. At Victoria and Fort Pitt to the east, and still more so at the R. C. mission of Lake St. Albert and Lake St. Ann to the west of Edmonton, the grain has suffered more or less frequently from the same cause. This enemy is a serious one, for against it man seems powerless. But admitting that there are frosts that cannot be avoided, and that no improvement will ensue on the general cultivation of the land, the draining of bogs, and the peopling of the country, there remain large and fertile tracts free from them, and, where the frosts are frequent, other crops than wheat can be raised, and the pasturage remains unrivalled.

It is only fair to the country to add, that the power of those frosts to injure must be judged not by the thermometer, but by actual experience. It is a remarkable fact, that frost which would nip grain in many other countries is innocuous on the Red River and Saskatchewan. Whatever the reason, and Mr. Spence in a recent pamphlet on " Manitoba and the North-west of the Dominion," has assigned several,—such as the dryness of the atmosphere, the heat-retaining character of the soil, and the sudden change of temperature that enables vigorous plants to bear an atmosphere at $20 °$ better than at $35 °$ when the latent heat of the earth and the plants has been given off,—the fact is undoubted. Due regard to times and seasons will also enable the farmer to escape very often the dangers peculiar to a locality. Thus, at Edmonton, if they sow late and the wheat is in the milk when the frost comes, it is injured. The remedy is to sow early.

Looking fairly at all the facts, admitting all the difficulties— and what country has not drawbacks—it is impossible to avoid the conclusion that we have a great and fertile North-west, a thousand miles long and from one to four hundred miles broad, capable of containing a population of millions. It is a fair land ; rich in furs and fish, in treasures of the forest, the field, and the mine; seamed by navigable rivers, interlaced by numerous creeks, and beautified with a thousand lakes; broken by swelling uplands, wooded hill-sides, and bold ridges; and protected on its exposed sides by a great desert or by giant mountains. The air is pure, dry, and bracing all the year round; giving promise of health and strength of body and length of days.   Here we have a home for our own surplus population and for the stream of emigration that runs from northern and central Europe to America.   Let it be opened up to the world by rail and steamboat, and in an incredibly short time the present gap between Manitoba and British Columbia will be filled up, and a continuous line of loyal Provinces extend from the Atlantic to the Pacific.

CHAPTER VII.

From Fort Edmonton to the River Athabasca.

August 28th.—It is proverbially difficult to get away in a
hurry from a Hudson's Bay fort, especially if outfit is required ;
but, we were furthered, not only by the genuine kindness of
Mr. Hardisty but by a false alarm that quickened every one's
movements, and so we got off early in the afternoon.

A report reached Edmonton in the forenoon, that the Crees
and Blackfeet were fighting on the other side of the river, a report based, as we afterwards learned, on no other ground than
that " some one " had heard shots fired, at wild duck, probably
enough. Where there are no newspapers to ferret out and
communicate the truth to every one, it is extraordinary what
wild stories are circulated ; and how readily they are believed,
though similar *on dits* have been found to be lies time and
again. As we would be detained with long pow-wows, if either
party crossed the river, every one helped us to hurry off. We
had to say good-bye not only to the Indians who had come from
Fort Pitt, and to Mr. McDougal and the gentlemen of the Fort ;
but also to Horetsky and to our botanist, as the Chief had decided to send these two on a separate expedition to Peace River,
by Fort Dunvegan, to report on the flora of that country, and
on the nature of the northern passes through the Rocky Moun-

tains. We parted with regret, for men get better acquainted
with each other on shipboard, or in a month's travel in a lone
land, than they would under ordinary circumstances in a year.
Souzie was more sorry to part with Frank than with any of the
rest of us. He had been teaching him Cree, and Frank had got
the length of twenty-four words which he aired on every possible occasion, to his tutor's unbounded delight. Souzie mounted
his horse and waited patiently at the gate of the Fort for two
hours, without our knowledge. When Frank came out he rode
on with him for a mile to the height of a long slope ; then he
drew up and putting one hand on his heart, with a sorrowful
look, held out the other ; and, without a word, turned his horse
and rode slowly away.

Our number was now reduced to four. We were to drive out
fifty miles to Lake St. Ann's, and " pack " our travelling stores
and baggage on horses there ; taking with us three new men,
and the faithful Terry, to whose cookery we had become accustomed, as eels are said to get accustomed to skinning. Mr.
Hardisty kindly accompanied us ten miles out, to the guard at
Lake St. Albert, to see that we got good horses. The road is
an excellent one, passing through a rolling prairie, dotted with
a great number of dried marshes on each side, from which immense quantities of natural hay could be cut.

Crossing the same Sturgeon River that we had crossed yesterday morning on our way to Edmonton, a hill rose before us
crowned with the Cathedral Church of the mission, the house of
the Bishop, and the house of the Sisters of Charity ; while, up
and down the river extended the little houses and farms of the
settlers. We called on Bishop Grandin and found him at home,
with six or seven of his clergy who fortunately happened to be
in from various missions. The Bishop is from old France. The
majority of the priests, and all the sisters, are French Canadians.
The Bishop and his staff received us with a hearty welcome,
showed us round the church, the school, the garden, and intro-

duced us to the sisters. The church represents an extraordinary amount of labour and ingenuity, when it is considered that there is not a saw mill in the country, and that every plank had to be made with a whip or hand saw. The altar is a beautiful piece of wood-work in the early Norman style, executed as a labour of love by two of the Fathers. The sacristy behind was the original log church and is still used for service in the winter.

This St. Albert mission was formed about nine years ago, by a number of settlers removing from Lake St. Ann's in hope of escaping the frosts which had several times.cut down their grain. It grew rapidly, chiefly from St. Ann's and Red River, till two years ago, when it numbered nearly one thousand, all French half-breeds. Then came the small-pox that raged in every Indian camp, and, wherever men were assembled, all up and down the Saskatchewan. Three hundred died at St. Albert. Men and women fled from their nearest and dearest. The priests and the sisters toiled with that devotedness that is a matter of course with them; nursed the sick, shrived the dying, and gathered many of the orphans into their house. The scourge passed away, but the infant settlement had received a severe blow from which it is only beginning to recover. Many are the discouragements, material and moral, of the fathers in their labours. Their congregation is migratory, spends half the year at home and the other half on the plains. The children are sent to school only when they have no buffalo to hunt, no pemmican to make, or no work of greater importance than education to set them at. The half-breed is religious, but he must indulge his passions. It is a singular fact that not one of them has ever become a priest, though several, Louis Riel among the number, have been educated at different missions, with a view to the sacred office. The yoke of celibacy is too heavy; and fiddling, dancing, hunting, and a wild roving life have too many charms.

The settlement now numbers seven hundred souls. The land

is good, but, on account of its elevation, and other local causes, subject to summer frosts ; in spite of these, cereals, as well as root crops, succeed when care is taken.   Last year they reaped on the mission farm twenty returns of wheat, eighteen of barley, sixteen of potatoes.   Turnips, beets, carrots and such like vegetables, grow to an enormous size.   A serious drawback to the people is that they have no grist mill ; the Fathers could not get them to give up the buffalo for a summer and build one on the Sturgeon.   They would begin it in the fall and finish it in the spring ; but the floods swept it away half-finished, and the Fathers have no funds to try anything on a solid and extensive scale.

The sisters took us to see their orphanage.   They have twenty-four children in it, chiefly girls ; two-thirds of the number half-breeds, the rest Blackfeet or Crees who have been picked up in tents beside their dead parents, abandoned by the tribe when stricken with small-pox.   The hair of the Indian boys and girls was brown as often as black, and their complexions were as light as those of the half-breeds.   This would be the case with the men and women also, if they adopted civilized habits.   Sleeping in the open air, with face often turned upward to a blazing sun, would soon blacken the skin of the fairest European.

Last Sunday we noticed, in the congregation at Victoria, that while some of the old Indians had skins almost as black as negroes, the young men and women were comparatively fair.   The explanation is that the young Crees are taking to civilized ways.   People at Fort Garry told us that when the troops arrived under Colonel Wolsely, some of them, who had slept or rowed the boats bare-headed under the blazing sun, were quite as dark-complexioned as average Indians.   The gentle Christian courtesy and lady-like manners of the sisters at the mission charmed us, while the knowledge of the devoted lives they lead must impress, with profound respect, Protestant and Roman Catholic alike.   Each one would have adorned a home

of her own, but she had given up all for the sake of her Lord
and His little ones. After being entertained by the bishop to
an excellent supper, and hearing the orphans sing, we were
obliged to hurry away in order to camp before dark. The
Doctor remained behind for an hour to visit three or four who
were sick in their rooms, and arrange their dispensary. Taking leave of Mr. Hardisty also, we drove on three miles and
camped. Five of us occupied one tent ; our own party of four
and Mr. Adams, the H. B. agent at Lake St. Ann's, who was
returning from Edmonton to his post.

August 29th.—Some of the horses were missing this morning, but an hour after sunrise all were found except Mr.
Adams' and another whose tracks were seen going in the St.
Ann's or homeward direction. Knowing that we would overtake them the start was made. After a third and fourth crossing of the Sturgeon river, we halted for breakfast. We then
crossed it for the fifth and last time, caught up to the two
horses quietly feeding near the wayside, dined at mid-day, and
rode on in advance with Mr. Adams to St. Ann's, leaving the
two carts to follow more leisurely. We reached the post an
hour before sunset, having ridden nearly forty miles, though,
as we had presented the odometer to Mr. McDougal, our cal-
culations of distances were now necessarily only guess work.
The carts got in an hour after, and the tent was pitched and
the carts emptied for the last time. From St. Ann's the road
is only a horse-trail through the woods, so often lost in marshes
or hidden by windfalls that a guide is required. Tents, for
the sake of carrying as little weight as possible, were discarded for the simple " lean to " ; and wheels for pack horses.
Our guide was Valad, a three-quarters Indian, and our packers—Brown, a Scotchman, and Beaupré, a French Canadian,
old packers and miners, and both first-rate men. They said
that the whole of the next day would be required to arrange
the pack-saddles, but they were told that we *must* get away
from the post immediately after dinner.

The road travelled over to-day was through a beautiful country, hilly and wooded, creeks winding round narrow valleys, and others that beaver dams had converted into marshes, on which were growing great masses of natural hay. The vegetation on the hill-sides was most luxuriant. The grass reached to the horses' necks, and the vetches, which the horses snatched at greedily as they trotted past, were from four to six feet high. The last twelve miles of the day's journey resembled a pleasure drive ; the first half amid tall woods through which the sunlight glimmered, with rich green underbrush of wild currant mooseberry and Indian pear, the ripe fruit of which we plucked from our saddles. Through these our road led down to the brink of Lake St. Ann's, a beautiful sheet of water, stretching away before us for miles, enlivened with flocks of wild duck and pelican on the islets and promontories that fringed it ; and then round the south-west side of the lake, for the last six miles, to Mr. Adams' house. Mrs. Adams had a grand supper ready for us in half an hour, and we did full justice to the cream and butter, and the delicious white-fish of Lake St. Ann's. This fish *(albus coregonus)* is in size, shape and taste very like the shad of the Bay of Fundy ; but very unlike it in the number and intricacy of its bones. It is an infinite toil to eat shad ; with all possible care little prickly bones escape notice and insinuate themselves into the throat ; but with white-fish a man may abandon himself to the simple pleasure of eating. Lake St. Ann's is the great storehouse of white-fish for this part of the country. It provides for all demands up to Edmonton. Last year thirty thousand, averaging over three pounds each, were taken out and frozen for winter use.

This was the worst place for summer frosts that we had yet seen. A field of potatoes belonging to the priest was cut down to the ground, and Mr. Adams pointed out barley that had been nipped two or three times, but from which he still expected half a crop.

August 30th.—" Packing " the horses was the order of the day till two o'clock, and Brown and Beaupré showed themselves experts at the work. A pack-saddle looks something like the miniature wooden horse used in our back yards for sawing sticks of cordwood. Wooden pads suited to the shape of the horse's back, with two or three plies of buffalo robe or blanket underneath, prevent the cross legs and packs from hurting the horse. All baggage, blankets, provisions, and utensils are made up into portable bundles as nearly equal in size and weight as possible. Each of the packers seizing a bundle places it on the side of the saddle, another bundle is put on the top between the two, where the log of wood to be sawed would be placed, and then the triangular-shaped load is bound in one by folds of shaganappi twisted firmly, but without a knot, after a regular fashion called the diamond hitch.

The articles which experience had shown to be not indispensable or not required for the mountains were now discarded, the object being to give as light loads as possible to the horses, that they might travel the faster. A horse with a hundred-weight on his back can trot without racking himself: when he has from one hundred and sixty to two hundred pounds he must be content to walk. If the horse is at all restive and breaks from the path, he crashes through dead wood and twists through dry till he destroys the load, or is brought up all standing by trees, that there is no getting through.

In the Mexican and United States Rocky Mountains, where a great deal of business has long been done with pack-horses, the saddles are of a much superior kind, called appara-hoes. With those the horses carry over three hundred pounds, and a day's journey is from twelve to fifteen miles. As our object was speed we dispensed with tent, extra clothing, tinned meat, books, etc., and thus reduced the loads at the outset to a hundred or a hundred and thirty pounds per horse. That weight included food for thirty days for eight men, and everything else that was absolutely necessary.

There was now before us a journey of five or six hundred miles, through woods and marshes, torrents and mountain passes; for we could not depend on getting supplies of any kind or fresh horses on this side of Kamloops; though there were probabilities of our meeting with parties of engineers between Jasper House and Yellow Head Pass.

Mr. Adams was of infinite service in all these arrangements. The luxuries of white-fish, fresh eggs, cream, butter and young pig bountifully served up for us at his table, were duly appreciated, but we valued still more highly the personal exertions, made with as much simplicity and thoughtfulness as if he had been preparing for his own journey. He was the last of the Hudson's Bay officers that we would be indebted to till we got to the Pacific slope, and parting from his post was like parting from the Company that has long been the mainstay of travellers, the only possible medium of communication, and the great representative of civilization in the vast regions of the North and North-west. From our meeting with the chief Commissioner at Silver Heights until our departure from St. Ann's we had experienced the hospitality of its agents, and had seen the same extended to all who claimed it, to the hungry Indian, and the unfortunate miner, as well as to those who bore letters of recommendation. It was on such a scale as befitted a great English corporation, the old monarchs and still the greatest power in the country.

At two P. M. all was ready; eight horses packed, eight others saddled for riding, and a spare horse to follow. Mr. Adams accompanied us a short distance; but, as the line of march had to be Indian file, we soon exchanged the undemonstrative good-bye with him, and plunged into the forest. For the first five miles the trail was so good that the horses kept at their accustomed jog-trot, though some of them were evidently unused to, and uneasy under their pack saddles. Valad rode first, two pack horses followed, Brown next, and so on till the

Chief or some other of the party brought up the rear of the long line on the seventeenth horse. If any of the pack-horses deviated from the road into the bush, the man immediately behind had to bring him back. The loud calls to the obstinately lazy or straying " Rouge," " Brun," " Sangri," " Billy," " Bischo," varied with whacks almost as loud on their backs, were the only sounds that broke the stillness of the forest ; for conversation is impossible with a man on horse-back in front of or behind you, and there is little game in these woods except an occasional partridge. After the first day, the horses gave little trouble, as they all got accustomed to the style of travelling, and recognized the wisdom of keeping to the road. Two or three old hands at the work always aimed at getting one of their companions between them and a driver, so that their companions might receive all the occasional whacks, and they share the benefit only of the loud calls and objurgations ; but the new ones soon got up to the trick, and their contentions for precedence and place were as keen as between a number of old dowagers before going in to dinner. These old hands carried their burdens with a swinging, waddling motion that eased their backs, and saved them many a rude jar.

In the course of the afternoon we passed one or two deserted tents, and "sweating booths," but no Indians. Three miserable starved-looking Stonies or Wood Indians had entered Mr. Adams' house while we were there, and, in accordance with invariable Indian etiquette, shook hands all round, before squatting on the kitchen floor and waiting for something to eat ; but with the exception of the few scattered round each of the Company's posts, who, as a rule, are invalids or idlers, we had not seen an Indian since leaving the Assiniboine, except the small camp near Moose-Creek and the Crees at Victoria. That they were buffalo hunting, or that their principal settlements are off the line of the main road does not give the whole truth. The Indians are dying out before the white man.

Now that the Hudson's Bay monopoly is gone, "free traders," chiefly from the south, are coming in, plentifully supplied with a poisonous stuff, rum in name, but in reality a compound of tobacco, vitriol, bluestone and water. This is completing the work that scrofula and epidemics and the causes that bring about scrofula and epidemics were already doing too surely : for an Indian will part with horse and gun, blanket and wife for rum. There is law in abundance forbidding the sale of intoxicating liquor to Indians, but law, without force to execute law, is laughed at by rowdies from Belly River and elsewhere.

The sweating booths referred to should have been explained before. They are the great natural luxury of the Indian, and are to be found wherever Indians live even for a week. There was scarcely a day this month that we did not pass the rude slight frames. At first we mistook them for small tents. They are made in a few minutes of willow wands or branches, bent so as to form a circular enclosure, with room for one or two inside ; the buffalo robe is spread over the frame work so as to exclude the air as much as possible, and whoever wants a Russian bath crawls into the round dark hole. A friend outside heats large stones to the highest point attainable, and passes them and a bucket of water in. The insiders pour the water on the stones, steam is generated, and, on they go pouring water and enjoying the delight of a vapour bath, till they are almost insensible. Doctor Hector thought the practice an excellent one, as regards cleanliness, health and pleasure; but the Indians carry it to an extreme that utterly enervates them. Their medicine-men enlist it in aid of their superstitions. It is when under the influence of the bath, that they become inspired ; and they take one or two laymen in with them, that these may hear their oracular sayings, and be able to announce to the tribe where there is a chance of stealing horses or of doing some other notable deed with good prospect of success. It is easy to

see, too, what a capital opportunity the medicine-man has, when
thus inspired to gratify his private malice or vengeance, or any
desire.   Many a raid and many a deed of darkness has been
started in the sweating booth.

The first five miles of the road, this afternoon, was a broad
easy trail, through open woods which showed fine timber of
spruce, aspen, and poplar, some of the spruce being over two
feet in diameter ; but had we formed from it any conclusion as
to our probable rate of speed, the next four miles would have
undeceived us.   Crashing through windfalls or steering amid
thick woods round them, leading our horses across yielding
morasses or stumbling over roots and into holes, with all our
freshness we scarcely made two miles an hour, and that with an
expenditure of wind and limb that would soon have exhausted
horse and man.   But the road again improved a little, and by
6.30 P. M., we had accomplished about twelve miles, and reached
a lake called Chain of lakes, or Lac des Iles, out of which the
Sturgeon river flows before it runs into Lake St. Ann's.   In
an open ground near the lake, covered thick with vetches, a
simple lean-to or screen for the whole company was constructed.
In the morning all decided that the lean to was a preferable
home to the round or closed tents we had hitherto used.   You
require for the former only a large cotton sheet in addition to
what the forest supplies at any time.   Two pairs of cross-poles
are stuck in the ground, as far apart as you wish your lodging
place for the night to be long ; a ridge pole connects these, and
then half-a-dozen or more poles are placed slanting against the
ridge pole.   Cover the sloping frame with your cotton sheet, or
in its absence, birch bark, and your house is made.   The ends
are open and so is the front, but the back is covered, and that,
of course, is where the wind comes from.   The ventilation is
perfect, and as your fire is made immediately in front, there is
no lack of warmth.

From this date the whole party had one tent of this descrip-

tion to sleep under, and one table to eat from. The days were
getting shorter, the horses could not go fast, and time had to be
economised in every possible way.

August 31st.—As packing eight horses takes twice as long
as harnessing twice the number, it was 6.30 P.M., before we
started. Hereafter, and for the same reason—the time needed
to pack and unpack,—only one halt and two spells per day
were to be made.

Six hours' travel at an average rate of three miles an hour,
brought us to the Pembina river. The road was through thick
woods and along the Chain of lakes, with an upward incline
until we came to the watershed between the Saskatchewan, and
the rivers running north-east into the McKenzie and through
it into the Arctic sea. The country then opened, and we could
see before us four or five miles to a ridge, on the other side of
which the guide said was the Pembina. The timber became
smaller as we advanced, till in the open it was poor and scrubby,
and the land here and over the drive to the Pembina looked
cold and hungry, with occasional good spots. In the neighbourhood of coal the land is usually poor, and we had been told
that the banks of the river showed abundant indication of coal
for sixty miles up and down from where the trail strikes.
After passing the Chain of lakes the road led along a small
round lake that empties on the other side ; and, soon after,
over a ridge from which a fine ampitheatre of hills, formed by
a bend of the river beneath, opened out before us, in the valley
of which we saw the broad shallow Pembina flowing away to
the north. The under-brush on the hill-sides had decided
autumn tints, the red and yellow showing early frosts. The
top of the opposite bank was a bold face of sandstone, with
what looked like enormous clusters of swallows' nests running
along the upper part ; underneath the sandstone, clay that had
been burnt by the spontaneous combustion of the coal beneath,
ash and burnt pieces of shale like red and white pottery on the

surface, half hidden by vegetation ; and down at the water's
edge a horizontal bed of coal.   We forded the river which is
about a hundred yards wide, and looking back saw on the east
side a seam of coal about ten feet thick, whereas on the west
side to which we had crossed only about four feet showed above
the water.   Pick in hand the Chief made for the coal, and finding a large square lump that had been carried down by the
river, he broke some pieces from it to make a fire.   In appearance it was much superior to the Edmonton seam ; instead of
the dull half-burnt look, it had a clean, glassy fracture like
cannel coal.   Carrying a number of pieces in our hands we
proceeded to make a fire and had the satisfaction of seeing them
burn, and of cooking our pemmican with the mineral fuel.   It
was evidently coal, equal for fuel, we considered, to inferior
Cape Breton kinds, burning sluggishly, and leaving a considerable quantity of grey and reddish ash, but giving out a good
heat.   Beaupré, who all this while had been washing sand from
the river in his shovel for gold, and finding at the rate of half
a cent's worth per shovel full, was amazed at our eagerness, or
that there should have been any doubt about its being coal.
He and his mates when mining on different rivers, had been in
the habit of making fires with it whenever they wished the
fire to burn all night ; and Brown said, that the exposure of
coal on Pembina was a mere nothing compared to that on the
Brazeau or North Fork of the North Saskatchewan ; that there
were seams eighteen feet thick there ; that in one canyon was
a wall of seam on seam as perpendicular as if it had been
plumbed, and so hard that the weather had no effect on it ; and
that on all the rivers, for some distance east of Edmonton, and
west to the Rocky Mountains, are abundant showings of coal.
This is perhaps the proper place to mention that on our return
to the east, Ex-Governor Archibald presented the Secretary
with a little box full that had been sent him as a sample from
Edmonton ; the sample was exactly like what we picked up in
the Pembina and tried with the results just stated.

The Secretary submitted it to Professor Lawson of Dalhousie College, Halifax, for analysis, and received a letter of which the following is an extract, and may be regarded as settling the question more favourably than we could have hoped for :

" My analysis of your coal is by no means discouraging :—

Combustible matter - - - - - - -	97.835 p. c.
Inorganic Ash - - - - - - - - - -	2.165 p. c.
Total	100.000

" The proportion of sulphur, chlorine, and other obnoxious impurities, " is quite small. The coal burns with a flame, and also forms a red cinder, " but is a slow burner ; and, although the absolute amount of ash is so " small, yet a much larger amount of apparent ash will be left in the grate " from imperfect combustion.   Yet, if we view this as a surface sample— " and such are invariably of inferior quality,—I think it offers great en- " couragement, for the percentage of ash is less than the average of the " best marketable coals in Britain. Of course this analysis of a very small " sample can only be regarded as a probable indication, not a demonstra- " tion, of the nature of the extensive beds of coal or bituminous shale " described in your letter."

The simple fact is that the coal deposits of the North-west are so enormous in quantity that the people were unwilling to believe that the quality could be good.

Here then is fuel for the future inhabitants of the plains, near water communication for forwarding it in different directions.

Captain Palliser also reports the existence of iron ore near several coal seams.

After dinner we rode on for three and a half hours to a good camping ground on the Lobstick river, about eleven miles from the Pembina ; and had the horses watered and everything made snug for Sunday before sunset.

On the way several creeks had to be crossed, or valleys where creeks had run till beavers dammed them up, and, as all had high steep banks, the work was heavy on the horses.   But the road so far had agreeably disappointed us.   It was not at all so

bad as travellers' tales had represented ; and we felt confident
that in another week Jasper House would not be far off, unless
the roads became very much worse. instead of fifteen days being
required as everyone at Edmonton and St. Ann's had said. So,
after a talk with Brown and Beaupré about their mining and
Blackfeet experiences, we threw ourselves down on a fragrant
grassy bed, a little tired, but in good spirits and glad enough
that we were not to be called early in the morning.

September 1st.—When we looked out at our wide open
door, between six and seven o'clock, a good fire was blazing,
and by it sat Valad smoking. He might have been sitting
there for centuries, so perfect was the repose of form and feature.

Brown enquired if he had seen the horses and the answer
was a wave of the hand, first in one direction and then in another, not only enough to say that he had, but also where they
were, without disturbing any of us who might be asleep.

He looked more like a dignified Italian gentleman than an
obscure Indian guide. With the lazy movements peculiar to
Sunday morning in a camp, one after another of his bed-fellows
shook himself out of his blanket. We had now time to look
around, and see what kind of a place we were camping on. A
bluff had stopped the course of the stream on its way east,
and made it swing round to the south. On the bluff, just at
the elbow, our tent was pitched. A rich grassy intervale along
the river, and vetches in a little valley on the other side of our
camp, gave good feed for the horses. On the opposite bank of
the stream, and a little ahead, stood three " lobstick " spruce
trees in a clump. From these probably the stream gets its
name. A lobstick is the Indian or half-breed monument to a
friend or to a man he delights to honour. Selecting a tall
spruce or some other conspicuous tree, he cuts off all the middle branches, leaving the head and feet of the tree clothed and
the body naked, and then writes your name or initials at the

root. That is your lobstick, and you are expected to feel highly flattered, and to make a handsome present in return to the noble fellow or fellows who have erected such a pillar in your honour.

There is an old superstition that your health and length of days will correspond to your lobstick's. As this belief proved inconvenient in some cases it has been quietly dropped, but the custom still flourishes and is greatly favoured by the half-breeds.

Whether such a simple way of getting up a monument is not preferable to piling brick upon brick to the height of a tree, to show how highly you honour a hero, is a question that might bear discussion.

At morning service the whole party attended. We took for granted that all could join in common prayer, and bear with profit the simplest truths of Christianity. With none of our former crews had we been on such friendly terms as with this one. The relation seemed more like that of a family than of master and servant.

The weather was beautiful. Last night it clouded up and in the early morning there was a light drizzle of rain, but not enough to wet the grass as much as if there had been the ordinary heavy dew of a clear night. The forenoon was cool enough to keep the black flies away, but they came out with the sun and the mosquitoes in the afternoon. At sunset the black flies vanish, but the mosquitoes keep buzzing round till the night is sufficiently cold to drive them off to the woods ; this usually happens about nine o'clock. The nights were so cold, though there was no frost, that we usually kept our clothes on, in addition to the double blanket. Our bag or boots served for pillow, and none of us was ever troubled with wakefulness, or complained in the morning that there had been a crumpled rose leaf under blanket or pillow.

There was little to mark this Sunday except the pleasant

peaceful enjoyment of it. The murmuring of the river over its pebbly bed was the only sound that broke the Sabbath stillness. The rest was peculiarly grateful after the week's hurry and changes; and the horses looked as well pleased with it as we. They ate till they could eat no more : and then they affectionately switched or licked the flies off one another, or strolled up to the camp to get into the smoke of the fire. Had they been able to speak, they would certainly have given thanks for the institution of a day of rest for beast as well as man.

We had one source of annoyance however. Two stray dogs had joined our party uninvited, a brown one at Edmonton, and a black at St. Ann's. They had been hooted, pelted and driven back, but after going on a mile or two further we would see them slinking after us again. Pemmican could not be spared, as we had sufficient for our own wants only, and to-day they looked particularly hungry. What was to be done with them? Go back they would not. To take them to Kamloops was out of the question. To let them die of starvation would be inhuman. There seemed nothing for it but to shoot or drown them, and though each and all of us promptly declined the part of executioner, their prospects looked so gloomy that Frank, who had pleaded for them all along, resolved to try and provide for them outside of our regular supplies. Getting permission to do what he could, he rigged a fishing line, and persuaded Brown and Valad to take a gun and try for beaver or duck. While all three were away, the brown was caught in the act of stealing pemmican. This aggravated their case, but, though all condemned, none would shoot. The hunters too came back empty handed, except with a pan-full of cranberries that Brown had picked, and that he stewed in a few minutes into a delicious jam. The dogs puzzled us, so we postponed further consideration of the problem till next day.

Instead of the usual three meals of pemmican, bread and tea, we had only two to-day, and a simple lunch at one o'clock. At six, dinner was served with all the delicacies we could muster. Berry-pemmican, pork and cranberry jam made a feast so delicious that no one thought of the dogs.

September 2nd.—Up at four and away at half-past five, or twenty minutes after sunrise. Another bright and sunny day, though the woods were so thick in some places that at one o'clock the dew was still on the grass.

Our first spell was six hours long. We crossed the Lobstick a little above our camp, and followed up its course without seeing it again to Chip Lake, from which it flows. The road ran through a fertile undulating country at first, then through inferior land which forest fires had desolated. There were few flowers or berries and no large trees. The dogs roused a great many partridges, but no one felt disposed to follow them into the bush. Brown shot a fine fat one from the saddle with his revolver and divided it between the dogs, so that they had a meal and therefore a respite for another day.

Our progress was so slow, averaging two miles an hour, that we were all dreadfully tired. The trail was not bad in itself, with the exception of a few small morasses, some of black muck, and others of a tenacious clay, but at every four or five yards a tree, or two or three branches were lying across, as firmly set by having been trodden on as if placed in position, and they prevented the horses from getting into a trot. These obstacles were not recent windfalls. They had evidently been there for years, and an expenditure of ten dollars a mile would clear most of them away. But the H. B. Company could hardly be expected to make a road for free-traders to Jasper House, and as it is everybody's business, not a hand is put to the work. Our dining place was at a small creek that runs into Chip Lake, a lake half as big as St. Ann's that the thick woods prevented our seeing. The ground was plentifully covered with creepers that yielded blueberries smaller and more pungent than those in the Eastern Provinces.

A little after two P. M., we crossed the creek, and wound up the opposite hill-side into a broken well-wooded country, the hollows in which were furrowed with beaver dams. After an hour of this we reached a hill top, from which a great extent of thickly wooded country opened out, first level and then with an undulating upward slope to the watershed of the McLeod. The horizon far beyond this slope in a due westerly direction was bounded by dim mountains, that we hailed with a shout as the long sought Rocky Mountains, but Beaupré checked the cheer by calling back that they were only the foot hills between the McLeod and the Athabasca. At any rate they were the out-liers of the Rocky Mountains, and in exactly a month from our saying goodbye to Governor Archibald at Silver Heights we had our first glimpse of them.

The road now descended to lower ground, and passed over the beds of old creeks destroyed by beavers. Had it not been for half-decayed logs lying across the path, the horses could have trotted the whole way. As it was, they made fully four miles an hour, in the afternoon spell of three and-a-quarter hours. Before five o'clock we came to a beautiful stream, and Valad advised camping, but the Chief, learning that there was a suitable place with good water and feed four miles farther on gave the word to continue the march. This ground, like much gone over in the morning, consisted of dry marsh, or sandy and gravelly ridges covered with scrub pine. It was part of the level region we had seen from the hill-top, and it had a deci-dedly poverty-stricken look. In an hour we had reached the camping place and prepared our lodging for the night, well pleased with the progress that had been made during the day. The spare horse, however, which as usual had been left to him-self to follow in his own way, was missing. Terry, who had brought up the rear, had seen him lounging and looking back, when within a mile of the camp. Beaupré at once started in pursuit, bridle in hand, but returned at dusk without him.

He had seen him near the creek we had crossed at five o'clock, evidently on his way home, or in a state of bewilderment, not knowing where he was going. Beaupré had tried to drive him into camp, but he plunged into the woods and refused to be driven back ; so Beaupré, afraid of losing the trail in the darkness, returned. As the horse could not well be spared, Valad was asked to go after him early next morning, try his luck and catch up to us before dark, while he went on under the guidance of Beaupré for the day.

The evenings were getting long now, and, after our slow and tedious journeying, it was pleasant to sit in the open tent before a great pine fire and talk about the work of the day, the prospects of to-morrow, and hear some story of wild western life from the men. Brown gave us the particulars of the horrible massacre of the Peigan Indians by Colonel Baker, the kindly views of it taken by the Montana citizens, and their memorial to Washington in his favour when he was threatened with court-martial. Brown and Beaupré themselves judged the massacre from a miner's standpoint.

But none of their stories of lawless and cruel deeds roused in us such indignation as what they told concerning villainies done recently in our own North-west. Perhaps the worst had happened only three weeks before our arrival at Edmonton, within one hundred yards of the Fort. A young Métis of eighteen summers, son of a well known hunter called Kiskowassis (or "day child," born in the day) had murdered his wife, to whom he had been married only a few months and who was enceinte. Last year he had slashed a woman with his knife in the wrist and made her a cripple for life. That was a small affair. But, having gone to the plains and formed an intimacy with another girl, he wanted to get rid of his wife. Luring her down to the river side, so that suspicion might fall on a party of Blackfeet camped on the other side, he stabbed but only wounded her, and she fled up the hill, he chasing and striking at her.

Some of the Blackfeet on the opposite bank cried *manoyo, manoyo* (murder), but there was no one near to help the poor creature, and soon a surer blow stretched her dead. This was too serious to be altogether passed over, so her brothers promptly called on Kiskowassis about it. Charley—the murderer—was not at home, but Kiskowassis acknowledged that he had gone too far, and proffered two horses that he extolled highly, the one as a hunter and the other as a carter, in atonement. The elder brother went out and came back in a few minutes, saying: "They're pretty good horses, I guess we'd better take them." And thus the affair was amicably settled; at the same price, as far as law on the Saskatchewan is concerned, Charley may go on and have his six wives more easily than Henry the eighth. An uncle of Charley, on the plains two months ago, shot a man who had offended him; and Beaupré extolled the whole family as "very brave." Charley had tried to enlist Beaupré last year in a promising enterprise of killing some Sursees who owned good horses; but Beaupré was not brave enough. There is a young brother, aged fourteen, who Beaupré says is sure to beat even Charley: "He is bound to steal a horse this very summer from the Blackfeet."

We asked Brown why at any rate the miners did not lynch Charley, since no one else acted. He said that there was such a proposal, but it was decided that as they were strangers enjoying the "protection" of the country, it would not be seemly to interfere.

September 3rd.—Awoke at four A.M., and found the fire burning brightly and Valad away in pursuit of the missing horse. Partly owing to his absence the start was an hour later than yesterday's. Leaving his saddle and some bread and pemmican on a tree we moved on. The trail was a continuation of the willow and alder marsh of last evening, but instead of being dry it was swampy, and the travelling heavy. The brown dog caught a musk-rat that made a meal for the two, and gave them another day's respite.

For the first eight or ten miles the road was almost wholly swamp, till a creek was crossed that runs into Chip or Buffalo Lake, and from it by the Lobstick into the Pembina. The water-shed of the McLeod then rose in a long broken richly-clothed slope. In five hours from camp, at an average rate of three miles an hour, Root River that runs into the McLeod was reached. The trail, which at no time was better than a bridle path, was so heavily encumbered in places with fallen timber that no trace of it could be seen. A rough path had to be broken round each obstacle, and sometimes Beaupré had difficulty in finding the trail again. Indian pears and moose-berries—the largest we had seen—grew along the hill-side, in such quantities that you could often fill your hand by leaning from the saddle, as the horse brushed past the bushes. We halted two hours and a half at Root River, and, as there was a birth-day at home, slap-jacks mixed with berry pemmican were made as a substitute for plumpudding, and, at dinner, the Chief produced a pint bottle of Noyeau, which had been stored for some great occasion, and Minnie's health was drunk in three table-spoonfuls a piece. Just as dinner was over, Valad made his appearance. He had a hard day of it following the track of the horse, but came up to him at our yesterday's dining place, moving quietly home-wards. Three times he turned him, but the horse always got away by dashing into the brush. Valad then went ahead and set a wooden trap on the road, but the horse avoided it, and Valad gave up the chase. On his way back he found that the squirrels had eaten his breakfast. Shouldering his saddle, he followed our trail, and rejoined us at two P.M., having walked forty-one miles and eaten nothing. His moccasins had been cut with the stumps and thorns ; but, though footsore in consequence, he made light of it and went to work with his usual promptness. Beaupré had been looking for half an hour, but quite in vain, among the long grass and shrubs, for a bit that had dropped off one of the bridles.

" We're all right now" was his judicious remark, when Valad
appeared, " the old man will smell it if he can't see it."

Our afternoon spell was heavy work ; crossing a branch of
the Root River, we came on a barren swamp, burned over so
thoroughly that there was not a trace of water nor of the trail
for two miles ; the once heavily-timbered slopes all round had
been devastated.   On our right a forest of bare poles, looking
in the distance like a white cloud, clung to the hill-side.   Dead
logs, poles, branches, strewed the ground so abundantly that the
horses could pick their steps but slowly.   After the barren,
came the last ascent, and so gradual was it that we did not
know when we were at the top, and then instead of a rapid descent to the McLeod, stiff marsh succeeded that got stiffer every
mile. The sun set before we got through half of the marsh, but
at one spot, a dry ridge intervening with good water near,
Valad advised camping.   In answer to our question, " how far
off is the McLeod still ?" he pointed to the sky saying " the sun
will be over more than half of that again before we see it."
This settled the question, though in a disappointing way, as it
put an end to the hope of getting to Jasper's this week.   Three
of the horses, too, were a little lame, and things did not look
quite as bright as when we started in the morning.

September 4th,—The three lame horses were looked at immediately after breakfast.   The cause of lameness in all three
cases was, that sharp strong stops cr splinters had run into or
just above their unshod hoofs ; we half wondered that some of
them had not pulled their hoofs off, in struggling to extricate
them from tough and sharp fibrous roots.   The splinters were
easily extracted from two, and, the third horse, allowing no one
near his hind leg, was managed dexterously by Valad.   Passing
one end of his shaganappi lasso twice round nis neck, he made
two turns of the other end round his body, and gradually slipped
those turns down over his hind legs, and tightened them.
Tightening the rope at his neck now, the horse resisted, but his

legs being tied, his own struggles with a little shove threw him, and when thrown he lay quiet as a lamb.

It had rained during the night, and the morning was cloudy. At 9 a.m. the rain came on again, after we had been two hours on the road, if the expression is allowable when there was no road. The rain made travelling across the muskeg still more difficult and uncomfortable. In six hours and a quarter we fought through ten miles, six or seven of them being simply over a continuous muskeg covered with windfalls. The horses stumbled over roots and timber to sink into thick layers of quaking moss, and sometimes through these to the springs underneath. The greater part of the ground bore tall beautifully shaped spruce and poplar, chiefly spruce, from one to three feet in diameter.

After crossing a little creek, the trail improved somewhat till it led to the ancient bank of the McLeod, at the foot of which yawned a deep pool with a bottom of tenacious clay, that had to be struggled through somehow. The horses sinking almost to their bellies, floundered in the mud at a fearful rate, with such effects on our clothes as may be conceived ; fortunately by this time we were quite indifferent on the subject of appearances. The river was only a hundred yards from this, but the trail led for half a mile up through a wooded intervale to the crossing. A little creek seamed the intervale, and the first open spot was strewed with as many chips as would furnish a carpenter's shop, beside several logs, two of them stripped of their bark and others cut into junks for transportation. We had disturbed a colony of beavers in their work of building a dam across the creek and of laying in their winter supplies.

The sight of the McLeod was a relief, for we had found the way to it a hard road to travel, as the Canadians who preceded Milton and Cheadle evidently had. The Chief came upon their testimony chalked with red keil on a large spruce tree in the swamp, five or six miles to the east of the river. Only the following words and half-words could be made out :—

AUGUST 10th, 1862, * * * * * *
* * * * * * * * * * * *
* * * * East Tilbury * * * *
* * * * * * * and * * *
* * * * * Robert Campb * *
* * * * * * * * * * * *
* * * * * * * for Cariboo *
* * * * * a hard road to travel.

Poor fellows ! some of them found the North Thompson a harder road.

The McLeod heads inside of the first range of the Rocky Mountains. Where we crossed, it is a beautiful stream about 110 yards wide, running north-easterly with a rapid current over a pebbly bed. Its breadth is not much greater than the Pembina, but it has three times the volume of water. At this season of the year, it can be forded at almost any point where there is a little rapid, the water in such places not coming up to the horses' necks. Crossing, we came upon a few acres of prairie, to the rich vetches on which the horses abandoned themselves as eagerly as our party did to the *réchaud* and tea that Terry hurried up. Fortunately too, the rain ceased, though the sky did not clear, and Valad made a big fire at which we dried ourselves partially. Brown advised that, as this was a good place, some provisions should be cachéed for those of the party who were to return from Jasper's ; and Valad, selecting a site in the green wood, he and Beaupré went off to it from the opposite direction, with about twenty-five pounds of pemmican and flour tied up, first in canvass and then in oil-skin, as the wolverine—most dreaded plunderer of cachés—dislikes the smell of oil. Selecting two suitable pine trees in the thick wood, they skinned (barked) them to prevent animals from climbing; then placing a pole between the two, some eighteen feet from the ground, they hung a St. Andrew's Cross of two small sticks from the pole, and suspended their bag from the end of one, that the least movement or even puff of wind would set it swinging. Such a caché Valad guaranteed against bird and beast of whatever kind. "And now," Beaupré summed up, " if no one finds that, we will be in good luck ; but if somebody finds it, we will be in bad luck; that's all."

Our course from this point was to be up the McLeod for nearly seventy miles of very bad road. As we had had enough of that for one day, we listened eagerly to Beaupré saying that it was possible to dodge the first eight miles by creeping along the shore of the river, and crossing and recrossing wherever the banks come down too close to permit travelling. Though Valad didn't know this way and Beaupré himself had not tried the crossings, having on a former occasion made the trip up the river in a canoe, and not by the shore, it was decided to try. A pleasant change on the forenoon's journey it proved to be, and quite a success; for we arrived at the proposed camping ground, after four crossings, before sunset. The river was low and the shore wide, consisting of rough pebbly stretches or sand bars, covered, near the bank, with wild onions, sand grasses, and creepers. Beaupré said that the sand would yield gold at the rate of a cent a shovelful, but that would give only $2 or $3 per day. Where the banks came near the river in bold bluffs, they showed sections chiefly of different kinds of clay and sandstone separated by black slate. No coal beds appeared except a four-inch seam that looked like coal, but may have been only a roof of shale to the coal beneath.

At the camp a roaring fire of pine logs was soon kindled, and a line hung along one side for our wet clothes ; but the steady drizzling rain recommenced and continued all night. We warmed ourselves at any rate, and turned in as comfortably as the circumstances permitted.

September 5th.—It rained steadily through the night and was drizzling in the morning. Though it hurts the horses' backs to saddle them when wet, there was no alternative, and so after getting ready with great deliberation, in hopes that it would clear up, we moved away at 7.30 A.M.

Our first spell was the hardest work of the journey, so far, with the least to show for it. We made about five miles, and it took as many hours to make the distance. The road followed the upward course of the McLeod, crossing the necks of land formed by the doublings of the river. These so called portages were the worst part of the road, though it was all so bad that it is invidious to make comparisons. The country was either bog or barren—both bad,—for the whole had recently been burned over, and every wind had blown down its share of the burnt trees. There was no regular trail. Each successive party that travelled this way, seemed to have tried to make a new one in vain efforts to escape the difficulties. Valad went ahead, axe in hand, and between natural selections and a judicious use of the axe, made a passage; but it looked so tangled and beset, that the horses often thought they could do better ; off they would go, with a swing, among the bare poles, for about two yards before their packs got interlaced with the tough spruce. Then came the tug ; if the trees would not give, the packs had to, and there was a delay of half an hour to tie them on again. We often wondered that the packs came off so seldom ; but Brown understood his business ; besides the trees had been burnt, and some of them were uprooted or broken with comparative ease. Of course the recent rains had not improved the going. Beaupré said that it had not been worse last summer, after the spring frosts had come out and the spring rains gone in. Take it all in all, the road was hopelessly bad,—deserving all the hard things that had been said of it,—and called for a large stock of the Mark Tapley spirit, especially when, by wandering from the trail, the horses got mired in muskegs or stuck between trees, or when the blackened tough spruce branches, bent forward by a pack horse, swung back viciously in the face of the unfortunate driver.

The road could only have been worse by the trees being larger ; but then it would have been simply impassable, for the windfalls would have barricaded it completely. The prospect, too, was dismal and desolate looking enough for Avernus or the richest coal fields : nothing but a forest, apparently endless, of blackened poles on all sides. Only when an angle or bend of the river came into view, was there any relief for the eye.

Towards midday, when every one's thoughts were on pemmican, " ho," " ho," was heard ahead, and two Indians appeared holding out hands to Valad. They had left Jasper's four days ago, and were bound for Edmonton, trusting to their guns or the berries to supply them with food on the way. The offer of a pemmican dinner turned them back with us for a quarter of a mile, to a little creek where the halt had to be called, though there was but poor feed for the horses among the blackened trees. The Indians had no dog, and were glad to take the black—as he would be useful in treeing partridges—back to Mr. Adams'. They promised also to drive home the spare horse if they could track him. We wrote a note by them to Mr. Adams, telling him what commissions we had entrusted them with. These Indians had straighter features and a manlier cast of countenance than the ordinary Wood-Indians. On inquiry, we learned that they were Iroquois from Smoking River, to the north of Jasper's, where a small colony has been settled for fifty years back. Their ancestors had been in the employment of the North-west Fur Company, and on its amalgamation with the Hudson's Bay, had settled on Smoking River, on account of the abundance of fur-bearing animals and of large game, such as buffalo, elk, brown and grizzly bears, then in that quarter.

After dinner, the march was resumed at the mile per hour rate. More discouraging was the fact that scarcely two-thirds of that modest speed was progress ; for the trail twisted like a ship tacking, so that at times we were actually progressing backwards. In struggling across creeks the difference between the Lowland Scot and the Frenchman came out amusingly.

Brown continued imperturbable, no matter how the horses went. Beaupré, the mildest mannered man living when things went smoothly, could not stand the sight of a horse floundering in the mud. Down into the gully he would rush to lift him out by the tail. Of course he got spattered and perhaps kicked for his pains. This made him worse, and he had to let out his excitement on the horse. Gripping the tail with his left hand, as the brute struggled up the opposite hill, swaying him from side to side as if he had been tied to it, he whipped with his right ; *sacre*-ing furiously, till he reached the top. Then feeling that he had done his part, he would let go and subside again into his mildest manners.

Towards evening the road improved so that the luxury of a smart walk was indulged in—with occasional breaks—for an hour or two. When we camped, the tally for the day was twelve miles, representing perhaps an air line of six or eight, for ten hours' hard work. A bath in the McLeod, and a change of socks followed by supper, put us all right, although the hope of seeing Jasper's before next Wednesday had completely vanished.

September 6th.—It rained last night, but the morning gave signs of a fair day. Renewed the march at 6.45 A.M. Yesterday's experiences were also renewed, except that the road as well as the day was better—enabling us to make two miles an hour. The road kept closer to the river, revealing many a beautiful bend or long reach. The timber was larger and less of it burnt. Poplar, cottonwood, and spruce, chiefly the latter, predominated. The opposite bank had escaped fires. Before noon, we got a glimpse of the mountains away to the south, and soon after reached a lovely bit of open prairie covered with vetches, honey-suckle, and rose-bushes out of flower. Here, the McLeod sweeps away to the south and then back to the north, and the trail instead of following its long circuit cuts across the loop. This portage is twenty miles long, and a muskeg in the middle—on one or

the other side of which we would have to camp to-night—is the
worst on the road to Jasper's.   Halted for dinner at the bend
of the river, having travelled nine of ten miles, Frank promising us some fish, from a trouty looking stream hard by, as a
change from the everlasting pemmican.   Not that any one was
tired of pemmican.   All joined in its praises as the right food
for a journey, and wondered why the Government had never
used it in war time.   It must be equal or superior to the famous
Prussian sausage, judging of the latter as we needs must, without having lived on it for a month.   As an army marches on
its stomach, condensed food is an important object for the commissariat to consider, especially when, as in the case of the
British Army, long expeditions are frequently necessary.   Pemmican is good and palatable uncooked and cooked, though most
prefer it in the *réchaud* form.   It has numerous other recom-
mendations for campaign diet.   It keeps sound for twenty or
thirty years, is wholesome and strengthening, portable, and
needs no medicine to correct a tri-daily use of it.   Two pounds
weight, with bread and tea, we found enough for the dinner of
eight hungry men.   A bag weighing a hundred pounds is only
the size of an ordinary pillow, two feet long, one and a half
wide, and six inches thick.   Such a bag then would supply
three good meals to a hundred and thirty men.   Could the same
be said of equal bulk of pork ?   But as Terry indignantly remarked : " The British Gauvirmint won't drame of pimmican
till the Prooshians find it out."

Frank came back to dinner with one small trout though
Beaupré said that he and his mate last summer had caught an
hundred in two hours, some of them ten pounds in weight.
Perforce we dined on pemmican, and liked it better than ever.

The sun now shone out, making the day warm and pleasant,
as September usually is in America.   At 2 p.m. got into line
again to cross the long portage.   The course was westerly, by
the banks of the stream called the Medicine, at the mouth of

which we had dined.   A great part of the road was comparatively free from fallen timber, so that we enjoyed the novelty
of a trot, and, except near two creeks that ran into the Medicine,—free from the still worse obstruction of muskegs.   An
hour before sunset, the Medicine itself had to be crossed, and
on the other side of it was the bad muskeg.   Beaupré drew a
long face when he saw the river, for the recent rains had made
it turbid and swollen to an unusual height, and this argued ill
for the state of the ground on the other side.   For the first
mile, however, we got on well enough, as the road took advantage of a ridge for two-thirds of that distance ; but then came
the dreaded spot.   It looked no worse than the rest, but the
danger was unseen.   Deep holes formed by springs abounded
underneath the soft thick moss, in which horses would sink to
their necks.   The task was to find a line of sure ground, and
by avoiding Scylla not to fall into Charybdis.   As Valad with
Indian, and Brown with Scotch caution were trying the ground
all round, Beaupré, leading his horse by the bridle dashed in
close to the swollen river, at a most unlikely spot, exclaiming :
" I'll chance it, any way."   The words were only out of his lips
when he fell into a pool up to his middle ; but undismayed, he
scrambled out, and keeping close to beds of willow and alder,
actually found a way so good that the rest followed him.   Only
one pack-horse sank so hopelessly deep, into a hole, that he had
to be unpacked and lifted out, Beaupré hoisting by the tail with
a mighty hoist—for the man had the strength of a giant.   An
hour after sunset, we arrived at an ascent where it was possible to camp, though the bare blackened half-burnt poles all
round gave a cheerless aspect to the scene.   All were too tired
to be critical ; thankful besides that the worst was over, and
that to-morrow, according to Valad there would be " un beau
chemin."

   To-day we had travelled twenty miles, representing probably
fourteen on the map.   As more could not have been done, no

one grumbled, though all devoutly longed for a more modern rate of speed. Crossing muskegs, it is impossible to hurry horses, and when fallen timber cannot be jumped or scrambled over, a single tree on the path may necessitate a detour of fifty yards to make five. How the heavily laden pack-horses of the Hudson's Bay Company get along such a road, is rather a puzzle.

September 7th.—Away from camp at 6:45 A.M.; and in less than two hours came again in view of the McLeod;—narrower and much more like the child of the mountains than at the first crossing. Instead of sand bars as there, ridges and masses of rounded stones and boulders are strewn along its shores, or piled up with drifted trees and rubbish in the shallower parts of its bed. The trail led up stream near the bank, descending headlong to the river two or three times, and then ascending precipitous bluffs that tested the horses' wind severely. From these summits, views of a section of the Rocky Mountains, sixty or seventy miles away to the south-west, rewarded our exertions, and were the only thing that justified Valad's phrase of "beau chemin." The deep sides of the mountains and two or three of the summits were white with snow, and under the rays of the sun one part looked green and glacier-like. We should have crossed and then recrossed the McLeod hereabouts to escape the worst part of the road, but Valad, to his intense mortification, missed the point where the trail led off to the ford. There was nothing left therefore but to keep pegging away at the rate of a mile an hour, up and down hill, through thick underbrush of willows and aspens that had sprung up round the burnt spruce and cotton-wood, which still reared aloft their tall blackened shafts.

At 1 o'clock, we dined beside the river on the usual breakfast and supper fare, having travelled twelve or thirteen miles in six hours and a quarter. Muskegs and windfalls delayed us most, the former being always near creeks, and worse than the latter. The only hard ground was on the sandy or gravelly ridges separating the intervening valleys, and on these, windfalls had accumulated from year to year, so that the trail in many places was buried out of sight. While at dinner clouds gathered in the west and quickly overspread the whole sky. This hurried our movements, but the rain was on––with thunder and lightning—in ten minutes. After the first smart shower, a lull followed which the men took advantage of to pack the horses, drying their backs as well as possible before putting on the saddles.

A little after 3 P.M., we were on the march and on rather a better road. Heavy thunder showers broken by gleams of sunlight dispelling the leaden clouds from time to time, gave a sky of wonderful grandeur and colour. The river and the finely wooded hilly country beyond, for hereabouts too the opposite banks had escaped the ravages of fire—probably because there was no trail and no travelling on that side, displayed themselves in magnificent panoramic views from every bluff we climbed, while far to the west and south-west beyond the hills, masses of clouds concealing the mountains but assuming the forms and almost the solidity of the mountains, made an horizon worthy of the whole sky and of the foreground. At sunset we descended for the last time to the river, and skirting it for two miles or crossing to long islets where the current divided itself, reached a beautiful prairie and camped under the shade of a group of spruce and poplars. This was the point Valad had aimed for, as a good place for the Sunday rest, chiefly because of the feed ; and here we were to take leave of the McLeod, and cross to the Athabasca—

> " No more by thee our steps shall be
>   For ever and for ever,"

or at least until there is a better road. From the watershed of the McLeod to this point was less than eighty miles, and to get over that distance had occupied four and a half days of the

hardest travelling. The tally of the week was 120 miles, and
every one was satisfied with it because more could not have
been done. And when, on the only occasion in the week on
which spirits were used, the whole party gathered round the
camp-fire after supper to have the Saturday night toasts of
" wives and sweethearts" and "the Dominion and the Railroad,"
immediately after " the Queen," the universal feeling was of
thankful content that we had got on without casualties, and
that to-morrow was Sunday. The men being without water-
proofs had not an inch of dry clothing on them, but they dried
themselves at the big fire as if it was the jolliest thing in the
world to be wet. Valad, under the influence of a glass of the
mildest toddy, relaxed from his Indian gravity and taciturnity,
and smiled and talked benignantly. " When with gentlemen"
he was pleased to inform us, " he was treated like a gentleman ;
but when with others he had a hard time of it." Poor Valad !
what a lonely joyless life he lived, yet he did his duty like a
man, and bore himself with the dignity of a man who lived close
to and learned the lessons of nature. Some will blame us for
giving toddy to an Indian, or for taking it ourselves, and perhaps more severely for not suppressing all mention of the fact.
Our only answer is that a little did us good and we were thankful for the good, and that the one merit this diary aspires to is
to be a frank and truthful narrative. It would have been mean
to have left Valad out ; and to show an Indian that it was
possible to be temperate in all things, possible to use a stimulant without abusing it, seemed to us on the whole a better
lesson to enforce practically, than to have preached an abstinence that he would have misunderstood.

September 8th.—Another day of rest, with nothing to
chronicle save our ordinary Sunday routine. But no,—this is
doing great injustice to the Doctor who eclipsed all his former
efforts, in the way of providing medical comforts, by concocting
a plum-pudding for dinner. The Doctor's prescriptions smelled

of the pharmacopœia as little as possible. Was an old woman
that he met on the way complaining of " a wakeness ?" Send
her a pannikin of hot soup. Were Valad's legs inflamed by
rubbing all day against his coarse trowsers in the saddle ?
Make him a present of a pair of soft flannel drawers. Was a
good Father at the mission in failing health ? Fatten him up
with rich diet, even on fast days. And finally, were we all
desirous of celebrating a birth-day, and did the thought make
us a little homesick, the only sickness that our own party ever
suffered from ? Get up a plum-pudding for dinner.

But how ? We had neither bag, suet, nor plums. But we
had berry pemmican, and pemmican in its own line is equal to
shaganappi. It contained buffalo fat that would do for suet,
and berries that would do for plums. Only genius could have
united plum-pudding and berry pemmican in one mental act.
Terry contributed a bag, and when the contribution was
inspected rather daintily, he explained that it was the sugar
bag, which might be used, as there was very little sugar left for
it to hold. Pemmican, flour and water, baking soda, sugar and
salt were surely sufficient ingredients ; as a last touch the
Doctor searched the medicine-chest, but in vain, for tincture of
ginger to give a flavour, and in default of that, suggested
chlorodyne, but the Chief promptly negatived the suggestion,
on the ground that if we ate the pudding the chlorodyne might
be required a few hours after.

At 3 p.m. the bag was put in the pot, and dinner was ordered
to be at 5. At the appointed hour everything else was ready ;
the usual *pièce de résistance* of pemmican, flanked for Sunday
garnishing by two reindeer tongues. But as we gathered round,
it was announced that the pudding was a failure ; that it would
not unite ; that buffalo fat was not equal in cohesive power to
suet, and that instead of a pudding it would be only boiled
pemmican. The Doctor might have been knocked down with a
feather ; Frank was loud and savage in his lamentations ; but

the Chief advised "more boiling," as an infallible specific in such cases, and that dinner be proceeded with.   The additional half hour acted like a charm.   With fear and trembling the Doctor went to the pot ; anxious heads bent down with his ; tenderly was the bag lifted out and slit, and a joyous shout conveyed the intelligence that it was a success—that at any rate it had the shape of a pudding. Brown, who had been scoffing, was silenced ; and the Doctor conquered him completely by helping him to a double portion.   How good that pudding was !   A teaspoonful of brandy on a sprinkling of sugar made sauce ; and there was not one of the party who did not hold out his plate for "more," though, as the Doctor belonged to the orthodox school of medicine, the first helping had been no homœopathic dose. To have been perfect the pudding should have had more boiling ; but no one dared hint a fault, for was not the dish empty ?   We at once named the place Plum-Pudding Camp, and Brown was engaged on the spot to make a better if he could at the Yellow Head Pass Camp.

In all respects save weather the day was as pleasant as our former Sundays ; but gusts of wind blew the smoke of the fire into the tent, and the grass was too thoroughly soaked with rain for pleasant walking.   The sun struggled to come out, but scarcely succeeded, and towards evening a cold rain, that would be snow on the mountains, set in.   Valad had pitched a separate camp for himself under a grove of pines, that sheltered him beautifully from the wind and rain.   So cozy was it that during the day one after another resorted thither, for a pipe or a quiet read, when eyes could no longer endure the big tent's smoke.

The usual morning and evening services were attended by all.   Each time that we united as one body in worship, our thoughts were raised from earth, and the bond that united us became stronger.

September 9th.—Up very early this morning, but it was 7 before we said goodbye to Plum Pudding Camp and the McLeod

river.   In packing horses, the more haste the less speed.   Any
twist of the shaganappi omitted is sure to avenge itself at the
most inconvenient place.   And as none but Brown and Beaupré
could do this work, it took a long time.

The night had been cold, and the grass in the morning was
crisp with frost, but the sun rose bright and soon dissolved the
hoar into dew.   We started in high spirits, under the warm rays
of the sun, with good hopes of soon seeing the Athabaska.   The
trail to it leads up an intervale of the McLeod for a mile, and
then crosses a hilly portage thirteen miles long.   The portage
consists of ridges of gravel intermixed with clay, supporting a
growth of pines and spruce large enough for railway or building
purposes.   At the bottom of each ridge is a creek of clear cold
water, running over black muck or whitish clay.   Half way
across, a lake that empties into the Athabaska lies under the
shadow of the Foot Hills ; and from this point successive steep
descents lead to streams running in deep valleys over pebbly
beds, and through the woods glimpses are had of blue wooded
heights on the other side of the Athabaska.   Instead of going
directly west to the river, the trail winds more to the south,
ascending the river at a distance from it, and we thus missed
the large alluvial flat a little north called Le Grand Bas-fond,
where is the only good grass for miles. At 1 o'clock we got our
first sight of the Athabasca, from a high bluff, and beyond it to
the south-west, fifty miles off, but seemingly close at hand, the
Rocky Mountains covered with snow.   It was time to halt,
but the pasture under the pines and spruces was so scant that
it would have been a mockery to turn the horses loose.   We
resolved therefore to keep moving and make only one spell for
the day.   For two hours longer the patient creatures toiled on,
as willingly as when fresh ; the trail winding for five or six
miles up and down the steep banks of the river, and crossing
several mountain streams, and for the next five going along a
smooth terrace of shingle, now a hundred feet above the river,

but once its bed.   Here the trail was so good that, with few in-
terruptions the jog trot was maintained.   At length on a burnt
tract, rich heavy bunch-grass—enough for the night—showed,
and the trail descending to another bench only ten feet above
the present bed of the river, we camped on the lower and drove
the horses back to the upper terrace after watering them.   In
a continuous march of ten hours about twenty-five miles had
been travelled.

Valad shook his head when he saw the white peaks and the
river.   He had never known the former so covered with snow,
nor the latter so swollen at this season of the year.   There must
have been severe weather in the mountains, with the probable
consequence for us, that instead of fording we would have to
construct a raft opposite Jasper House.

The Athabasca at this early point of its course is nearly as
large as the Saskatchewan at Edmonton, of the same clay
colour, and running with a more rapid current.   It varies in
breadth according as it is hemmed in by cliffs of sandstones,
shales, and clay ; or as its shores expand into intervales or broad
terraces rising one above the other.   These successive terraces
are marked very distinctly in several places on both sides of the
stream.   Dr. Hector measured their heights with the aneroid
at Le Grand Bas-fond, and found that the three lowest and most
distinctly marked were fifteen, a hundred, and two hundred
and ten feet above the alluvial bottom of the valley, while one
still higher, not so uniformly distinct, was three hundred and
seventy feet.   These terraces are covered with spruce and pine.

From the terrace above our camp, the mountains seemed
immediately beyond the wood on the opposite side of the river.
They towered up in a grand silver-tipped line closing the western horizon so high up, that the sun always sets here more than
half an hour sooner than on the plains.

At length we had come to the bases of the Rocky Mountains,
and the sight of them was sufficient reward for all the toil of
the preceding fortnight.

While hacking with his axe at brush on the camping ground, just where our heads would lie, Brown struck something metallic that blunted the edge of the axe. Feeling with his hand he drew out from near the root of a young spruce tree, an ancient sword bayonet, the brazen hilt and steel blade in excellent preservation, but the leather scabbard half eaten as if by the teeth of some animal. It seemed strange in this vast and silent forest wilderness thus to come upon a relic that told, probably, of the old days when the two rival fur companies armed their agents to the teeth, and when bloody contests often took place between them. Brown presented the treasure trove to the Chief, for his museum, as a memento of the Athabasca, and from it, this our forty-fourth camp, since leaving Thunder Bay, received the name of Bayonet Camp.

To-night we rest under the protection of the Rocky Mountains.

CHAPTER VIII.

The Rocky Mountains.

September 10th.—The Athabasca fell six inches during the
night. Got away from camp at 7:30 A.M., and for two hours
had a delightful ride to Prairie River. The trail ran along a
terrace of shingle or alluvial flats, and was free from fallen
timber and muskegs. Most of the flowers were out of blossom,
but in the spring and summer these open meadow-like places
must be gay with anemones, roses, vetches, and a great variety
of compositæ—none now in bloom, except a light-blue aster
that had accompanied us from the North Saskatchewan, and all
the way through the wooded country. The burnt ground
shewed a brilliant crimson flower from which red ink is made,
and which we had seen on the Matawan.

Few, however, thought of plants to-day or of anything but
the mountains that stood in massive grandeur, thirty miles
ahead, but on account of the morning light, in which every
point came out clear, seemingly just on the other side of each
new patch of wood or bit of prairie before us.

They rose bold and abrupt five or six thousand feet from the
wooded country at their feet,—the western verge of the plains,
the elevation of which was over three thousand feet additional
above the sea,—and formed in long unbroken line across our
path, save where cleft in the centre down to their very feet, by

the chasm that the Athabasca, long ago forced, or found for itself. " There are no Rocky Mountains" has been the remark
of many a disappointed traveller by the Union and Central
Pacific Railways.   The remark will never be made by those
who travel on the Canadian Pacific ; there was no ambiguity
about these being mountains, nor about where they commenced.
The line was defined, and the scarp as clear, as if they had been
hewn and chiselled for a fortification.   The summits on one side
of the Athabasca were serrated, looking sharp as the teeth of a
saw ; on the other, the Roche à Myette, immediately behind
the first line, reared a great solid unbroken cube, two thousand
feet high, a " forehead bare," twenty times higher than Ben
An's ; and, before and beyond it, away to the south and west,
extended ranges with bold summits and sides scooped deep, and
corries far down, where formerly the wood buffalo, and the elk,
and now the moose, bighorn, and bear find shelter.   There was
nothing fantastic about the mountain forms.   Everything was
imposing.   And these too were ours, an inheritance as precious,
if not as plentiful in corn and milk, as the rich plains they
guarded.   For mountains elevate the mind, and give an inspi-
ration of courage and dignity to the hardy races who own them
and who breathe their atmosphere.

> For the strength of the hills we bless thee
> Our God, our fathers' God.
> Thou hast made our spirits mighty
> With the touch of the mountain sod.

The scene had its effect on the whole party.   As we wound
in Indian file along the sinuous trail, that led across grassy bas-
fonds under the shadow of the mountains that were still a day's
journey distant, not a word was heard, nor a cry to the horses
for the first half-hour.   Valad led the way, clad friar-like in
blue hooded capote which he wore all regardless of the fact that
the sun was shining ; Brown next, in rugged miner costume
half-leathern half-wollen, and Beaupré in the same with a

touch of colour added ; the Chief and the Doctor in their yellow
moose-hide jackets ; even Terry, who of late invariably brought
up the rear, ceased to howl " git out o' that " to the unfortunate
animal he sat upon, dropped his stick, and put his pipe in his
waistcoat pocket. He had seen Vesuvius, the Himalayas and
the Hill of Howth, but they were " nauthin to this." Before
us, at times, a grove of dark green spruce, and beyond the sombre wood, the infinitely more sombre grey of the mountains ;
where the wood had been burnt, the bare blackened poles
seemed to be only a screen hung before, half revealing, half
concealing, what was beyond. The mountains dwarfed and relieved everything else. There was less snow than had appeared
yesterday, the explanation being that the first and least elevated mountain range only was before us now that we were near,
whereas, when at a greater distance, many of the higher summits beyond had been visible.

Soon after crossing Prairie River, the trail led away to the
east from the Athabasca among windfalls of the worst kind, or
muskegs, and up and down steep banks. Little progress was
made for the next two hours, but the mountain air told so on
our appetites that at midday a halt of an hour and a half was
imperatively demanded, although it had to be on the borders of
a swamp among blackened poles.

After dinner we resumed the march and soon crossed another
Prairie River, formed apparently by the union of three streamlets, winding by different valleys down a wooded range that lies
at the foot of the mountains, and extends east by north for some
distance. The view of the mountains all this afternoon more
than made up for the difficulties of the road. Instead of being
clearly outlined, cold, and grey as in the morning, they appeared indistinct through a warm deep blue haze ; we had come
nearer, but they seemed to have removed further back.

When on the other side of Prairie River, the wooded range
from which it flowed was on our left, and the high wooded hills

beyond the Athabasca on our right. Woods and hills in front closed up the lower part of the gorge from which the Athabasca issued, and completely divided the Rocky Mountains into two ranges, right and left ; thus an amphitheatre of mountains closed round while we were making for the open that yawned right in front.

At 4.30 P.M., the order was given to camp ; Frank and Valad went off to hunt, and the Chief and the Secretary to climb a hill and note the surrounding country. Bear and fresh moose tracks were seen by the latter two, and fresh otter trails leading down into the river. On their return they fell in with Frank carrying a beaver ; he and Valad had fired at two and shot one. The Doctor in their absence had fished in primitive style, with a tent pole and twine and a hook baited with pemmican, and had caught two fine trout. Having this varied provision, supper without *réchaud* was unanimously decreed, and Valad set to work on the beaver and Terry on the fish. In fifteen minutes Valad had the animal skinned, boned, the whole of the meat stretched out in one piece on a brander of sticks and exposed to the fire to grill ; the tail on another stick, and the liver on a third. We waited impatiently for supper, the Secretary making toast of Terry's under-done bread to keep himself from murmuring. In due time everything was ready, and the five who had never tasted beaver, prepared themselves to sit in judgment. The verdict was favourable throughout ; the meat tender, though dry, the liver a delicious morsel, and the tail superior to moose-muffle. Within an hour after that beaver had been industriously at work on his dam, he formed part of the interior economy of eight different stomachs, and scarcely a scrap was left to show what he once had been. More sudden and complete metamorphosis is not in Ovid. The trout were excellent, so that it may be understood that a straight meal was made. In honour of the event of the evening, this, our forty-fifth, was named Beaver Camp.

Having lost an hour and a half of sunlight to-day, we made arrangements to start early to-morrow for a long spell.

This was to be our last night on the plains. To-morrow night we would be in the embrace of the mountains.

September 11th.—Away this morning at 6.15 A. M., and halted at 1 P. M., after crossing the Rivière de Violon or Fiddle river, when fairly inside the first range. It was a grand morning for mountain scenery. For the first three hours the trail continued at some distance east from the valley of the Athabasca, among wooded hills, now ascending, now descending, but on the whole with an upward slope, across creeks where the ground was invariably boggy, over fallen timber, where infinite patience was required on the part of horse and man. Suddenly it opened out on a lakelet, and right in front, a semi-circle of five glorious mountains appeared ; a high wooded hill and Roche à Perdrix on our left, Roche à Myette beyond, Roche Ronde in front, and a mountain above Lac Brulé on our right. For half a mile down from their summits, no tree, shrub, or plant covered the nakedness of the three that the old trappers had thought worthy of names ; and a clothing of vegetation would have marred their massive grandeur. The first three were so near and towered up so bold that their full forms, even to the long shadows on them, were reflected clearly in the lakelet, next to the rushes and spruce of its own shores. Here is scene for a grand picture equal to Hill's painting of the Yo Semite Valley. A little forther on, another lakelet reflected the mountains to the right, showing not only the massive grey and blue of the limestone, but red and green colourings among the shales that separated the strata of limestone. The road now descended rapidly from the summit of the wooded hill that we had so slowly gained, to the valley of the Athabasca. As it wound from point to point among the tall dark green spruces, and over rose bushes and vetches, the soft blue of the mountains gleamed through everywhere, and when the woods parted, the mighty column of Roche à Perdrix towered a mile above our heads, scuds of clouds kissing its snowy summit, and each plication and angle of the different strata up its giant sides was boldly and clearly revealed. We were entering the magnificent Jasper portals of the Rocky Mountains by a quiet path winding between groves of trees and rich lawns like an English gentleman's park.

Crossing a brook divided into half a dozen brooklets by willows, the country opened a little and the base and inner side of Roche à Perdrix were revealed ; but, it was still an amphi theatre of mountains that opened out before us, and Roche à Myette seemed as far off as ever. Soon the Rivière de Violon was heard brawling round the base of Roche à Perdrix and rushing on like a true mountain torrent to the Athabasca. We stopped to drink to the Queen out of its clear ice-cold waters, and halted for dinner in a grove on the other side of it, thoroughly excited and awed by the grand forms that had begirt our path for the last three hours. We could sympathise with the enthusiast, who returned home after years of absence, and when asked what he had as an equivalent for so much lost time,—answered : " I have seen the Rocky Mountains."

After dinner, a short walk enabled us to take bearings. The valley of the Athabasca from two to five miles wide, according as a sandy bas-fond or intervale along its shore varied in width, extended up to the west and south, guarded on each side by giant forms. We had come inside the range, and it was no longer an amphitheatre of hills, but a valley ever opening, and at each turn revealing new forms,, that was now before us. Roche Ronde was to our right, its stratification as distinct as the leaves of a half opened book. The mass of the rock was limestone, and what at a distance had been only peculiarly bold and rugged outlines, were now seen to be the different angles and contortions of the strata. And such contortions ! One high mass twisting up the sides in serpentine folds ; another bent in great waving lines, like petrified billows. The colouring, too, was all that artist could desire. Not only the dark green of the spruce in the corries, which turned into black when far up, but autumn tints of red and gold as high as vegetation had climbed on the hill sides ; and above that, streaks and patches of yellow, green, rusty red, and black, relieving the grey mass of limestone ; while up the valley, every shade of blue came out according as the hills were near or far away, and summits hoary with snow bounded the horizon.

There was a delay of three hours at dinner, because the horses, as if allured by the genii of the mountains, had wandered more than a mile up the valley ; but at four o'clock all was in order again and the march resumed. A wooded hill that threw itself out between Roches à Perdrix and à Myette had first to be rounded. This hill narrowed the valley, and forced the trail near the river. When fairly round it, Roche à Myette came full into view, and the trail led along its base.

Myette is the characteristic mountain of the Jasper valley. There are others as high, but its grand bare forehead is recognized everywhere. It is five thousand eight hundred feet above the valley, or over nine thousand feet above the sea. Doctor Hector with the agent in charge of Jasper House climbed to a sharp peak far above any vegetation, three thousand five hundred feet above the valley, but the great cubical block which formed the top towered more than two thousand feet higher. A hunter who has given his name to the mountain, is the only one that ever ascended this cube. He made the ascent from the south side, every other being absolutely inaccessible. Doctor Hector gives the following description of the composition of Myette : "It is composed of a mass of strata, which have at one time formed the trough of a huge plication, viz. :

ft.

(a) Hard compact blue limestone and shale, with nodules of iron pyrites.. } 2,000

	ft.
(b) Fossil shales almost black......... ….................. ……...	300
(c) Hard grey sandstone……........…. …. ….................…......	100
(d) Shales towards the upper part with green and red blotches	500
(e) Cherty limestone and coarse sandstone obscured by timber	3,000

The ridge we had ascended is formed of cherty limestone and capped by yellow shales with beds of black sandstone forming the highest point."

The views this afternoon from every new point were wonderfully striking. Looking back on Roche à Perdrix it assumed more massive proportions than when we were immediately beneath. A huge shoulder stretched up the valley, one side covered with bare poles grey as itself, and the other with sombre firs. From it the great summit upreared itself so conspicuously that it filled the back ground and closed the mouth of the valley. Valad in grave tones told the story of his old partner—an unfortunate half-breed—who, when hunting bighorn on its precipitous slopes, twenty-two years ago, was carried over one of them on a snow-slide and dashed in pieces.

A good photographer would make a name and perhaps a fortune, if he came up here and took views. At every step we longed for a camera. On the opposite side of the river a valley opened to the north, along the sides of which rose mountain after mountain with the clearly defined outlines that the secondary formation of the rocks gives to them. On the same side the Range from Roche Ronde was continued further up the Athabasca by a hump-shaped rock, and then by a vast mass, like a quadrilateral rampart, with only two sides of the square visible, the sides furrowed deep, but the line of the summit unbroken. At the base of this—Roche Suette—is Jasper's House, and opposite Roche Jacque's showed as great a mass, with two snow-clad peaks, while the horizon beyond seemed a continuous bank of snow on mountain ranges. But the most wonderful object was Roche à Myette, right above us on our left. That

imposing sphinx-like head with the swelling Elizabethan ruff of
sandstone and shales around the neck, save on one side where
a corrugated mass of party-coloured strata twisted like a coil
of serpents from far down nearly half way up the head, haunted
us for days.   Mighty must have been the forces that upreared
and shaped such a monument.   Vertical strata were piled on
horizontal, and horizontal again on the vertical, as if nature
had determined to build a tower that would reach to the skies.
As we passed this old warder of the valley, the sun was setting
behind Roche Suette.   A warm south-west wind as it came in
contact with the snowy summit formed heavy clouds, that threw
long black shadows, and threatened rain ; but the wind carried
them past to empty their buckets on the woods and prairies.

It was time to camp, but where ?   The Chief, Beaupré, and
Brown rode ahead to see if the river was fordable.   The rest
followed, going down to the bank and crossing to an island
formed by a slew of the river, to avoid a steep rock, the trail
along which was fit only for chamois or bighorn.   Here we
were soon joined by the three who had ridden ahead, and who
brought back word that the Athabasca looked ugly, but was
still subsiding, and might be fordable in the morning.   It
was decided to camp on the spot, and send the horses back a
mile for feed.   The resources of the island would not admit of
our light cotton sheet being stretched as an overhead shelter,
so we selected the lee side of a dwarf aspen thicket, and spread
our blankets on the gravel ; a good fire being made in front to
cook our supper and keep our feet warm through the night.
Some of us sat up late, watching the play of the moonlight on
the black clouds that drifted about her troubled face, as she
hung over Roche Jacques ; and then we stretched ourselves
out to sleep, on our rough but enviable couch, rejoicing in the
open sky for a canopy, and in the circle of great mountains that
formed the walls of our indescribably magnificent bed chamber.
It had been a day long to be remembered.   Only one mishap

had occurred ; the Chief's bag got a crush against a rock, and his flask, that held a drop of brandy carefully preserved for the next plum-pudding, was broken. It was hard, but on an expedition like this the most serious losses are taken calmly and soon forgotten.

September 2nd.—We slept soundly our first night in the mountains, and after a dip in the Athabasca and breakfast, Valad went off on horse-back to try the fords. Though the river had fallen six inches since last night, he found it still too deep for pack horses, and there was nothing for it but to construct a raft,—a work of some difficulty when there is no auger and only one axe to cut down the wood. We had time now to take a good view from our Island Camp. Looking forward, Roche Jacques closed the horizon on the left ; to his right and further up the river, the Pyramid Rock barred the way, a graceful conical shaped mountain like Schiehallion, but grander, his front-face a mass of snow. Between these two our road lay after crossing the river. Opposite the camp to the north, the hump of Roche à Bosche, stood out prominently ; separated from it by the Indian Snake River, and two or three miles further up stream, the great wall of Roche Suette, at the foot of which Jasper House is situated, blocked the western way.

The forenoon looked as if it meant rain. Sunrise gilded with fire the tops of the mountains ; but the light soon died away. Clouds and mists gathered round Roches Jacques and Suette, but hung there instead of coming down, and the white face of the Pyramid Rock, that divided the two, stood out clear and untouched by the rolling vapour.

The Chief made some pencil sketches, while the men went up stream a mile to a suitable part of the river and worked hard preparing a raft till 10.30 A.M., by which time they had enough logs for the purpose cut and carried down to the bank. Returning to camp for an early dinner of tea and cold pemmican, they then packed the horses, carried everything up to the

raft and unpacked there.   Fifteen or sixteen logs bound together by three strong crosspoles, and tied each to each with
folds of rope, composed the raft.   Between the crosspoles a
number of smaller ones were laid, to serve for a floor and keep
the luggage from getting wet.   The Chief and the two packers
were then left to manage the raft, and the rest stripped to the
middle and rode across—Centaur like—driving before them the
unsaddled pack-horses.   At the crossing the river is divided
by sand bars into three parts, and at two of these the water
reached to the pommel of the saddle.   All got over safely,
though there was some danger on account of the strength of the
current; and the raft followed, after a delay caused by the
weight of the cargo necessitating the addition of two big logs to
make the ship float lightly enough.   A ride of two miles took
us to Jasper's, where we arrived exactly fifteen days after leaving Edmonton, two of them days of rest and a third lost by the
obstruction of the Athabasca.   It is hardly fair to speak of it
as lost however, for there was no point at which the delay of a
day was so little unacceptable to us.   The mountains of the
Jasper valley would have repaid us for a week's detention.

  This station is now all but abandoned by the Hudson's Bay
Cy.   It was formerly of considerable importance, not only from
the number of fur-bearing animals around, but because it was
the centre of a regular line of communication between Norway
House and Edmonton on the one side, and the Columbia District and Fort Vancouver on the other.   An agent and three or
four men were then stationed at it all the year round.   Even in
Dr. Hector's time the house must have been of a somewhat pre-
tentious order, for he speaks of it as " constructed after the
Swiss style, with overhanging roofs and trellised porticoes."
Now there are only two log houses, the largest propped up before and behind with rough shores, as if to prevent it being
blown away into the river or back into the mountain gorges.
The houses are untenanted, locked and shuttered.   Twice a year

an agent comes up from Edmonton to trade with the Indians of the surrounding country and carry back the furs.

The Chief expected to meet at this point, or to hear some tidings of one of his parties that had been instructed to explore from the Pacific side of the mountains in the direction of the Jasper valley. As no trace of any recent visit could be found, we moved on up the Athabasca ; the trail leading along the sandy beach of Lake Jasper for two miles to a little opening on the hill side above, where as there was a species of small bunch-grass growing, and no one knew of feed farther on, camp was pitched for the night.

Our four miles' travel to-day on the west bank of the river was a succession of magnificent mountain views. After crossing the Athabasca the valley of Rocky River, which runs into it, opposite Jasper House, opened out extending away to the south-east, bordered on both banks by ranges of serrated bare peaks, while seemingly in the very centre rose a wooded conical hill. Round all these, masses of mist were enfolding themselves, and the sun shining at the same time brought out the nearest in clear relief.

Jasper House itself is one of the best places for seeing to advantage the mountains up and down the valley. It is situated on a pretty glade that slopes gently to the Athabasca, sufficiently large and open to command a view in every direction. Roche à Myette, distant five or six miles, is half concealed by intervening heights and is here less conspicuous than elsewhere even when seen from greater distances, but a gleam of sunlight brightens his great face and makes even it look lightsome. A score of miles to the south, the Pyramid Rock gracefully uplifts its snowy face and shuts in the valley, the space between being filled by the mountains of Rocky River and the great shoulders of Roche Jacques. Looking westerly, and behind the House, is Suette, his rampart rising cold, stern, and grey above his furrowed sides. Other peaks overhang the

valley to the north, and between them deep wooded valleys are
dark as night. Separated from these by the Snake Indian
River, the true proportions of Roche à Bosche are seen for the
first time. Away to the south the masses of snow on the Pyramid speak of coming winter.

There is a wonderful combination of beauty about these
mountains. Great masses of boldly defined bare rock are united
to the beauty that variety of form, colour, and vegetation give.
A noble river with many tributaries, each defining a distinct
range, and a beautiful lake ten miles long, embosomed three
thousand three hundred feet above the sea, among mountains
twice as high, offer innumerable scenes, seldom to be found
within the same compass, to the artist.

Valad informed us that the winter in this quarter is wonderfully mild, considering the height and latitude ; that the Athabasca seldom if ever freezes here, and that wild ducks remain
all the year instead of migrating south, as birds farther east
invariably do. The lake freezes, but there is so little snow that
travellers prefer fording the river to trusting to the glare ice.

Our tent was pitched among firs on a slope above Lake
Jasper. Gusts of wind came from every point in the compass,
and blew about the sparks in a way dangerous to the blankets,
but before we were well asleep rain began to fall and dispelled
all apprehensions on the score of fire.

September 13th.—The rain that had been brewing yesterday
came down last night in torrents. One awakened to find the
boots at his head full of water ; the feet of another, the head of
a third, the shoulders of a fourth, were in pools according to the
form of the ground, or the precautions that each had taken
before turning in. The clouds were lifting, however, and
promised a fine day, and nobody cared for a little wetting, but
everybody cared very much, when the Chief announced that
the flour bag was getting so light that it might be necessary to
allowance the bread rations. That struck home, though there
was abundance of pemmican and tea.

The trail led along Lake Jasper and was so good that we made the west end of the lake, which is ten miles long, in two hours. Practically we were now without a guide; for Valad had not been beyond Jasper House for twenty years, and twice before dinner he missed the trail. Every mile we advanced revealed new features. Roche Jacques rises on the opposite side of the lake, and one deep valley in his sides would be bright as an autumn garden, up to the line of snow; the next, sombre with firs. Each of those valleys is seamed transversely by a number of streamlets, that divide it into a succession of plateaux rising higher and higher till the wall of steep bare rock is reached.

But there is no sharp line dividing vegetation from the naked rock. A belt of harder rock intervening breaks the forest; one or two hundred feet above, the trees may reappear in a long thin streak along the side of the mountain, like a regiment in line, or in a dense grove, like a column; and a different stratification above stops them again. The same change of strata probably accounts for the absence of snow from belts which have snow above and beneath them; far away these bare belts look like highways winding round the mountain. Behind, Myette reared his head over us, seemingly as near as ever; the Pyramid Mountain supported by a great rampart of rock, from which his lofty head rose gracefully, still closed the view; and a cluster of snow clad peaks surrounded him at a respectful distance. From time to time we passed through woods growing along the sides of burns rushing down into the lake. The woods prepared us for fresh prospects beyond, so that the eye had a perpetual feast.

At one point the trail led up some steep rocks, and from these charming views of the lake and the mountains were had. Towards the west end, a lakelet, separated from lake Jasper by two low narrow pine clad ridges, presented in its dark green waters, that reflected the forest, a striking contrast to the light sunny grey of the larger lake reflecting the sky.

Rounding the lake, the trail was encumbered with fallen timber, and from this point to the halting place for dinner at two o'clock we travelled slowly, doing altogether not more than eighteen or nineteen miles in the seven and a quarter hours. At the end of Lake Jasper, a strath, from two to five miles wide, which may still be called the Jasper Valley, bends to the south. Our first look up this valley showed new lines of mountains on both sides, closed at the head by a great mountain so white with snow that it looked like a sheet suspended from the heavens. That, Valad said, was " La montagne de la grande traverse," adding that the road to the Columbia country up the formidable Athabasca Pass, lay along its south-eastern base, while our road would turn west up the valley of the River Myette. He mentioned the old local titles of the mountains on this side, but every passer-by thinks that he has a right to give his own and his friends' names to them over again.

In going through the woods we saw several broken traps. This was a famous place in the olden times for trappers, and on that account a foaming torrent that comes down between Pyramid Rock and three great crags to the north, like Salisbury Crags, Edinburgh, on a large scale, is called Snaring River.

Some of the timber here is three feet in diameter, chiefly fir, but near Snaring River a growth of small pines has sprung up on burnt ground.

This torrent will be remembered by us because of the danger in crossing it, and because beside it we found the first traces of one of the parties we expected to meet in the Jasper valley. It is a foaming mountain torrent, with a bed full of large round boulders which it piles along its banks, or hurls down its bed to the Athabasca. These make the footing so precarious that if a horse falls, there is little hope for him or his rider. Valad crossed first. As the water came up to his horse's shoulder, and the horse stumbled several times, it was evidently risky. Just at

this moment, Brown who had gone down stream to look for
another ford, called out that he saw footprints of men and horses.
Off went the Chief, and at the same moment Valad screamed
across the torrent that white men had just been there.   All
followed the Chief, and Valad came back at a lower crossing.
The traces of three men and three shod horses (showing
that they did not belong to Indians) were clearly made out
going down in the direction of the Athabaska ; but though
guns were fired as a signal, no response was heard ; and the
word was passed to cross at the lower ford.   Beaupré took
some pemmican in his pocket, as a precaution, in case all hands
but himself were lost ; notwithstanding the omen, we reached the
other side safely, and pushed across a pine flat, and then a
quaking bog like Chatmoss to a little lake, with treacherous
quicksands on its shore and in its bed.   On the other side is an
extensive sandy bas-fond where we halted for dinner, sorely
regretting that the men who were on their way to Jasper's for
the very purpose of meeting us, had missed us by being on a
different trail or on no trail, for as the old one had been burnt
over, neither party had found it.   But the packs were scarcely
off the horses' backs when a Shuswap Indian rode up the bank
so quietly, that he was in our midst before we saw him, and
after the usual hand-shaking, delivered a slip of paper to the
Chief.   Hurrah ! it was from Moberly, and stated that he had
just struck fresh tracks and had sent back this Indian to learn
who we were.   Valad spoke to the Indian in Cree, and Beaupré in French, but he was from the Pacific side and only shook
his head in answer.   Brown then tried him in Chinook, a barbarous lingo of one or two hundred words, first introduced by
the Hudson's Bay agents, for common use among themselves
and the Pacific Indians ; and generally spoken now all through
Oregon, B. Columbia, and the north, by whites, Chinese, Indians, and all nationalities.   The Shuswap's face brightened,
and he answered in Chinook to the effect that Moberly was five

or six miles back : that they had come three days' journey from their big camp, where there were lots of men and horses. Brown asked if they had enough to eat at the camp ; " Oh ! hy-iu, muck â muck ! hy-iu iktahs !" " Lots of grub, lots of good things"—was the ready answer. He was offered some pemmican and took it, but said that he had never seen such food before. A note was at once sent back to Moberly that we would move on, and that he would probably overtake us on the morrow.

After dinner the march was resumed for seven miles up the valley. On the east side a succession of peaks resembling each other with the exception of one—Roche à Bonhomme—hemmed us in : while on the west, with lines of stratification parallel to lines on the east side, the solid rampart at the base of the Pyramid rose so steep and high, that the snowy summit behind could not be seen. The valley still averaged from two to five miles wide, though horizontal distances are so dwarfed by the towering altitude of the naked massive rocks on both sides, that it seemed to be scarcely one fourth of that width. What a singularly easy opening into the mountains, formed by some great convulsion that had cleft them asunder, crushed and piled them up on each side like cakes of ice, much in the same way as may be seen in winter on the St. Lawrence or any of our rivers, on a comparatively microscopic scale, in ice-shoves ! The Athabasca finding so plain a course had taken it, gradually shaped and finished the valley, and strewn the bas-fonds, which cross-torrents from the hills have seamed and broken up. It looks as if nature had united all her forces to make this the natural highway into the heart of the Rocky mountains.

Myette and all his companions of the first range, that had become so familiar to us in the last few days, were completely hidden by the turn of the Athabasca ; and the mountains ahead, that had shown at the bend, were also hidden from view ; but at sunset we came to another bend that the river makes again to the west, and *La grande montagne de la traverse* came fully out in his snowy raiment, and the Pyramid peeped over the great wall, that girds his body and flows down over his feet, to see our backs. We turned with the river and, after going another mile encumbered with fallen timber, camped on a terrace overlooking the river and surrounded on all sides with snow-capped mountains. As this was to be our last night by the Athabasca, and perhaps the last on the eastern slope of the mountains, we named this camp, the forty-eighth from Lake Superior, Athabasca."

September 14th.—The trail this morning led along the Athabasca for seven miles, to where the Myette runs into it, opposite the old Henry House. With the exception of a difficulty soon after starting, caused by the disappearance of the trail near the river, and the forcing a path through thick brush till we found it again, the road was excellent ; passing for four or five miles over beautiful little " prairies," which had not been touched as yet by the frost, and on which bunch grass grew,—and for the next two or three miles through pines, so well apart from one another that it was easy to ride in any direction. The day was warm and sunny, and the black flies that had left us for a week reappeared here. This valley, which seemed as beautiful on the other side of the river, is so completely sheltered, that the winter in it must be very mild.

The highest mountains that we had yet seen, showed this morning away to the south in the direction of the Athabasca Pass, and " the Committee's Punch Bowl." This Pass is seven thousand feet high, and snow lies on its summit all the year round, but our road led westward up the Myette ; and, as the Athabasca here sweeps away to the south, under the name of Whirlpool river, the turn shut out from view for the rest of our journey, both the valley and the mountains of the Whirlpool.

With the Myette bad roads began again. Just as they com-

menced, Moberly caught up to us, having ridden on in advance
of his men. He had left Victoria, Vancouver's Island, for the
Columbia, having organized large provision-trains in the spring
on pack-horses, and brought them on over incredible difficulties to " Boat Encampment," at the most northerly bend of the
Columbia. From Boat Encampment they were to cross to the
Athabasca Pass and move on to the Jasper valley, to afford
autumn and winter supplies to the parties operating from that
centre. He himself had crossed in advance direct to the lake
on the other side of the Yellow Head Pass, where he met one
of the parties under his command, making a trail in the direction of the Pass from the west. Hearing nothing about us
from them, he had loaded three horses with flour and bacon,
and come on to meet us; but by taking the river trail from
Snaring River, he had missed us yesterday. Except the two
Iroquois on the MacLeod, his was the first face we had seen
since leaving St. Ann's, and to meet him was like re-opening
communication with the world, although we, and not he, had
the latest news to give.—How welcome he was, we need not
say !

The first five miles up the Caledonian valley, as the valley of
the Myette is called in the old maps and in Dr. Hector's journals, we made in about three hours, and a little after midday
halted for dinner. Fallen timber was the principal cause of the
slow rate, though the steep sharp rocks hurt the horses so much,
that they had to tread softly and slowly. The rocks are hard
rough sandstone, with a slaty or a peculiar pebbly fracture.
The trail so far was scarcely worthy of the bad name travellers
had given to it, and we began to imagine that the remaining
fifteen miles to the Yellow Head Pass could be made before
nightfall. Moberly quietly said that it was a fond imagination,
and that if the next five miles were got over by dark he would
be satisfied, as it had taken him a whole day to make seven
miles on his way down. Myette has such unpretending portals,

especially when compared with the magnificent ranges about the Athabasca, it's current is so quiet near the mouth, and the valley so short that no one would forecast any formidable difficulties, in ascending it to the Pass. But the afternoon proved that the valley is worthy of its old name Caledonian, if the name was meant to suggest the thistle or the " wha' daur meddle wi' me !"

The Myette has a wonderful volume of water for its short course. It rushes down a narrow valley fed at every corner by foaming fells from the hill-sides, and by several large tributaries. A short way up from its mouth it becomes simply a series of rapids or mad currents, hurling along boulders, trees and debris of all kinds. The valley at first is uninteresting, but five miles up and for much of the rest of the way, is picturesque, two prominent mountains, that rise right above the Pass and the lake at the summit, closing it in at its head.

Moberly's three men and horses came up as we were rising from dinner, and they passed on ahead, axes in hand, to improve the trail a little. It certainly needed all the improvement it got, and a good deal more than they could give in an afternoon. Long swamps that reminded us of the muskegs on the McLeod, covered with an under-brush of scrub birch, and tough willows eight to ten feet high, that slapped our faces, and defiled our clothing with foul-smelling marsh mud, had to be floundered through. Alternating with these, intervened the face of a precipice, the rocky bed and sides of the river, or fallen timber stumps and blackened poles, to climb, scramble over, or dodge. No wonder that Milton and Cheadle bade adieu to the unkindly Myette with immense satisfaction. We had to cross and recross the river or parts of it seven or eight times in the course of the afternoon, for the train sought low levels and avoided ascending the bluffs and walls of rugged rock that rise sheer from the water. The middle ten miles of the Caledonian valley present formidable difficulties for a road of any kind.

Four hours' hard work took us over five miles, and by that time every one was heartily sick of it, and full of longing to reach Moberly's camp. As we stumbled about on a patch recently burnt over, one of his Indians, whom he had thoughtfully sent back, met and guided us to a desolate looking spot, the best camping ground he had been able to find. Some little grass had sprung up on the blackened soil, and no one was disposed to be particular. Supper was left in the hands of Tim— Moberly's Indian cook—and he prepared a variety of delicacies that made up for all other deficiencies ; bread light as Parisian rolls, Columbia flour being as different from Red River as Tim's baking from Terry's ; delicious Java coffee, sweetened with sugar from the Sandwich Islands, that now supply great part of the Pacific coast with sugar ; and crisp bacon, almost as great a luxury to us as pemmican to Moberly's men. All the hardships of the afternoon were forgotten as the aroma of the coffee steamed up our nostrils, and when Tim announced that he had oatmeal enough to make porridge for breakfast, our luck in meeting him was declared to be wonderful, and Caledonia Camp was voted the jolliest of our forty-nine. An hour after, the united party gathered round the kettle to drink the three Saturday night toasts, with three times three and one cheer more.

Consulting Moberly about the programme for next day, he advised that we should move on in the morning four miles to the last recrossing of the river, and rest there for the day, for the two reasons, that by so doing we would get good feed for the horses, and probably fall in with the camp of his trail makers, who worked in advance of the surveying party. Both reasons were so good that the advice was taken *nem. con.*

September 15.—Had the promised porridge for breakfast, and found it quite up to our anticipations. Left the Caledonia Camp at eight a.m. for our Sabbath day's journey. As every one needed rest and was tired of the Myette and its swamps, willows and rocks, the sight of the crossing was hailed with general joy, and all the more when those in front called out that there was a fresh trail on the other side. Sure enough, as Moberly had expected, the trail party had reached the river, and their camp was only a quarter of a mile off. Our difficulties had come to an end, we supposed, for there would be a reasonably good trail now all the way to Kamloops; and the North Thompson canyons need no longer be dreaded. The conclusion proved to be somewhat hasty, but it cheered us at the time. We rode up to the camp, and gave and received hearty greetings. An old-countryman named McCord was at the head of the trail party. He had pitched tents for the Sunday rest on a gentle incline beside the river, which flowed without rapids all the way from our last camp. We had been at the entrance of the Yellow Head Pass then, for though the actual summit is six miles farther west than where we met McCord, there was little of a rise from our last night's camp. The two mountains that we had seen from near the bottom of the valley, closing its head, now appeared as the southern peaks of a noble ridge that bounded the pass to the north. The nearer to us of the two was almost conical and the other resembled the frustum of a cone, serrated into a number of peaks, like a cross-cut saw, the big teeth in the centre and the small ones at the ends. These two mountains on which the snow rests the whole year are still nameless. As to the most prominent points on the Canadian Pacific Railway, we would suggest that the statesmen who have been most identified with the project should have the honour of giving names to them.

After a hearty lunch, on pork and beans—favourite dish of miners and axemen—divine service was held. The congregation consisted of twenty-one men, including English, Scotch, Irish, Indians from both sides of the Rocky Mountains, and representatives of all the six provinces of the Dominion. We joined in singing Old Hundred and in common prayer, and a sermon was

then preached—not very short on the plea that the majority of
the congregation had not heard a sermon for three months.
As usual the worship had the effect of awakening hallowed
associations, and making us feel united in a common sacred
life. In the evening all hands of their own accord gathered
round our tent to share in the family worship.

McCord had selected his camping ground judiciously. Good
wood, water, and pasture in his immediate neighbourhood; a
beautiful slope covered with tall spruce, amid which the tents
were scattered; an open meadow and low wooded hills to the
northwest round which the low line of the pass winding in the
same direction, could easily be made out; and the horizon,
bounded by a bold ridge which threw out its two great peaks to
overhang the pass. This was one of the most picturesque spots
in the Caledonian Valley, combining a soft lowland and wood-
land beauty, with stern rocky masses, capped with eternal
snow. We were 3,700 feet above the sea, but the air was soft
and warm. Even at night it was only pleasantly cool. We
were all delighted with this our first view of the Yellow Head
Pass. Instead of contracted canyon or savage torrent raging
among beetling precipices as we had half feared, the Pass is
really a pleasant open meadow. So easy an ingress into the
heart of the Rocky Mountains as that by the Jasper Valley, and
so favourable a pass as the Yellow Head could hardly have
been hoped for.

Dinner was ordered for six o'clock and Brown set to work on
his pemmican plum pudding. It had to be made so large, that
at six o'clock it required at least another hour's boiling. Fortunately McCord's cook, in ignorance of what Brown was about,
had prepared at his fire a genuine old fashioned plum-pudding;
and full justice was done to this, till the pemmican one was
ready. It was then proposed to keep it for breakfast, but the
Dr. was impatient to put Brown's skill to the proof, and an
hour after dinner, all gathered around our tent, to try the

second pudding and decide on Brown's reputation. Terry in preparing the sauce had used salt instead of sugar, and the Dr. was accused of having put him up to the mistake to spoil the dish ; but the pudding was a decided success, though eaten under the great disadvantage of no one being very hungry. Altogether this was a great day. The pleasure of meeting friends, of believing that our difficulties were practically at an end, the establishment of communication with the Pacific parties, the beauty or the prospect, the general good feeling, the quiet Sunday rest, the common worship, all contributed to heighten our enjoyment ; and to make us rise from our second plum pudding with the plough boy's sentiment in our hearts if not on our lips : " I'm fu,' and as thankfu'."

CHAPTER IX.

Yellow Head Pass to the North Thompson River.

September 16.—Our aim to-day was to reach Moose Lake where Mohun's party was surveying. The distances given us were : six miles to the summit of the Pass, six thence to Yellow Head Lake, four along the Lake, and fourteen to Moose Lake. These we found to be correct except the last which is more like sixteen than fourteen, and unfortunately Mohun's party was near the west end of Moose Lake, and this added eight more, so that instead of thirty, we had to do forty. Besides, not having been informed that the second half of the trail was by far the worst, no extra time was allowed for it, and hence we had five hours of night travelling that knocked up horses and men, more than a double day's ordinary work would have done. The day began well and ought to have ended well, but instead of that, it will always be associated in our minds with the drive to Oak Point from the North-west Angle on July 30th. Worse cannot be said of it.

The first half of the day was more like a pleasure trip than work. The six miles to the summit were almost a continuous level, the trail following the now smooth-flowing Myette till the main branch turned north, and then a small branch till it too was left among the hills. A few minutes after, the sound of a rivulet running in the opposite direction over a red pebbly bottom was heard. We had left the Myette flowing to the Arctic Ocean, and now came upon this, one of the sources of the Fraser hurrying to the Pacific. At the summit, Moberly welcomed us into British Columbia, for we were at length out of " No-man's land," and had entered the western province of our Dominion. Round the rivulet running west, the party gathered, and drank from its waters to the Queen and the Dominion. No incline could be more gentle than this from the Atlantic and Arctic to the Pacific slope. The road wound round wooded banks, a meadow with heavy marsh grass extending to the opposite hill. There had been little or no frost near the summit, and flowers were in bloom that we had seen a month ago farther east. The flora was of the same character on both sides of the summit; eight or nine kinds of wild berries, vetches, asters, wild honey-suckle, &c. Good timber, the bark of which looked like hemlock, but that the men called pine, covered the ground for the next few miles to Yellow Head Lake. This beautiful sheet of water, clear and sparkling up to its firm pebbly beach, expanding and contracting as its shores recede or send out promontories, was called Cowdung Lake formerly, but ought to bear the same name as the Pass. Towards the western end where we halted for dinner, its woods have been marred by fires that have swept the hill sides, but wherever these have kept off, its beauty is equal to, though of a different kind from, Lake Jasper. Low wooded hills intersected with soft green and flowery glades rise in broken undulations from its shores. Above and behind the hills on the south side, towers a huge pinnacle of rock, the snow on whose summit is generally concealed by clouds or mist. On the north, the two mountains that we had seen yesterday, bounding the pass on that side, and which had been hidden all the forenoon by the woods at their base, through which the trail runs, now looked out from right over our heads ; riven masses of stratified rock, in a slightly curved line, forming a gigantic cross-cut saw. Through the Pass, slate cropped out in several places, and boulders of granite strewed the ground, but granite was not observed *in situ*. Probably, slate is what gold miners term the bed rock, and Brown and Beaupré pointed out quartz veins that they had no doubt were gold-bearing.

After dinner the trail, from the nature of the soil, was so rough that the horses could go only at a walk of three miles an hour. It ran either among masses of boulders, or through new woods, where the trees and willows had been cut away, but their sharp stumps remained. It was dark before we reached the east end of Moose Lake, and if all our party had been together, we would certainly have camped beside one of the many tributaries of the Fraser, that run down from the mountains on both sides, after it emerges from Yellow Head Lake, and make it a deep strong river before it is fifteen miles long. One of those mountain feeders that we crossed was an hundred feet wide, and so deep and rapid in two places, that the horses waded across with difficulty. Our company, however, was un_ fortunately separated into three parts, and no concerted action could be taken. Moberly and the Doctor had ridden ahead to find Mohun's Camp and have supper ready ; the pack-horses followed three or four miles behind them ; and the Chief, Frank, and the Secretary were far in the rear, botanising and sketching. Every hour we expected to get to the Camp, but the road seemed endless. In the dense dark woods, the moon's light was very feeble, and as the horses were done out, we walked before or behind the poor brutes, stumbling over loose boulders, tripped up by the short sharp stumps and rootlets, mired in deep moss springs, wearied with climbing the steep ascents of the lake's sides, knee-sore with jolts in descending, dizzy and stupid from sheer fatigue and want of sleep. A drizzling rain had fallen in showers most of the afternoon, and it continued at intervals through the night ; but our exertions heated us so much that our clothes became as wet, on account of the waterproofs not allowing perspiration to evaporate, as if we had been thrown into the lake ; and thinking it less injurious to get wet from without than from within, we took off the waterproofs, and let the whole discomfort of the rain be added to the other discomforts of the night.   The only consolation was that the full moon shone out occasionally from rifts in the clouds, and enabled us to pick a few steps and avoid some difficulties.   At those times the lake appeared at our feet, glimmering through the dark firs, and shut in two or three miles beyond by precipitous mountains, down whose sides white torrents were foaming, the noise of one or another of which sounded incessantly in our ears till the sound became hateful.

At length the camp-fire glimmered in the distance.   But to crown this disastrous day, there was no feed about Mohun's camp, and his horses had left a few days previously for Tête Jaune Cache.   His men had a raft made on which to transport their luggage and instruments up to the east end of the lake, as their first work for to-morrow.   They had completed the survey along the west end and centre.   Our poor horses most of which had now travelled eleven hundred miles, and required rest or a different kind of work, had had a killing day of it, and there was no grass for them.   Reflecting on the situation was not pleasant, but a good supper of corned-beef and beans made us forget our own fatigue.   After supper, at 2 p.m., wrapping dry blankets round our wet clothes, and spreading waterproofs over the place where there were fewest pools of water, we went in willingly for sweet sleep.

The Doctor had completely forgotten his fatigue before our arrival under the influence of a present of the spoon and fishing line of Milton and Cheadle's " Headless Indian."   One of the packers had found the skeleton, and had also found the head lying under a fallen tree, a hundred and fifty yards from the body. As the body could not have walked away and sat down minus the head, the explanation of the packers was that Cheadle's Assiniboine on his unsuccessful hunt for game had killed and eaten the Shuswap, and turned the affair into a mystery by hiding the head. Poor Mr. O'B., of whom we heard enough at Edmonton to prove that his portraiture is faithfully given in " the North-west Passage by land," will accept this solution of the mystery if no one else will. The Doctor put the old horn spoon, and the fishing line—a strong native hemp line, among his choicest treasures, and took minute notes of the position of the grave that he might dig up the head.

The two descriptions in Milton and Cheadle that have been generally considered apocryphal, and that have discredited the whole book to many readers, are those concerning Mr. O'B., and the headless Indian. Not only did we find both verified, but the accounts of the country and the tale of their own difficulties are as truthfully and simply given as it was possible for men who travelled in a strange country, chiefly in quest of adventures that they intended to publish, and who naturally wished to get items with colour for their book. The pluck that made them conceive, and the vastly greater pluck that enabled them to pull through such an expedition was of the truest British kind. They were more indebted than they perhaps knew as far as " Slaughter Camp," to the trail of the Canadians who had preceded them, on their way to Cariboo ; but from that point, down the frightful and unexplored valley of the North Thompson, the journey had to be faced on their own totally inadequate resources. Had they but known it, they were beaten as completely as by the rules of war the British troops were at Waterloo. They should have submitted to the inevitable and starved. But luckily for themselves and for their readers they did not know it ; and thanks to Mrs. Assiniboine, and their own intelligent hardihood that kept them from giving in, they succeeded where by all the laws of probabilities they ought to have disastrously failed.

We had now crossed the first range of the Rocky Mountains, and were on the Pacific slope, on the banks of the river that runs into the Pacific Ocean.   One or two of our party seemed to think that difficulties were therefore at an end ; that all that had to be done now was to follow the Fraser to its mouth, as so great a river would be sure to find the easiest course to the sea.   A party of gentlemen ignorant of the geography of the country, and deserted by their guides in endeavouring to cross the Rocky Mountains a few years ago, farther south, argued similarly when they struck the Columbia River.   " So great a river cannot go wrong : its course must be the best ; let us follow it to the sea."   And they did follow its northerly sweep round the Kootanie or Selkirk mountains, for one or two hundred miles, till inextricably entangled among fallen timber, and cedar swamps, they resolved to kill their horses, make rafts or canoes, and trust to the river.   Had they carried this plan out, they would have perished, for no raft or canoe can get through the terrible canyons of the Columbia.   But fortunately two Suswap Indians came upon them at this juncture, and though not speaking a word that they knew, made them understand by signs, that their only safety was in retracing their steps, and by getting round the head waters of the Columbia, reach Fort Colville by the Kootanie Pass.

Just as the Columbia has to sweep round the Selkirk group, so in a similar way far north or north-west, the Fraser loops round the Gold Mountains.   Those two groups may be considered one, with a gap or long break between the northern bend of the Columbia and the point called Tête Jaune Cache, where the Fraser has to turn to the north.   It is evident then that the true course for a traveller, from Yellow Head Pass to the west, since he cannot cross the Gold Mountains, which stretch in line across his direct path, is to turn south-east a little, try for a road by this gap, and overcome the Gold Mountains by flanking them.

The reader must understand that besides intervening groups and spurs with distinct names, and important enough to be often considered distinct ranges, there are two main mountain chains that have to be traversed in going to the Pacific,—the Rocky Mountains proper and the Coast Chain or Cascades. These two run apparently parallel to each other, but they really converge towards the north till they ultimately become one chain. "The distance between the axis of the two chains on the line of the Union and Central Pacific Railways is about 900 miles, while on the lines surveyed for the Canadian Pacific it varies from 300 to 400 miles." With regard to a passage over or through these great ranges, the railway in the United States has to climb to plateaux that are nearly as high as the summits. On Canadian territory the mountains themselves are higher than in the south, but they are cloven by river passes. We have seen how easy is the passage from the east through the Rocky Mountains proper by the valleys of the Athabasca and Myette. The average height of the mountains above the sea is nine thousand feet; but the height of the Yellow Head Pass is only three thousand seven hundred feet. On each side of the valleys the mountains act as natural snow-sheds.

Is there a similar pass through the Cascades? Passes in abundance, but unfortunately not one like the Yellow Head. We can get to the Cascades only by a long detour north or south, and the nearer we get the more formidable they look. And first, how to reach them? We follow the Fraser from the Yellow Head Pass, to Tête Jaune Cache. There we expect to see the Gold range stretching in unbroken line before us, forcing the Fraser far to the north, and us somewhat to the south-east and then the south. Oh! for a direct cut through to the Cariboo gold fields like that which the Athabasca cleaves the Rocky Mountains with! In the mean time our course from

Tête Jaune Cache, will be to slip in between the Gold and Selkirk groups till we strike the North Thompson, and continue
the flanking process, by going down its banks southerly till we
get to Kamloops at the junction of the North and South Thompson, where we can recommence our westerly course, along the
comparatively low lying fertile plateau, extending between the
western slope of the first chain and the Cascades. West of this
plateau we rejoin the Fraser, and accompany it through the
Cascades to the Sea.

September 17.—We are now in the heart of the Rocky
Mountains, nearly a day's journey on from Yellow Head Pass,
with jaded horses, and a trail so heavy that fresh horses cannot
be expected to average more than twenty miles of travel per
day.

This morning the consequences of last night's toil and
trouble showed plainly by a multitude of signs. Breakfasted
at 9 A. M., started from Moose Lake Camp at midday, and
crawled ahead about four miles, the horses lifting their feet so
spiritlessly that at every step we feared they would give out.
At an open glade here, the feed was pretty good, though
cropped close by the dozen horned cattle, kept for the purpose
of furnishing fresh beef for Mohun's party, and it was decided
that it would be wise to camp.

The delay was not lost time, however vexatious the mis-
management that necessitated it. The chief had to receive reports about all that had been done by the engineers in this
quarter, inspect the line of survey and the drawings that had
been made ; and give instructions not only for Moberly's parties, but through him for others. Besides, we needed a long
night's rest, and a big fire to dry our clothes and blankets before going farther. For assurances were volunteered all round
that we had a full fortnight of no holiday travel before reaching Kamloops.

Mohun accompanied us until we should fall in with the pack-train on its way up from the Cache, in order to arrange about an exchange of our jaded and unshod horses for others fresh and shod.

Moose Lake that we struck last night, is a beautiful sheet of water, ten or eleven miles long, by three wide. It receives the Fraser, already a deep strong river fully a hundred and fifty feet wide, and also drains high mountains that enclose it on the north and south. The survey for the railway is proceeding along the north side, where the bluffs though high appeared not so sheer as on the south. The hillsides and the country beyond support a growth of splendid spruce, black-pine, and Douglas fir, some of the spruce the finest we had ever seen. So far in our descent from the Pass, the difficulties in the way of railroad construction are not formidable nor the grades likely to be heavy. Still the work that the surveyors are engaged on requires a patience and forethought that few who ride in Pullman cars on the road in after years will ever appreciate.

September 18th.—Away from camp at 8 o'clock. Soon after, struck the Fraser, rushing green and foaming through a narrow valley, closed in by high steep rocks wooded beneath, and bare from half-way up. As we advanced, a change in the vegetation, marking the Pacific slope, began to show distinctly. The lighter green of cypress mingled with the darker woods till it predominated—white birch and small maples also coming in. Our jaded horses walked quietly along, at the two-and-a-half miles per hour step, on a trail heavy at the best, across mountain streams rushing down to join the Fraser, the worst of them roughly bridged with logs and spruce boughs; around precipitous bluffs and hills, and through mud-holes sprinkled heavily with boulders. Frequently we came on the stakes of the surveying party who had used the trail where there was but one possible course for any road. After travelling nine miles Mohun invited us to tie our horses to the trees, and go down two hundred yards to see the first canyon of the Fraser. A canyon

is simply a mountain gorge in which the river is obliged to contract itself, by high rocks closing it in on both sides. A river,
however, is not needed to form a canyon ; for walled rocks,
enclosing a narrow waterless valley constitute a canyon. At
this first canyon, the rocks closed in the river for some hundred
yards to a width of eight feet, so that a man could jump across.
Down this narrow passage the whole of the water of the river
rushed—a resistless current, slipping in great green masses
from ledge to ledge, smashing against out-jutting rocks, eddying
round stony barriers, till it got through the long gate-way. In
some cases these canyons are merely rocks near the stream ; in
others they are bluffs extending far back, or perhaps one great
bluff that had formerly stretched across the river's bed, and had
been riven asunder. In either case they present formidable
obstacles to railroad construction.

A mile beyond, we came to the Grand Fork of the Fraser,
where the main stream receives from the north-east a tributary
important enough to be often considered its source. It flows in
three great divisions, through a meadow two miles wide, from
round the bases of Robson's Peak—the monarch of the mountains hereabouts—and his only less mighty satellites whose
pyramidal forms cluster in his rear. A mile from the first division we came to the second, and found the first section of
Mohun's pack-train in the act of crossing it towards us. The
first section consisted of horses ; the second—of mules led by a
bell horse—under the supervision of Leitch, the chief packer,
followed a mile behind. A general halt was called, and Leitch
sent for. No difficulty was found in making new arrangements.
He gave us four fresh pack horses, five saddle horses, and two
packers, and took all our horses, and Brown, Beaupré and Valad
to help him—Valad being specially entrusted with the duty of
taking back six horses of the Hudson's Bay that were among
ours. This was an entire reorganization, and again Terry was
the only one of the old set that remained with us. He wished

to go on to Cariboo to make his fortune at the mines there. A vision of gold nuggets, picked up as easily as diamonds and rubies in Arizona, more than any sentimental attachment to us was at the root of his steadfastness. But it grieved all to part from the other three, and they seemed equally reluctant to turn their backs on us. Beaupré's only consolation was that he would get pemmican again, for he declared that life without pemmican was nothing but vanity; and we had made the huge mistake of exchanging our pemmican with McCord for pork. The next day and every day after we rued the bargain, but it was too late. Beaupré and Valad had suffered grievously in body from the change, and for an entire day had been almost useless. The Doctor was reduced practically to two meals a day, for he could not stand fat pork three times. Indeed all, with the single exception of Brown, lamented at every meal, as they picked delicately at the coarse pork, the folly of forsaking that which had been so true a stand-by for three weeks. The Chief gave Brown and Beaupré letters to Moberly, the latter having returned to the Jasper valley two days ago. Valad made his adieus, and received the gratuity that the Chief gave him, with a dignity that only an Indian or a gentleman of the old school could manifest. And so exeunt Brown, Beaupré and Valad.

It was only two P.M. when Leitch came up; but his horses had been travelling all day, and as we were in a good place for feed, he advised that camp should be pitched, and no movement onward made till the morrow. This was agreed to, the more readily because the Chief had further instructions to write and send back by Mohun, and because the clouds that had been floating over the tops of the hills all day, and obscuring the lofty glacier cone of Robson's Peak, began to close in and empty themselves. Looking west down the valley of the Fraser the narrow pass suddenly filled with rolling billows of mist. On they came, curling over the rocky summits, rolling down to the forests, enveloping everything in their fleecy mantles. Out of

them came great gusts of wind that nearly blew away our fires
and tents ; and after the gusts, the rain in smart showers.
Once or twice the sun broke through, revealing the hill sides,
all their autumn tints fresh and glistening after the rain, and
the line of their summits near and bold against the sky ; all,
except Robson's Peak which showed its huge shoulders covered
with masses of snow, but on whose high head clouds ever
rested.

September 19th.—It rained during the night, and the morning looked grey and heavy with clouds ; but the sun shone
before eleven o'clock, and the day turned out the finest since
crossing the Yellow Head Pass.   At 7.30 A.M. got off from
the camp, giving a last cheer to Brown, Beaupré and Valad ;
and casting many a longing look behind to see if Robson's Peak
would show its bright head to us.   But only the snow-ribbed
giant sides were visible, for the clouds still rested far down
from the summit.   Three miles from camp, beside the river, at
a place called Mountain view, his great companions stood out
from around him ; but he remained hidden, and reluctantly we
had to go on, without being as fortunate as Milton and Cheadle.

Our new horses were in prime condition ; but the road for
the first eleven miles was extremely difficult ; and last night's
rain had made it worse.   The trail follows down the Fraser to
Tête Jaune Cache, when it leaves the river and turns south-east
to go to the North Thompson, at right angles to the main course
we had followed since entering the Caledonian Valley.   The
Fraser at the same point changes its westerly for a northerly
course, rushing like a race horse, for hundreds of miles north,
when it sweeps round and comes south to receive the united
waters of the North and South Thompson, before cutting
through the Cascade Range and emptying into the ocean.
Tête Jaune Câche is thus a great centre point.   From it the
valley of the Fraser extends to the north, and the same valley
extends south by the banks of the Cranberry and of the Canoe

Rivers to the head of the Columbia,—a continuous valley being
thus formed parallel to the Rocky Mountains, and separating
them from the Gold and Selkirk groups.

Our first spell to-day was eleven miles over a road so heavy
that it cost our fresh horses three and a half hours' tough work.
The trail hugged the banks of the river closely, passing through
timber of the finest kind—spruce, hemlock, cedar (a different
variety from the white or red cedar in the eastern provinces)
white birch and Douglas fir. An old Iroquois hunter, known
in his time as Tête Jaune or Yellow Head, probably from the
noticeable fact in an Indian of his hair being light coloured, had
wisely selected this central point for cacheing all the furs he got
in the course of a season on the Pacific slope, before setting out
with them to trade at Jasper House. He has given his sobri-
quet forever, not only to the Câche, but to the pass and the
lake at the summit. At the Câche, lofty, glacier clothed mountains rise in all directions up and down the valley of the Fraser, the Cranberry, and the Canoe—enough peaks to hand down
to posterity the names of all aspiring travellers and their
friends for the next century. The Gold Mountains form in unbroken line right across our path, forbidding any further progress west, and forcing us to go south-east to flank them, as
they force the Fraser to the north. To our great comfort there
is stationed at the Câche a large boat of the C. P. R. S. Into it
were pitched saddles and packs, and we rowed ourselves across
while the horses swam. The Fraser, at this early stage of its
course, is as broad and strong as the Athabasca below the Jasper
valley. As the packs were off the horses, we halted for dinner,
and at one o'clock were on our way again, hustling at a great
rate to make up for the slow progress of the last two days. Jack
and Joe, our new packers, proved to be no idlers. The one was
a New Brunswicker who had spent years among the Rocky
Mountains, chiefly in the United States ; the other an Ontarian, settled in British Columbia,—both sharp active fellows,

knowing a good deal of human and still more of horse nature.

Our second spell was twenty miles, south-east and south to the crossing of the Canoe River. The trail here was in excellent condition, and for the great part of the way a buggy might have been driven on it. A sandy ridge like a hog's-back runs up the east side of the valley of the Cranberry, and the trail is along it's top. This valley is the connecting link between the Fraser and Canoe rivers. The valley of the Canoe is another and larger link, extending to Boat encampment ; at the northern end of the valley of the Columbia. Before us, as we journeyed south with a little easting, snowy peaks rose on each side of the valley, dwarfing it in appearance to an extremely narrow width ; while right ahead a great mountain mass that marked the beginning of the main valley of the Canoe, seemed to close our way. The trees struggled far up the sides, fighting a battle with the bare rocks and the snows,—the highest trees heavily dusted with last night's snowfall. Crossing a little stream called the McLennan that issues from a pass in the side hills, we rounded Cranberry Lake and saw the valley of the Canoe stretching far up in the direction we had been going, while our road was across the river and up the dividing line S. S. W. to Albreda Lake and River.

Although only five o'clock, the sun was now setting behind the mountains to the west from which the Canoe issues, and the road was heavy with recent rainfall, boulders and mudholes, so that there was no use of pushing on much farther. At the Crossing of the Canoe, there was a raft on the other side, but as the river had fallen two feet in the course of the day, we tried the ford and found it quite practicable,—the water not coming much higher than the horses' shoulders ; so that the Crossing which had so nearly cost Lord Milton and Mrs. Assiniboine their lives did not delay us ten minutes.

The rapidity with which these mountain torrents increase or decrease in depth is an astonishing feature to those who hav been accustomed only to lowland rivers. A warm day melts the snows high up, and there is an increase in depth by the afternoon of from six inches to two or three feet. A cold night succeeds, and down the stream falls by morning. That the Canoe had fallen during the day was proof that though warm in the valley, the air was cold in the mountains. The high mountains not only protect the valleys from much of the cold, but also from much of the snow. They act as natural snow fences. As the sun had now disappeared, though his light still shone on the double range of high peaks stretching away down the Canoe, camp was pitched on the other side of the river, Jack and Joe proving themselves as expeditious and obliging as Brown and Beaupré. It was amusing to listen to the slang terms of the Pacific that garnished their talk. " Spell " we found had crossed the mountains, and " spelling place " and a " good spell " were as common on the· one side as the other. But Jack's call to his horses was new to us. " Git," the abbreviated form of our " get up " and Terry's " git up out o' that," was the only cry ever addressed to them, and the sound of it would quicken their walk into a trot when no other words in the language would have the slightest effect. This transatlantic sententiousness and love of abbreviations, from which come their " Sabre cuts of Saxon speech," characterized all their conversation. Without intending the faintest disrespect, they addressed the Doctor always as " Doc." " Good morning, Doc," meant no more than " good morning, my lord " would mean. Even the grandeur of the mountains did not secure to them their name in full. " They call them ' the Rockies,' " said Jack, jerking his head in their direction, with an air that indicated that no further information was required about such things. Every adjective and article that could in any way be dispensed with was rejected from their English ; and if syllables could be lopped off long words so as to bring them down to one syllable, the axe was unsparingly applied. San Francisco was always

" Frisco," and Captain—a name applied indiscriminately to
every stranger—never longer than " Cap."

September 20th.—Up early this morning and, after breakfast
on bread and pork—very unlike Irish pork—for not a solitary
streak of lean relieved the fat, got away before the sun had
looked out over the mountains.   From our camp a singular
radiation of valleys could be observed.   That of the Canoe ran
almost north and south, inclining more to the west up stream.
Between the west and south, the valley of one of its tributaries
joined it.   Along this tributary, called the Camp River—from
the fact of one of the surveying parties wintering on it last year
—our course was to be to-day.   Between the east and north
the valley of the Cranberry, along which we had travelled yesterday afternoon, extended away to the Fraser.

Our aim to-day was to reach the North Thompson.   Between
our camp and it, thirty-three miles of bad road had to be
travelled.

Broad gravel benches, supporting a growth of small black
pines, rose one above another like terraces, the highest attaining
a height of four or five hundred feet.   Up these the trail led,
heading across to Camp River.   Similar benches of sand or
gravel, or of sand mixed with boulders, are a characteristic of
all the rivers of British Columbia.   They are distinctly defined
as the successive banks of the smallest as well as of the largest
rivers.   Those along the Canoe show that a much greater volume of water once flowed over or rested in the valley.   It may
be that the Columbia, before the present canyons through which
it now runs to the south were riven, flowed thus far or farther
north.

It seemed to us a great mistake that the old Indian trail had
not been abandoned here, and a new trail made.   The terraces
are so steep and high, and the descent on the other side to the
valley of Camp River so sudden, that the only explanation we
could suggest of the trail facing up and down instead of round-

ing them, was that Tête Jaune had first made it when chasing
a chamois or bighorn, and that he and all others thereafter,
McCord's party included, were too conservative, to look for
another and better way.

At the summit of the divide, Camp River flows opposite ways
from the two ends of a sluggish lake, the part that runs down
to the Thompson assuming the name of the Albreda. The
valley is narrow and closed in at its south-west end by the
great mass of Mount Milton which fronted us the whole day.
This mountain that Dr. Cheadle selected to bear the name of
his fellow traveller is a mass of snow-clad peaks that feed the
little Albreda with scores of torrents, ice-cold and green coloured, and make it into a river of considerable magnitude before
it flows into the Thompson. It is on the south of the Albreda
and not on the north as stated by them, and the trail winds
round its right or north side, leaving it on the left. Soon
after entering the valley of Camp River we saw it before us,
towering high above the hills that enclosed the narrow valley,
and seeming to bar our further progress to the south and south-
west. A semi-circle of five peaks, enclosing a snowy bosom,
forms the left side ; and, next to these, four much higher rise,
the highest and largest in the centre showing a broad front of
snow like a field, inclined down till hidden by a forest of dark
firs on a range of lower hills. Our road which at first was up a
narrow fire-desolated stony valley, led next round the base of
these lower hills, and from the difference of soil and of elevation, changed from a succession of bare, stony ridges, into a succession of mud-holes and torrents—bridged, fortunately for us,
by the trail party—till we came to the first crossing of the
Albreda. The timber here was of the largest size, but many of
the noblest looking cedars were evidently not of much worth
from internal decay. It was after sunset when we passed over
the wooded slopes and along the banks of the river, and as the
dark forest opened here and there, one white peak after an-

other came out through a broad rift in the wooded hills. The underbrush consisted chiefly of a great variety of ferns of all sizes, from the tiniest to clusters six feet high, or of the broad aralea which so monopolized all light and moisture where it grew that there was no chance for grass. In some marshes a water-lily, with leaves three feet long, in seed at this season, hid the water as completely as the aralea the ground. Everything on the Pacific slope is on a large scale,—the mountains, the timber, the leaves, the ferns, and the expectations of the people.

It was still eight miles to the crossing of the Thompson. Since starting in the morning we had halted only once, yet had made barely twenty-five miles. But as the fast gathering darkness, twice as deep because of the forest, compelled it, our fifty-fifth camp from Lake Superior was pitched beside the Albreda.

September 21st.—Up this morning at 4.30, in the dark, and on the road two hours later. The days were now so short, because of the season of the year and the mountain-limited horizon, that as it was impossible to travel on the trail after nightfall, the most had to be made of the sunlight.

The trail for the first eight miles was as bad as well could be, although a great amount of honest work had been expended on it. Before McCord had come through, it must have been simply impassable except for an Indian on foot,—worse than when Milton and Cheadle forced through with their one pack-horse at the rate of three miles a day ; for the large Canadian party had immediately preceded them, whereas no one attempted to follow in their steps till McLellan in 1871, and in the intervening nine years much of the trail had been buried out of sight, or hopelessly blocked up by masses of timber, torrents, landslides, or *debris*. Our horses, however, proved equal to the work. Even when their feet entangled in a network of fibrous roots, or sunk eighteen inches in a mixture of bog and clay, they would make gallant attempts at trotting ; and by slipping over rocks, jumping fallen trees, breasting precipitous ascents with a rush, and recklessly dashing down the hills, the eight miles to the crossing of the Thompson were made in three hours.

The early morning was dark and lowering, and at eight o'clock a drizzle commenced which continued all the forenoon. Struggling through sombre woods and heavy underbrush, every spray of which discharges its little accumulation of rain on the weary traveller as he passes on, is disheartening and exhausting work. The influence of the rain on men and horses is most depressing. The riders get as fatigued as the horses; for jumping on and off at the bogs, precipices, and boulder slides thirty or forty times a day is as tiresome as a circus performance must be to the actors.

We crossed the Thompson at a point where it divides into three, the smallest of the three sections being bridged with long logs, the two others broad and only belly deep, as Jack phrased it. Riding down the west side, too wet and tired to notice anything, the men in advance passed a blazed tree with a piece of paper pinned to the blaze; but the Secretary, being on foot, turned aside to look; and read,—

> "In V's Cache
> There is a box for S. Fleming
> or M. Smith."

He at once called out the good news, and V's Cache in the shape of a small log shanty was found hard by. Jack unroofed it in a trice and jumped in; and among other things, stored for different engineering parties, was the box. A stone broke it open, and as Jack handed out the contents, one by one, a general shout announced their nature.—-Candles and canned meats; good. "Hooray," from the rear! Two bottles of Worcester sauce and a bottle of brandy! better; sauce for the fat pork and for the plum-pudding next Sunday. Half a dozen of Bass' Pale Ale, with the familiar face of the red pyramid brand! Three times three and one cheer more! After this crowning mercy, more canned meats, jams, and a few bottles of claret evoked but faint applause. The wine and jams were put back again for Mr. Smith. Four bottles of the ale, a can of the preserved beef, and another of peaches were opened on the spot, and Terry producing bread from the kitchen sack, an impromptu lunch was eaten round the Cache, and V's health drunk as enthusiastically as if he had been the greatest benefactor of his species. As the *finale*, we deposited the empty bottles and cans at the foot of the blazed tree, and wrote

> " Gratefully received
> The above ;
> *Vide infra.*"

On one side, " God bless V !" and on the other, " *Si vis monumentum, despice,*" and decorating the paper with red and blue pencil marks as elaborately as time and our limited resources permitted, we rode off with merry hearts, the rain ceasing and the sun shining out at the same time as if to be in unison with our feelings. Is it necessary here to implore the ascetic and the dignified reader to be a little kind to this ebullition on our part. It was childish, perhaps, but then what were we but babes in the wood ? Circumstances alter cases ; and our circumstances were peculiar. We would have gushed over a mere acquaintance, had he come upon us in that inhospitable valley, those melancholy woods, under those rainy skies. Probably we might have fallen on the neck and wept over an old friend. Is it wonderful that the red pyramid looked so kindly, and touched a chord in our hearts ?

Two miles farther on, the sound of a bell was heard. Jack said that it must be the bell-horse of another pack-train ; but in a few minutes a solitary traveller, walking beside his two laden horses, emerged from the woods ahead. He turned out to be one John Glen—a miner on his way to prospect for gold on hitherto untried mountains and sand-bars. Here was a specimen of Anglo-Saxon self-reliant individualism more striking than that pictured by Quinet of the American settler, without priest or captain at his head, going out into the deep woods or virgin lands of the new continent to find and found a home. John Glen calculated that there was as good gold in the mountains as had yet come out of them, and that he might strike a new bar or gulch that would pan out as richly as Williams Creek, Cariboo ; so putting blankets and bacon, flour and frying-pan, shining pickaxe and shovel on his horses, and sticking revolver and knife in his waist, off he started from Kamloops to seek fresh fields and pastures new. Nothing to him was lack of company or of newspapers ; short days and approach of winter ; seas of mountains and grassless valleys, equally inhospitable ; risk of sickness and certainty of storms ; slow and exhausting travel through marsh and muskeg, across roaring mountain torrents and miles of fallen timber ; lonely days and lonely nights ;—if he found gold he would be repaid. Prospecting was his business, and he went about it in simple matter-of-course style, as if he were doing business on 'change. John Glen was to us a typical man, the modern missionary, the martyr for gold, the advance guard of the army of material progress. And who will deny or make light of his virtue, his faith, such as it was ? His self-reliance was sublime. Compared to his, how small the daring and pluck of even Milton and Cheadle ! God save thee, John Glen ! and give thee thy reward !

Glen was more than a moral to us. He brought the Chief a letter from the Hudson Bay agent at Kamloops, of date August 24th, informing him that our personal luggage from Toronto *via* San Francisco had arrived, and would be kept for us. This was another bit of good fortune to mark the day.

In hopes of getting to Cranberry marsh, twenty-two miles down from the crossing, we pushed on without giving the horses any rest except the lunch half-hour at V's Cache ; but the roads were so heavy that when within four miles of the marsh the packers advised camping. The horses continued to go with spirit; but the long strain was telling on them, and they had to be our first consideration. The road had seemed to us—if not to the horses—to improve from V's Cache; but it was still a hard road to travel, the valley of the Thompson being almost as bad as the valley of the Albreda. In our eighteen miles along it to-day, there was not a mile of level. It was constant up and down. as if we were riding over billows. Even where the ground was low, the cradle hills were high enough to make the road undulating. The valley of the Thompson is very narrow for a stream of its magnitude; in fact it is a mountain gorge rather than a valley. Only at rare intervals is there a bit of flat or meadow or even marsh along its banks. High wooded hills rise on each side; and, beyond these, a higher range of snowy peaks, one or another of the highest of which peeps over the woods at turns of the river, or when the forest through which you are toiling opens a little to enable you to see. The forest is of the grandest kind—not only the living but the dead. Everywhere around lie the prostrate forms of old giants, in every stage of decay, some of them six to eight feet through, and an hundred and fifty to two hundred feet in length. Scarcely half-hiding these are broad-leaved plants and ferns in infinite variety, while the branchless columnal shafts of more modern cedars tower far up among the dark branches of spruce and hemlock, dwarfing the horse and his rider, that creep along across their interlaced roots and the mouldering bones of their great predecessors.

It was not five o'clock when we camped; but the sun had set in the narrow valley, and it was quite dark before the horses had been driven to the nearest feed, and the tent put in order for the night. Terry set to work as usual to hurry up the tea; but to his and our dismay there was no tea kettle. It had fallen by the way from the pack to which it was tied. Jack was sure he had seen it on, four miles back; but as " *Nulla vestigia retrorsum*" was our motto, whatever the loss sustained, no one proposed to turn back and look for it; and our only other pot—the one used for pork and porridge boiling and all other purposes—was laid under requisition for the tea. The two frying pans had also had their handles twisted off; but Joe tied the two handles together and made a pair of pinchers out of them that would lift one; and Terry notched a crooked stick and made a handle for the other. Supper was prepared with these extemporised utensils. The Doctor and Frank fried slap-jacks and then boiled canned goose in the one pan. Terry fried pork in the other; and boiled dried apples in the pot before making the tea in it. The Chief and the Secretary assisted with bland smiles and words of encouragement, and by throwing a few chips on the fire occasionally : and a jolly supper, between the open tent and the roaring fire, was the grand finale.

September 22nd.—The first meal this morning, there being only one pot, was a plate of porridge, eaten after a dip in the ice-cold Thompson. Two hours after Terry announced *déjeuner à la fourchette*. The Doctor and Frank roused themselves from their second sleep to enjoy it; but Jack was absent. Not taking kindly to the porridge, he had gone off without saying a word, in search of the missing kettle, and service was postponed till his return.

Looking round at the site of our camp, we could see nothing on our own side of the river but a willow thicket, and the dense forest rising beyond. On the other side, and up stream, a snow-clad, round topped mountain looked over the lower hills. Four or five miles down stream a lofty pyramid showed us its snowy face, with a twin peak a little to the south, and a great shoulder also snow-covered, extending farther beyond in the same direction. This "biceps Parnassus" we inferred was Mount Cheadle, and in honour of the man the camp was dubbed Camp Cheadle.

Before mid-day Jack returned in triumph with the tea kettle
—which he had found less than four miles back—slung across
his shoulders.   A cup of tea was at once made in it for him as
reward.   The Dr. now prepared the pudding, and when it was
deposited in the pot for its three hours' boil, the bell was rung
for divine service.

Just as the Secretary commenced, the pot to the dismay of
every one tumbled over.   Half-a-dozen hands were instinctively
stretched out, but Terry put it right, with the coolness of a
veteran, and the service proceeded with no more trouble,
except that gusts of wind blew the smoke into our eyes, making
Jack in particular weep enough to gratify any preacher.

Dinner was ordered for four o'clock, and it need hardly be
said, the pudding was a success.   It rolled from the bag on to
the plate, in the most approved fashion of oblong or rotund
puddings.   The Dr. garnished it with six ferns for the six Provinces of the Dominion.   The Chief produced V's brandy,
poured some over the pudding and applying a match, it was set
on the table in a blaze of blue light, that gladdened every one
with old memories.

Before sunset, the wind had blown away the clouds and the
snowy mist that had been falling up on the mountains.   When
it was dark the stars came out in a clear sky, promising fine
weather on the morrow.   After some general talk and calcula-
tions as to whether we could get to Kamloops for next Sunday,
in which hope weighed down the heaviest improbabilities, all
gathered round the hearthstone fire for family worship.   It was
the time that we always felt most solemnized; thankful to God
for his goodness to us, praying His mercy for our far away
homes, and drawn to one another by the thought that we were
in the wilderness, with common needs, and entirely dependent
on God and each other.

CHAPTER X

Along the North Thompson River to Kamloops.

September 23rd.—Jack rose this morning at 3 a.m., and made up the fire by kicking the embers together and piling on more wood. In a quarter of an hour after, all hands were up—folding blankets and packing. We breakfasted by moonlight, and would have been off at once, but two of the horses had wandered, and it was some time before they were found. Jack tracked them to an island in the river, and had to wade across for them.

This was the first occasion on which any of the horses had strayed even a short distance from the bell. They had always kept within sound of it on the journey and during the night. The bell is hung round the neck of the most willing horse of the pack, and from that moment he takes the lead. Till he moves on, it is almost impossible to force any of the others forward. If you keep back your horse for a mile or two when on the march, and then give him the rein, he dashes on in frantic eagerness to catch up to the rest. Get hold of the bell-horse when you want to start in the morning, and ring the bell and soon all the others in the pack gather round.

We had never seen the gregariousness of horses so strongly exhibited as in the case of those Pacific pack-trains. And the mule shows the sentiment or instinct still more strongly. A bell-horse is put at the head of the mule train, and the mules follow him and pay him the most devoted loyalty. If a strange dog comes up barking, or any other hostile looking brute, the mules often rush furiously at the enemy, and trample him under foot, to shield their sovereign from danger or even from insult. Altogether the bell-horse was a novelty to us, though his uses are so thoroughly understood here, that Jack and Joe were astonished at our asking any questions about so well established an institution.

The night had been frosty, and the ground in the morning was quite hard, but after we had been on the road for an hour, the sun rose from behind Mount Cheadle, and warmed the air somewhat, though it continued cold enough all day to make walking preferable to riding. For the first four miles the road was similar to Saturday's. We then came to a mountain stream, towards the mouth of which the view opened and showed us Mount Cheadle rising stately and beautiful from the opposite bank of the Thompson. What had seemed yesterday a great shoulder stretching to the south was now seen to be a distinct hill, but in addition to the cone or pyramid with the twin heads of Mount Cheadle, a third and lower peak to the north-east appeared. Beyond the stream is Cranberry marsh. The trail here goes along the beach for a short distance, and then turns into the woods and hills, giving us a repetition of Saturday's experiences. Eight miles from camp we crossed another and larger stream on the other side of which the valley widened and the country beyond opened. The landscape was softer and the wild myrtle and the garden waxberry mixed with the ruder plants that had held entire possession of the ground farther up. Eight miles more brought us to open meadows along the banks of the river, overgrown in part by willows and alders, and in part covered with marsh grass. Here a halt of two hours for dinner was called. We had travelled about sixteen miles in five hours, and had only ten more to travel, to reach Goose Creek, where camp was to be pitched for the night. It was expedient

SKULL OF THE HEADLESS INDIAN.

to get there as early as possible, that the horses might have a good feed, for there would be no grass along to-morrow's road, which was said to be the worst between Yellow Head Pass and Kamloops.

During the last two or three days the river had fallen very much, and at our halting place it was eight or nine feet below its high water mark. The valley was wide enough to enable us for the first time to see on both sides the summits of the mountains that enclosed it. At this point they are remarkably varied. A broad deep cleft in the heavily timbered hills on the west side of the river, showed an undulating line of snowy peaks, rising either from or behind the wooded range ; and the opposite side was closed in nearer the river by a number of separate mountains, from four to six thousand feet high, that folded in upon or rose behind one another.

The afternoon drive was along a level, for the next six or seven miles to Blue River, where our progress was slow from the stubs or short sharp stumps of the alders, that dotted and sometimes completely filled up the trail. Blue River gets its name from the deep soft blue of the distant hills, which are seen from its mouth well up into the gap through which it runs. A raft is kept on this river for the use of the survey. We made use of the Cache or shanty on the bank, opening it for a small supply of beans and of soap. A diligent search was made for coffee but without result.

The timber here is small and much of it has been destroyed by fires. After crossing the river, the trail winds round a bluff that extends boldly to the Thompson. Timber that had fallen down the steep face across the trail delayed us several times. Frank shot a large porcupine as it was climbing a tree, and pitched it on the kitchen pack to be tried as food. Three miles more brought us to Goose Creek where we camped an hour before sunset. This was the spot the Doctor had been told to **examine** for the bones of the headless Indian, and therefore as soon as he had unsaddled his horse, he selected a shingle shaped stick, and, without saying a word, set off on his exploration with all the mystery and deliberation of a resurrectionist.   In a few minutes he came on a bit of board with the following inscription pencilled on it :—

"Here lie the remains of the 'Headless Indian,' discovered by Lord "Milton and Dr. Cheadle, A.D. 1863.   At this spot we found an old "tin kettle. a knife, a spoon, and fishing line ; and 150 yards up the "bank of river we also found the skull, which was sought for in vain by "the above gentlemen.

"T. Party, C. P. R. S.

"June 5th, 1872."

Scratching the ground with his wooden spade the Dr. was soon in possession of the skull, and of the rusty scalping knife that had been thrown in beside it, and finding the old kettle near, he appropriated it too, and deposited all three with his baggage as triumphantly as if he had rifled an Egyptian tomb. Terry did not like the proceedings at all, and could only be reconciled to them on the plea that they might lead to the discovery of the murderers ; for nothing would persuade him that the man's head had dropped off, and been carried to a distance by the wind or some beast.   He had seen heads broken, or cut off, but he had never heard before—and neither had we as far as that goes—of a head rolling off; and therefore concluded that "there had been some bad work here."

Frank and Jack skinned the porcupine, and prepared it for cooking.   A leg being spitted and broiled before the fire as a test morsel, was pronounced superior to beaver ; and the carcass was consigned to Terry, who decided to cut it up, parboil, and fry it for breakfast.

September 24th.—There was no need to look at the thermometer when we got up to know that there had been frost.   Every one felt it through the capote and pair of blankets in which he was wrapped.   The Chief rose at midnight and renewed the fire.   Frank then got up and curled himself into a ball within

a few inches of the red embers. At 3 A.M. all rose growling,
stamping their cold feet, lingering about the fire, lighting pipes,
and considering whether washing the face wasn't a superstitious
rule to be occasionally honoured in the breach rather than the
observance. Everything was done slowly. It was nearly sunrise before any one even thought of looking at the thermometer,
which then indicated 17 ° : not so very low, but we had been
sleeping practically in the open air, and in a cold wind with
rather light covering. Three-quarters of an hour were spent in
cooking the porcupine ; and as it did not come up to our expectations, from inherent defects or Terry's cooking, very little of
the meat was eaten ; and no one proposing to carry a piece in
his pocket for lunch, it was left behind,—the only thing in the
shape of food that had been wasted by us on the journey.

At 6.15 we were on the march, expecting a heavy day's work,
as the road lay over the Great Canyon that had all but defeated Milton and Cheadle's utmost efforts, and past the " porte
d' enfer " of the Assiniboine. The first three miles after crossing the Creek were partly round and partly over a heavy bluff;
and the next five along the river, which ran like a mill-race
between high hills. These hills on our side afforded space for
the road either along their bases, or on the first bench above.
The next ten or twelve miles were to be through the dreaded
canyon ; a pass as much more formidable than Killiekrankie as
the Thompson is greater than the Garry. While climbing the
first bluff near the entrance to the canyon, the bell-horse of a
pack-train was heard ahead. Fortunately there was space for
us to draw aside and let the train pass. It was on its way up
to Tête Jaune Cache with supplies, and consisted of fifty-two
mules led by a bell-horse, and driven by four or five men, representing as many different nationalities. Most of the mules
were, with the exception of the long ears, wonderfully graceful
creatures ; and though laden with an average weight of three
hundred pounds, stepped out over rocks and roots firmly and

lightly as if their loads were nothing.   This was the first train
that had ever passed through the canyon without losing at least
one animal.   The horse or mule puts its foot on a piece of in-
nocent-looking moss ; underneath the moss there happens to be
a wet stone over which he slips ; at the same moment, his broad
unwieldly pack strikes against a rock, outjutting from the bluff,
and as there is no room for him to recover himself, over he
goes into the roaring Thompson, and that's the last seen of him
unless brought up by a tree halfway down the precipice.   Two
months before a mule fell over in this way.   The packers went
down to the river side to look for him, but as there was no
trace to be seen, resumed their march. Five days after, another
train passing near the spot heard the braying of a mule, and
guided by the noise looked, and found that he had fallen on a
broad rock half way down, where he had lain for some time
stunned.   Struggling to his feet, fortunately for him the appa-
raho got entangled round the rock, and held him fast till he
was relieved by the men of the train from his razor bridge over
the flood.   This was a more wonderful deliverance than that
of Bucephalus when abandoned by Mr. O'B.

For several miles, the river here is one long rapid, dashing
over hidden and half-hidden rocks scattered over every part of
its bed.   The great point of danger is reached at " Hell Gate."
A huge arch had once stretched across the present channel, and
had been rifted asunder, leaving a passage for the river not
more than thirty feet wide.   The rock looked as if it had recently parted, a depression on the one side exactly fitting into
an overhanging rock opposite, looking as if a counter convulsion might groove and tongue the two together again. Through
this passage the river raged, and the whole force of the current
ran under the overhanging black rock, so near its roof that at
high water the river is forced back.   From this point the canyon continues for six or seven miles down, at one point the
opposing rocks being only fifteen feet apart. The river there

boils and spurts up as if ejected from beneath out of a hydrau-
lic pipe.

Half a mile below Hell Gate, a bell was again heard ahead.
This to our great delight belonged to a mule train accompanying
Mr. Marcus Smith—the deputy of the Engineer-in-Chief on the
Pacific side.   Our pack-horses were sent on while we halted to
exchange greetings and news.   Mr. Smith was on his way to
Tête Jaune Cache to try and find a pass across the Gold range.
He had spent the greater part of the summer on the Pacific
coast, in the Cascades, and the Chilcoten district in order to
find a practicable line for the railway from Bute Inlet through
to Tête Jaune Cache.   After a long consultation and a lunch of
bread and cheese—cheese produced by Smith and eaten so freely
by us who had not tasted any for two months, that Smith rue-
fully declared our lunch to be " cheese—and bread," the Chief
advised him to return with us to Kamloops, as it was too late
in the season to adventure into the heart of the Gold range
from the east side.   The two parties accordingly became one.

Following up our pack-horses, we came in the course of the
next few miles to the bottom of the canyon, and all at once to
a totally different aspect of the river and road. The river ceases
to descend rapidly for the next twelve miles, and the valley
opens out to a breadth of two or three miles.   The road runs
along this level ; but, though a great improvement on the
breakneck hills we had been going up and down all day, the
clumps of willow and alder stubs and roots kept the horses from
venturing on much beyond a walk,—except the Secretary's, a
mad brute called the fool which dashed on after the bell at such
a rate that the rest of the party in following more slowly
looked round to pick up the remains.   The river here, as if
exhausted with its furious racing, subsides into a smooth broad
lake-like appearance, calmly reflecting everything on its banks.
Hence the name of this district—" Stillwater."   Four miles
along this brought us to our men unpacking the horses at the

point agreed on in the morning.   Half a mile ahead, they said,
were the tents of the U. and V. parties who had been surveying
all summer between Kamloops and Tête Jaune Cache.   They
had met at this central point, the work on both sections being
just finished.   Going on to their camp, we found Mr. John
Trutch, the engineer in charge of both parties, and our friend
V.   Their encampment seemed to us a great affair, unaccustomed as we had been for weeks to new faces.   Each party
consisted in all of sixteen or eighteen men, with two Indians,—
one the cook's slavey, and the other—slavey to the officer in
charge, and general messenger.   Besides the two parties there
was a third in charge of the pack train, so that the valley was
alive with men and mules ; all busy packing up to start for
Kamloops in the morning.   Most cordial were the greetings on
both sides.   They at once set to work to prepare supper for us,
though they had had their own already, and men were sent back to
bring our tent down beside their encampment.   The latest news
was eagerly asked and given.   The news that delighted us most
was the victory of the Canadian team at Wimbledon in the
competition for the Rajah of Kolapore's cup against eight
picked shots of the United Kingdom.   The names of the eight
were read out, and a special cheer given for Shand of Halifax,
who scored highest.

A mighty supper was soon announced.   Never were men in
better condition for the table.   Beefsteak, bacon, stuffed heart,
loaf bread, and a bottle of claret ; a second course of fried slices
of the remains of a plum-pudding, seasoned with blueberry-jam
made by themselves, a feast the memory of which shall long
gladden us !   There was so much to talk and hear about, such
a murmur of voices, the pleasant light of so many fires, the prospect of a warm, sound sleep, and of more rapid journeying hereafter, that there was nothing wanting to make our happiness
complete, except letters from home, and those were at Kamloops, not far away,

September 25th.—Rose refreshed, and as ready for a Highland breakfast as if we had not eaten an English dinner last
night.   It was arranged that Mr. Trutch should accompany us
to Kamloops, V. remaining behind to bring on everything, and
that at the Clearwater River, sixty-two miles distant, we should
take the survey boat and go down the Thompson for the
remaining seventy-three miles to Kamloops.

As the Chief had letters to write to different parties, it was
nine o'clock before we got away from the pleasant Stillwater
Camp.   Our pack-horses had gone on two hours before with
instructions to camp at Round Prairie, twenty-five miles from
Stillwater.

Soon after starting, we caught up to the beef-cattle and the
pack-train of mules that had gone in advance with U's camp.
As the trail is narrow, and mules resent being passed on the
road—occasionally flinging their heels back into the face of the
too eager horse—it took some time and engineering to get
ahead ; but when this was accomplished we moved at a rapid
walk, breaking now and then into a trot.   From the canyôn to
Clearwater the trail steadily improved.   Our morning journey
was for ten miles along the grassy or willow covered meadow
on the west side of the Thompson's Stillwater. The river looked
like a long lake.   The sand over the trail and the *debris* strewn
around showed that, in some years at any rate, the river over-
flowed the low meadow.

We halted for lunch at the south end of the Stillwater, fortunately coming on U's advance party, who supplied us with
some bread, while the Doctor produced two boxes of sardines
he had prudently " packed."   One of the men gave Mr. Trutch
a pair of willow grouse he had shot the day before.   British
Columbia boasts of having seven or eight varieties of the grouse
kind, the most abundant being the sage hen, the blue grouse,
the ptarmigan, and the spruce partridge or fool-hen, that is
oftener knocked over with a stick than shot.

After its long repose the Thompson now begins to brawl and prepare for another rush down hill. Its height above sea level at the bottom of the canyôn is 2,000 feet, and at Kamloops 1,250. It falls more than two-thirds of this 750 feet of difference in the forty-five miles immediately above Clearwater. In the seventy-three miles below Clearwater the fall is only 240 feet. The meadow now ceased, and the valley contracted again. We could easily understand the dismay with which Milton and Cheadle beheld such a prospect. The valley had opened below Mount Cheadle as if the long imprisonment of the river, and with it their own, was coming to an end; but the Great Canyôn had hedged it in again more firmly than ever. Next at Stillwater, and down for twelve or fourteen milles, everything looked as if the river, wearied with its long course between high overhanging hills, was at last about to emerge into an open country of farms and settlements; but again the hills closed in, and the apparently interminable narrow valley recommenced.

There was no gloom, however, in our party. No matter what the road, the country or the weather, everything was on our side; fair trail, friendly faces, commissariat all right, and the prospect of a post office before the end of the week. The day was warm and sunny; the climate altogether different from the rainy skies and cold nights higher up the slope; and we were assured that an hundred miles farther down stream, no rain ever fell except an occasional storm or a few drops from high passing clouds—an assurance more welcome to us than to intending settlers.

The aspect of the hills too was changing. They were lower and more broken, with undulating spaces between, giving promise of escape to the imprisoned traveller, sooner or later. Distinctly defined benches extended at different points along the banks, and on these the trail was comparatively level. About 4 p.m. we came to a bit of open called Round Prairie, and found the men unpacking for the night, as there was no other good place for the horses nearer than sixteen miles off.

This had been the easiest day's journey since entering the mountains, for though we had travelled twenty-four miles, there was no fatigue, so that it was really like one of the pic-nic days of the plains. The early camping gave another chance to read the papers, of which every one took advantage, devouring with avidity papers nearly two months old.

September 26th.—It rained heavily this morning, and the start from camp was made with the delays and discomforts that rain produces. The cotton tent weighs thrice as much as when dry. The ends of the blankets, clothes, some of the food, the shaganappi, etc., get wet. The packs are heavier and the horses' backs are wet; and it is always a question whether or not water-proofs do the riders any good. This morning one of the pack-horses could not be found. Everything had to be packed on the three others ; Jack remained behind to look for the fourth, and soon found the poor brute sheltered from the rain, in a thicket near where the bell had been.

The country to-day resembled that of yesterday ; but even where it opened out, the steady drizzle and the heavy mists on the hills hid everything. Cedars had entirely disappeared, and the spruce and pines were comparatively small. The aralea gave place to a smaller leaved trailer with a red berry like the raspberry ; and a dark-green prickly-leaved bush like English holly, called the Oregon grape, and several grasses and plants new to us covered the ground.

Six miles from camp we came to Mad River, a violent mountain affluent of the Thompson, crossed by a good bridge ; and ten miles farther on to Pea Vine Prairie, where as the rain ceased and enough blue sky "to make a pair of breeches" showed, the halt for dinner was called. Here we saw for the first time the celebrated bunch-grass, which has no superior as feed for horses or cattle ; especially for the latter, as the beef that has been fed on it is peculiarly juicy and tender. The name explains its character as a grass. It consists of small narrow blades—ten to fifty of them growing in a bunch from six to eighteen inches high, and the bunches so close together in places that at a distance they appear to form a sward. The blades are green in spring and summer, but at this season they are russet grey, apparently withered and tasteless, but the avidity with which the horses cropped them, turning aside from green and succulent marsh grass and even vetches, showed that the virtue of the bunch-grass had not been lost.

The clouds now rolled up like curtains from the hills, and the sun breaking out revealed the river, three or four hundred feet below, with an intervale on each side that made the valley at least two miles across to the high banks that enclosed it. There was a bend in the river to the west, so that we saw not only a little up and down, which is usually all that can be seen on the North Thompson, but round the corner ; a wide extent of landscape of varied beauty and soft outlines. The hills were wooded, and the summits of the highest dusted with the recent snow, that had been rain-fall in the valley. Autumn hues of birch, cottonwood, and poplar blended with the dark fir and pine, giving the variety and warmth of colour that we had for many days been strangers to, and which was therefore appreciated all the more. The face of the bank on which we stood presented a singular appearance. It was of whitish clay mixed with sand, the front hard as cement by the action of the weather ; there had been successive slides of the bank behind in different years, but the old front had remained firm, and was now standing out along the face, away from the bank, in pyramidal or grotesque forms, like the trap of basalt rocks, spires, and columns along the east coast of Skye, springing from debris at the base. Similar strange forms of cemented whitish clay are to be found in several places on the Fraser.

As Smith and Trutch now messed with us, the different cooks contributed to the common stock and to the cooking, with the two advantages of greater variety to the table, and greater speed in the preparation. After a short halt at Pea Vine we got into the saddle again, and made ten miles before sunset ; the trail leading across sandy benches intersected by numerous little creeks, the descent to which was generally so direct that every one had to dismount, both for the down and the up hill stretch. Camp for the night was pitched at one of these creeks, twelve miles to the north of the Clearwater, and Frank who had become quite an adept at constructing camp fires, built up a mighty one, at which we dried wet clothes and blankets. Our camp presented a lively scene at night. Great fires before each tent lit up the dark forest, and threw gleams of light about, that made the surrounding darkness all the more intense. Through the branches of the pines, the kindly stars—the only spectators—looked down on groups flitting from tent to tent or cumbered about the many things that have to be cared for even in the wilderness, cooking, mending, drying, overhauling baggage, piling wood on the fire, planning for the morrow, or taking notes. How like a lot of gypsies we were in outward appearance, and how naturally every one took to the wild life ! A longing for home and for rest would steal over us if we were quiet for a time, but a genuine love for camp life, for its freedom and rude happiness, for the earth as a couch and the sky for a canopy, and the wide world for a bed-room, possessed us all ; and we knew that, in after days, memory would return, to dwell fondly over many an old camping ground by lake or river side, on the plains, in the woods, and among the mountains.

September 27th.—Six miles travel like yesterday's brought us this morning to Raft River, a broad stream, whose ice-cold pellucid waters indicated that it ran from glaciers, or through hard basalt or trap rock that yielded it no tribute of clay to bring down ; and six miles more along gravelly benches to the Clearwater, whose name is intended to express a similar character, and the difference between itself and the clay coloured Thompson it empties into. The Clearwater is so large a stream that after its junction, the Thompson becomes clearer from the admixture. At the junction there is a depot of the C.P.R. Survey, with a man in charge, and a three ton boat used to bring up supplies from Kamloops, which we had arranged with V. to take down, leaving Jack and Joe to bring along the horses, at a leisurely pace. From Clearwater to Kamloops by the trail is between seventy and eighty miles, and by the river probably ninety. Aided by the current we hoped to row this in a day and a half, and so get to Kamloops on Saturday night. V. had given us four men to row the boat, and as she lay at the river bank, the loads were taken from the horses' backs, and thrown in without difficulty.

After dining in front of the shanty, we said good-bye to Jack and Joe, and gave ourselves up to the sixth lot of men we had journeyed with since leaving Fort Garry, and the fourth variety of locomotion ; the faithful Terry still cleaving to the party, and really seeming to get fond of us, from force of habit, and the contrast of his own long tenure of service with the short periods of all the others.

At two P.M., twelve got into the boat ; our five, the crew, Smith, Trutch, and his man Johnston, who was to steer and help Terry. Up to two o'clock the day had been cloudy and cold, but the sun now came out, and we could enjoy the luxury of sitting in comfort, talking or reading, knowing too that no delay was occasioned by the comfort. The oars were clumsy but the men worked with a will, and the current was so strong that the boat moved down at the rate of five or six miles an hour, so that after four and a half hours, Trutch advised camping, though there was still half an hour's twilight, for at the same rate we would easily reach Kamloops on the morrow.

In this part of its course the river did not seem materially larger, or different from what it was much farther up. It still ran between high rugged hills, that closed in as canyons at intervals. Its course was still through a gorge rather than a valley.

Any expanse was as often up on a high terrace, that had once been its bed, as down along its present banks. Seventeen miles from the Clearwater we passed the Assiniboine's bluff, a huge protuberance of slate that needs only a similar rock on the other side to make it a formidable canyon. At some points the forms of the hills varied so much that the scene was picturesque and striking, but these hills are merely outliers, and not high enough to impress, or to do away with the feeling of monotony.

Our crew were expert in managing a boat and in putting up a tent. Before dark everything was secured, and we lay down for the last time in this expedition—in our lean to—*sub Jove frigido*. This—our Thompson River Camp—was the sixtieth from Lake Superior, and as we wrapped the blankets round us, a regretful feeling that it would probably be the last, stole into every one's mind.

September 28th.—Raining this morning again, but as there were no horses to pack, it was of less consequence. By 7:30 the boat was unmoored and we were rowing down the river, having fifty-two miles by the survey line and probably sixty-five by the river to make before night. Behind and above us the clouds were heavy, but we soon passed through the rainy region to the clearer skies that are generally in the neighbourhood of Kamloops. For the first half of our way the river scenery was very similar to that of yesterday, except that the flats along the banks were broader and more fertile, and the hills covered more abundantly with bunch grass. A few families of Siwashes, as Indians on the Pacific slope are called, in barbarous Chinook,—probably from Sauvages, are scattered here and there along the flats. Their miserable little tents looked like salmon smoking establishments ; for as the salmon don't get this far up the river till August and September, the Siwashes catch and dry them for winter use very late in the year.

Small pox has reduced the number of Siwashes in this part of the country to the merest handful. A sight of one of their winter residences is a sufficient explanation of the destructiveness of any epidemic that gets in amongst them. A deep and wide hole is dug in the ground, a strong pole with cross sticks like an upright ladder stuck in the centre, and then the house is built up with logs, in conical form, from the ground to near the top of the pole, space enough being left for the smoke and the inmates to get out. Robinson Crusoe-like they use the ladder, and go in and out of the house during the winter by the chimney. As this is an inconvenient mode of egress, they go out as seldom as possible ; and as the dogs live with the family, the filth that soon accumulates can easily be estimated, and so can the consequence, should one of them be attacked with fever or small pox. They boast that these houses are " terrible warm," and when the smoke and heat reach suffocation point, their remedy is to rush up the ladder into the air, and roll themselves in the snow for a few minutes. In spring they emerge from their hibernation into open or tent life ; and in the autumn they generally find it easier to build a new house or bottle to shut themselves up in, than to clean out the old one. This practice accounts for the great number of cellar-like depressions along the banks of the river ; the sites of former dwellings resembling the sad mementoes of old clans to be seen in many a glen in the Highlands of Scotland, and suggesting at the first view that the population in former years had been very large. But as one Siwash family may have dug out a dozen residences in as many years, the number of houses is no criterion of what the tribe numbered at any time.

For the first ten or fifteen miles of to-day's course, the river ran rather sluggishly. The current then became stronger, and as it cut for several miles through a range of high hills that had once stretched across its bed, there was a series of rapids powerful enough to help us on noticeably. The valley here became a gorge again. Emerging from the range at mid-day, Trutch pointed out blue hills in the horizon, apparently forty or fifty miles ahead, as beyond Kamloops. We halted for twenty minutes to take a cold lunch, and then moved on.

An hour before sunset we came to the first sign of settlers,— a fence run across the intervale from the river to the mountain, to hinder the cattle from straying. Between this point and Kamloops there are ten or eleven farms—" ranches " as they are called on the Pacific slope—all of them taken up since Milton and Cheadle's time. The first building was a saw-mill about fifteen miles from Kamloops, the proprietor of which was busy sawing boards to roof in his own mill, to begin with. Small log cabins of the new settlers, each with an enclosure for cattle called " the corral " close to it, next gladdened our eyes, so long unused to seeing any abodes of men. For all time the names and technical expressions on the Pacific coast are likely to show that settlement proceeded from the south and not across the mountains. But such Californian terms as ranch, corral and others from the lips of Scotchmen sounded strangely in our ears at first.

Stock raising is the chief occupation of the farmers here ; for though the ground produces the best cereals and vegetables, irrigation is required as in the fertile plains and valleys of California ; and the simplest method of irrigating—even where a stream runs through the farm—is expensive in a country where farm labourers and herdmen get from $30 to $75 a month and their board ; and where stock raising pays so well on account of the excellence of the natural grass. Common labourers on the roads in British Columbia get $50 a month, about $20 of which they pay for board ; and teamsters and packers from $100 to $150.

The farmers who have settled on the North or South Thompson are making money ; and beef commands higher prices every year. As there are very few white women most of the settlers live with squaws—or Klootchmen as they are called on the Pacific ; and little agricultural progress or advance of any kind can be expected until immigration brings in women accustomed to dairy and regular farm-work, to be wives for white men.

The ranches taken up are near little creeks that supply water to irrigate them. In the valley of the South Thompson are large extents of excellent land, ready for the plough, that will not be settled on till it is proved that water can be profitably raised from the river, or be had from wells in sufficient quantity. Neither way has yet been tried, simply because all the land along the creeks has not yet been taken up, and there has been no necessity for experimenting.

As we drew nearer Kamloops, characteristics of a different climate could be noted with increasing distinctness. A milder atmosphere, softer skies, easy rolling hills ; but the total absence of underbrush and the dry grey grass everywhere covering the ground were the most striking differences to us, accustomed so long to the broad-leaved underbrush and dark-green foliage of the humid upper country. We had clearly left the high rainy, and entered the lower arid, region. The clouds from the Pacific are intercepted by the Cascades, and only those that soar like soap-bubbles over their summits pass on to the east. These float over the intervening country till they come to a region high enough to intercept them. Thus it is that while clouds hang over Kamloops and its neighbourhood, little rain or snow falls. The only timber in the district is a knotty red pine, and as the trees grow widely apart, and the bunch-grass underneath is clean, unmixed with weeds and shrubs, and uniform in colour, the country has a well-kept park-like appearance, though there is too little of fresh green and too many signs of aridity for beauty.

The North Thompson runs smoothly for ten miles above Kamloops, after rippling over a sudden descent, and making a sharp bend round to the north-west and back again to the south·

In the afternoon a slight breeze had sprung up, and a tent was hoisted for a sail : but the wind shifted so frequently that more was lost than gained by it, and at sunset we took it down and trusted to the heavy oars. We had only four or five miles to make when it became so dark that the shoals ahead could not be seen ; and as none of the crew knew this part of the river, the steering became mere guess-work, and the Doctor as the lucky man was put at the helm. We grounded three or four times, but as the boat was flat-bottomed, and the bed of the river hard and gravelly, she was easily shoved off. The delays were provoking, all the more because there might be many of them ; but about 8 o'clock, the waters of the South Thompson, running east and west, gleamed in the darkness at right angles to our course. The North branch, though the largest, runs into the South branch. A quarter of a mile down stream from the junction is Fort Kamloops.

The boat was hauled in to the bank ; and Trutch went up to the Fort. Mr. Tait, the agent, at once came down, and with a genuine H. B., which is equivolent to a Highland, welcome, invited us to take up our quarters with him. Gladly accepting the hospitable offer, we were soon seated in a comfortable room beside a glowing fire. We were at Kamloops ! beside a Post Office, and a waggon road ; and in the adjoining room, the half dozen heads of families resident in or near Kamloops were holding a meeting with the Provincial Superintendent of Education, to discuss the best means of establishing a school. Surely we had returned to civilization and the ways of men !

Were we to judge from what we have seen of the country along the Fraser and Thompson rivers, the conclusion would be forced on us that British Columbia can never be an agricultural country. We have not visited, however, the Okanagan and Nicola Districts, or the Chilcoten Plains ; and we have heard good accounts of the fertility of the former, and the rich park like scenery of extensive tracts in the latter. But the greater part of the mainland is, " a sea of mountains "; and the Province will have to depend mainly on its rich grazing resources, its valuable timber, its fisheries, and minerals, for any large increase of population. The part of the country lying between the western slope of the Rocky Mountains and the Cascades is an elevated plateau " varying in breadth but probably averaging over one hundred and twenty miles," and in length extending from the boundary line north to Chilcoten lake. This extensive intervening plateau or series of pleateaux is extremely valuable as a stock-raising country, and with the aid of irrigation would produce great quantities of cereals.

The indications are that it once was submerged under water, with the hill tops then showing as islands, and with the long line of the Cascades separating the great elevated lake from the sea. In process of time clefts riven in the Cascades made ways for the waters to escape. By these clefts the Fraser, the Ho mathco, the Skeena, and the Bella Coula now run in deep gorges through granite and gneissic or trap and basalt rocks to the sea. Originally the waters emptied by a series of falls the magnificence of which it is scarcely possible to conceive. The successive subsidences of the water are now shown by the high benches of gravel and silt along the river valleys, and on account of the great depth cut down by the rivers, there are no bottom lands or meadows worth speaking of. As a general rule, with only a few exceptions, all the water channels are found in deep gorges, and for this reason the great rivers of the Province cannot overflow their banks. They must be content with rising higher up the steep hill-sides, between which, for the greater part of their course, they are pent.

CHAPTER XI

From Kamloops to the Sea.

September 29th.—A long sleep in real beds under a rafted roof, and a dip in the Thompson prepared us for such a break- fast as we never expect to eat again. Turtle soup out of a gold spoon is meagre fare compared to Kamloop's beef. After a few samples at breakfast, we were willing to subscribe to all that had ever been said in favour of bunch-grass as feed for the cat- tle of kings. Mealy potatoes, eggs, and other luxuries that need not be mentioned, lest those who never knew want should scorn our simple annals, explained satisfactorily the process by which Dr. Cheadle added forty-one pounds to his weight in a three week's stay at Kamloops. The dip was a pleasure too and not merely the duty it had sometimes been felt. Though the branches of the river are united, the currents of the two keep distinct for several miles down ; and the Fort being on the south side, we bathed in the South branch, which is so much warmer than the North that in summer, people who are anx- ious for cold water often cross in a canoe to the other side for a bucketful.

Soon after breakfast, people began to assemble for the public worship that had been intimated immediately on our arrival.

The service was held in the dining room of the fort. About thirty attended :—our own party, several gentlemen from other parts of the Province, the seven or eight inhabitants of Kamloops, and four or five farmers from the neighbourhood. Mr. Tait's two little girls represented the female population of the place ; for the three or four white women of the settlement were either absent from home or otherwise unable to attend ; and the men who lived with Klootchmen did not bring them to church. It may seem wonderful that these prosperous farmers should not have white wives ; but the remoteness of the place must be remembered, and they say, too, that the Victoria girls are unwilling to give up the pic-nics and gaieties of the capital for farm life and hard work in the interior. Of course there are no servant girls at Kamloops. A young Chinaman, answering to the common name of John, was cook and maid of all work at the fort ; and he did the work in a quiet, pleasant, thorough way, that made us wish to steal him for our own use.

Lunch at one, and dinner at five o'clock came in not too rapid succession, though a walk to the nearest hill-top was all that even the most energetic of the party took in the interval. From the hill-top is a magnificent view of the country around Kamloops : the North Thompson valley for twenty miles up ; the South Thompson extending to the east, and the united stream running west for seven miles, when it expands into a beautiful sheet of water, eighteen miles long, called Kamloops Lake. The hills in the neighbourhood have the clean, cultivated, park-like appearance that we noticed yesterday ; and several farms on the flats, at the junction of the two branches, gave a look of life and field work, to which, as well as to the universal soft mellow colouring imparted by the bunch grass, our eyes had long been unaccustomed. Ten miles away among the hills, on the opposite or north side of the Thompson, is the guard, with the four or five hundred horses of the fort, which, had time allowed, we would have visited, to compare the horses with

those of the plains.   One keeper suffices for the guard, for the
horses cluster in bands round their own stallions, and give no
trouble except when some, being required for use or sale, have
to be separated from the rest.   On such occasions, the whole
guard has to be corralled or penned, and the selection made.   It
would be impossible for a thief to steal one except by corralling
the band.   Last year the Company was offered $12,000 for
their Kamloops collection of horses. The offer was not accepted,
but it gives us an idea of the value of animals that cost their
owners only the pay of one keeper.

Our Sunday dinner was again crowned with a pemmican
plum-pudding.   The Doctor had fraternized with John and
prepared it as a surprise.   Nothing can be said concerning its
excellence more forcible than that it stood the test of being
eaten after Kamloops beef.   Few guessed the ingredients of the
pudding, but all praised it as having a peculiar flavour.

Dinner was scarcely over when people began to assemble for
the evening service that had been announced in the forenoon.
It was rough, mighty rough, on some of the party round the
table, this sudden transition from material to spiritual food.
The Doctor looked beseechingly at the Secretary, and formed
on his lips without syllabling it a word that could easily be interpreted "short !"   But he, with callous indifference, preached
for nearly an hour, because the congregation was larger than
in the morning, and would not get a sermon again for six
months.

September 30.—On Saturday night our disappointment had
been intense on learning that there were no letters or papers for
us.   All grumbled, and one threatened to leave out the last
half of the weekly toast of sweethearts and wives ; but hearing
that the paymaster of the Canada Pacific Railway Survey had
left Victoria for up country, we comforted ourselves with the
hope of meeting him with the budget in his pocket at Cache
Creek, where the Kamloops road joins the Cariboo waggon road
or at Ashcroft six miles farther down the Thompson.

Ashcroft is fifty-five miles from Kamloops, and if we were to get there to-night, an early start was necessary. But the proverbial difficulty of getting away in a hurry from a Hudson Bay fort held good. New arrangements require to be made ; men taken on or paid off ; horses or boat, and baggage to be seen to ; instructions to be left ; and all the time loafers and interviewers are in the way. We took advantage of odd minutes to be weighed, and a table giving our respective weights at Toronto and Kamloops is enough to prove that the expedition had not told severely on our physique.

Weight at Toronto, July 16.	At Kamloops, Sept. 30.
The Chief - - - - 174 lbs.	177 lbs.
The Doctor - - - - 184 "	187 "
Frank - - - - - 142 "	160 "
The Secretary - - - 142 "	160 "

Or a sum total, for the four, of 42 lbs. gain.

The order for the day was to row down twenty-five miles to Savona's ferry at the foot of Kamloops Lake, and there take horses to Ashcroft.

It was 8 o'clock before a start from the fort was effected, and a head wind springing up soon after, our rate of progress was slow. The river gradually expands into the Lake, and the scenery would be exceedingly beautiful were it not for the grey and arid or California look that vegetation presents. The hills are diversified in form and colouring, as they are in age ; some heavy bluffs of trap and basalt jutting out into the lake, intermingled with carboniferous rocks ; and beyond them elevated plateaux, composed of a silt of mingled sand and clay, retreat in more or less distinctly defined terraces. These plateaux again have been broken and twisted by small streams and side waters. On those broken narrow winding plateaux, and the hill sides that bound them, is abundant grazing for ten times the number of cattle or sheep now seen on them.

While rounding the great bluff on the south side of the Lake, the wind—which generally blows directly either up or down stream—blew so freshly up that the boat made little or no headway. We landed at midday, resolving to take to the horses if they could be seen on the other side of the bluff, and leave Terry in the boat to look after the luggage. Fortunately Mr. Tait had accompanied Jack (who had made a forced march from Clearwater, arriving at Kamloops on Sunday afternoon), and noticing that the wind kept the boat back, they waited for us in a little cove beyond the bluff, nine miles from the ferry. We gladly mounted into the saddle again, and in an hour and a half reached the end of the lake, where the Thompson issues from it as a broad deep noble-looking river. Ferrying across, a council was held at Savona's to decide what was to be done. It would be sunset before refreshment could be taken ; and it looked a little Dick Turpin-ish to start at such an hour for a thirty mile ride over a new road in a cloudy moonless night. Learning, however, that the Governor had been on his way to Kamloops to meet us, but had turned back to Ashcroft on hearing that we would probably be there to-night, our usual word "Vorwärts" was given. A jolly-looking Boniface and Mrs. Boniface hurried up a capital supper of Kamloops beef and vegetables, coffee and cake ; and promised one "that would make the hair curl" to any who could remain over night. Such a temptation, aided by a variety of circumstances, induced Smith to remain ; but at 6 o'clock the rest of us were in the saddle.

Four hours after, we reached Cache Creek, having rested only ten minutes on the way at the house of a French Canadian settler. The road followed the course of the Thompson, except for the last six or eight miles, when it turned a little northerly up the valley of the creek that runs into the Buonaparte, a tributary of the Thompson. There are good farms along the road, but night and the fact that it was after harvest made it necessary to accept the testimony of others on the point. The ground is a sandy loam, and will produce anything if irrigated, and nothing without irrigation. At Cache Creek the hotel was full, as it generally is, because at a junction of several roads. There was a letter for us from the Governor, and his trap waiting to take us on to Ashcroft. After waiting a little at Cache Creek to give the Doctor time to examine a patient, we got into the trap, and reached Ashcroft Hotel at 11 o'clock, and in half an hour after were in bed. The Governor had taken up his quarters at Senator Cornwall's, hard by, and would see us in the morning.

October 1st.—After breakfast, a decision had to be come to with regard to our future movements in British Columbia. The Governor, not expecting our arrival so soon, had concluded that we would not be able to take the steamer to San Francisco till the 27th inst. He had aranged to accompany us to Bute Inlet on the 11th, and advised us to visit in the interval the Upper Fraser river and Cariboo. It was important, however, that we should leave Victoria a fortnight earlier, if at all possible, and that necessitated our going on directly to New Westminster. No special object would be served by the Chief visiting Cariboo. The Governor, therefore, very kindly waived his own wishes, and telegraphed to Victoria for a steamer to meet us on Saturday at Burrard's Inlet.

We had now to wait a day at Ashcroft for an express to Yale, where the steamer to Mew Westminster connects with the stage coach from Cariboo. Nothing would be gained by going on at once, for there would have to be delay at Yale, if not here. We therefore spent the day in seeing the country, and in the evening dined at Senator Cornwall's.

The country about Ashcroft is sparsely peopled, and men accustomed to the rich grassy plains on the other side of the mountains, might wonder at first sight that it is peopled at all. In appearance, it is little better than a vast sand and gravel pit, bounded by broken hills, bald and arid except on a few summits that support a scanty growth of scrub pines. The cattle had eaten off all the bunch-grass within three or four miles of the road, and a poor substitute for it chiefly in the shape of a bluish weed or shrub, called sage grass or sage bush has taken its place. The cattle eat this readily, and fare well on it in winter ; but it grows thinly, dotting rather than covering the sandy soil, and giving a pepper and salt look to the near hill-sides. This poor looking land however is no more a desert than are the rich valleys of California. Like them, it will grow anything, if irrigated. Unfortunately the clouds pass and repass, driving forward only to sail high up, and beyond to the mountains, or to eddy back ; but even with this great drawback, and the high price of labour, and the lack of capital, farming pays well. There is abundance of water in the Thompson to irrigate all those arid slopes.

At lunch to-day a lumberer from the other side of the river came in and enquired for the Doctor. A log had fallen on a Chinaman employé, and broken his leg. As there was no Dr· within a hundred miles, the employer had come over to telegraph for a druggist 30 miles off, as the nearest approach to a regular practitioner. "John," he said, "was a wonderful Chinaman ; he would as lief live with him as with a white man." The Doctor went at once on the errand of mercy, and having to extemporise everything required for setting the leg, it was eight o'clock at night before he got back. He reported the patient to have exhibited the greatest fortitude, and to be doing well.

All the domestic servants we had seen as yet were Chinamen. They are paid from $20 to $45 a month, but as servant girls ask nearly as much, John is usually preferred. Though all gamble and most smoke opium, such vices do not materially interfere with their duties as servants. They are bowling out not only the cooks and servant girls, but the washer-women on the Pacific coast, and we must look to them as the future navvies and miners of our West. There are 18,000 of them in San Francisco out of a population of 160,000; 60,000 in California, and about 100,000 altogether on the Pacific side of North America. It would have been difficult to build, and it would now be difficult to work the Union Pacific Railway without them. Is it wonderful then that there should be a prejudice against them in the breasts of the white working-classes they are supplanting? The true-blue Briton of last century hated the French, because "they were all slaves and wore wooden shoes." Why should not the Yankee or Irish labourer hate the Chinese, when they not only wear wooden shoes, but are the best of workmen, cleanly, orderly, patient, industrious and above all cheap?

This evening we met Judge O'Reilly, whose praises had been often sung by Brown and Beaupré, in contrast with judges on the other side of the boundary line. "There isn't the gold in British Columbia that would bribe Judge O'Reilly," was their emphatic endorsement of his dealings with the miners. They described him, arriving as the representative of British law and order, at Kootanie, immediately after thousands had flocked to the newly discovered gold mines there. Assembling them, he said that order must and would be kept; and advised them not to display their revolvers unnecessarily, "for, boys, if there's shooting in Kootanie, there will be hanging." Such a speech was after the miners' own heart, and after it there were no disturbances in Kootanie.

The judge in his turn praised the miners, as manly, law abiding fellows. He never had the least difficulty in preserving order among the thousands gathered from all quarters of the earth, though the available force at his back usually consisted of two constables.

Left this morning for Lytton, forty-eight miles down stream, in an express, as the mail waggon from Cariboo was sure to be full of passengers at this season of the year. The waggon road on which we travelled is the principal public work of British Columbia; constructed as a government work with great energy soon after the discovery of the Cariboo gold mines. It was a very creditable undertaking, for most formidable engineering difficulties had to be overcome at the Canyons of the Fraser and the Thompson, and the expense to an infant colony was necessarily heavy. The waggon road is an enduring monument to Sir James Douglas—the first Governor of the Province—a man worthy to rank with those Roman generals and governors who were the great road-makers of the old world.

Before its construction there was only a trail to Cariboo, along which the gold hunters toiled night and day, driving pack-horses that carried their blankets and provisions, or if too poor to afford horse or mule, packing everything on their own backs. Men have been known to start from Yale on foot, for the gold fields, with 150 lbs. weight on their backs, and when they got to their destination, their difficulties only commenced. Gold was and is found in every sandbar of the river and in every creek; but it had to be found in large quantities to enable a man to live. A pound of flour cost a dollar and a half, and everything else sold at proportional prices. The gold was in largest quantities near the bed rock, and this was generally covered with a deposit of silt from five to forty feet thick, containing but little of the precious metal near the surface. The country presented every obstacle to prospecting. Range upon range of stern hills wooded from base to summit, through which a way could be forced only with incredible toil, and at the daily risk of starvation; it is little wonder that the way to Cariboo, and the country itself proved to be the grave of many an adventurous gold seeker. A few made fortunes, in a week or a month, which as a rule they dissipated in less than a year; hundreds gathered moderately large sums, which they took away to spend elsewhere; thousands made wages; and tens of thousands, nothing. It had been the same in California, when gold was discovered there; but then the masses who were unsuccessful could not get out of the country, and they had—fortunately for themselves—to hire out as farm servants and herdmen. In British Columbia they could get back to Oregon and California, and back they went, poorer than they had come, but leaving the Province little the better for their visit.

At various points on the river, all down the road, miners are still to be found. These are chiefly Siwashes and Chinese, who take up abandoned claims, and wash the sand over again, being satisfied with smaller wages than what contents a white man. Their tastes are simple and their expenses moderate. None of them dream of going to the wayside hotels, and paying a dollar for every meal, a dollar for a bed, a dollar for a bottle of ale, or twenty cents for a drink. The Chinaman cultivates vegetables beside his claim; these and his bag of rice suffice for him, greatly to the indignation of the orthodox miner. The Siwash catches salmon in his scoop net from every eddy of the river, and his wife carries them up to the house and makes his winter's food. These two classes of the population, the one representing an ancient civilization, the other scattered nomads with almost no tribal relationships, resemble each other in appearance so much that it would be difficult to distinguish them, were it not for the long tail or queue into which the Chinaman braids his hair, and which he often folds at the back of his head, instead of letting it hang down his back. The Pacific Indian is Mongolian in size and complexion, in the shape of the face, and the eyes. He has neither the strength of limb, the manly bearing, nor the dignity so characteristic of the Indians on the east side of the Rocky Mountains, but he is quite as intelligent, and takes more readily to civilized ways.

Salmon are the staple of the Siwash's food, and these are so abundant that they generally sell them for ten to twenty five cents apiece; and ten cents in British Columbia is equivalent to a penny elsewhere, for there is no smaller coin than the ten cent piece in the Province. Servants here and on the Fraser river would probably bargain as they used to bargain when hiring in Scotland, that they were not to be expected to eat salmon oftener than four times a week, if there was the slightest necessity of their making any stipulation. But masters and mistresses know their places too well to dream of imposing that or any other condition on them. We passed several Chinamen travelling along the road, each man carrying all his worldly goods suspended from the ends of a pole slung across one of his shoulders. So habituated are they to this style of carrying weight, that when they possess only one bundle, inconvenient to divide, they are said to tie a stone to the other end of the pole to balance the load. Whether this is meant as a joke or not, I shall leave as a puzzle to my readers.

Next to the bold and varied scenery, the chief objects of interest to a stranger travelling down the Thompson and the Fraser, especially after entering the Cascade range, are the Indian graves. Whatever these poor people can accomplish in the way of architecture or art, is reserved for their dead. A house better than they live in is built, or a good tent erected, and in it are placed the valuables of the deceased,—his gun, blanket, food ; in front hang scalps, or bright shawls, and white flags ; his canoe is placed outside, and beside it the hide of his horse or mule over a wooden skeleton ; rude painted images representing the man, woman, or family, as the case may be, are ranged in front. It is an article of faith with them that no Indian ever desecrated or robbed a grave ; and this is probable enough, for seldom has an Indian been known to steal or disturb even the cache of another, though the cache of dried salmon on the Pacific slope is usually hung on a tree by the wayside. The provincial law very properly imposes severe penalties on those who violate Indian graves ; but that the temptation may not be too strong, the canoe is generally riddled, and the lock of the gun taken off, before being deposited beside the dead. All those possessions so valuable in the eyes of a Siwash are left exposed to the winds of heaven and the beasts of the forest, and the age of the grave can be read in the condition in which you find them.

Driving for three hours over a country resembling that round Ashcroft, we came to Cook's Bridge, where the Thompson is crossed, and soon after to the foot hills of the Cascade range. Everywhere the soil looked poor and arid ; yet everywhere that cultivation was attempted, it produced cereals, roots, and fruits of the best kind. Tomatoes, water and musk melons ripened in the open air; and no farmer has fewer than fifty head of cattle, while some have ten times as many. Now, however, we were about to enter another rainy region, and the heavy mists resting on the hill-tops ahead, were the first indications of the change. The river's narrowness about Ashcroft had astonished us ; but here it contracted still more, looking smaller than either its North or South branch away up at Kamloops. What it is forced to lack in breadth it makes up in depth. As the rocky outliers of the mountains cannot be levelled into meadows, the river has to dam itself up their sides or dig a deeper ditch. The road followed its course, winding along the bases of the hills, or climbing over the canyôns, while far down, so immediately under us, that a stone could be dropped into the deep water, the river lay, like a green serpent, now at peace, and now rearing a crested head to pierce deeper into the overlapping barriers before it.

Towards sunsetting, cold rain with strong gusts of wind came on ; and as the road was often only a narrow ledge, cut out of the side of a precipice, we were thankful when the driver pointed out a hill in front, as the one on the other side of which was our resting place, the village of Lytton, at the junction of the Thompson with the Fraser.

We soon saw the lights of the village, and drove up to a house, the mean outside of which gave little promise of the good things for the inner man, in the dining room. M. Hautier, a Frenchman, and his pretty little Flamand wife, kept the house, and had comfortable rooms prepared for us, and a *petit goût de mouton* for supper.

October, 3rd.—The village of Lytton can scarcely be considered worthy of its aristocratic name. A single row of frail unpainted sheds or log shanties, the littleness and rickettiness of which are all the more striking from the two noble rivers that meet here and the lofty hills that enclose the two valleys, is the sum total of Lytton. Its population of perhaps an hundred souls is made up of Canadians, British, Yankees, French, Chinamen, Siwashes, half-breeds ; all religions and no religion.

To judge by the outside appearance of the village, there must be something rotten in its state. No sign of progress ; the use of paint or whitewash considered a sin ; though perhaps, even whitewash would be too good for such tumble down little huts. But go into the hotel, and all is changed. The inside is as different from what the outside would lead you to expect, as if it was the house of a rich Jew, in the middle ages. All the comforts of the Saut-market are to be had, and everyone, inside and outside the house, appears able to pay for them. A dirty looking miner calls for drinks all round, at twenty-five or fifty cents a drink, and considers himself half insulted if ony one in the room declines the friendly invitation. " Go through the form so as not to give offence," whispered a gentleman to the Doctor, as he saw him backing away from the freely proffered claret, champagne and brandy. The meat, fish, vegetables, and sweets on the table are all excellent, and well cooked. There are no poor men in the Province, and no such thing as bad living known. The explanation of this contrast, huts in which the tenants live like fighting cocks—is that none of the people came here to stay. They came to make money and then return home. Therefore it is not worth their while to build good houses or furnish them expensively ; but they can afford to live well, and the gold miner's maxim is eat, drink, and be merry, for to-morrow we die.

This state of things has been the millstone round the neck of British Columbia. The discovery of gold in 1858, on the Fraser, brought the first rush of people to the mainland, and resulted in the formation of the colony. All California was delirious. Thirty thousand men left the States for the Fraser, or, as it was more popularly called, " the Crazy River." The rush to Pike's Peak was nothing to the rush for Victoria. But in the course of the next two or three years, the thousands died or drifted back again, and only the tens remained. Then, in 1862 the Cariboo mines were discovered, and the second rush was greater than the first; but again, not an emigration of sober, steady householders, whose aim was to establish homes, and live by their own industry, but of fever-heated adventurers from all parts of the world—men without a country and without a home. San Francisco was deserted for a time. Thousands sold their lots there, and bought others in Victoria or claims in Cariboo. Cariboo was four hundred miles from the sea, and there was no road but an old Indian trail, winding up and down mountains and precipices, across deep gorges and rivers, through thick woods without game; but the obstacles that would have stopped an army were laughed at by miners. Of course the wave soon spent itself.

From that day, until recently, the colony has been going back, or as some gloomily say, getting into its normal condition. Within the last ten years, millions of dollars in solid gold have been taken out of the colony. No one thought of remaining in it except to make a fortune; no one was interested in its political life; no one of the thousands of foreign immigrants became a subject of the Crown. It was a mere finger-joint separated from its own body. But all this is now changing. With Confederation came the dawn of a brighter future; and, although British Columbia may never have the population of California or Oregon, an orderly development is commencing that will soon make it rank as a valuable Province of the Dominion.   It has the prospect of being no longer a dissevered limb, but of being connected by iron, as well as sympathetic, bands with its trunk ; and it is already receiving the pulses of the larger life. Had the Columbia River, instead of the 49th parallel been made its Southern boundary line, *i.e.*, had it received its natural and rightful boundary instead of a purely artificial one, it could compete with California in cereals as well as in gold mining. But in this, as in every case of disputed lines in America, U.S. diplomatists knew the value of what they claimed, and British diplomatists did not.   Every one in the Province believes that they lost the Columbia, because the salmon in it would not take a fly.   At the time of the dispute, when the Secretary for War was using brave words in the House of Commons, the brother of the Prime Minister happened to be stationed on the Pacific coast, and fished in the Columbia without success, because the salmon were too uneducated to rise to a fly.   He wrote home that " there was no use making a fuss about the country for it wasn't worth a ———."   And so the worthless region, now considered the most valuable on the Pacific, was gracefully given up.   And why not, when it was the privately if not publicly announced aim of a school of British politicians to get rid of the whole of British America, and thus gradually work out Benjamin Franklin's problem of how " a great nation may be made into a very little one."   But enough of this.   We still have more good land than we know what to do with.

Our first spell to-day was thirty-two miles down the Fraser from Lytton to Boston Bar, once a sand-bar celebrated for its rich gold deposits, and still rich enough to be washed by Chinamen and even a few not over-ambitious whites.   The road for the first ten or eleven miles ran chiefly across broken gravelly benches ; and then over, or when possible, around canyons that overhung the river.   The highest of these was Jackass Mountain, a huge bluff of pudding stone, probably so called because before the waggon-road was made, the old Indian path must have been strewn with the carcases of gold seekers' mules. The road now is at an elevation of seven or eight hundred feet above the river; and a thousand feet higher up may be seen a bridge at one time only two feet wide, stretched, like a spider's web, across a deep gulch on the old trail. Many a miner, in 1862, had crawled across this on his hands and knees, with heavy packs on his shoulders, well knowing that if he slipped, there was nothing to save him from rolling and pitching over sheer perpendicular rocks, from point to point, for eighteen hundred feet into the Fraser.

> " Had you seen these roads before they were made,
>   You would lift up your hands and bless General Wade,"

is a couplet well known to every tourist in the Highlands of Scotland. Sir James Douglas is the General Wade of British Columbia, and his name should be on the mile-stones of its waggon-road. The boast of the Colonists that no country in the world with so small a population and revenue ever constructed such good roads through so difficult a country is quite legitimate; and no one but a man possessed of great administrative ability and iron will could have done the work.

The waggon road, in many places, had to be hewed sideways out of the rock, or cloven through it, or built up with log or mason work in the hollows; and the cribbing is now so much out of repair, that one could not help feeling uneasy. The heavy rain last night had brought down boulders on it from the rocks above and loosened the soil at its outward edge, leaving but little firm ground for the waggon between the mountain and the edge of the bank. The slightest carelessness or recklessness in driving would have hurled the whole of us into the deep muddy torrent that rolled along swiftly at the bottom of the gorge. But the ribands were in the hands of a steady New Brunswicker, who had been on the road since it was built, in

summer and winter, day-light and dark, storm and shine, and
who had never once missed time or come to grief in any way.
Steve and a brother New Brunswicker, who drove the mail-
coach, were now, as they deserved to be, partners in the concern. Better whips there are not; and we cordially recom-
mend tourists who wish to travel over a road far more grand
and picturesque than the celebrated Corniceé between Genoa and
Nice, to trust themselves to either of them.

We dined at Boston Bar; and by one o'clock were on the
road again, hoping to get over the remaining twenty-four miles
to Yale before dark. The scenery all the way was of the same
frightfully grand character as it had been for most of the forenoon, with the exception of a small patch of open ground here
and there, cultivated by an enterprising settler, and on which
fruits and roots of the finest kinds grow readily. Eleven miles
from Yale we crossed to the west side of the Fraser over a
pretty suspension bridge, and, a mile beyond had to halt. A
gang of men were busy rebuilding the bridge over a strong
mountain torrent, called Spuzzum's Creek, from a patriarchal
Siwash chief of that ilk, who had gathered a colony around him
near the bridge, in decent looking huts superior to those of the
town of Lytton; and as only the stringers had been laid, there
seemed nothing for it but to camp, or cross on foot and walk to
Yale through a thick drizzle which has commenced. Several
of the huge freight waggons used in British Columbia, each
drawn by. twelve or sixteen oxen, and fully a hundred pack
mules had come on before us, to cross; but having been told
that there was no chance, their drivers had unharnessed, or
unpacked them, and were idling about. Steve, however,
was equal to the occasion. He offered ten dollars if the men
would stop their work and place loose planks across the stringers. The bargain was struck, and in an hour the job was done.
Steve unharnessed his horses and walked them across, and the
men dragged after him not only his waggon, but also the

mail coach which by this time had caugh up to us. A number of Siwashes were engaged on the bridge, and seemed to work on a footing of equality with the whites, with the grand exception that their wages were only $20 a month, while the whites got from $40 to $60 and their board. The general report was that the Siwash was a good fellow, obedient and industrious as long as he had a mind to work, if liquor could be kept from him ; but that liquor made him mad. He could neither resist it nor stand it. Again we were struck with the Asiatic cast of countenance ; and some of them were handsomer, from having decidedly straighter noses, than any Chinaman we saw. But the Fraser and Lilloet Indians are said to be the best in the Province, the best featured and the most industrious.

It was not quite dark when we saw the lights of Yale. Our first resort was to the Post Office armed with authority from the Governor to open the Kamloops bag. No difficulty was made, and in it were found letters and papers for everyone of the party but the Secretary. Unfortunate man ! Never did Briton look more like pariah than he as he sat looking gloomily at the others.

October 4th.— At Yale, we said good bye to horses. Henceforth, steam, the nineteenth century horse, would carry us down the river, along the coast, and across the continent homewards. Canoe and barge, buck-board and cart, saddle and pack-horse, buggy and express waggon belonged to the past of the expedition.

To-day the steamer *Onward*, that runs twice a week down the Fraser from Yale, was to take us to New Westminster, the Capital of British Columbia previous to its union in 1866 with Vancouver's Island. There, another steamer connects for Victoria, but our intention was to examine some of the harbours on the mainland before crossing to Vancouver's Island. The *Onward's* usual hour of starting is 7 A.M., but she delayed

to-day till noon to oblige several gentlemen who had come up
the river as far as Hope, to examine a new silver lead discovered in the mountains seven miles back from that settlement,
and who wished to get back to Victoria this week.   The delay
gave us time to walk round Yale and up the river.   The village itself has a neat, clean, thriving appearance, as if its
inhabitants had settled down to live in the country.   The scenery in the neighbourhood is of the grandest kind, varying with
every bend of the river.   Hills rise in gradual wooded slopes
for five, six or eight hundred feet ; and above, bald rocks shoot
up plumb for ten or twelve hundred feet higher.   The valley is
narrow, affording but little room for the farmer.

The steamer started at noon, and nine hours after reached
New Westminster, distant 95 miles.   The current is so strong
that she could run down in six hours, while it takes two days
to work up.   None of the stopping places are of much importance, though one or two are reported to be growing, especially
the agricultural settlement of Sumass, which is beginning to
supply New Westminster and Victoria with beef cattle.   A
little more work on that line is what the Province needs most ;
for at present, instead of keeping her gold within her own borders, she has to export it all to buy the necessaries of life.

Soon after passing Hope, where every one got specimens of
the new silver mine, the Fraser turns from its southerly to a
south-westerly and then a westerly course ; and the valley begins
to broaden and give some room and verge for farms.   But the
good land near the river does not amount to much.   The Fraser
has gold in its sandbars, and salmon by the hundred thousand in
its pools and channels ; but spite of its great length and force,
the mountains between which it forces its way are too powerful
for it to accomplish the usual work of rivers.   It cannot overflow, no matter how immense the volume of water it rolls
down to the sea ; it can only rise higher up the sides of its rocky
barriers.   We could see the high water mark twenty-five feet
above the present level.

On board the *Onward* we met Chief Justice Begbie, another name held in profound respect by the miners, Siwashes, and all others among whom he has dealt out justice. Judge Lynch has never been required in British Columbia, because Chief Justice Begbie did his duty, and maintained the dignity of his Court as effectually as if it had been held in Old Westminster. It is a grand sight to a rightly constituted mind when two or three policemen scatter a street mob. It must have been a grander to see a British Judge backed by one or two constables maintaining order at the gold mines among the tag-rag and bob-tail, the rough and tumble, fever-heated classes of miners, gamblers, claim jumpers, and cutthroats who congregate at such places. For " the yellow fever" seizes upon the most daring and the most abandoned of humanity, the strongest and the weakest. And where there is no previously settled population to enforce order, what can be expected round every rich creek and gulch but a miniature Norfolk Island without the keepers? In such communities, especially at the outset, justice or even a little more than justice is true mercy. That Scotch Lord Braxfield who gleefully told an unfortunate wretch that " he would be nane the waur o' a little hanging," would have been a very guardian angel in California in 1849. It is a proud thought to us that British America has proved herself a worthy daughter of the Old Mother in her judiciary ; that in no Province has a judge ever been accused as corrupted or corruptible. In British Columbia the difficulties in the way of preserving order were greatest, yet the laws have always been respected and enforced, and two or three constables proved sufficient for every emergency. The results have been simply marvellous. *The Times* Cariboo correspondent could write in 1862 :—" As to security of life, I consider it just as safe here as in England." Every week for the last nine years the mail coach has carried a box or boxes of gold dust from Cariboo with no defender but Steve or his partner ; and though running thrcugh a country roamed over by the lawless of every nation, where ambuscades could be planned at every turn, where for long stretches there is neither house nor shanty, it has never been plundered nor even attacked. Though comparisons are odious, they ought to be made sometimes. It is almost impossible to take up a newspaper, published on the other side of the line, without reading accounts of violent deeds in the gold fields or of mail-coaches plundered. One fact that came under our own notice is sufficiently illustrative. On our return, the train stopped for an hour at Ogden, in the Utah Territory. The first thing that attracted our attention was a series of placards on the railway station describing four different cases of highway robbery in the territory that month, and offering rewards varying from hundreds to thousands of dollars for the discovery of the highwaymen.

They tell many good stories in British Columbia of the Chief Justice's dignity on the Bench, and the terror he inspires. The last we heard ought to be true. He sternly told a witness who hesitated considerably, that he believed he was prevaricating. —" And h-how can a fellow h-help prevaricating who has l-lost his front teeth ?' was the half-frightened response of the poor man, expecting nothing less than an order for his instant execution.

On our arrival at New Westminster several gentlemen of the place waited on the Chief to offer him a public dinner. He felt obliged to decline, with thanks for the courtesy ; and after making arrangements to start for Burrard's Inlet in the morning, we turned into our berths in preference to going to an hotel.

October 15th.—The programme for the day was to drive nine miles across the spit of land, on one side of which is New Westminster, to Burrard's Inlet ; see as much of the inlet as possible ; and when the steamer that the Governor had telegraphed for arrived, proceed in her to Bute Inlet, visiting on

the way the surveying parties who had been at work all summer on the coast. Several New Westminster gentlemen accompanied us to Burrard's Inlet; and as the member for the
district, the senior member for Victoria, and a senator from
Cariboo were in town, the Chief invited them to join us in our
coasting trip to the north.

As this enlargement of the party occasioned an hour's delay,
there was time to look round New Westminster, before starting.
The population of the little town is less than a thousand, but
the importance of a town in America is not estimated so much
by its population, as by its position and the extent of country
it supplies. New Westminster is the only town on the delta
of the Fraser, and as the delta may be said to extend east and
west from Sumass to the sea, and from Boundary Bay on the
south to Burrard's Inlet on the north, or over sixty miles in
length by twenty in breadth, a district including much land fit
for agriculture, the population and importance of the country
and town are sure to increase. Its being near the mouth of the
Fraser, a river seven hundred miles long, does not help it much,
not only because the Fraser drains comparatively little land
adapted for cultivation, but because the entrance is intricate on
account of the tortuous channel and shifting shoals that extend
out for some distance into the Gulf of Georgia. The excellent
harbour of Burrard's Inlet, nine miles to the north, will therefore be generally preferred for shipping purposes. This has
been already proved to a certain extent. The New Westminster proprietors of a large steam saw-mill finding Burrard's
Inlet the fitter port for their shipments of lumber, transferred
the machinery and set up their mill on the north side of the
Inlet; so that now little or nothing is exported from New
Westminster, except fish and cattle from the neighbouring settlements. A practically unlimited quantity of fish ought to be
exported; for salmon go up the Fraser from the sea in countless numbers. They are said to be inferior in quality to those

of the Atlantic coast, though we did not think so, and they would probably be quite as good for canning. The first trade we saw this morning was a Klootchman selling four salmon for twenty-five cents ; and that in a country where twenty-five are less valuable than ten cents in the Eastern Provinces. A sturgeon in the fish market weighed over 300 lbs. They are sometimes caught from six to nine hundred weight, and the flavour of this fish is considered by many superior to salmon. But the Province is young, and requires capital and exterprise before it can compete on a large scale with the fish-curing establishments on the Columbia River.

We paid a visit to the assaying office, and the agent in charge explained the process by practical illustrations. Where there is no assay office, the miner in selling his gold is at the mercy of itinerant dealers. Now he takes his precious dust or nuggest to the office, where it is fused into ingots and the exact market value of each ingot stamped on it for a quarter per cent, or $1 for $400. The New Westminster office assayed last year of the products of the Fraser mines $100,000. The Cariboo office of course does a much more extensive business.

At 10 A.M. the united party started for Burrard's Inlet, and arrived in two hours. A lover of ferns would be charmed with this bit of road, so surprising a variety can be gathered, especially near the Inlet. Many, such as the shield, the winter, the rock, the lady fern and the bracken, are similar to those found in the Atlantic provinces, but other varieties were altogether new to us.*

A steamer, so diminutive and toy-like that each man stepped on board tenderly for fear of upsetting or breaking her, was in waiting to take us across the Inlet to the large saw-mill of

---

* A small collection chiefly made about Burrard's Inlet, includes the following varieties, besides two new ones that we could not make out :—Polypodium vulgare ; P. Dryopteris ; Asplenium Trichomanes ; Allosorus crispus ; Cystopteris montana ; C. fragilis ; Pteris Aquilina ; Blechnum boreale ; Polystichum acrostichoides ; P. Lonchitis ; Lastrea dilatata ; Botrychium Virginicum ; B. Lunaria ; B. lunarioides.

Messrs. Moody, Diety and Nelson. Thirteen million feet of lumber were exported last year from this, and about as much from another mill on the south side of the inlet owned by a company. All the lumber is the famous Douglas Fir. Logs four to five feet in diameter were being hauled up and sawed by two circular saws, the one placed vertically over the other, as it is easier to work on such huge subjects with two ordinary sized than with one very large saw. The workmen represented the various nationalities scattered everywhere along the Pacific coast, Whites, Chinese, Siwashes and Kanakas or Sandwich Islanders.

The aborigines work well till they save enough money to live on for some time, and then they go up to the boss and frankly say that they are lazy and don't want to work longer. They are too unsophisticated to sham sickness, or to strike. Another habit of the richer ones, which to the Anglo-Saxon mind borders on insanity, is that of giving universal backshish or gifts to the whole tribe, without expecting any return save an increased popularity that may lead to their election as Tyhees or chiefs when vacancies occur. An old fellow, big George, was pointed out to us as having worked industriously at the mill for years till he had saved $2,000. Instead of putting this in a Savings Bank, he had spent it all on stores for a grand "Potlatch," summoning Siwashes from far and near to come, eat, drink, dance, be merry, and receive gifts. Nearly a thousand assembled ; the festivities lasted a week ; and everyone got something, either a blanket, musket, bag of flour, box of apples, or tea and sugar. When the fun was over, big George, now pennyless, returned to the mill to carry slabs at $20 a month. His reputation mounted to an extraordinary height because of so magnificent a potlatch, and he stood a good chance of the Tyheeship ; but two rivals, Supple Jack and Old Jim, were preparing to outdo him ; and if Siwashes are at all like civilized beings, the "popularis aura" shall fill their sails before long.

Very naturally Siwashes measure all excellence by the grub or gifts they get. It is said that when a Bishop lately visited a tribe that one of his missionaries had laboured among for some time, they all gathered to meet him, being told that he was "hyass Tyhee" or great chief of the praying men. The Bishop addressed them at great length, and apparently with effect, but when done, a grave and reverend fellow rose and snuffed out his lordship with half a dozen words, which in vernacular Chinook, are even more emphatic than in any slang English they can be rendered into, "lots of gab; no grub, no gifts; all gammon." A delightful gentleman to convert, certainly!

The workmen at the mill live in comfortable little houses, perched on rocks at the foot of a lofty wooded hill overhanging the shore. There is no soil except what has been made on the beach from chips and sawdust. Round the nearest point is a small tract diligently cultivated by a few Chinamen. The men have a large reading-room with a harmonium, and a well selected library. No intoxicating liquors can be sold on the premises. Their pay is good and they save money. The manager of the mill on the other side of the Inlet told us that he would give $200 a month to any competent overseer we would send him.

The woods all round these shores are well stocked with deer. The usual way of hunting is to send the dogs into the woods, and drive the deer down into the harbour, where they are at the mercy of the sportsman. The overseer informed us that in this way he could shoot a deer any day within two hours.

After lunch, we embarked on a large steamer belonging to the mill for a sail round the Inlet. At this moment, the *Sir James Douglas*, the steamer the Governor had telegraphed for, arrived from Victoria. The captain came on board to put himself at the orders of the Chief, and it was arranged to start with him as soon after midnight as possible. In the meantime he proceeded with us down the Inlet.

Burrard's Inlet is naturally divided into three divisions, that are really three distinct harbours. The saw-mills are on the opposite shores of the middle one. This middle harbour narrows at both extremities, and an outer and a further inner harbour are thus made. We had time to visit only the outer and the middle, both safe and capacious harbours, with easy entrance and good anchorage. At seven P.M. we got back to the mill, and after dinner said good-bye to the New Westminster gentlemen who had kindly accompanied us. The little cabin of the *Sir James Douglas* was to be our dining and sleeping room for the next week, our last week, for after it the home stretch would begin.

———

The little that we saw of the mainland of British Columbia does not warrant us to say much about it as a field for emigrants. There can be no reasonable doubt that it can support in comfort a much larger population than it now has. The resources of the colony are considerable, but all its industries are in their infancy, cramped from want of capital, and obliged to compete with the immense and consolidated establishments of similar industries on the other side of the boundary line. Its distance from the countries that supply emigrants, and the expense of travelling from place to place, on account of the magnificent distances within the Province itself, are great drawbacks. But on the other hand, the high price paid for labour, the ready market for all products of the soil, and the healthiness of the climate are immense attractions to the ordinary class of emigrants. While lumbering, mining, and the fisheries offer the richest prizes to men of capital and experience, mechanics and the labouring classes can command such wages that the economy of a few years puts them in the position of small capitalists. Farm labourers especially ought to be able to buy and stock good farms of their own out of the savings of four or five years ; and then they are comfortable and independent for life. We heard the province styled the poor man's paradise ; and as 10 per cent is given everywhere, with undoubted security, for the use of money, the rich man has no reason to be dissatisfied.

CHAPTER XII.

The Coast, and Vancouver's Island.

October 6th.—Before any of us came on deck this morning,
the good *Sir James Douglas* had steamed out of Burrard's Inlet,
and past the lofty mountains that enclose the deep fiords of
Howe Sound and Jervis Inlet, into the middle of the Straits of
Georgia. Our first sight was of the Island of Texada on our
right, and the bold outline of Vancouver's Island farther away
on our left.

After breakfast, divine service was held in the cabin. On
those inland waters of the Pacific that folded themselves round
rocky mountain and wooded island, we, who had come four
thousand miles from the Atlantic, united our voices in common
prayer with fellow subjects who call these shores of the vaster
Ocean of the West, their home. Again, all found that prostration
before Him, who is our Father, and also King of Nations, not
only evokes the deepest feelings of the human heart, but purifies
them. The tie of a common nationality, especially if the nation
has a great history, is holy. The aim of our work was to bind
our country more firmly together, and this thought elevated the
work ; while worshipping together made us feel more power-
fully than any amount of feasting and toasting the flag that
inhabitants of the same Dominion, subjects of the same

Sovereign, and heirs of the same destinies, must ever be brothers.

Towards mid-day, our course took us out of the Straits of Georgia, north-easterly up into Bute Inlet, another of those wonderful fiords of unknown depth that seam this part of the Pacific coast. The chart makes it 40 fathoms deep, with a mark over the figures signifying that the naval surveyors had sounded to that depth without finding bottom.

The object of going up this Inlet, the proposed terminus for the Railway, was to enable the Chief to get such a birds-eye view of it as he had already obtained of the prairie and the mountain country, and at the same time to meet two parties of the Survey, who had been at work in this quarter all summer.

On the question of which is the best western terminus, there are two great parties in British Columbia, one advocating the mainland, the other Vancouver's Island. On the mainland, Burrard's Inlet is the favourite. If a harbour on Vancouver's Island be chosen, then the railway must eventually cross to the shores of Bute Inlet. The advocates of the Island termini— Victoria, Esquimalt, and Alberni,—asserted that it was a simple matter to cross the Straits of Georgia to the mouth of Bute Inlet by Valdes Island, which on the map does seem to block them up almost completely ; then, that the line could be made along the shore of the Inlet to the mouth of the Homathco River, and up its course, through the Cascades, to the Chilcoten plains. Two main routes had therefore to be surveyed : one, from the mouth of the Fraser River, and up the Thompson ; the other, from Vancouver's Island across to Bute Inlet, and, up the Homathco to the upper Fraser, whence the line could be carried to Fort George or the North Thompson valley, if no direct passage across the Gold-range to the Canoe River, or Tête Jaune Cache could be found.

A short time after the latter survey was commenced, the engineer reported that Valdes Island, although represented on the charts as one, really consisted of a group of three islands. The naval surveyors had seen channels piercing into Valdes Island, but had not followed them up, their business being to lay down the soundings only along the through channels, and Valdes Island, not having been explored, had always been considered an unit. The discovery of the true state of the case complicated the question, and necessitated a hydrographic survey of four or five instead of two Narrows. This was work for one party, the line up Bute Inlet being assigned to another, and up the Homathco through the Cascades to a third.

On board the *Sir James Douglas* we had the member for New Westminster, a zealous advocate of Burrard's Inlet, and the member for Victoria—a true believer in an Island terminus. To a student of human nature it was amusing to notice with what different eyes each looked at or refused to look at the difficulties of the rival routes. The former gazed exultingly on the high bluffs and unbroken line of mountains, that rose sheer from the waters of Bute Inlet. But his sarcasms were invariably met by a counter reference to the canyons of the Fraser and the Thompson.

There was not one of us who had ever seen anything like the Inlet we steamed up this afternoon. The inlets which cut deep into this coast, from the straits of Fuca northward for twelve degrees of latitude, probably resemble the fiords of Norway, but none of our party could speak of those from personal observation.

It is a singular fact that, while there is not a single opening in the coast for seven hundred miles north of San Francisco, except the bad harbour of Astoria at the mouth of the Columbia river, the next seven or eight hundred miles should be broken by innumerable inlets. The case is paralleled on the Atlantic side of North America. From Florida to Maine there are very few good ports, while north of Maine, embracing the coast of New Brunswick and Nova Scotia there are scores.

The openings in the iron-bound coast of Nova Scotia are not unlike those on the Pacific side, except that on the Atlantic the indentations do not cut so deep into the land, and the shores are low.

Up into the very heart of the Cascade range through a natural passage, which could not have been formed by the ocean, for the coast is protected here from its erosions by Vancouver's Island, we sailed to-day for forty miles, over water almost as deep under our keel as the snow-capped mountains that hemmed the passage were high above our heads. The Inlet varies in breadth from one to two-and-a-half miles, and for the greater part of its length a ship may sail close enough to the shore for a man to jump to the rocks.

A mist, followed by a drizzling rain, came on early in the afternoon, and hid the summits of the mountains, but the gleam of scores of white cataracts could be seen; and, like furrows amid the dark spruce, the clean sides of the rocks in long straight lines showed where avalanches had swept everything before them into the deep waters below. Half way up the Inlet we saw a tent on the shore. A whistle brought its tenant out to us in a canoe; he proved to be a commissary who had preceded X party a few miles, in order to make necessary arrangements for their advance. An hour after, we passed camp X., but as the mist had thickened and our captain had never been in these waters before, he steamed on without stopping, for Waddington harbour at the head of the Inlet. This point he reached after dark, and at once sent a boat's crew ahead to sound for an anchoring place. After some delay, between seven and eight P.M., the boatswain held up a lantern in the boat to indicate where soundings had been found. Steaming up to the light the anchor was let go in twenty-five fathoms, quarter of a mile from the shore and from the head of the Inlet.

October 7th.—A magnificent view awaited those early on deck this morning. Nearly two hours were spent in weighing anchor, and then the steamer went round the harbour to enable us to see it on all sides. Rain had fallen steadily through the night, and, now that it had ceased, mist clouds hung about the great masses of rock that on all sides rose perpendicular into the region of eternal snow. Here and there, rifts in the mist, as it was broken by projecting peaks, revealed mountain sides curtained with glaciers. The only sound which broke the awful stillness was the muffled thunder of cataracts, multiplied by last night's rain, gleaming far up among the scanty pines, washing down the slippery rocks in broad white bands, or leaping from bluff to bluff an hundred feet at a time, for more than a thousand feet down to the sea. We were at the head of Bute Inlet. The salt sea water could cut no deeper into the range that guards the western side of our continent. The mountains stood firm except where the Homathco cuts its way through, in a deep gorge, sentinelled on each side by snow-clad warders.

By this water-highway the late Mr. Waddington had urged the Government of British Columbia to make their road to Cariboo. On their adopting the Fraser River route, he organized a private company and began construction of Bute Inlet Road, so convinced was he, that its superiority would attract the travel between Cariboo and the outside world, and that a toll on goods carried over it would repay the Company. His project was a steamer from Victoria to the head of Bute Inlet, and a waggon road thence up the Homathco to Cariboo; the distance being 175 miles less this way than by the Fraser. After spending $60,000 on surveys and on trail making, his men were murdered in 1864 by a tribe of Indians to whom provocation had been given. The Government secured the arrest of the murderers, and had them hung up at Quesnel mouth; but, from that day, the Coast and Chilcotin Indians have been regarded as dangerous and blood-thirsty. The C. P. R. parties who travelled the country this year, had no trouble however; and Mr. Smith reports that the Chilcotins are the manliest and most intelligent Siwashes he has seen in the Province.

From the description that Mr. Smith gave us of the scenery on the Homathco, we would fain have landed and gone at least a few miles up the river : but time did not permit.   He had worked up from the head of the Inlet through the Cascades in July last, overcoming by sheer determination not to be beaten—all difficulties of forest, canyons, torrents, and Indians ; getting surveys at great risk of neck and limb, by felling trees across deep chasms from one to two hundred feet wide, and letting men down by ropes to the foot of high cliffs.   The following extracts from one of his private letters to the Chief give more vivid pictures than any plate can, of scenes up the river. Here is what he says of the canyons, 31 miles from the head of the Inlet, and immediately above the rope ferry used by Mr. Waddington :—" I commenced the survey of the canyon, following the river on the new trail commenced by Waddington, as far as it went,—about half a mile,—when it terminated at an inaccessible bluff on which blasting had been commenced.   The scene here is awfully sublime.   The towering rocks, thousands of feet high ; serrated and broken by dark chasms—far above these again the snow-clad peaks, connected by huge glaciers ; out of which issued torrents that fell in cascades ; and in a deep gorge beneath a mountain torrent—whirling, boiling, roaring, and huge boulders always in motion, muttering, groaning like troubled spirits, and ever and anon striking on the rocks, making a report like the booming of distant artillery.   But with all this wildness, there is the fresh beauty of vegetation. Wherever there is a crevice, to the base of the snow-clad peaks were clumps of evergreen trees, and lower down wherever a handful of soil could rest it was sprinkled with wild flowers amongst which bloomed the sweet lily of the valley."

After getting through "the core of the Cascade range," he came upon " the murderers' camp, where thirteen of Waddington's men were murdered eight years ago.   The spot looks as if it had never before been visited by man since the massacre.

The number of tents could be counted by the cedar bark forming the beds. Strewed around were various tools,—a black-
smith's anvil, sledge-hammers, crowbars, grindstone, vice, picks,
and half a dozen shovels carefully placed against a tree ready
for the morrow's work ; also pieces of clothing, amongst which
were at least one pair of woman's boots—too surely indicating
the source of the trouble." This last clause suggests the origin
of more than one " Indian atrocity." It's always a fair question to ask : " Who struck the first blow ?"

The forenoon was spent by us in coasting down the northerly
side of the Inlet until we came to camp X. After inspecting
their work we proceeded on our way down, Mr. Gamsby, the
engineer in charge, accompanying us. He reported that the
Indians, far from giving any trouble, had been of material
assistance in many ways, acting as servants or messengers, and
selling deer, wild fowl, and fish, at moderate prices. He pointed
out a stream, running into the Inlet on the east side, at the
mouth of which, on a recent visit, he had seen hundreds of
thousands of dead salmon strewn along the shore ; while thousands of crows, kites, vultures, and eagles filled the air. In
similar places, such sights must have been common when white
men first came to the country. These Pacific waters swarm
with fish, that struggle up brawling streamlets to spawn, in
spite of rapids, cascades, rocks, and shallows. No wonder that
people, who have only eaten salmon caught inland, say that the
Pacific varieties are inferior. They were good when they
entered the river's mouth ; but, when caught a few hundred
miles up the Fraser, often the head is bruised by rocks and
falls, and the scales, fins, and even the tail rubbed or worked
off. No wonder that half of them perish by the way, and that
none return to the sea. It is asserted everywhere in British
Columbia, that none of the salmon entering the Fraser river,
and even the smaller streams, ever return to the sea.

We were struck with the beauty of Gamsby's canoe, and

THE HAMATHCO BELOW THE DEFILE

indeed of all the Indians' canoes on this coast. Each is a model
of architectural grace, although the lines reminded us of Chinese
or Japanese rather than of British models. The canoes are
generally made out of a single large log, formerly scooped out
with chisel and stone mallet, gimlet, from bird's bone, and
muscle shell or stone adze. After scooping out the log, they
used to steam it in the following primitive manner : Fill it
with water, throw in heated stones to make the water boil, and
at the same time build a bark-fire round the outside. The
wood gives several inches, until the central part of the canoe
is made broader at the top, and the requisite curvature secured
to its sides. Light cross pieces are inserted from side to side
to improve the form ; outside and inside are then painted ;
ornamented figure-head and raised stern piece set on ; and the
canoe is complete.

By midday the mouth of Bute Inlet was gained, but instead
of returning in the direction of Burrard's Inlet, we ran through
Arran Rapids in order to pass round the north side of Valdes'
Inland. At every turn, the beautiful views which an archipelago affords, met our eyes. The islands of every possible
variety of form, were wooded from lofty summits to the brink
of deep channels. At one time we were in cross-roads where
four different channels opened out, north, south, east, and west ;
soon after in a narrow winding strait, or shooting swiftly
through tidal rapids, or in a broad bay where snowy peaks could
be seen behind the green foothills. After passing through Seymour
Narrows, where, if there is to be a continuous line from an Island
terminus, the bridge between Valdes' and Vancouver must be built,
we rounded into a beautiful land-locked harbour, called Menzies
Bay, and cast the anchor for the night. Between the Narrows
and the Bay, the tents of Y. party were picturesquely pitched,
on an open easy slope, under the shadow of the forest. A
whistle from the steamer brought Mr. Michaud on board, and,
after dinner all rowed off to his encampment, the Chief to in-

spect plans, the rest to see the camp. As compared with the others, Y. party has been in clover from the beginning of their work. They were near Victoria, had a monthly mail, and could renew their supplies as they ran out. Their storehouse filled with bags of flour, flitches of bacon, pork, molasses, split peas, beans, pickles, and a keg of beer, suggested good cheer; while any day, they could buy from the Indians a deer, weighing from 120 to 160 lbs., for one or two dollars; and salmon, trout, wild-geese, duck, or mallard, for trifling sums. They had no deer-meat in camp to-day, but they generously presented us with two wild geese, each weighing ten or eleven lbs.

October 8th.—Our programme for the day was to reach Nanaimo Coal Mines as soon as possible, for the steamer's bunkers needed replenishing, and we wished to see something of the mines, which promise to be of more benefit to British Columbia than the gold-fields. Accordingly at 4 a.m. the anchor was weighed.

We were now getting into waters familiar to our captain; for strange as it may appear, not one on board with the exception of Mr. Smith, had ever been up Bute Inlet or round Valdes Island before this trip. Nothing shows more clearly the imperfectly developed condition of the Province than such a fact. Her representative men, those most likely to be best acquainted with her resources, know little beyond their own neighbourhood or the line of their one waggon-road. Distances are so great, the means of communication so limited, and the mountainous character of the country renders travelling so difficult, that the dwellers in the few towns and settlements have hitherto seen but little of the Province as a whole.

When we appeared on deck about 7 o'clock, the steamer was running down the Straits of Georgia, over a rippling, sun-lit sea. The lofty Beaufort range, on our right, rose grandly in the clear air, every snowy peak distinct from it neighbour, and the blue sky high above the highest. Victoria, and the twin peaks Albert Edward and Alexandra, ranging from 6,000 to over 7,000 feet in height, were the most prominent; but the noble serrated range as a whole, more than separate peaks, caught the eye. The smaller Islands to the left were hidden by a fog-bank that gradually lifted. Then stood out, not only islet after islet in all their varied outline, but also the long line of the Cascade range behind. Yesterday had been charming from 10 o'clock, when the sun pierced through the mists; but to-day was all white. A soft warm breeze fanned us, and every mile disclosed new features of scenery, to which snow-clad mountain ranges, wooded planes, and a summer sea enfolding countless promontories and islands, contributed their different forms of beauty. The islands are composed of strata of sandstone and conglomerate; the sandstone at the bottom worn at the water line into caves and hollows; the conglomerate above forming lofty cliffs that are wooded to the summit and over-hang winding inlets and straits most tempting to a yachtsman. From the southern point of Valdes Island down to Nanaimo, a considerable area of low lying and undulating land extends between the central mountain range of Vancouver's Island and the Straits of Georgia, well adapted for farming purposes. At two points, Comox and Nanoose, settlements have been formed within the last few years, but where there is one settlement there ought to be twenty, if the island is to raise its own grain and hay, and to cease sending out of the country all its wealth. There is little or no immigration to Vancouver's Island, and little has been done to induce it, or to smooth the way for those who arrive. When an immigrant reaches the country, he finds it diffi-cult to obtain information as to where there is good land to take up; and how is it possible for him to go out among a sea of moun-tains to search for a farm? The island should be thoroughly sur-veyed according to the simple system long practised in the United States, and lately adopted in Manitoba; the amount of good land known, divided into sections and subsections, and numbered ; so that, on arriving at Victoria, the immigrant could go into the Crown Land office, learn what land was pre-empted, and where it would be expedient for him to settle. There are many obstacles in the way of immigrants reaching this distant colony, and therefore special efforts are required to bring them, and to keep them when they come ; for, until there is a large agricultural population, the wealth of the country must continue to be drained out of it, to buy the necessaries of life and every other article of consumption, from Oregon, California, Great Britain, and elsewhere.

We were sorry at not being able to visit Comox. Testimony was unanimous concerning the good quality of the land, the accessibility to markets, and the prosperity of the settlers, notwithstanding the short time they have been in the country.

By noon we had left the Beaufort range behind, and Mount Arrowsmith came into view ; while far ahead on the mainland, and south of the 49th parallel, what looked a dim white pyramid rising to the skies, or a white cloud resting upon the horizon, was pointed out to us by the Captain as Mount Baker. Soon after we rounded into the northern horn of Nanaimo harbour, called Departure Bay, and drew alongside the pier, where a lately organized Company is shipping coal from a new seam that has been opened, three miles back from the point of shipment.

Landing, and leaving the steamer to coal, most of us walked by a trail to Nanaimo through the woods, along a channel that connects Departure Bay with the old mines. The channel, which is an excellent roadstead, is between the mainland of Vancouver and a little island called Newcastle, on the inner side of which another excellent coal mine, within ten feet of navigable water, has just been opened. There are two seams at Newcastle, averaging three feet each, and separated by three feet of fire clay, which, as the miners proceed, becomes thinner, the coal seams becoming thicker. From this convergence it is supposed that the clay will soon give out, and the two seams of coal unite into one. Near this Newcastle mine is a quarry of light-coloured freestone of excellent quality, which is sure to be of immense service and value in the near future. There is no such freestone quarried on the Pacific coast; and its convenience for shipping makes it doubly valuable.

At Nanaimo proper is a population of seven or eight hundred souls,—all depending on the old or Douglas mine. The manager informed us that they would probably ship fifty thousand tons this season, while last year they shipped less than thirty thousand; and that, next year, they would be in a position to ship an hundred thousand or more. They could give employment to fifty or sixty additional men at once, at wages averaging from two to three dollars a day. A new seam, nine feet thick, had lately been discovered below the old one; and we went down the shaft three hundred feet to see it. The coal was of the same excellent quality as that of the old mine, which is the best for gas or steam purposes on the Pacific coast. But the miners had come upon a fault in the seam, caused by the dislocation of the strata, immediately above and below, intruding a tough conglomerate rock that they were now cutting away in the hope of its soon giving out. The coal measures, which these few seams now worked represent, extend over the whole eastern coast of Vancouver Island, and, like those on the east of the Rocky Mountains, are cretaceous or of tertiary age. They are considered as valuable as if they were carboniferous.

It is provoking to know that the agricultural settlements in the neighbourhood, which, though small, are the most extensive on the island, are not able to supply the present population of Nanaimo with food; and that no steps are taken to bring in new settlers, though there is abundance of good land all round. If this state of things continues, even though the mining population of Vancouver's Island increase ten fold in as many years, most of the wealth will be sent out of the county, as was the gold of Cariboo, and the country in the end be as poor as ever.

Nanaimo does not look like a coal mining place. The houses are much above the average of miners' residences in Britain or in Nova Scotia. They are scattered about, often in picturesque situations, with gardens, and not in long, mean, soot-covered rows, laid out with the idea that men who see nothing of beauty underground cannot be expected to appreciate it above. The view of the Cascades range, on the other side of the Straits, is almost equal to the view of the long semi-circular line of the Alps from Milan. At sunset, when warmed with the roseate light, or, a little later, when a deep soft blue has displaced the *couleur de rose*, the beauty contrasts painfully with the ash heaps and tenements of a mining village. Though not a believer in the " God made the country ; man made the town " sentiment, the contrast irresistibly suggests the words.

October, 9th.—Another day of glorious weather ; such weather as Vancouver's Island has, almost without interruption, from March till October or November ; warm enough for enjoyment, and cool enough for exercise. Our course was down the Gulf of Georgia to Victoria ; past the agricultural districts of Cowichan and Saanich on the Vancouver side, and the various islands that line the mainland on our left. Mount Baker was the great feature in the landscape all day. We could hardly help feeling envious that the United States instead of ourselves possessed so glorious a landmard ; especially as it still bears the name of the British Naval Officer in Capt. Vancouver's ship who first saw it, and is in the country that was formally taken possession of for the British Crown in 1792, and that had been, up to 1846, held by a British Company. Indeed, it is difficult to conceive of any plausible excuse that the United States could have brought forward, in claiming the country round Puget's Sound. They knew its value, and the British Premier, not only did not, but his brother had said that the whole country was not worth much ; for the salmon wouldn't take a fly.

On the fourth of April, 1792, the birthday of King George III., after whom he had named the Straits of Georgia, Captain Vancouver took formal possession for His Majesty of all the waters of Puget Sound, and of the coast north and south along which he had sailed. All the prominent capes, points, harbours, straits, mountains, bear to this day the names of his lieutenants and friends, just as he named them on his great voyage. He changed nothing. As the old Portuguese navigator, Juan de Fuca, had discovered the Straits of Fuca, his name was honourably preserved, and as Vancouver met a Spanish Squadron that had been sent out to give up Nootka and other Spanish claims on the coast of Great Britain, he adopted the names that the Dons had given to any channels or islands, such as Valdez, Texada, Straits of Melaspina, etc. Puget Sound he named from his second lieutenant ; Mount Baker from his third ; Cape Mudge from the first ; Mount Rainer from Rear Admiral Rainer ; Capes Grey and Atkinson, Burrard, Jervis, and Bute Inlets, Fort Discovery, Johnstone's Channel, and a hundred others, were all alike named by him ; and if Britain had no right to those south of the 49th parallel, she had no right to those farther north.

Still more astonishing : in 1846 when Britain yielded the Columbia River and the whole Pacific side of the continent up to the 49th parallel, not a single citizen of the United States had settled to the north of the Columbia. Swarms from the Western States had flocked into Oregon in the ten preceding years of joint occupation, and so the Government at Washington might plead the will of the settlers against the Imperial rights of Britain ; but that plea could have carried them, at the farthest, only to Astoria. If Oregon had to be ceded, the Columbia River should have been the boundary.

It may be said that all this is a reviving of dead issues, out of place and useless now.   But the history of the past throws light on the present, and is a beacon for the future.   Had the San Juan difficulty been viewed, not merely in the light of the literal wording of the Treaty of 1846, but in the light of all the facts, the decision of the Emperor of Germany must have been different.

Before noon we entered the Haro Strait that separates San Juan from Vancouver's Island.   Between the northern part of the Haro Channel and Vancouver's Island, are several islets and two narrow channels, that ships going to Victoria may take.   South of these, there is nothing between San Juan and the southern extremity of Vancouver, but the Haro Strait, six or seven miles wide.   It is therefore evident that while San Juan would be useless to Britain for military purposes, its possession by the United States is a menace to us ; for it commands the entrance to British waters, British shores, a British river, and British Province.   There is a hill on San Juan about a thousand feet high, a battery on which would command the whole Strait.

The sail down the Straits of Haro was all that a pleasure party on board a steam yacht could have desired.   On the mainland, the long line of the Cascades or Coast range broken by the Delta of the Fraser extended to the south,—though dwarfed into comparative insignificance by the mighty mass of Mount Baker, rising up in the midst.   Farther south, the line swept round the deep gulf of Puget Sound, then north-westerly and away as far west as the entrance of the Straits of Fuca, under the name of the Olympian range.   When under the lee of San Juan the snowy pyramid of Mount Baker looked out on us over the Island, while far to the south, in the back ground of the Olympian range, the dim form of Mount Rainer was seen lifting itself up in the sky.   Rounding the southern point of Vancouver's Island, we came to the spit of land that is cut into by the harbour of Victoria and four miles further west by the much superior harbour of Esquimalt. We steamed first into Victoria to get letters and telegrams, and proceeded immediately to Esquimalt, returning by land, over a good macadamized road.

The harbour of Victoria has a narrow entrance, is small, inconveniently shaped, and accommodates only vessels of eighteen feet draught of water ; but as Esquimalt is near enough to serve as an additional harbour, Victoria does not suffer. Esquimalt harbour is a gem ; not very large, but the anchorage is excellent, and it has all the other requisites of a first-class harbour ; and in the Royal Roads outside, along the coast as far as Race Rocks, any number of ships can ride safely. In Esquimalt, one U. S. and four British men-of-war lay, two of the latter having been just paid off. Not Esquimalt, but the foreign port of Valparaiso is the headquarters of the Pacific squadron. Esquimalt is our own, our interests are along the coast, coal is near, China and Japan only fifteen days distant, and the Admiral could be in daily communication when necessary with the Home authorities. The only reasons assigned on the other side are that British Commercial interests in South America are par-amount, and that sailors desert at Esquimalt and get off easily to the States. The same reasons ought to be conclusive against Halifax as the head-quarters of the North American squadron, and in favour of adopting Rio or some other South American port in its stead.

The terms of confederation with the Dominion included a guarantee of the interest on £100,000 stg. for ten years from the completion of the work, for a first-class Graving Dock at Esquimalt, and the Provincial Government has taken steps to commence its construction.

On our return to Victoria in the afternoon, one of the first persons we met in the street was Terry. Having no further need of his services, we had parted with him last week at New Westminster. He had gone on to Victoria direct and had monopolized the lionizing intended for the whole party ; had been interviewed about our marvellous north-west passage by land, with results as given in the newspapers, that spoke quite as much for Terry's imagination as for his memory. He had conjured up a Canyon on the Canoe River twenty miles long, where no Canyon is or ever had been ; had described us as galloping down the Yellow Head Pass till arrested by the sight of quartz boulders gleaming with gold, and rocks so rich that Brown and Beaupré had deserted to go back and mine ; and, with many another fact or fancy equally readable, made the hearts of reporters glad. Drinks had been the reward, and the consequences to Terry proved serious. For on the first day after being paid in full at the office in Victoria for his long trip, he had been plundered of every dollar. He was now looking round for work ; and before we left Victoria, hired as general servant on board a ship going north. Thus disappeared Terry into space. Should any one in future wish to engage him, we hereby certify him as a good servant, a good tailor, a good cobbler, and indeed anything but a good cook, the post which, unfortunately for us, he filled. But even of cookery he knows something ; for he engaged with us as cook in order that he might learn the business ; and he experimented on us long enough to learn the rudiments. In his own words, " he never liked being boss ; but could be understrapper to any one," and such a man is a treasure in America.

A walk through the streets of Victoria showed the little capital to be a small polyglot copy of the world. Its population is less than 5,000 ; but almost every nationality is represented. Greek fishermen, Kanaka sailors, Jewish and Scotch merchants, Chinese washermen, French, German and Yankee restaurant-keepers, English and Canadian officeholders and butchers, negro waiters and sweeps, Australian farmers and other varieties of the race, rub against each other, apparently in the most friendly way. The sign-boards tell their own tale :

" Own Shing, washing and ironing ;" " Sam Hang," ditto ;
" Kwong Tai & Co., cigar store ;" " Magasin Français ;" Teu-
tonic Hall, lager beer ;" " Scotch House ;" " Adelphic " and
" San Francisco " saloons ; " Oriental " and " New England "
restaurants ; " What Cheer Market," and " Play me off at ten-
pins," are found within gunshot, interspersed with more com-
mon-place signs.

The senior member for the city had invited several gentlemen
to dine with us at the Colonial Hotel at 5 o'clock.   A better
dinner could not be served in Montreal.   We were only sorry
that we had to leave at 7, to go on board the *Sir James Douglas*
and proceed to Alberni Channel, one of the proposed termini
on the west coast of Vancouver's Island.   But time was
precious, as the San Francisco steamer was expected to be in
every hour.   Parting with Mr. Smith, and adding the second
member for Victoria to our number, we went down to our little
steamer and started on this, our last expedition.

October 10th.—The distance between Victoria and the Pacific by the Straits of Fuca is sixty miles.   The *Sir James Douglas* made that by midnight, and then turned north for the
spacious Archipelago of Barclay's sound, from the head of
which Alberni Canal, or to use the modern word Channel, a
deep narrow fiord like those on the main land, cuts its way up
into the interior of Vancouver's Island.   Barclay sound has
three entrances, separated from each other by groups of islets
and rocks, and as the nearest is the best for ships from the
south, the Captain intended to run up by it into Alberni.   The
weather during the night was so favourable that he over-ran
his distance, and never having been in the sound before, he
waited for daylight to compare the coast with the charts.
Those who came early on deck had thus an opportunity of seeing the Pacific breaking on the iron shores of Vancouver.
Away behind us the great ocean stretched unbroken to Japan
and China, sleeping peacefully—under the morning light that

was shining over the mountains to the east—with no motion save a slow voluptuous roll of long billows that seemed gentle enough to be stayed by a child's hand. But to know their strength, even in a calm, turn and look where these same billows meet the headlands. Over the first they break with a heavy roar; and then, as if amazed to be resisted, they gather up their forces and rush with a long wild leap, like white-maned war-horses charging, among the inner breakers, to meet the fate that a gallant ship would meet if it mistook the entrance to the sound. When a gale is blowing from the west, the surf must be tremendous, for there is nothing to break the roll of the Pacific for 2,000 miles; but the entrances into the Sound are wide, and one or two lighthouses would obviate all risk. The most prominent mark about the southern entrance at present is Ship Island, probably so called from a number of bare trees on it like the masts of a ship. Beyond the coast line a bold range of serrated mountains runs along the centre of the island, like a backbone, north and south, into the heart of which Alberni Channel pierces.

Passing up the sound, several canoes with from two to half-a-dozen Indians in each hailed us with friendly shouts. They are squat in shape, dirtier, more savage, with a more decided cross-eye than the Indians on the mainland. In all probability this side of America was peopled from Asia, and not necessarily round by Behring's Straits and the Aleutian Islands. Even in this century Japanese junks, dismasted in a typhoon or otherwise disabled, after drifting for months about the North Pacific have stranded on the American continent or been encountered by whaling ships, and the survivors of the crews rescued, in cases where all had not perished of hunger.

There are two or three trading posts and several Indian villages on Barclay Sound. The traders come to the posts in schooners at certain seasons of the year, and trade for peltries, seal-oil, and fish. The scenery along the sound and up the channel resembles Bute Inlet, except that the hills do not rise so sheer and high from the water and the wood is better. There are also larger extents of open alluvial ground at the mouths of the streams that run into the sea, and along the valleys between the hills that they drain. At the head of Alberni is the Sumass, a river of considerable size that drains large lakes in the interior and is said to be bordered by extensive tracts of fertile soil. At its mouth is enough good land for several farms, but there are no settlers. An English Company formerly worked saw mills at this point, from which in 1862 over eight million feet of lumber were exported. The working of the mills has been abandoned, as the speculation did not pay, and the premises are now going to ruin. A walk round showed us one reason at least of the failure. Too much money had been sunk in house, orchard, outhouses, and other fixtures and improvements that yielded no return. No sane man would have started on such a scale with his own money. It was a sorry spectacle to see so many good buildings doorless and windowless, falling into decay or broken up by the Siwashes for wood to burn. In a country whose lumbering interests require development it is too bad that capitalists should be deterred by such an example.

Alberni harbour offers such decided advantages as a terminus that it may prove a formidable rival even to Esquimalt.

After a bath in the harbour, the water being wonderfully warm for the time of year, we steamed out into the Ocean again, and got back in time to see a glorious sunset on the Pacific. The twilight continued for an hour after; a band of carmine that shaded into orange and, higher up, into mauve, lingering so long over the horizon that we ceased to look at it, and only when turning into our berths, noticed that it had given way to the universal deep blue of the night sky. The sea was smooth and the night calm and beautiful as the preceding; and in consequence we were at the wharf in Victoria

harbour between four and five A. M., to the astonishment of
the citizens who had not expected us back till the afternoon or
next day.

October 11th to 14th.—It had been assumed that the *Prince
Alfred* steamer would leave Victoria for San Francisco on the
twelfth ; but her day was changed to the fourteenth as she had
to go to Nanaimo to coal. We had thus three days to spend
in Victoria instead of one, and so great was the hospitality of
the people that three months might have been spent enjoyably.
Various as are the nationalities and religions represented in
Victoria, the people are wonderfully fused, and there is a
general spirit of mutual toleration, kindness, and active good
will that makes it a pleasant town to live in. Like the whole
colony it is a poor man's paradise. Everyone seems to have
plenty of money ; and every kind of labour receives enormous
prices. There is no copper currency, and the smallest silver
piece is what is called "a bit"; the ten cent and the English
sixpence, though of different values, being alike called bits, and
given to children or put in church-door plates (there are no
beggars) as cents or coppers are in other countries. This
absence of small coins has much to do with the general cost of
living, and the indifference to small profits characteristic of all
classes here. The merest trifle costs a bit ; and though there
are 25 and 50 cent pieces in currency, yet, if anything is worth
more than a bit, with a lofty indifference to the intermediate
coins, the price is generally made a dollar. Emigrants on
landing, and men with fixed incomes, are the chief sufferers
from this state of things ; for as mechanics, labourers, and
servants are paid accordingly, they like it, and speak with
intensest scorn of the unfortunates who would divide a bit because they perhaps think it too much to give for a paper of
pins or an apple. "John" who comes across the Pacific to
make money and then return to the flowery land doesn't heed
their scorn ; and so, most of it was reserved before Confedera-

tion for canny Canadians who received the flattering appella-
tion of North American Chinamen; Californians being as well
supplied with gold and as lavish with it as the Victorians
themselves.

All this was very well in the halcyon days of the young
Province, when gold-dust was accounted as nothing; when
miners who had been six months in Cariboo would come down
to the capital and call for all the champagne in an hotel to wash
their feet; eat £10 notes as pills, or as a sandwich with a slice
of pork, or light their pipes with them; and when town lots
commanded higher prices for the moment than in 'Frisco.   But
the tide turned; the gold flowed out of the country to buy the
champagne, and more necessary articles, instead of being spread
abroad among resident farmers, or manufacturers; Cariboo
yielded less abundant harvests; and the inflated prosperity of
Victoria collapsed.   Lots that had been bought at from $10,000
to $25,000 have been sold since, it is said, for $500; the 15,000
people who lived around the city in tents have taken flight, like
wild geese, to more southern climates; and the then reputed
millionaires are now content with a modest business.   The
virus, however, is still in the blood of the Victorians.   They
half expect that the good old times, when every man got rich
without effort on his part, will come again; that something
will turn up; new mines or the railway being now the chief
objects of reliance, to make business brisk.   This delusion,
which belongs to the gambling rather than the true trading
spirit, retards the growth of the city; for it makes men hold on
to house and business lots, or demand sums for them far
beyond their value.   Great part of the four miles between
Esquimalt and Victoria is owned by a company called
" the Puget Sound."   This land is held at prices too high
for settlers or gardeners to buy, and thus it is that the
suburbs do not present the cultivated appearance that might
have been expected from the soil and fine climate.   High prices

for land and for everything else in and around the town, and extreme difficulty of obtaining information about good land elsewhere ; what condition of affairs could be more discouraging for emigrants or intending settlers ?

An infusion of new blood is required. At present the classes that ought to come are servant girls, labourers, mechanics, miners, farm-servants, and such like, for these would get remunerative employment at once ; and, gradually, land would be taken up, and money be diffused in so many hands that there would be a healthy flow instead of the present comparative stagnation and universal waiting for better times.

In looking at Victoria and the surrounding coast the situation is so commanding that it is difficult to avoid speculating a little as to its probable future. The island is at the end of *the west* and the beginning of *the east.* Behind it, over the mountains, stretch the virgin plains of our North-west, extending to the Great Lakes. Fronting it are the most ancient civilizations and the densest masses of humanity on the surface of the globe. With such a position, the harbours, minerals, fish, and timber of this colony become important. If the " golden gate" be one passage-way between the Old World and the New, the straits of Fuca and its harbours, the channels of Vancouver's Island and the inlets of the mainland are many. To our railway terminus will converge the products of Australia and Polynesia, as well as of China and Japan ; and all that the busy millions of Great Britain need can be sent to them across their own territory, independently of the changing phases of the Eastern question.

Let there be a line of communication from the Pacific to the St. Lawrence through a succession of loyal Provinces bound up with the Empire by ever-multiplying and tightening links, and the future of the Fatherland and of the Great Empire of which she will then be only the chief part is secured. With such a consummation in view, should not he be considered an enemy to the Common-weal who would dissever the western or American portion of so great an Empire from its foundation, from its capital and centre, simply because a belt of ocean intervenes ; a belt too that is becoming less of an obstacle every year. For in a few years we shall have a railway with but one break from the Pacific coast to the extreme easterly side of Newfoundland, and thence daily steamers will cross the Atlantic in a hundred hours. Canada will be as near London as Scotland and Ireland were forty years ago. It will be easier to make the journey from Victoria to London than it was to make it from the North of Scotland at the beginning of the century. These results, however marvellous, will be due to steam alone. How much nearer to the core of the Empire may not Canada be considered with the means of instantaneous telegraphic communication extended to every part of the Dominion ?

But it would be unworthy of our past to think in this connection only of material progress and national consolidation and security. Loftier have ever been the aims of our forefathers. It is not enough for us to allow Chinamen to come to our shores merely that, while living, they may do our rough work cheaply, repelled the while from us by injustice and insult, and that when dead a Company may clear money by carrying their bodies back to their own land. A nation to be great must have great thoughts ; must be inspired with lofty ideals ; must have men and women willing to work and wait and war for an idea. To be a light to the dark places of the earth ; to rule inferior races mercifully and justly ; to infuse into them a higher life ; to give them the good news that makes men blessed and free, believing that as the race is one, reason one, and conscience one, there is one Gospel for and unto all ; nothing less than this was the thought—deeply felt if sometimes inarticulately expressed—of our great ancestors in the brave days of Old. And it is ours also. By the possession of British Columbia and Vancouver's Island we look across into the very eyes of four hundred millions of heathen, a people eager to learn, acute to investigate, and whom the struggle for existence in thronged centres has made tolerant, patient, and hardy. Can we do nothing but trade with them?

October 14th.—To-day we left Esquimalt by the *Prince Alfred* on the home stretch, friends on the wharf giving us kindly parting cheers. A delightful voyage of four days down the coast brought us to San Francisco ; a wonderful city for its age, though not equal to Melbourne, the only other city in the world it ought to be compared with. Doubtless it is a fine thing to escape frost and snow ; but some people would endure all the snow-storms of Quebec or Winnipeg rather than one sand-storm in Frisco.

On Saturday morning, Oct. 16th, we breakfasted at the Lick House, San Francisco. On Saturday the 26th we breakfasted at home in Ottawa.

———

And how does the country crossed by the Union and Central Pacific Railways compare with our own North-west, has been asked us since our return? Comparisons are odious and therefore the answer shall be as brief as possible. The Pacific slope excepted, for there is nothing in British Columbia to compare with the fertile valleys of California, everything is so completely in our favour that there is no comparison except the old racing one of " Eclipse first and the rest nowhere.'' California itself, though its yield of wheat in favourable years is marvellous, is not a country to rear a healthy and hardy race. There is no summer or autumn rain-fall ; the air is without its due proportion of moisture ; and the lack of moisture is supplied by dust. The people look weary, and used up. In the course of a generation or two, unless a constant infusion of fresh blood renews their strength, the influences of climate must tell disastrously not only on their physique but on their whole spirit and life.

Are Anglo-Saxons secure from falling into the same sleepy and unprogressive state, that the energetic Spaniards, who first settled the country, soon sank into?

But when we leave California and travel from twelve to fifteen hundred miles, through Utah, Nevada, Wyoming, and Eastern Nebraska, the contrast with our North-west is startling. Certainly population has been attracted to various points over this vast region. The Mormons with infinite toil and patience, have made the deserts of Utah bring forth food for man and beast, but they are deserts nothwithstanding, and yield nothing unless carefully irrigated ; and the mean houses of logs or adobé —or sun-dried clay bricks,—and the unintelligent careworn countenances of the people do not testify very eloquently in favour of Utah. The State of Nevada is rich in minerals, especially in silver ; and the railway has been the means of developing these to a great extent, while the export of the bullion supplies to the railway a considerable local traffic. Along the Humboldt, and in side valleys, large herds of stock are fed ; and in parts of Wyoming and Eastern Nebraska stock raising is carried on with profit. But what a country to live in ! Everywhere it has a uniform dry, dusty, what an Australian writer would call " God-forsaken " look. For more than a thousand miles not a tree or shrub except sage-brush or grease-wood, relieves the desolation. And yet this is the country that guide books describe as if it were the garden of the Lord, and to which they summon the millions of Europe. As we sat in the railway train and read the description of the land we were passing through ; read of boundless tracts of the finest pasturage in the world ; of free soil on which anything and everything could be raised, of slopes that would yet be clad with vines and bear the rarest fruits ; and then looked out of the window and saw limitless stretches of desert or semi-desert, high, arid, alkaline plateaux, dotted scantily with miserable sage-brush, hundreds of miles without a blade of grass, a soil composed of disintegrated lava and hard clay, or disintegrated granite or sandstone, or a conglomerate of the two, we could hardly believe our eyes. The American desert is a reality. It is unfit for the growth of cereals or to support in any way a farming population, because of its elevation, its lack of rain, and the miserable quality, or to speak more correctly, the absence of soil. The enterprise that ran the pony express, that constructed telegraphs and a line of Railway across such a country is wonderful ; but not half so wonderful as the faith that sees in such a desert an earthly paradise, or the assurance that publishes its vision of what ought to be, for a picture of what is, or the courage that volunteers the sacrifice of any number of foreigners to prove the sincerity of its faith.

In a word, after reaching the summit of the first range of mountains, from the Pacific, the Railway in the United States has to cross more than a thousand miles of desert or semi-desert. According to the evidence of our senses, whatever guide-books may say to the contrary, we discovered on the home stretch that the great west of the United States practically ceases with the valley of the Missouri and of its tributary, the Platte.

CHAPTER XIII.

Our Country.

The preceding chapters are transcribed—almost verbally—from a Diary that was written from day to day on our journey from ocean, ocean-ward. The Diary was kept under difficulties. Notes had to be taken, sometimes in the bottom of a canoe and sometimes leaning against a stump or a tree ; on horseback in fine weather, under a cart when it was raining or when the sun's rays were fierce ; at night, in the tent, by the light of the camp-fire in front ; in a crowded wayside inn, or on the deck of a steamer in motion.

As may be seen by a reference to the Itinerary in the Appendix, our Diary commenced at Halifax on the Atlantic coast on July 1st, the sixth anniversary of the birth-day of the Dominion, and closed at Victoria on the Pacific coast on October 11th. The aggregate distance travelled by one mode of locomotion or another was more than five thousand miles, a great part of it over comparatively unknown, and therefore supposed to be dangerous country. We recrossed the Continent to our starting point by rail, the Secretary arriving at Halifax on November 2nd, having thus accomplished the round trip of nine or ten thousand miles in four months. None of us suffered from Indians, wild beasts, the weather, or any of the hardships incidental to travel in a new and lone land. Every one was physically better on his return than when he had set out. And yet there had been no playing on the road. We cannot charge ourselves with having lost an hour on the way ; and Manitobans, Hudson's Bay Officers, and British Columbians all informed us that we made better time between Lake Superior and the Pacific than ever had been made before.

It is only fair to the public to add that the writer of the Diary knew little or nothing of our North-west before accompanying the expedition. To find out something about the real extent and resources of our Dominion ; to know whether we had room and verge for an Empire or were doomed to be merely a cluster of Atlantic Provinces, ending to the west in a fertile but comparatively insignificant peninsula in Lake Huron, was the object that attracted a busy man from his ordinary work, on what friends called an absurd and perilous enterprise. All that is claimed for the preceding chapters is, that they record truthfully what we saw and heard. And having read since the works of Professor Hind, Archbishop Taché, Captain Palliser and others, we find, that though these contain the results of much more minute and extended enquiries and scientific information which renders them permanently valuable, they bring forward nothing to make us modify our own conclusions, or to lessen the impression as to the value of our North-west, that the sight of it produced in our minds.

We are satisfied that the rugged and hitherto unknown country extending from the Upper Ottawa to the Red River of the North, is not, as it has always been represented on maps executed by our neighbours, and copied by ourselves, impracticable for a Railway ; but entirely the reverse ; that those vast regions of Laurentian and Huronian rocks once pronounced worthless, are rich in minerals ; and that in the iron background to the basin of the St. Lawrence, hitherto considered valuable only for its lumber, great centres of mining and manufacturing industry, shall in the near future spring into existence.

Beyond these apparently wilderness regions we came upon the fertile belt, an immense tract of the finest land in the world, bounded on the west by coal formations so extensive that all other coal fields are small in comparison. Concerning this central part of the Continent, we have testified that which we have seen, and as a summary it is sufficient to quote Hind's emphatic words, Vol. II., p. 234 :

" It is a physical reality of the highest importance to the interests of " British North America that a continuous belt, rich in water, woods and "pasturage can be settled and cultivated from a few miles west of the " Lake of the Woods, to the passes of the Rocky Mountains ; and any "line of communication, whether by waggon road or railroad, passing " through it, will eventually enjoy the great advantage of being fed by an "agricultural population, from one extremity to the other."

Concerning the country from the mountains to the sea, it is unnecessary to add anything here. The mountains in British Columbia certainly offer obstructions to Railway construction ; but these obstacles are not insuperable, and, once overcome, we reach the Canadian Islands in the Pacific, Vancouver and Queen Charlotte,—in many respects the counter parts of Great Britain and Ireland, the western outposts of Europe,—rich in coal, bituminous and anthracite, and almost every variety of mineral wealth, in lumber, fish, and soil, and blessed with one of the most delightful climates in the world.

And now we might take farewell of the reader who has accompanied us on our long journey, but before doing so, it seems not unfitting to add a few words concerning the routes of our fellow-travellers who parted from us at Forts Garry and Edmonton ; concerning those men whom we found engaged on the survey and the general impressions left on our minds by all that we saw and experienced.

The Colonel spent ten days in Manitoba. Leaving Fort Garry, he travelled rapidly to Edmonton by the same trail that we had taken, in the hope of overtaking us before we had left

for the mountains.   Finding on his arrival that we had started
seven days previously, he decided to proceed 145 miles south-
west to the Rocky Mountain House ; thence through the country of the Blackfeet, to cross the mountains by North Kootenay
Pass ; and thence into Washington Territory, U.S., and viâ
Olympia to Victoria.   He accomplished the journey successfully,
though detained for two or three days by a snow-storm at the
foot of the mountains ; but as the delay enabled him to shoot a
large grizzly bear that approached within a few yards of his
camp, he had no reason to regret it much.   His southerly
march from Edmonton gave him the opportunity of seeing the
western curve of the fertile belt—the rainbow of the North-
west—and he speaks of it, especially of that portion through the
Blackfeet country, extending for about 300 miles along the
eastern bases of the Rocky Mountains towards the international
boundary line, with a varying breadth of from 25 to 80 miles,
as the future garden of the Dominion ; magnificent in regard
to scenery, with soil of surpassing richness ; and in respect of
climate, with an average temperature during the winter months,
15 ° higher than that of the western portion of the Province of
Ontario.

    We are now able to speak concerning the northwestern
curve of the fertile belt as positively as of the district to the
south which the Colonel traversed. At Edmonton, the Chief sent
Botanist and Horetzky northwards, with instructions to proceed
by Forts Assiniboine and Dunvegan and across the Rocky
Mountains by Peace River, the one to make then for the Upper
Fraser, and the other to go still farther north and reach the sea
by the Skeena or Nasse River.   They also succeeded in their
journey ; and their reports more than confirm the statements of
previous writers with regard to the extraordinary fertility of
immense prairies along the Peace River, the salubrity, and the
comparative mildness of the climate.   It is quite clear that
exceptional climatic causes are at work along the eastern flank

of the Rocky Mountains, north as well as south of Edmonton. Whether the chief cause be warm moist winds from the Pacific or a steady current of warm air under the lee of the mountains, analogous in the atmosphere to the Gulf stream in the ocean, or whatever the cause, our knowledge is too imperfect to enable us to say. But the salient facts are undoubted. At Fort Dunvegan, six degrees north of Fort Garry, and nearly thirteen north of Toronto, the winters are milder than at Fort Garry; and as for the seven months, from April to October, the period of cultivation, according to tables that have been carefully compiled, Dunvegan and Toronto do not vary more than about half a degree in mean temperature, while as compared with Halifax, N.S., the difference is $1°69$ in favour of Dunvegan. Our two fellow-travellers assured us also that they had seen nothing between the Red River and Edmonton to compare with the fertility of soil and the beauty of the country about Peace River. They struck the mighty stream below Dunvegan and sailed on it up into the very heart of the Rocky Mountains, through a charming country, rich in soil, wood, water, and coal, in salt that can be gathered fit for the table, from the sides of springs with as much ease as sand from the seashore; in bituminous fountains into which Sir Alexander McKenzie and Harmon both say that "a pole of twenty feet in length may be plunged, without the least resistance, and without finding bottom," and in every other production that is essential to the material prosperity of a country.

The following extract from the Journal of our Botanist gives a graphic description of what Peace River itself is :—"This "afternoon we passed through the most enchanting and sublime "scenery. The right bank of the river was clothed with wood- "spruce, birch and aspen, except where too steep, or where there "had been landslides. In many places the bank rose from the "shore to the height of from 300 to 600 feet. Sandstone cliffs "300 feet high often showed, especially above Green Island.

" The left bank was as high as the right, but instead of wood,
" grassy slopes met the view ; but landslides always revealed
" sandstone.   In places the river had cut a passage through the
" sandstone to the depth of 300 feet and yet the current indi-
" cated little increase.   The river was full from bank to bank,
" was fully 600 yards wide, and looked like a mighty canal cut
" by giants through a mountain.   Up this we sped at the rate
" of four miles an hour, against the current, in a large boat be-
" longing to the Hudson's Bay Co'y.; propelled by a north-east
" gale."

When we remember that the latitude of this river and the
richest part of the country it waters is nearly a thousand miles
north of Lake Ontario, the language we have used about it may
sound exaggerated because the facts seem unaccountable.   But
the facts have been long on record.   The only difficulty was the
inaccessibility of the country.   In Harmon's Journal are such
entries as the following :—

" Peace River, April 18, 1809.—This morning the ice in the
" river broke up."   *

" May 6.—The surrounding plains are all on fire.   We have
" planted our potatoes, and sowed most of our garden seeds."

" July 21.—We have cut down our barley ; and I think it
" is the finest that I ever saw in any country."

" October 6.—As the weather begins to be cold, we have
" taken our vegetables out of the ground, which we find to be
" very productive."

Another year we have the following entry :

" October 3.—We have taken our vegetables out of the
" ground.   We have 41 bushels of potatoes, the produce of one
" bushel planted the last spring.   Our turnips, barley, etc.,
" have produced well."

---

* April 30th is shown by the public records, to be the mean time of opening of navigation at Ottawa, between 1832 and 1870.   During that period, 38 years, April 17th was
the earliest and May 29th the latest days of opening.

In the journal of a Hudson's Bay Chief-factor published last year by Malcolm McLeod, Ottawa, is the following extract concerning the climate of Dunvegan, from the records of the celebrated traveller and astronomer—Mr. David Thompson:

" Only twice in the month of May, 1803,—on the 2nd and " 14th, did the thermometer fall to 30 °. Frost did not occur " in the fall till the 27th September."

"It freezes," says Mr. Russell, "much later in May in " Canada; and at Montreal, for seven years out of the last " nine, the first frost occurred between 24th August and 16th " September."

In Halifax, N. S., the writer has seen a lively snow-storm on the Queen's birthday; and almost every year there is frost early in June.

Similar quotations could be given from other writers, but they are unnecessary. We know that we have a great Northwest, a country like old Canada—not suited for lotus-eaters to live in, but fitted to rear a healthy and hardy race. The late Hon. W. H. Seward understood this when he declared that " vigorous, perennial, ever-growing Canada would be a Russia behind the United States." Our future is grander than even that conceived by Mr. Seward, because the elements that determine it are other than those considered by him. We shall be more than an American Russia, because the separation from Great Britain to which he invites us is not involved in our manifest destiny. We believe that union is better than disunion, that loyalty is a better guarantee for true growth than restlessness or rebellion, that building up is worthier work than pulling down. The ties that bind us to the Fatherland must be multiplied, the connection made closer and politically complete. Her traditions, her forms, her moral elevation, her historic grandeur shall be ours forever. And if we share her glory, we shall not shrink even at the outset from sharing her responsibilities.

A great future beckons us as a people onward. To reach it, God grant to us purity and faith, deliverance from the lust of personal aggrandizement, unity, and invincible steadfastness of purpose. The battles we have to fight are those of peace, but they are not the less serious and they are surely nobler than those of war. The victories we require to gain over all forms of political corruption, the selfish spirit of separation, and those great material obstacles in the conquest of which the spirit of patriotism is strengthened. It is a standing army of engineers, axemen and brawny labourers that we require, men who will not only give a fair day's work for a fair day's wage, but whose work shall be ennobled by the thought that they are in the service of their country, and labouring for its consolidation. Why should there not be a high *esprit de corps* among men who are doing the country's work, as well as among those who do its warfare? And why should the country grudge its honours to servants on whose faithfulness so much depends? "There is many a red-coat who is no soldier," said the Duke of Wellington. Conversely, there are true soldiers who wear only a red shirt.

This thought leads us to make mention of the men who have been engaged for the last two years in connection with the Canadian Pacific Railway Survey, the pioneers of the great army that must be engaged on the construction of the work and on whom has devolved the heavy labour that commonly falls to the lot of an advance-guard. On our journey we met several of the surveying parties, and could form some estimate of the work they had to do. We could see that continuous labour for one or two years in solitary wilderness or mountain gorges as surveyor, transit-man, leveller, rodman, commissary, or even packer, is a totally different thing from taking a trip across the continent for the first time, when the perpetual novelty, the spice of romance, the risks and pleasures atone for all discomforts. Here are one or two instances of the spirit that animates the body.

The gentleman now at the head of party X. had commenced work in charge of another party between Lake Superior and the Upper Ottawa. He remained out during the whole summer and winter in that trackless rugged region, previously untrodden by white men, and rarely visited by Indians. After a severe winter campaign, he completed the difficult and hazardous service entrusted to him. On his return in the spring he was told that it was desirable that he should go to British Columbia without delay ; and, though he had not spent two weeks with his family in as many years, he started at once.

Near the end of the year just closed the Chief was called upon to send a party to explore the section of country between the North Saskatchewan, above Edmonton, and the Jasper valley. It was deemed advisable to examine this wild and wooded district in the winter season, on account of the numerous morasses and muskegs which rendered it next to impassable at any other season. The party most available for this service had been engaged during the summer and winter of 1871 and the whole of 1872 in the lake region east of Manitoba, and had returned to Fort Garry after completing satisfactorily their arduous work. The Chief asked, by telegraph, the Engineer in charge if he was prepared to start at short notice for the Rocky Mountains on a prolonged service. Almost immediately after sending this message, the following telegram was received from the gentleman referred to : " May I have leave of absence to return home for a few weeks on urgent private business ?" This was at once followed by another : " Your message received. I withdraw my application for leave. I am prepared to start for the Rocky Mountains with my party. Please send instructions." It was evident that the first two telegrams had crossed. The members of party M., notwithstanding what they had gone through, away from friends and the comforts of society, were ready to undertake a march of a thousand miles still farther away, in the dead of a Canadian winter.

And what was the journey? They knew that it implied hardships such as Captain Butler encountered, and which he so graphically describes in " The Great Lone Land." They knew that it meant a great deal more. The journey over, they were only at the beginning of their work, and the work would be infinitely more trying than the journey itself.

These are only two instances out of many of that " Ready, aye, Ready" spirit, which the British people rightly honour as the highest quality in their soldiers, from the lowest to the highest grades. With respect to the ordinary everyday work that has to be done, our cwn little experience gave us some idea of its discomforts. Among the mountains, there is hardly a day without rain, except when it snows. Leather gives way under the alternate rotting and grinding processes that swamps and rocks subject it to. Mocassins keep out the wet about as well as an extra pair of socks. Clothes are patched and re-patched until lock, stock and barrel are changed. At night you lie down wet, lucky if the blanket is dry. In the morning you rise to a rough breakfast of tea, pork and beans. When relations at home are just enjoying the sweet half-hour's sleep before getting up, you are off into the dark silent woods, or clambering up precipices to which the mists ever cling, or on the rocky banks of some roaring river, getting back to camp at night tired and hungry, but still thankful if a good day's work has been accomplished. And this same thing goes on from week to week,—working, eating, sleeping. Books are scarce, for they are too bulky to carry; no newspapers and no news—unless fragments from three to six months old, strangely metamorphosed by Packers and Indians, can be dignified by the name of news. Nothing occurs to break the monotony save rheumatism, festered hands or feet, a touch of sickness, perhaps scurvy, if the campaign has been long; the arrival of a pack-train with supplies, or some such interesting event as the following, which we found duly chronicled on a blazed tree, between Moose Lake and Tête Jaune Cache:—

"BIRTH."

" Monday, 5th August 1872.

" This morning at about 5 o'clock 'Aunt Polly,' bell-mare
" to the Nth. Thompson trail party's pack-train, was safely de-
" livered of a Bay Colt, with three white legs and white star on
" forehead. This wonderful progeny of a C. P. R. Survey's
" pack-train is in future to be known to the racing community
" of the Pacific slope, as Rocky Mountain Ned."

The Sunday rest and the next meal, are almost the only
pleasures looked forward to ; and the enjoyment of eating
arises, generally, not from the delicacies or variety of the fare ;
for even fat pork, porridge, bread and coffee, need all the zest
that hard work and mountain air can supply, in order to be
thoroughly enjoyed three times a day, week in and week out.

In addition to all the extraordinary discomforts attending
this class of work there are the dangers to life, inseparable from
the great extent of the work undertaken, and the rapidity with
which it was begun and pushed forward ;—extensive fires in the
forest ; the risks of starvation or the risk of drowning, while
endeavouring to make the passage of lakes and rivers in a frail
canoe or on a raft.

This survey work implies more than hardships and hazards.
Already it has connected with its history a mournful death-
roll. At the outset, some tribes of Indians were expected to
give trouble. On the contrary, they have for the most part
been friendly and helpful. When nearly a thousand men were
engaged directly or indirectly on the work, and scattered over
pathless regions over a whole continent, it would not have been
wonderful had supplies failed to reach some parties, and death
by starvation occurred. In no case has such a disaster yet happened. But there are forces that can neither be organized nor
bribed. Fourteen men have been destroyed by the elements ;
seven by fire, and seven by water ; destroyed so completely that
no trace has been found of the bodies of ten.

One party,—seven in number,—engaged in carrying provisions north of Lake Superior, was surprised by the widespread forest fires that raged over the west in the autumn of 1871. The body of only one of its number could be discovered.

In the spring of 1872, a party that had finished its work well, after an arduous winter campaign far up the Ottawa beyond Lake Temiscamang, prepared to return home. The gentleman in charge and one of his assistants separated from the rest, to take on board their canoe two others who had been previously left at a side post prostrated with scurvy. The four were known to have started down the river. That was the last seen of them, though the upturned canoe was found, and it told its own tale of an upset, by rock or rapid or awkward movement of the sick men, into ice-cold lake or river.

In the Autumn of 1872, three others, on their way to begin their winter's work, were shipwrecked and drowned in the Georgian Bay.

All those men died in the service of their country as truly as if they had been killed in battle. Some of them have left behind wives and little children, aged parents, young brothers or sisters, who were dependent on them for support. Have not those a claim on the country that ought not to be disregarded?

That this work is too seldom looked at from any other save the wages point of view, is our excuse for putting the real state of the case warmly. Who are the men whose disciplined enthusiasm enables them to manifest the self-sacrifice we have alluded to? Many of them are men of good birth and education, who have chosen the profession of Engineering as one in which their talents can be made in a marked degree subservient to the material prosperity of mankind. Others have chosen it because of its supposed freedom from routine, and the prospect it is thought to offer of novelty, adventure, and such a roving life as every young Briton or Canadian, with any of the old blood in his veins, longs for.

And what wages do these men receive ? Simply their pay by the month ! They do not know whether they will have the satisfaction—that every man interested in his work has the right to look forward to—of seeing their work finished by themselves. Even after the preliminary surveys are completed, and the work placed under contract, the tenure of office is insecure. Sometimes a clamour is raised against the presumed extravagance of the Government, when the newspapers have nothing more stirring to write about, or when some reporter fancies he has not received due attention. At other times, some unprincipled contractors conspire to effect the removal of men, whose only fault is that they have performed their duty faithfully. From these or other similar causes, engineers in the public service are sometimes unjustly sacrificed. And, if remonstrance is made, the answer is ready : " They received their pay for the time they were employed, and others, quite as competent, are ready and willing to take their places." Yes, and the same might be said of the officers and men of the British army, but they are treated very differently. The work of one of the military expeditions, such as the Abyssinian or Red River, which have shed such lustre on the British name, is not more arduous. The heaviest part of a soldier's duty on such expeditions, it is well known, is the long laborious marching. The work of engineers on the survey is a constant march ; their shelter, even in the depth of winter, often only canvass ; they have sometimes to carry their food for long distances, through swamps and over fallen trees, on their backs ; and run all the risks incidental to such a life, without medical assistance, without notice from the press, without the prospect of plunder or promotion, ribands or pensions. To be sure there is the work of *construction* only, and the world has always given greater prominence to the work of *destruction*.

To *construct* is " the duty that lies nearest us." " We therefore will rise up and build." Our young Dominion in grappling with so great a work has resolutely considered it from a national and not a strictly financial point of view; knowing that whether it pays directly or not, it is sure to pay indirectly. Other young countries have had to spend, through long years, their strength and substance to purchase freedom or the right to exist. Our lot is a happier one. Protected "against infection and the hand of war" by the might of Britain, we have but to go forward, to open up for our children and the world what God has given into our possession, bind it together, consolidate it, and lay the foundations of an enduring future.

Looking back over the vast breadth of the Dominion when our journeyings were ended, it rolled out before us like a panorama, varied and magnificent enough to stir the dullest spirit into patriotic emotion. For nearly 1,000 miles by railway between different points east of Lake Huron ; 2,185 miles by horses, including coaches, waggons, pack, and saddle-horses ; 1,687 miles in steamers in the basin of the St. Lawrence and on Pacific waters, and 485 miles in canoes or row-boats ; we had travelled in all 5,300 miles between Halifax and Victoria, over a country with features and resources more varied than even our modes of locomotion.

From the sea-pastures and coal-fields of Nova Scotia and the forests of New Brunswick, almost from historic Louisburg up the St. Lawrence to historic Quebec ; through the great Province of Ontario, and on lakes that are seas ; by copper and silver mines so rich as to recall stories of the Arabian Nights, though only the rim of the land has been explored ; on the chain of lakes, where the Ojibbeway is at home in his canoe, to the plains, where the Cree is equally at home on his horse ; through the prairie Province of Manitoba, and rolling meadows and park-like country, out of which a dozen Manitobas shall be carved in the next quarter of a century ; along the banks of

> A full-fed river winding slow
> By herds upon an endless plain,

full-fed from the exhaustless glaciers of the Rocky Mountains, and watering "the great lone land;" over illimitable coal measures and deep woods; on to the mountains, which open their gates, more widely than to our wealthier neighbours, to lead us to the Pacific; down deep gorges filled with mighty timber, beside rivers whose ancient deposits are gold beds, sands like those of Pactolus and channels choked with fish; on to the many harbours of mainland and island, that look right across to the old Eastern Thule "with its rosy pearls and golden-roofed palaces," and open their arms to welcome the swarming millions of Cathay; over all this we had travelled, and it was all our own.

> " Where's the crowd that would not dare
> To fight for such a land ?"

Thank God, we have a country. It is not our poverty of land or sea, of wood or mine that shall ever urge us to be traitors. But the destiny of a country depends not on its material resources. It depends on the character of its people. Here, too, is full ground for confidence. We in everything "are sprung of earth's first blood, have titles manifold." We come of a race that never counted the number of its foes, nor the number of its friends, when freedom, loyalty, or God was concerned.

Two courses are possible, though it is almost an insult to say there are two, for the one requires us to be false to our traditions and history, to our future, and to ourselves. A third course has been hinted at; but only dreamers would seriously propose " Independence " to four millions of people, face to face with forty millions. Some one may have even a fourth to propose. The Abbé Sieyes had a cabinet filled with pigeon-holes, in each of which was a cut-and-dried Constitution for France. *Doctrinaires* fancy that at any time they can say, " go to, let us make a Constitution," and that they can fit it on a nation as readily as new coats on their backs. There never was a profounder mistake. A nation grows, and its Constitution must grow with it. The nation cannot be pulled up by the roots,—cannot be dissociated from its past, without danger to its highest interests. Loyalty is essential to its fulfilment of a distinctive mission,—essential to its true glory. Only one course therefore is possible for us, consistent with the self-respect that alone gains the respect of others ; to seek, in the consolidation of the Empire, a common Imperial citizenship, with common responsibilities, and a common inheritance.

With childish impatience and intolerance of thought on the subject, we are sometimes told that a Republican form of Government and Republican institutions, are the same as our own. But they are not ours. Besides, they are not the same. They are not the same in themselves ; they are not the same in their effects on character. And, as we are the children even more than we are the fathers and framers of our national institutions, our first duty is to hold fast those political forms, the influences of which on national character have been proved by the tests of time and comparison to be the most ennobling. Republicanism is one-sided. Despotism is other-sided. The true form should combine and harmonize both sides.

The favourite principle of Robertson of Brighton, that the whole truth in the realm of the moral and spiritual consists in the union of two truths that are contrary but not contradictory, applies also to the social and political. What two contrary truths then lie at the basis of a complete National Constitution ? First, that the will of the people is the will of God. Secondly, that the will of God must be the will of the people. That the people are the ultimate fountain of all power is one truth. That Government is of God, and should be strong, stable, and above the people, is another. In other words, the elements of liberty and of authority should both be represented. A republic is professedly based only on the first. In consequence, all appeals are made to that which is lowest in our nature, for such appeals are made to the greatest number and are most likely to be immediately successful. The character of public men and the national character deteriorate. Neither elevation of sentiment, nor refinement of manners is cultivated. Still more fatal consequences, the very ark of the nation is carried periodically into heady fights; for the time being, the citizen has no country; he has only his party, and the unity of the country is constantly imperilled.

On the other hand, a despotism is based entirely on the element of authority. To unite those elements in due proportions, has been and is the aim of every true statesman. Let the history of liberty and progress, of the development of human character to all its rightful issues, testify where they have been more wisely blended than in the British Constitution.

We have a fixed centre of authority and government, a fountain of honour above us that all reverence, from which a thousand gracious influences come down to every rank; and, along with that immovable centre, representative institutions, so elastic that they respond within their own sphere to every breath of popular sentiment, instead of a cast-iron yoke for four years. In harmony with this central part of our constitution, we have an independent judiciary instead of judges—too often the creatures of wealthy adventurers or the echoes of fleeting popular sentiment. More valuable than the direct advantages, are the subtle indirect influences that flow from our unbroken connection with the old land, those living and life-giving forces that determine the tone and mould the character of a people. Ours are the old history, the graves of forefathers, the flag they died for, the names "to which a thousand memories call," the Queen whose virtues transmute the principle of loyalty into a personal affection.

SANDFORD FLEMING'S OVERLAND EXPEDITION.

ITINERARY.

Journey from Halifax, on the North Atlantic, to Victoria, on the North Pacific, between July 1 and Oct. 11, 1872.

DATE.	DESIGNATION OF PLACES BY THE WAY.	ESTIMATED MILES TRAV'D.					
		LAND.		WATER.		TOTAL.	
		Rail	Horses	Steamer	Canoe		
1872							
July 1.	From Halifax, along the route of the Intercolonial Railway, under construction and partly in operation, to Rivière du Loup.	To Truro	61				
		" Moncton....	50	76			
		" Miramichi..	19	....	115		
		" Bathurst..........	....	45			
		" Metapedia..	....	80			
		" Rimouski	....	110			
		" Riv. du Loup......	....	66			
							622
July 9.	From Riviere du Loup along the Grand Trunk, St. Lawrence & Ottawa and Northern Railways to Collingwood.	" Quebec.....	126				
		" Montreal..........	166				
		" Ottawa............	166				
		" Toronto...........	275				
		" Collingwood.......	94				
							827
16.	From Collingwood by steamer through the Georgian Bay, Lake Huron and Lake Superior to Thunder Bay.	" Owen Sound......	....	....	45		
		" Killarney..........	....	....	100		
		" Bruce Mines.......	....	....	135		
		" Sault St. Marie.....	....	....	50		
		" Michipicoten Island	....	....	115		
		" Nepigon...........	....	....	150		
		" Thunder Bay......	....	....	100		
							695
22.	From Thunder Bay along the Dawson route to Fort Garry. *Camp No. 1.						
23.		" Shebandowan......	....	45			
24.	" 2.	" Brule Portage.....	....	....	....	60	
25.	" 3.	" Camp Ignace......	....	....	....	35	
26.	" 4.	" American Portage.	....	....	....	61	
27.	" 5.	" Rainy Lake........	....	....	....	60	
28.	" 6.	" Hungry Hall	....	....	....	90	
29.	" 7.	" Island Camp.......	....	....	....	8	
29.	" 8.	" Northwest Angle..	....	....	....	70	
30.	" 9.	" Oak Point.........	....	80			
31.	" 10.	" Government House	....	30			
							539

Carried Forward...... 2,683

*Camps numbered from Lake Superior.

ITINERARY—Continued.

DATE.	DESIGNATION OF PLACES BY THE WAY.		ESTIMATED MILES TRAV'D.				
			LAND.		WATER.		TOTAL.
			Rail	Horses	Steamer	Canoe	
1872							
			Brought forward	....	....	....	....	2,683
Aug. 1.	From Fort Garry to Stone Fort and back.		To Government House	....	40			
							40
		Camp.						
2.	From Fort Garry	No. 11.	" White Horse Plains	....	33			
3.	to Fort Ellice.*	" 12.	" Rat Creek.	....	37			
4.		" 13.	" Three Creeks......	....	24			
5.		" 14.	" Camp Assiniboine..	....	40			
6.		" 15.	" Salt Lake..........	....	41			
7.		" 16.	" Qu'Appelle........	....	45			
							220
8.	From Fort Ellice to	" 17.	" Broken Arm River.	....	31			
9.	Fort Carlton.	" 18.	" Lonely Tree........	....	43			
10.		" 19.	" Little Touchwood..	....	41			
11.		" "	" "	....	"			
12.		" 20.	" Touchwood........	....	43			
13.		" 21.	" Quill Lake Plain...	....	42			
14.		" 22.	" Round Hill........	....	43			
15.		" 23.	" S. Saskatchewan...	....	46			
16.		" 24.	" Fort Carlton......	....	18			
							307
17.	From Fort Carlton	" 25.	" Bears Paddling La..	....	38			
18.	to Fort Pitt.	" "	" "	....	"			
19.		" 26.	" Jack-fish River....	....	48			
20.		" 27.	" English River......	....	41			
21.		" 28.	" Fort Pitt Guard....	....	40			
							167
22.	From Fort Pitt to	" 29.	" Moose Creek......	....	40			
23.	Fort Edmonton.	" 30.	" Snake Lake........	....	42			
24.		" 31.	" Victoria Mission...	....	40			
25.		" "	" "	....	"			
26.		" 32.	" Deep Creek........	....	44			
27.		" 33.	." Fort Edmonton....	....	27			
							193
28.	From Fort Edmon-	" 34.	" St. Albert..........	....	11			
29.	ton to Jasper	" 35.	" St. Anns'..........	....	39			
30.	House.	" 36.	" Round Lake.......	....	12			
31.		" 37.	" Lobstick Creek....	....	29			
Sept. 1.		" "	" "	....	"			
2.		" 38.	" Valad's Camp......	....	26			
3.		" 39.	" Camp Minnie......	....	23			
4.		" 40.	" McLeod River Camp	....	17			
5.		" 41.	" Indian Camp......	....	12			
6.		" 42.	" Muskeg Camp......	....	20			
7.		" 43.	" Plum Pudding C'mp	....	21			
8.		" "	" "	....	"			
9.		" 44.	" Bayonette Camp...	....	25			
10.		" 45.	" Beaver Camp......	....	17			
11.		" 46.	" Island Camp.......	....	26			
							278
			Carried Forward......					3,888

*Distances between Fort Garry and Edmonton were measured by "Odometer."

ITINERARY.—Continued.

DATE.	DESIGNATION OF PLACES BY THE WAY.		LAND. Rail	LAND. Horses	WATER. Steamer	WATER. Canoe	TOTAL.
1872							
		Brought forward.	....	....	....	....	3,888
Sept 12.	From Jasper	Camp No. 47. To Jasper Lake	....	4			
13.	House to Yellow	" 48. " Athabaska Camp...	....	25			
14.	Head Pass.	" 49. " Caledonian Valley..	....	17			
15.		" 50. " Yellow Head Camp.	....	4			
							60
16.	From Yellow Head	" 51. " Moose Lake Camp.	....	40			
17.	Pass to Kam-	" 52. " Herd Camp........	....	4			
18.	loops.	" 53. " Camp Fraser.......	....	13			
19.		" 54. " Canoe River.......	....	31			
20.		" 55. " Albreda Camp......	....	25			
21.		" 56. " Camp Cheadle,....	....	26			
22.		" " " " "	....	"			
23.		" 57. " Headless Indian....	....	23			
24.		" 58. " Camp V .-.........	....	24			
25.		" 59. " Round Prairie......	....	24			
26.		" 60. " Bunch Grass Camp.	....	26			
27.		" 61. " Camp Thompson...	....	12	....	25	
28.		" 62. " Kamloops....	....	....	..	60	
							333
29.	From Kamloops to New	" Kamloops..........	....				
30.	Westminster.	" Cornwalls	....	38	....	16	
Oct 1.		"	....	"			
2.		" Lytton.............	....	48			
3.		" Yale...............	....	56			
4.		" New Westminster...	....	....	95		
							253
5.	From New Westminster to	" Burrard Inlet......	....	8	32		
6.	Victoria. On board the	" Waddington Harbor	....	....	190		
7.	steamer "Sir James Doug-	" Seymour Narrows..	....	....	80		
8.	las."	" Nanaimo...........	....	....	100		
9.		" Victoria............	....	....	80		
							490
10.	From Victoria to Alberni,	" Pacific Ocean.......	....	....	150		
11.	Aarclaay Sound and back	" " "	....	....	150		
	Str. "Sir James Douglas."						300
		Total Mileage....	957	2185	1687	485	5,314

SUMMARY.

			Miles.
Distance	travelled	by Railway................	957
"	"	Horses, including waggon, pack and saddle horses......	2,185
"	"	Steamers —on St. Lawrence and Pacific waters..........	1,687
"	"	Canoes or row-boats................................	485

From Halifax to Victoria 〉 ....Total miles 5,314
between July 1st and Oct. 11th. 〉

APPENDIX

The last chapter of *Ocean to Ocean* explains why the writer accompanied the expedition to which he acted the part of Secretary, and how it came to pass that the book was written. The Dominion is now four years older. Our North-west is not the almost unknown country it then was. True, the work of colonization and of building a railway from Lake Nipissing to the Pacific has not proceeded at the lightning express rate that was prophesied ; but neither the prophecy nor its failure is to be wondered at. In 1867, public men and the press joined in affirming that trains would run from Halifax to Montreal in three years ; and the Maritime Provinces took action on the strength of the anticipation. But though the Intercolonial Railway is only five hundred miles long, and passes through a country which has been partially settled for one or two generations, and runs near the open sea, it was not completed till 1876. Need we wonder much should three decades instead of one pass away before the Canada Pacific is opened for through-traffic ? However, during the last four years considerable progress has been made ; and in giving to the public a second edition of *Ocean to Ocean,* an appendix is called for, to show where we now stand.

The settlement of the North-west, on which the success of

the great exterprise depends, cannot proceed rapidly until access by rail is given to the outside world of intending emigrants. The average emigrant is a poor man. He is likely therefore to have a large family. He carries his household goods with him. That he be taken from his old to his proposed new home at the smallest possible expense and with few changes and breakings of bulk is simply indispensable. In 1872, every one expected that the desired result would be in a measure attained by the completion of the railway from St. Paul's, Minnesota, to the Boundary Line. A well informed London Times correspondent wrote that " 1873 will certainly see the railway track at Fort Garry, and that thus will be opened the rich Canadian territory of Manitoba and the fertile valley of the Saskatchewan." But this certainly depended on the willingness of the Dutch bondholders to advance more money without prospect of immediate repayment, and was dissipated by their determination not to do so, to which determination they still resolutely adhere. The terminus of the track remains where it was ; and emigrants have still to travel on foot or in their waggons for two or three hundred miles over the prairie, or betake themselves to the Red River boats in order to reach Winnipeg. Possibly the first great link of the Canada Pacific Railway, extending from Thunder Bay on Lake Superior to the crossing of the Red River may be built before there is communication by rail through Minnesota ; and as giving direct access to Manitoba through our own territory and affording the most direct outlet for surplus farm produce are objects of paramount importance, the construction of this link four hundred and fourteen miles long—is being energetically proceeded with. Its course is well to the north of the Dawson road which our party canoed over; by a shorter route ; and through a country much more favourable than was at one time thought possible. Works of construction, except about Rat Portage or the crossing of the Winnipeg River, will be light, and what is of even more importance—remarkably easy ascending gradients have been secured. "The more this portion of the railway can be made to convey cheaply the products of the soil to the navigation of the St. Lawrence, the more will the field be extended within which farming operations can be carried on with profit on the fertile plains. The information obtained suggests that it will be possible to secure maximum easterly ascending gradients between Manitoba and Lake Superior within the limit of twenty-six feet to the mile, a maximum not half so great as that which obtains on the majority of the railways of the Continent." (Progress Report, 1874).

Respecting the line as a whole and the character of the difficulties to be overcome, the Chief Engineer's statements are equally satisfactory. He reports that "the practicability of establishing railway communication across the Continent wholly within the limits of the Dominion is no longer matter of doubt. It may indeed be now accepted as a certainty that a route has been found, generally possessing favourable engineering features, with the exception of a short section approaching the Pacific coast; which route, taking its entire length, including the exceptional section alluded to, will on the average show lighter work, and will require less costly structures than have been necessary on many of the railways now in operation in the Dominion." The Yellow Head has been definitely determined upon as the best pass through the first range of the Rocky Mountains. By it "a railway can be carried from the North Saskatchewan to the central plateau of British Columbia with gradients as light as those on railways in Ontario, and with works of construction scarcely heavier than on the Intercolonial line. We are thus enabled to project a satisfactory route from the railway system of the Atlantic Provinces to a point within about two hundred miles of the Pacific tide water." The character of the climate about the eastern approach to the Yellow Head Pass may be judged from

the fact given in the Report that one hundred horses and mules
engaged on the survey, nearly starved when they reached the
Jasper valley, were turned out in mid-winter to shift for themselves, not a single death occurred, and they all resumed work
in March in fair condition.   The extraordinary significance of
this fact will be appreciated when it is remembered that the
Jasper valley is 3,300 feet above the level of the sea or very
nearly as high as the Pass, and about ten degrees of latitude
farther north than Toronto.

All this is extremely satisfactory ; but the difficulties on the
last two hundred miles referred to—the western end of the
Canada Pacific Railway—are sufficient of themselves to make
the undertaking a formidable one for a richer country than
Canada.   An army of engineers has been employed among the
mountains of British Columbia since 1871 ; the Cascades have
been pierced by seven lines of survey; every attempt has been
made to wrest from them the secret of an easy passage to the
ocean ; but, though the outlook has more than once been promising, the attempts have failed.   There is no direct, and no easy
pass.   On any one of the projected lines construction will in-
volve enormous outlay.   It is understood that the route that
the Government favours is to follow the Fraser River from
Tête Jeaune Cache to Fort George and thence to strike across
to the head of Bute Inlet.   As Lord Dufferin has pointed out,
this means that eventually the railway must be carried down
the bold rocky shores of the Inlet, across to Vancouver's
Island, and on to Esquimalt.

Once built, the difficulty of operating the railway in winter
will be found just where construction threatens to be most difficult—the western slopes of the two great mountain chains in
British Columbia.   " Except in these localities, it will have on
an average considerably less snow than existing railways have
to contend with."

By the time it is built, let us trust that a population shall have entered our North-west sufficiently large to ensure enough traffic to pay working expenses. The prospect is good ; but should the prospect not be realized, the Canada Pacific—irrespective of the cost of construction—would be a white elephant of portentous dimensions to Canada. At present the Dominion has a population of about 900 for every mile of railway constructed, and that is found to be anything but a paying average. But even on that basis, our North-west should have a population of one and a quarter to one and a half millions by the time the line is opened from the Pacific to Lake Superior. Of course the safe policy would be, not to begin construction from the Pacific side till a million of people had actually settled in the North-west ; and it is a question whether more liberal terms might not be offered to British Columbia than have yet been suggested to obtain the delay. It cannot be the true interest of any member of the body that the body should suffer and even run the risk of destruction. But if such delay is impossible, it is clear that the speedy completion of the link between Thunder Bay and Red River, and a vigorous colonization policy constitute the key to the position.

In view of the obligations which Canada has assumed, obligations that no party dreams of repudiating though there may be legitimate differences of opinion as to the mode in which they should be fulfilled, the question of paramount importance is—what are the capabilities of the North-west for settlement ? On this point, what has been proved in the course of the past four years ? Have the views then taken by the author after a rapid ride across the country been borne out by the experiences of settlers and explorers ? Have the difficulties in the way of colonization on a large scale become greater or less as they were approached ?

These questions can be easily answered. I have alluded to one cause or delay that has operated against a more speedy settlement of Manitoba. Another, the grasshopper plague—has proved to be a more serious drawback than the settlers in 1872 contemplated. But, this excepted, all reasonable expectations then entertained have been fulfilled. This Appendix is not intended to serve as a guide book for emigrants. To those who wish a recent and readable book of that kind, Hamilton's " Prairie Province " is recommended. All that can be done here is to give a few facts and conclusions in the way of a general review.

The grasshoppers are dreaded in all the border States and Territories of America as the locusts were by the Jews in the days of Joel the prophet. Their first appearance in the Red River valley, of which we have any account, was in the year 1818. The Scotch settlers, brought out under the auspices of the Earl of Selkirk, suffered severely from their ravages in 1818, 1819 and 1820. Thirty-six years elapsed before their next invasion ; and that was followed by a six years' respite. From 1867 to 1870, and from 1873 to 1875, they did much damage. This year Manitoba has been entirely free from their ravages ; and the people generally believe that they have entered on another period of exemption, and that should the pests re-appear, the settlers will be sufficiently numerous and well organized to stamp them out. Those who are desirous of learning about the grasshoppers, their origin, range, flight, swarming, and the best means of prevention to be adopted by the settlers attacked, I would refer to Mr. G. M. Dawson's Report in connection with the British North America Boundary Commission (p. 304-311). No scientific work of such permanent value as this Report has been presented to the Government of the Dominion so far as known to me. While the Report is valuable as a contribution to the Natural History—especially the geology—of America, the lucid style and the concluding chapters on the capabilities of the country with reference to settlement, make it interesting to the general reader. Mr. Dawson concludes that Manitoba from its more northerly position and proximity to the great forest regions appears to be less liable to wide-spread visitations of the grasshoppers than the regions further south, and that—as in those more exposed regions much has been done to limit or prevent their ravages—they can be successfully fought in Manitoba when population has increased and the settlers have learned to combine against the common enemy.   It is also satisfactory to know that the North Saskatchewan country is not subject to their visitations.

While everyone now assigns to the grasshoppers their due weight, other obstacles, once dreaded, have become less formidable as they were approached.   Notwithstanding fears and the declarations of authorities that neither the Red River nor the Saskatchewan could be utilized for steam navigation, steamers do navigate both rivers.   The business done by the Red River Steamboats is so lucrative that one trip to Winnipeg has been known to repay the owners the whole cost of the vessel.   The practicability also of direct steam navigation from the City of Winnipeg to the north of Lake Winnipeg, a distance of 360 miles, has been demonstrated, and different trips have been made from above the Grand Rapids at the mouth of the Saskatchewan for 800 miles to Fort Edmonton.   It is now certain that the Saskatchewan and Lakes Winnepegosis and Manitoba can be utilized for traffic and intercourse by means of small steamers ; that the Mossy Portage—four miles long—between Cedar Lake on the Saskatchewan and Lake Winnepegosis, and Meadow Portage—one and a-half miles long—between Lakes Winnepegosis and Manitoba, could be easily improved, and the Channels at Coal and Tobin's Rapids be deepened at small expense.   The extent of the water system immediately available is indeed marvellous.

Again, notwithstanding the declared opinion of a high authority that a telegraph line could not be constructed because there was not a sufficient supply of wood for posts on the plains, there is now telegraphic communication from Lake Superior to

Winnipeg and thence to the bases of the Rocky Mountains. This difficulty, too, is solved in the good old fashion, *solvitur ambulando*.

In 1859, the Edinburgh *Review* proved conclusively that the proposal to form the Red River and Saskatchewan country into a Crown Colony was a wild and wicked notion ; that hailstones, Indians, frosts early and late, want of wood and water, rocks, bogs, and such like amenities made settlement impossible. The answer is that in spite of the difficulties in the way of getting to the country, and in spite of the unexpected vivacity of the grasshoppers, the population of the Red River Valley has increased in four years from 12,000 to 40,000, and the population of Winnipeg from 700 to about 7,000. With regard to the healthfulness of the climate, the pleasantness of the long winters, and the fertility of the soil, travellers and residents have borne unvarying testimony. For the production of cereals, pulse, and root crops, and as a stock-raising country, there seems to be no better anywhere. The yield for 1876 is the best proof. A summary in the Toronto *Daily Globe* of a minute account in the Manitoba *Free Press* gives the following averages for the Province as a whole : Wheat, 32½ bushels per acre ; barley, 42½ ; oats, 51 ; peas, 32 ; potatoes, 229 ; turnips, 662½. Such is the result, although the unusually severe and late rains damaged the crops, and other drawbacks peculiar to the season operated to lower the average. On newly broken-up ground where the old sod had never rotted, the yield was small ; and many of the settlers had to sow old and decayed seed because of the grasshopper ravages the preceding year. The significance of an average like 32½ bushels of wheat to the acre will be best understood in the light of the following rough calculation by Mr. Dawson : "As a measure of the possible agricultural capacity of this great valley, take one-half of the entire area, or 3,400 square miles equalling 2,176,000 acres, and for simplicity of calculation, let it be supposed to be sown entirely in wheat. Then, at the rate of 17 bushels per acre—which according to Prof. Thomas, is the average yield for Minnesota—the crop of the Red River Valley would amount to 40,992,000 bushels," (p. 278). The total crop of Manitoba for 1876 is: wheat, 480,000 bushels; barley, 173,000; oats, 380,000; peas, 45,000; other grains, 5,000; potatoes, 460,000; turnips and other roots, 700,000.

With respect to the vast country beyond that North-West of which Manitoba is only the threshold, we have much more definite information than we had, and every year adds to our store. Beside the township surveys which have already extended far beyond the Province, a special survey of meridians and bases is also going on. The lines are laid down northerly and westerly, and the work is intended to extend to Peace River. The objects of the survey are to establish a practicable ground work for the extension of township surveys at any point along the line of railway where they may be required, to facilitate the location of the land grant along the line of railway, to obtain a systematic knowledge of the resources of the country, and to furnish information as to geographic position and topography required for the accurate mapping of the northwest. With this last object in view, the position of the bases and meridians in the series are being definitely checked from time to time by means of a continuous triangulation carried on over the most favourable belt of country that can be found, under the personal direction of Mr. Lindsay Russel. The astronomic station on the 49th parallel at Pembina has been adopted as the point of departure for this triangulation.

Descriptive extracts from the Reports of Township surveys in Manitoba and the North-West Territory extending to Fort Ellice have been published. These Reports mention the nature of the surface of each township surveyed, the kind and quality of the soil and timber, the supply of water afforded by lakes, streams, springs, and wells, with such other information as the intending settler requires most. Hundreds of townships in regular succession have been thus described by the surveyors, and scarcely a score are declared unfit for settlement. The land is usually pronounced "of good quality" or "the finest quality," "sandy loam," "deep dry loam," or "good black loam," "level," "rolling" or "undulating prairie," "excellent," "very rich," or "first-class."

Still further west than the valley of the Assiniboine, settlements are springing into existence, especially on the banks and at the confluence of rivers. The half breeds are selling their farms on the Red River, moving west and establishing themselves on the Qu'Appelle, the Saskatchewan and its tributaries, and as far away as Peace River. These hardy *bois-brulés* will always be the advance guard of the great army of regular immigrants. Our old fellow-traveller, the much lamented Rev. George McDougal, writing in October 1875 describes in simple glowing language the fertility of the prairie from the lower Saskatchewan south-westerly to within sight of the Rocky Mountains, over which he himself had just travelled as a messenger of peace from the Government to the Indians. Writing from near the confluence of the Red Deer and Bow Rivers, he says : "A great change has come over the scene in the last fifteen months; men of business had found it to their interest to establish themselves on the banks of our beautiful river. A stock raiser from across the mountains had arrived with several hundred head of cattle. And now on the very hills where two years ago I saw herds of buffalo, the domestic cattle gently graze, *requiring neither shelter nor fodder from their master all the year round.*" Concerning the country that extends from the lower Saskatchewan north-westerly to Peace River, Prof. Maconn is even more emphatic. In his Report (1873) he asserts that "the prairie country extends all the way from the lower Saskatchewan by Lac La Biche across the Athabaska to Slave Lake, and thence to the mountains. Here then is a strip of country over 600 miles in length, and at least 100 in breadth, containing an area of 60,000 square miles, which has a climate no way inferior to that of Edmonton. . . . Regarding the quality of the soil throughout the entire region, my note-book is unvarying in its testimony. I took every opportunity to examine the soil and always found it deep and fertile."

But it was only after Mr. Maconn visited Peace River in 1875, when he had time to explore the country fully, that his evidence regarding that far North-land becomes positively wonderful. The entire district along Peace River for a distance of 760 miles, in a belt of 150 miles wide on each side, or an area of 252,000,000 acres, is as suitable for the cultivation of grain as Ontario. Besides the peculiar excellence of the country for cereals, he had found thousands of acres of crystallized salt, so pure that it was used in its natural state by the H. B. Company. Coal abounded in the richest veins, and was interstratified with hemalite or iron ore yielding fifty per cent. Thousands of acres of coal oil fields were found. The tar lying on the surface of the ground was ankle deep. Miles and miles of the purest gypsum beds cropped out of the river banks. No wonder that he considers Peace River to be the richest part of Canada. While such facts have been given as respecting the valley of the Red River and Assiniboine, of the Saskatchewan and its tributaries, and even of the great Peace River, in what was formerly considered the far, foreign North, the testimony concerning our Southern boundary is more favourable than was expected. All along the 49th parallel of latitude, between the Red River valley and the bases of the Rocky Mountains, the country was believed to be only a treeless, rainless desert, a continuation of the great American desert, extending in a triangular shape well into our North-West. Mr. G. M. Dawson in his Report describes the three prairie steppes along the boundary line (p. 269--300) and shows that most of the first, and much of the second is good.

Even with regard to the third steppe he says : " The explorations in connection with the Boundary Survey have served to shew that this country, formerly considered almost absolutely desert, is not—with the exception of a limited area—of this character ; that a part of it may be of future importance agriculturally, and that a great area is well suited for pastoral occupation and stock farming." Of course he believes that the progress of settlements will be from the valley of the Red River to the Saskatchewan, following that to its head, and that the great pastoral area of the plains south of the Fertile Belt will be entered from the North.

Another matter that pressed itself on our attention four years ago, was the apparent absence of fresh water in many extensive districts. This difficulty, too, has been solved. " It is found that there are few regions where ordinary wells of moderate depth do not succeed in finding ample supplies of water ; and this not only far removed from the rivers, but in their immediate vicinity, though the water level of the stream may be considerably lower than that of the bottom of the well. The rather impervious nature of the prairie sub-soil renders it probable that these wells are supplied either by intercalated coarser layers, or,—as appears to be more likely—by water circulating in fissures ; which, formed originally by the cracking of the soil at the surface, often penetrate its homogeneous mass to a considerable depth." In the vicinity of the City of Winnipeg boring has been extensively carried out ; water is reached at an average depth of fifty feet, and it rises to within a few feet of the surface. The general section met with is thus stated :

Black Loam - - - - - - - - - -	about 4 feet.
Yellow mud and sand - - - - - - -	" 6 "
Blue mud and alkali - - - - - - - -	" 30 "
Limestone concrete, resembling the bed of a river, and carrying water - - - - -	

Wherever there is alkali in the soil the well is tubed round to prevent infiltration.

Another difficulty to which we called attention—the exist_ence of great areas of treeless prairie, can be solved slowly but surely, as has been done in Minnesota and elsewhere by the exertions of settlers, encouraged by Government. The late Minister of the Interior devoted special attention to this subject, and as he has been appointed Governor of the North-West, he will be in a position to encourage the systematic planting of trees, and to prevent or limit the prairie or forest fires that have been hitherto so destructive. The good effects of extensive tree-planting on the soil and on the climate can be hardly over-estimated. Professor Maconn says : " One consequence of trees being planted will be a greater rain-fall, and as a consequence of greater rain-fall, the salts in the soil will be dissolved and carried off from the surface and salt plants disappear. This is no fancy sketch, as it is a fact in physical geography that to clothe the land with trees gives a greater rain-fall, and takes away the salt. Any person acquainted with the history of Palestine and North Africa, knows that what were the most fruitful countries in the world two thousand years ago are now barren saline wastes. The cause is well known. The trees were cut down, none were planted in their place, the sun evaporated the rain before it had time to percolate the soil, salts accumulated, and in the course of time the land was given up to perpetual barrenness." This subject also is exhaustively discussed in Mr. Dawson's Report (p. 311 to 324).

The Indian question is the only remaining one upon which anything need be said, and it deserves a chapter or a volume to itself. Since *Ocean to Ocean* was written there have been two Indian wars in the United States, one with the Modocs and another with the Sioux. Captain Jack and Sitting Bull have shown what loss and expense a handful of savages can inflict on a great nation, and we should give heed to the lesson. When our neighbour's house is on fire it becomes us to be on the alert. Other facts indicate how deeply the honour and the interest of the Dominion is involved in preserving undisturbed our traditional friendly relations with the Indian tribes on both sides of the Rocky Mountains. Here is one fact that points a moral :—During the two years that the Boundary Commission was doing its work, the scientific men engaged by the U. S. Government required the protection of a large military force, whereas the British Canadian party engaged on the other side of the line had no escort and were never disturbed !

The first steps taken by the Dominion Government to protect the Indians from ill-treatment and from whiskey, were in 1873, when Acts were passed for the establishment of the Mounted Police Force, and prohibiting the introduction of intoxicating liquors into the Territories. These Acts and the action consequent upon them, have been attended with the happiest results. Order reigns throughout the North-west. The fact that men charged with the murder of Indians have been brought a thousand miles across the great lone land and lodged in the Winnipeg prison to await their trial, shows the length of the arm of Canada, and that the life of the Indian is as sacred in the eye of the law as the life of any other subject of the Queen. The trading posts and forts, established by outlaws and desperadoes from the Western States on the Bow and Belly Rivers, that were demoralizing the Indians, have been completely broken up. Some of the border ruffians and whiskey traders have been caught, fined or imprisoned, and their stock of buffalo robes—when they had such—confiscated. Others have recrossed the line, disgusted with British institutions. The Assistant Commissioner in charge at Fort MacLeod reports " the complete stoppage of the whiskey trade throughout the whole of this section of the country, and that the drunken riots which in former years were almost of daily occurrence, were now entirely at an end." He reports that the Indians—Blackfeet, Assiniboines and Crees—are very intelligent men, very hospitable, and very friendly ; and that they appreciate highly the boon conferred on them by the Government in establishing the Force among them. " Their delight is unbounded when I tell them that I expect to remain with them always." The Force is usually stationed at Forts Pelly, Carlton, Edmonton, Walsh and MacLeod.

Up to 1872 only two treaties had been made with the Indians in our North-west. By the first the Indian title was extinguished in Manitoba ; and in a wide region north and west of the Province, by the second. Partly in consequence of more favourable terms subsequently granted to Indians elsewhere, and partly in consequence of the non-fulfilment of what were known as " Outside Promises," the Indians included in those treaties became dissatisfied. A memorandum containing certain understandings, it seems, had been appended to the original draft of the treaty, and this had not been sanctioned. But the Indians never forget. They felt that they had been cheated. The Government wisely adjusted the difficulty by directing that the memorandum should be considered part of the Treaties. The annual payment to each Indian included under them was raised from $3 to $5 ; a further annual payment of $20 allowed to each Chief ; and a suit of clothing every three years to each Chief and Herdman.

Since 1872, five other treaties have been made by Governor Morris with different tribes of Indians. In October, 1873, Treaty No. III was made at the north-west angle of the Lake of the Woods with the Salteaux tribe of the Ojibbeways, by which the country between Ontario and Manitoba—now forming the Territory of Kewatin—was ceded. In September, 1874, Treaty No IV was made at Qu'Appelle Lakes with the Crees, Salteaux, and mixed breeds, by which 75,000 square miles were ceded. In September, 1875, Treaty No. V was made at

Behren's River and at Norway House with the Saltaux and Swampy Cree tribes, extinguishing their title to the territory all round Lake Winnipeg. And this year treaties have been made with the Plain Crees at Fort Pitt, by which the Indian title over the remainder of the North-west, except the country of the Blackfeet, has been extinguished. The Blackfeet are to be dealt with next year, when Governor Morris' experience of Treaty-making ought to be sufficient to qualify him for dealing even with the Eastern question. The Blackfeet have always taken rank as perhaps the boldest and bravest tribe in America, and it was therefore thought that they would give trouble sooner or later; but we have learned that they desire our friendship and protection. Keep whiskey from them, and they keep the peace.

What is the secret of our wonderful success in dealing with the Indians? It can be told in very few words. We acknowledge their title and right to the land, and a treaty once made with them we keep it. Lord Dufferin has pointed out what is involved in our acknowledgment that the original title to the land exists in the Indian tribes and communities. " Before we touch an acre, we make a treaty with the chiefs representing the bands we are dealing with, and having agreed upon and paid the stipulated price . . . we enter into possession, but not until then do we consider that we are entitled to deal with an acre." It is well that this should be clearly understood, because the Indians themselves have no manner of doubt on the subject. At the North-west Angle, chief after chief said to the Governor : " This is what we think, that the Great Spirit has planted us on this ground where we are, as you were where you came from. We think that where we are is our property." And they have wonderfully English notions about all that the possession of the land involves; that the land includes the buildings on it, and that trespass is not allowable. When Mr. Dawson, one of the Commissioners, at the outset of the negotiations,

told them how desirable it was for them to have a treaty, they
answered him very plainly, that there were other matters that
ought to be settled first; that promises had been made to them
when the road was built that had not been fulfilled; and that
they regarded, therefore, all the houses on the line, and all the
big boats on the waters as theirs, till they were recompensed for
them. The only answer his Honour could give to them was
to fall back on first principles that would make the hair of
an English Squire or Judge stand on end—" wood and water "
he assured them, " were the gift of the Great Spirit, and were
made alike for the good both of the white and red man." Being
well assured that the land is theirs, they demand compensation
for it as a right. And who will question their right? Those
vast rolling prairies, those gently sloping or bold broken hills,
those sparkling lakes covered with wild fowl and stocked with
fish, are theirs by inheritance and by possession. They did not,
after the fashion of white men divide their property up into
separate estates. Had they done so, no one would have ques-
tioned their title. But that the country that has always yielded
them support is their own and not ours, they fairly and rightly
believe. The tribe holds the land and the wood and the water
for common use. And it is only fair that, before arranging to
run our railroads through it, or inviting European emigrants to
go in and take possession, we should meet the Indians in
friendly council, buy their rights and extinguish their title.
They are ready to meet us half-way. Though brave and proud,
they are willing to admit our superiority. Though few in number, and every year becoming fewer, they would be formidable
as enemies, for they are magnificent horsemen, and could support themselves on the great plains where ordinary troops
would starve. Though born hunters, and almost as fond of a
buffalo run as of fire-water, they are, under missionary influence, betaking themselves in some places to agriculture and
stock-raising, and their most intelligent men see that it is nec-

essary for them to abandon their nomad for a settled life if they are to exist alongside of white men.   Hitherto the buffalo has been to them what the potato was to the Irish before the great famine.   The buffalo has been more ; house, clothing, harness-leather, cordage, thread, as well as food.   But the buffalo is beginning to be a less certain element.   The buffalo disappears before civilization, and Chippewa, Cree and Black-foot must be civilized, or they too will disappear.

Some people smile at the notion of treaties with a few thousand half-naked, painted savages.   And to him who sees only the ludicrous in anything different from his own use and wont, the scene may appear a travesty of treaty-making.   Any infringement on his rights would be a serious matter.   But how can anything be important to an Indian ?   My friend, the Indian is a man, and God has implanted the sense of justice in the breasts of all men.   To the Indian his land or fishing ground is as important as it would be to you, and the memory of his fathers may be as sacred.   Said the Lac Seul Chief at North-west Angle : " We do not wish that any one should smile at our affairs, as we think our country is a large matter to us."

Something more than making a treaty is needed.   It must be kept to the letter and in the spirit.   I am not aware that the Indians ever broke a treaty that was fairly and solemnly made. They believe in the sanctity of an oath ; and to a Christian nation, a treaty made with true believers, heretics, or pagans, with mosque-goers or church-goers, should be equally binding. The words of Mawedopinias, who with Pou-wa-say, had car-ried on the negotiations that resulted in the North-west Angle Treaty, show that their eyes are open when they treat with us, and that their covenants are meant to be sacred.   The business having been completed, he stepped up to the Governor and said : " Now you see me stand before you all ; what has been done here to-day has been done openly before the Great

Spirit, and before the nation, and I hope that I may never hear anyone say that this treaty has been done secretly ; and now, in closing this Council, I take off my glove, and in giving you my hand, I deliver you over my birth-right and lands ; and in taking your hand I hold fast all the promises you have made, and I hope they will last as long as the sun goes round and the water flows, as you have said." The Governor took his hand and said : " I accept your hand, and with it the lands, and will keep all my promises in the firm belief that the treaty now to be signed will bind the Red man and the White together as friends forever." The copy of the treaty was then prepared and duly signed. The hereditary Chieftain, who is said to have seen a hundred summers, was brought forward to sign it first. The Governor handed him the pen. He hesitated and said that he expected to have been paid the money. " Take my hand," said the Governor, at the same time extending it, " see, it is full of money." He looked in his face, took the offered hand, and signed the treaty.

To break a treaty made with these old lords and sons of the soil would be worse than to break one made with a nation able to resent a breach of faith.

The speech of the Governor-General to the people of Victoria last September made known to all Canada that there is one Province in the Dominion where the Indians feel themselves aggrieved ; because the fundamental principle of British and Canadian policy had been ignored by the Provincial Government in its dealings with them. " In British Columbia, except in a few cases under the jurisdiction of the H. B. Company, or under the auspices of Sir James Douglas, the Government assumed that the fee-simple of as well as the sovereignty over the land resided in the Queen. Hence interferences with the prescriptive rights of the Indians, and dissatisfaction on their part." The annual reports of the Department of the Interior have been full of this subject for several years past, but the gravity of the situation has not been understood by the public. How very grave it is, one declaration of Mr. Powell, the Indian Commissioner, shows : " If," he reports, " there has not been an Indian war, it is not because there has been no injustice to the Indians, but because the Indians have not been sufficiently united." He also reports that the Indian bands at Nicola and Okanagan Lakes wholly declined to accept any presents in the summer of 1874, lest by so doing they should be thought to waive their claims for compensation for the injustice done them in relation to the land grants.

What makes this worse and worse is that the Indians of British Columbia greatly outnumber the white population, that they contribute to a very marked extent to the financial prosperity of the Province, and that they have made astonishing progress wherever pains have been taken to teach them anything useful. The following table, taken from Commissioner Powell's Report, gives a comparative statement of their exports for 1874 and 1875 of fish, fish oil and furs :

	1874.		1875.
Fish	$69,665 00	Fish	$114,170 00
Oil...............	44,453 00	Oil...............	19,816 00
Furs.............	307,625 00	Furs............	411,810 00
Cranberries	2,011 00	Cranberries......	3,568 00
	$423,754 00		$549,364 00

Nearly the whole of the above exports are contributed by Indians. Mr. Lindeau, the Commissioner of the Mainland Division of the Province, writes in his last Report that the Chief of the Lower Fraser Indians addressed him at a recent interview in the following language : " You told us that our Great Mother the Queen was good and powerful, and we believed you. We know that she has only to speak to this Government and our lands must be fixed (defined) ; we wonder why our Great Mother does not speak. We want you to tell her

what we have said. We were promised 80 acres of land to
each family, and now we are treated like children and put off
with 20 acres, which is not enough if we are to do like the
white men. Shall we be obliged to turn to our old ways?"
The Chief spoke in a tone of deep earnestness. He is a remarkably intelligent, clever man. The comfortable appearance
of the dwellings of his tribe, and the neat and substantial
church erected and finished by himself at his own village speak
well for his industry and skill. The Indians of British Columbia, as a rule, are sober, industrious, self-reliant, and law-abid-
ing. They labour in the saw-mills, the logging camp, the field,
the store, in fact in every department where labour is required,
and are fairly remunerated.

Lord Dufferin has paid a just tribute to the wonderful success of the Rev. Mr. Duncan at Metlakatlah—a man whom
the Church of England may well class with the Selwyns and
Pattesons,—" of the neat Indian maidens in his school, as
modest and as well dressed as any clergyman's daughters in
any English parish," and " of scenes of primitive peace and
innocence, of idyllic beauty and material comfort " in an Indian community under the administration of a judicious and
devoted Christian missionary. A gentleman who cannot speak
like His Excellency, but who has had a longer acquaintance
with the Indians of British Columbia, and who has employed
hundreds of them on surveys and other work, writes me as
follows concerning the Nicola Lake, and Thompson and Lower
Fraser Indians, many of whom are under the missionary care
of the Rev. Mr. Good : " They are a most promising community, and doubtless much is due to Mr. Good's teaching. They
are not only regular in their devotional exercises, but industrious, honest, sober, and tidy in their persons and dress. And
they are the most spirited Indians I have yet met in B. C. It
was one of their Chiefs who refused the presents of the Commissioner, for fear that by accepting them he might prejudice

the claims of his tribe for lands which they believed had been unjustly taken from them and sold by the Local Government; and one of his Klootchmen knocked a cigar out of his hand, which he had accepted, and crushed it with her foot." To plunder such people of their land, village sites, fishing stations, burial grounds, or favourite resorts, would be a blunder as well as a crime. The policy that has succeeded in all the other Provinces and Territories of the Dominion must be applied to British Columbia, and in no Province are we likely to see more splendid results.

The brief review that has been now given is enough to show that progress is being made in connection with the great work of the Colonization of the North-west and the construction of the work that is to bind all Canada together with links of steel from Ocean to Ocean, and that there are good grounds for hoping that—as difficulties are cleared out of the way, the progress shall be at an increasingly rapid rate. Four years is not a long period in the history of a country; and to hasten surely, it is necessary to hasten slowly. The present rate is rapid enough to satisfy reasonable expectations. And the writer believes that the growth of true national feeling throughout every part of our wide-extended glorious Dominion—unattended possibly with as many ebullitions of sentiment as some would like—more than corresponds to the material progress we are making, and that every Canadian, while legitimately cherishing pride in the past and present, may look forward confidently to the future of his country.

THE END

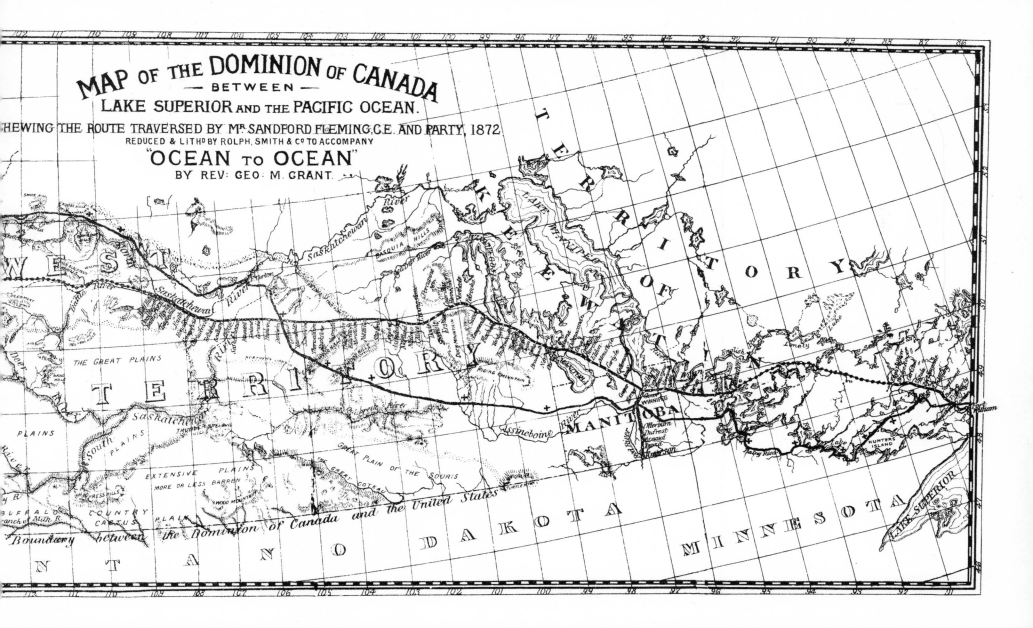

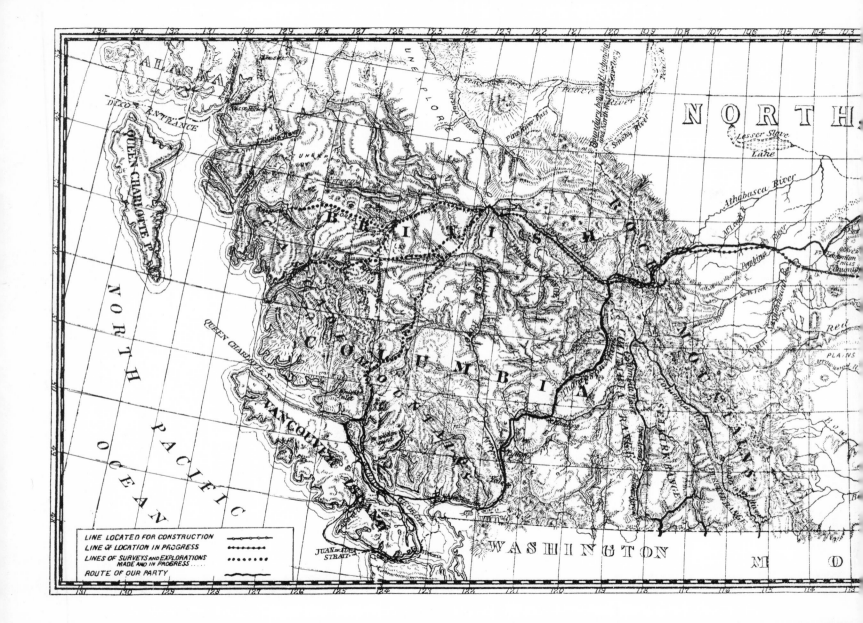

LINE LOCATED FOR CONSTRUCTION
LINE OF LOCATION IN PROGRESS
LINES OF SURVEYS AND EXPLORATIONS
MADE AND IN PROGRESS
ROUTE OF OUR PARTY

DATE DUE			

BUREAU OF ILLUSTRATION BUFFALO NY